ADVICE FROM Kathryn Falk—
and more than 100 romance authors, editors, and agents

MARY BALOGH * JENNIFER BLAKE * BARBARA
BRETTON * SUZANNE BROCKMANN * STELLA
CAMERON * MILLIE CRISWELL * EMMA DARCY * JUDE
DEVERAUX * KATHLEEN EAGLE * SUZANNE FORSTER *
JULIE GARWOOD * TESS GERRITSEN * HEATHER GRA-
HAM * VIRGINIA HENLEY * BEVERLY JENKINS * SANDRA
KITT * JOHANNA LINDSEY * LINDA LAEL MILLER *
TERESA MEDEIROS * PAMELA MORSI * CONSTANCE
O"BANYON * JANETTE OKE * BERTRICE SMALL *
KATHERINE SUTCLIFFE * ANNE STUART * AND MORE…

"*Romantic Times* is the bible of romantic fiction." —*USA Today*

"Lively, interesting, thorough…the definitive aspiring romance
writer's self help book." —*New York Daily News*

"Kathryn Falk's new book is amazing. No one can organize things
like she does."—Barbara Cartland

"I tell all new writers to call Kathryn and then do everything she tells
them to do. I always take her advice."—Heather Graham

"*How to Write a Romance for the New Markets*…. provides invaluable
advice on the options for writing Ethnic Romances as well as promoting them."—Sandra Kitt

"How to Write for the New Markets is a book I'm proud to contribute to and recommend. "—Jude Deveraux

"I advise all aspiring writers to study this book if they want to write
a multicultural romance." —Beverly Jenkins

"This book is a must read for every writer of romance."
—Walter Zacharius, Founder/CEO, Kensington/Zebra Books

"Pushing the limits of romance novels and propelling the genre into the 21st century has never been more intelligently presented."—Dara Joy

"This book puts inspirationals and all the other off-shoot sub-genres clearly within reach of new writers."—Lori Copeland

"European romance authors will now be better prepared for the future…."—Nick Robinson, President, Scarlet Books, England

"This new handbook is as helpful and educational as the original *How to Write a Romance and Get It Published*."
—Alicia Condon, Editorial Director, Leisure Books.

"*How to Write a Romance for the New Markets* contains the basics for understanding the ongoing changes in romance publishing."—Pesha Rubinstein, agent

"I recommend this book to all new romance writers. Kathryn encourages excellence and gives everyone an opportunity to meet the challenge." —Patti Steele-Perkins, agent

"No one has survived longer in the same job in the romance industry than Kathryn Falk and me. This new book gives writers the benefit of her vision and experience." —Katherine Orr, VP Public Relations, Harlequin/Silhouette

"*How to Write a Romance for the New Markets* helps to explain how Kathryn and Romantic Times have kept the romance industry evolving into the 21st century and they're unstoppable." —Bertrice Small

"I truly wish every aspiring romance writer would read—no, *study*—this book before putting pen to paper, or fingers to a keyboard." — Gary M. Frazier, Editor-in-Chief, Genesis Press, Inc.

"Kathryn has always been the new writer's helpmate. I call her my fairy godmother." —Judith McNaught

KATHRYN FALK, LADY OF BARROW is the Founder/CEO of *Romantic Times Magazine,* an affiliate with Barnes and Noble of *RomanticTimes.com.*

She is the author of *Miniature Needlepoint and Sewing Projects for Dollhouses, Love's Leading Ladies, How to Write a Romance and Get it Published, Romance Readers Handbook, How to Write Young Adult Novels,* and *How to Write Horror.*

Following the tremendous success of *How to Write a Romance and Get it Published* in 1983, Kathryn began a Manuscript Evaluation Service (in conjunction with *Romantic Times Magazine*). Over the years, this service has helped hundreds of new writers see their manuscripts through to publication.

The same year, she also launched the annual *Romantic Times Booklovers Convention,* which presents intensive writing courses and networking opportunities for aspiring writers. The event has given thousands of these aspiring writers, as well as readers and booksellers the chance to meet and mingle with authors, publishers, cover models and illustrators as it sponsors the Mr. Romance Cover Model Pageant, a costume competition and a book fair as part of the festivities.

In addition, Kathryn leads the *Lady Barrow Tours* on regular visits to England, Scotland and Ireland. In partnership with Carnival Cruise Lines she organizes writers' theme cruises.

In Alvin, Texas, for the benefit of her father and others afflicted with Alzheimers, she has created a home care complex known as Barrow Village—opened for those who seek a pampered environment for their aging parents. She has established a Lady Barrow Antique Flea Market and Auction House to support the project.

Kathryn is a leading collector of antique Lotus Slippers and memorabilia related to China's bound-feet ladies. She travels between homes in New York, Texas, Austria and her village of Barrow in Suffolk, England.

She takes her duties as Lady of Barrow seriously and is exercising her 16th century manorial right to "market and fayre" by organizing a Medieval fair in Barrow during July of 2001. This is to be held as part of the festivities for the first International Booklovers' Convention to be held in Cambridge, England. The event will mark the celebration of Barbara Cartland's 100th birthday and the 20th anniversary of the establishment of *Romantic Times Magazine*.

Time Magazine, in its December, 1998 "Builders and Titans" issue, included Kathryn as one of the business geniuses of the past century.

HOW TO WRITE A ROMANCE

FOR THE NEW MARKETS

AND GET IT PUBLISHED

BY KATHRYN FALK

VOLUME 1

PREPARING TO WRITE

Genesis Press, Inc.

GENESIS PRESS, INC.
315 Third Avenue North
Columbus, Mississippi 39701

How To Write A Romance For The New Markets

ISBN 0-7394-0834-8

PRINTED IN THE UNITED STATES OF AMERICA

First Edition

DEDICATED TO

The loyal readers of Romantic Times Magazine, and the villagers of Barrow, England.

And to Kenneth Rubin, still . . . and always, my knight in shining armor.

ACKNOWLEDGEMENTS

I want to thank publisher Wil Colom, Ann Peach, Judith Kohnen, and all the wonderful authors who answered my request for advice to new writers. Some of the articles have appeared previously in *Romantic Times* magazine and some are originals for this book.

Contributors

Victoria Alexander

Bridget Anderson

Amanda Ashley

Mary Balogh

Gerri Benninger

Jo Beverley

Jennifer Blake

Susan Bontley

Barbara Bretton

Suzanne Brockmann

Toby Bromberg

Anita Richmond Bunkley

Linda Cajio

Stella Cameron

Marilyn Campbell

Linda Castle

Meg Chittenden

Wil Colom

Lori Copland

Millie Criswell

Jennifer Cruisie

Emma Darcy

Jude Deveraux

Thea Devine

Jennifer Dunne

Kathleen Eagle

Lynne Emery

Leslie Esdaile

Gwynne Forster

Suzanne Forster

Lori Foster

Dorothy Garlock

Julie Garwood

Tess Gerritsen

Nancy Gideon

Heather Graham

Lucy Grijalva

Gay G. Gunn

Shirley Hailstock

Sylvia Halliday

Crystal Wilson Harris

Robin Lee Hatcher

Lorraine Heath

Dee Hendrickson

Virginia Henley

Donna Hill

Sandra Hill

Martha Hix

Tami Hoag

Christine Holden

Linda Hyatt

Peggy Jaegly

Beverly Jenkins

Donna Julian

Marcia King-Gamble

Mary Kirk

Sandra Kitt

Karen Morrison Knox

Judith Kohnen

Susan Krinard

Jane LaMunyon

Jill Marie Landis

Sinclair LeBeau

Johanna Lindsey

Merline Lovelace

Tess Mallory

Teresa Medeiros

Linda Lael Miller

Jeanne Montague

Kathleen Morgan

Pamela Morsi

Elizabeth Goldsmith Musser

Constance O'Banyon
Janette Oke
Sara Orwig
Catherine Palmer
Susan Paul
Ann Peach
Chris Peirson
Kayla Perrin
Susan Elizabeth Phillips
Tori Phillips
B. K. Reeves
Mildred E. Riley
Evelyn Rogers
Hebby Roman
Kate Ryan

Sharon Sala
Dallas Schulze
Danny Sinopoli
Carol J. Sheridan
Gloria Dale Skinner
Christine Skye
Bertrice Small
Heywood Smith
Deb Stover
Anne Stuart
Katherine Sutcliffe
Jane Toombs
Chassie West
Al Zuckerman
and more . . .

Table of Contents

Part One – The Art of Writing Romance

Chapter I – Before You Begin . . .

Chapter II – Craft & Technique – Reviewing the Basics

Chapter III – Building Character and Emotion

Chapter IV – Sensual Writing

Chapter V – Researching Romances

Chapter VI – A Writer's Life: Inspiration and Consolation

Part Two – The New Markets

Chapter VII – Innovative Trends

Chapter VIII – The Multi-Cultural Market

Chapter XI – Romantic Suspense

Chapter XII –Appendices

Foreword

When I wrote *How to Write a Romance and Get It Published*, today's romance novel industry was in its infancy. It was 1980, and everything and everyone was new to the game. We were pioneers and didn't realize it! This was the major reason the book was fun to compile. There were no "laws" on the romance-writing frontier, so we made them up as we went along. I sat down and figured out what the book needed in order to turn readers into writers, and it sold. A prominent hardcover publisher, Crown, brought out my opus to great fanfare in 1983. It was the first "how-to" of this burgeoning genre, and everyone liked the style.

How to Write a Romance and Get It Published carved out a life of its own. Both media response and strong sales stunned the publisher; they quickly sold out the first 23,000 hardcover copies. In 1984 New American Library bought the mass-market rights, the book was brought out in paperback and went through numerous printings, selling more than 100,000 copies—and it's still in print.

I was to discover through the years that nearly every newly published romance author had first studied my book. They would show me dog eared well marked copies and tell me how it kept them going or got them started.

That's still a thrill for me.

In 1990 I was asked to update the source section (agents, editors, addresses, telephone numbers, etc.) Many new sub-genres were emerging as I met the deadline, thus compelling me to replace many of the old articles with new ones. The new version proved to be as successful as the original and is still a constant seller for my publisher, now called Penguin Putnam. (See, even my publisher changed!)

The essence of *How to Write a Romance and Get It Published* has remained timeless and intact—a basic how-to-write, step-by-step instruction guide for getting started on your first romance novel, presented through the letters of an ambitious young would-be writer named Rosie.

But now, the 21st century is upon us and the time has come to prepare new writers for a new age—one that includes the Internet and incredible software, regional publishers, new sub-categories, new twists on tried-and-true sub-genres, heroes of every shape and form, heroines who push the sensual envelope, plots that reflect a spiritual and religious revival, and a growing admiration for psychological mysteries.

Every week, piles of letters arrive at *Romantic Times Magazine* with requests from around the world for information about how to write romance novels. Like acting or painting, romance writing is a dream occupation—if you don't mind being glued to the computer or dictating like Barbara Cartland and Sidney Sheldon. The letter writers I hear from are usually women, or men who have wives who want to write. They have seen or heard about the remarkable romance market statistics:

120 new books published each month

48% of paperback sales

The average reader spends over $1,200 a year on books.

The average reader buys 20 – 40 books a month.

Romance readers have better sex lives!

In the middle of all these letters, I heard from Rosemarie, the daughter of Rosie, who inspired my original *How to Write* book. Like many of the new writers I meet these days, Rosie's daughter is living a multicultural existence and networks already with other book lovers and aspiring writers. And like her mother before her, Rosemarie has inspired me. I am about to set forth with Rosemarie and her roommates—and you, I hope—on a new voyage of romance-writing discovery, replete with information that will take you all from yesterday, through today and into tomorrow.

This book, *How to Write a Romance for the New Markets and Get it Published*, is designed to help writers better understand the genre as it is published today. I believe that this guide supplements my first book and can further help new writers save precious time, avoid frustration, and help them survive through the rough patches. I have asked some wonderful writers to give you the benefit of their experience in explaining the most common problems they have encountered—along with timely solutions.

Now I'd like you to meet my friends in romance publishing who have always been generous with advice. If this book shows you the warmth and friendship within our industry, then I have really done my job.

Good luck and keep writing!

Kathryn Falk, Lady of Barrow
Romantic Times Magazine
55 Bergen Street
Brooklyn, New York 11201
Tel.: (718) 237-1097
E-mail: BarrowLady@aol.com

*"Romance is a constantly evolving genre.
You can see its shifting trends from year to year.
No matter which direction this metamorphosis
takes us, there is one thing of which I'm certain—
romance is here to stay. People love to dream,
and as long as we have dreamers,
we'll have a need for storytellers."*
—Julie Garwood

PART ONE

THE ART OF WRITING ROMANCE

"There's nothing to writing. All you do is sit down at the typewriter and open a vein."
—Red Smith

Rosemarie Kelly,
San Francisco, CA

Dear Ms. Falk,
You don't know me, but you know my mother, Rosie, the lady who wrote letters to you in the early 1980's and was featured in your book, *How to Write a Romance and Get It Published.* Your advice worked! Avon published her three books, *Ambrosia, Chastity Morrow,* and *For Honor's Lady,* but, as you may have heard, family problems cropped up, illnesses, and eventually other priorities came first and she dropped out of writing.

I think I have inherited her talent and want to become a romance writer, too. I learned a lot growing up around her. I'm an avid reader and usually read about eight romances a month. I also read your magazine, *Romantic Times,* from cover to cover, especially relishing the great reviews of all the new romances. And I do mean ALL. It's become very clear to me there is a lot of competition, not only for getting published in the first place, but also for shelf space in bookstores, and so I wonder about *my* chances of being published. I don't want to start out by being discouraged, but this is all quite daunting when there are more than 100 new romances on the shelves each month!

To tell you a little bit about myself: I left home after college and now teach in a private school in San Francisco. I share a slightly cramped apartment in Chinatown with two roommates, Jade Ling and Sierra Cole, who also read romances. We met in a bookstore and decided to start a little "writer's colony." We have each taken writing courses locally. Our dream is to someday write novels full-time.

We have a big favor to ask of you. Will you help us learn how to pursue writing seriously in today's marketplace? I know you answered almost everything about writing for my mom in your previous book, so we can still use that book as a basic "How to Write" manual. However, she warns me that things are different now: characters and story lines have changed radically and the "mid-list," where she started, is shrinking.

Anything extra you can add to what was in your first book will be greatly appreciated by all of us.

Sincerely,
Rosemarie

CHAPTER 1

BEFORE YOU EVEN BEGIN

Kathryn Falk, Lady of Barrow
Romantic Times Magazine
Brooklyn, New York

Dear Rosemarie,

It was a delight hearing from you. Send my regards to your mother. We miss her in the romance biz; she was quite a talent. You probably do have writing in your blood—story-telling talent is quite often handed down through generations.

You and your roommates are fortunate to be living in such a colorful city. San Francisco is one of the greatest book-selling capitals of the country so you're in an exciting environment for beginning writers.

I will be most happy to help all of you embark upon novel writing.

To do that I am going to combine what I have learned by being part of the romance industry for the past 18 years, with the cumulative knowledge of a lot of good friends of mine. Some of them are romance's superstars, others quite new on the scene, but each is a writer with special knowledge to share with you. Between us all, we should be able to give you a great deal of worthwhile and necessary advice on how to write for the *new* markets—the ones which quickly turn into . . . *tomorrow's* markets.

Your mother is correct indeed, Rosemarie; much has changed since she started out.

Writing wonderful romance novels for these new markets will take a lot of study and work, but I'm sure you know all that. You must be prepared to keep up with all the new books and market news as we go along.

Writing novels requires a proper start and that can be a tricky proposition. Considerable deliberation and thought should go into approaching the writing of a romance (or other types of popular fiction), or you will be spinning your wheels and feeling frustrated.

Too many new writers do "stream-of-consciousness" writing at the computer and wind up with weak premises and flabby chapters, never finishing what they start. Enthusiasm alone won't make you write a good book.

Here are two important rules for getting started:

Do not write a word until your outline is solidly thought out.

Do not get overly enthusiastic and consider leaving your job until you are well-enough established.

One author had a contract for a book and thought she was on her way, but two years later had to return to her old job. I see her name once again on books, so it seems like she did learn how to juggle a job and writing. In the beginning, so must you!

Then there's the story of a famous author who got a huge advance for two books and used all the money to renovate a large estate. A few years later, the next contract was for far less money, and the end of the story is sad. Eventually the author sold off the house and now lives in the gatehouse, watching the new owners drive by.

Forewarned is forearmed.

I have asked some exceptional writers to start you off on the right foot by helping you to fully understand the impact of romance and your responsibility to the craft. Emma Darcy, one of the best-selling romance writers with more than sixty million books in print, will tell you about the most important thing to keep in mind if you are going to be a successful author—*your readers*. You may feel it's

7

a bit early to think about readers when you haven't even written a book yet, but believe me, readers assure your success (or failure).

Gerry Benninger will set you straight on the importance of respecting the genre. Catherine Palmer will lead you through the magic and rituals of romance, and the great Virginia Henley puts in a plea for passion. In addition, there are one or two further surprises from other wonderful novelists.

I hope you enjoy the enclosed articles. They represent the best sentiments of the genre, and I hope you find these women as inspirational as I have over the years.

Good Luck to you, Sierra, and Jade on your writing odyssey.

Kathryn

"Well-crafted romances transport me to distant eras and diverse locales. They introduce me to pirates and queens, rogues and hosts. Some make me cry; others make me laugh out loud. They enrich my life and provide a quiet reward at the end of a difficult day.

Karen Morrison Knox
Reader . . . Writer

* * *

"Kathryn asked me to help get you off on the proper foot, and I am happy to offer some guidance. New writers are an important addition to the genre. Always remember that the reader is your touchstone."

Never Lose Sight of the Reader

By Emma Darcy

Never lose sight of your reader when you write a romance novel. Readers have always dictated whether a book is successful or not. Romance readers—as opposed to outsiders commenting on the genre—do not think all romance books are the same. So what, to each of them, makes an outstanding book . . . one that they will buy and keep and treasure?

It touches them—*personally*—in ways that make them feel good, with truths they recognize and empathize with and values they hold dear. It will have characters they like and can identify with, a story that reflects a situation they understand and perhaps have lived through themselves, (or would like to live through), plus the overall impact of satisfaction that comes with the sense of everything turning out right—the kind of rightness they want to feel.

Your success as a romance author will be measured by what the readers *feel* about your books. You might be proud of a beautifully crafted story. You *ought* to take great personal satisfaction in writing a book that interests you. However, it will fail in the market place if it does not deliver what the reader wants to get from it.

I have often been asked the question: "Don't you feel guilty about raising readers' expectations of love in their real lives?" My answer contains the core of understanding that romance authors must have if they are to write a successful book for readers. No, I don't feel guilty, because I don't raise expectations. My stories reflect what readers want themselves, what they dream of having or experiencing, even if only in a fantasy world. The more truly I reflect the readers' hearts and minds in my stories, the more those books are loved.

That's the truth of it. If I could digest all the fan letters I've received from readers over the years into a few lines, those lines would be: *You touched my heart. You made me feel for the hero and heroine. Brought smiles and tears. Believable characters—true to life. A warm, beautiful story—couldn't put it down," and "the man of my dreams."* These are key points to the readers' enjoyment of a romance. Note how they relate to *feelings*.

Writing a romance is not easy. It is not a matter of simply constructing a clever, action-packed story with a set of interesting characters who do interesting things. It is the most personal soul stripping exercise any author could set out to do. To touch the hearts of readers we must expose our own, injecting our innermost feelings and thoughts and beliefs into the characters and situations we write about. It is the only possible way of striking that chord of truth that is so necessary for real, deep-down communication. We form a bond of intimate sharing with our readers. We create a world they'd like to live in and people they'd love to be or meet. And for a little while, we are together in the private life we hold within.

I think of my readers as a sisterhood that stretches all around the world. When I'm writing a romance they are sitting on my shoulder overlooking every word, every scene, every development of the relationship. I ask them, "Does this situation interest, intrigue, entertain, enthrall you? Is this what you'd say—or love to say—in these circumstances? Where do you want these people to go now? Is it right for you if I let their passions run away with them at this point?"

The sense of "rightness" is so important. Hit a false note and you lose the readers. You break the chord that keeps them with you. The prime task of a romance author is to keep the readers "inside" with everything that's happening in your story—characters, motivations, values, action, time, place, circumstance, and most of all, the emotions being expressed.

Romance writing is about understanding people and giving them understanding. For me, the greatest regard for what I do comes when readers write and thank me for giving them a new insight or showing them a different way of dealing with a problem in their real-life relationships.

Human behavior—that which drives people to do what they do,

want what they want—is precisely what an author explores in the romance genre. There is nothing shallow or formulaic about it. Within the context of a man and woman coming together with love and commitment, there are millions of stories to be told.

Readers certainly don't want the same story to be told over and over again. Although the ending is predictable—has to be if we are to deliver absolute satisfaction—readers don't want the body of the book to be too predictable. An author who cares about her readers will pile on surprises and keep building suspense over what is going to happen next. However, never forget, the surprises should be like birthday gifts, something new, delightful, charming and heart touching—what the reader will be pleased to get, even though she's not expecting it.

I've seen authors in this genre write one great book and never repeat that success with the rest of their works. The reason, I believe, is very simple. They "lucked into" touching the readers' hearts that first time instead of realizing it was what they had to do *every* time. The readers make no excuses for authors who fail them. They just stop buying their books.

There is one golden rule for success in this business.
Never lose sight of your reader.

"Tis the good reader that makes the good book; in every book he finds passages which seem confidences or asides hidden from all else and unmistakably meant for his ear; the profit of books is according to the sensibility of the reader; the profoundest thought or passion sleeps as in a mine, until it is discovered by an equal mind and heart.
Ralph Waldo Emerson
* * *

"If you're going to be writers of romances, never doubt it is the most honorable of professions. My advice to new writers is respect the genre deeply and learn to deal with its critics as soon as possible."

Romance as Literature

By Gerry Benninger (Romantic Times Reviewer)

There are two kinds of literature according to scholars: escapist and interpretive. This division is scholars' way of ensuring they don't waste valuable time reading, dealing with, or discussing something that is not worthy of their time and attention. Only "interpretive" literature is "deep/worthy" enough to challenge "the keen mind." Escape is to be left to the undemanding, non-critical masses. As everyone knows, romance has been consigned to the escape vacuum, labeled by many as having no redeeming value.

This attitude keeps the romance genre from being considered "respectable," so romances are automatically dismissed and never examined further. Millions of stories are brushed off as being two and not three-dimensional. Nevertheless, romances (and some are better than others) can be viewed as a modern legacy of perhaps the most brilliant period in English language literature: the Romantic Movement, which included Tennyson, Byron, and Austen.

Most prose and poetry borrow from romantic form, philosophy, and symbolism, and modern romances most fully realize this influence. The most striking aspects the genre preserves are individualism, emotion's validity (not against reason, but to balance its demands), and the importance of imagination.

The romance genre has mythological depth. And one day, when the genre is finally understood for its possibilities rather than being dismissed without examination, individual books will shine forth with powerful themes, and the practice of reclassifying romances as some other genre in order to have them taken seriously, will cease.

"All good books are alike in that they are truer than if they had really happened, and after you are finished reading one you will feel that all that happened to you and afterwards, it all belongs to you; the good and the bad, the ecstasy, the remorse and sorrow, the people and the places and how the weather was. If you can get so that you can give that to people, then you are a writer."

Old Newsman Writes
From *Esquire* (December, 1934)
* * *

"Kathryn once printed this article in RT and says it gives new writers a perfect image of the beauty inherent in the craft of novel writing. When you finally start writing, prepare your romance novel with care and love, and it will be a gift well worth receiving."

The Rituals of Romance

By Catherine Palmer

A good cup of tea, like a good book, involves two people. One is the giver; one is the receiver. Growing up in Africa as the daughter of missionaries, I had many opportunities to take tea with my friends who lived in villages out in the bush.

I will never forget the blind Maasai tribeswoman who made tea for me over an open fire inside her hut. When she held out the cup, she cradled it in both hands in the African sign of blessing. As I sipped the tea, heavily laced with milk and sugar, I knew I had been given a gift worth savoring. In the same way, I have written each of my novels with the care I pray will make them truly blessed gifts to my readers. Like my Maasai friend, I first assemble all the ingredients. Second, I prepare them. Then I give with both hands.

Gathering ingredients is never easy. To make a cup of *chai* in Africa, someone must walk many miles to buy sugar and tea. A cow must be milked. Water—that precious commodity—must be drawn from a hole dug in a dry riverbed. Gathering ingredients for a good book takes similar diligence. The writer must be willing to research all elements of the novel—from historical background to details of daily life.

Would-be writers have told me, "I'll just write contemporary novels, because I won't have to do any research." My contemporary romances have compelled me to research rock climbing, archaeology, steroids, elephants, and adoption. In fact, I was so caught up in my study of adoption that my husband and I decided to adopt a little boy from a Romanian orphanage. Our son, Andrei, will testify that every author needs to do her research!

Ingredient gathering also involves learning how to plot and how to create believable characters. Before every book, I compile a binder filled with research, character sketches, and plots. I want to give my readers the best I have to offer.

When I sat in the smoky interior of my Maasai friend's hut, I observed the care she took in the preparation of tea. Her sightless eyes could not protect her as she stirred her fire. Her callused fingers placed the pot of water on the coals, added tea leaves and poured in milk and sugar. Then she took the steaming pot in her bare hands and poured her gift into the cup.

A writer's labors at preparing the gift of a book must show no less care. These days I write in a well-equipped downtown office. I now earn enough money to help my family and Uncle Sam both. It wasn't always this easy. I have written at my kitchen table with my baby crawling between my feet. I earned so little one year my accountant asked me why I bothered. I have written for five publishing houses and seven editors. Imprints that had bought and scheduled my books have folded. New editors have come into projects and rejected my writing. Reviewers have written scathing commentaries that nearly crushed me. The process of writing has never been easy.

Even though I thank God for the blessings of my current stability, I can say that writing still involves a great deal of work. Like all working women, a writer learns to balance the demands of her career with the needs of her family. Being a published writer means contracts, deadlines, correspondence, budgets, and galley proofs.

But published or unpublished, being a writer means writing. Every day. Even when you don't feel like it. A writer who wants to give her readers the best gift must write. No matter what.

When my Maasai friend held out her cup of tea, I knew she was blessing me. In the same way, when a reader takes my book, opens to the first page and begins to read, I pray she will feel a sense of all the love and care that went into its preparation.

I offer my books with both hands in a blessing that conveys my respect for any reader. And when I receive letters saying my words touched a heartstring, made someone laugh or cry or stand up against injustice, then I am blessed greatly in return.

If you're going to become a romance writer, write with dedication to your craft.

If you're a reader, accept each new book as a gift. Light a candle, prop up your feet, open a book and pour a cup of tea.

"So you want to be a writer? Whenever someone tells me that this is her/his goal, I offer one simple piece of advice: <u>Don't give up your day job</u>!"

Don't Give Up Your Day Job—Yet!

By Dallas Schulze

When I tell aspiring writers, "Don't give up your day job," it always gets a laugh, which makes me feel terribly witty, but it's a valid piece of advice. Being a full-time writer sounds like a dream come true and there are some pretty neat perks. You don't have to dress up to go to work. In fact, you don't have to dress at all. I know a lot of writers who work in their pajamas. You don't have to punch a time clock, or fight commuter traffic, and you set your own hours.

So why not quit the 9-5 grind and embrace this halcyon lifestyle? Well, there's the inherent uncertainty of the writing life. Markets shift, styles change, editors come and go, publishers go under. All this is out of your control. You could sell four books to an editor who adores your work, then she quits and the next editor just doesn't share her good taste. A bad cover, a screw-up in shipping, or, heaven forbid, a less than stellar piece of writing and your numbers drop, your income along with it.

The other reason to hang onto the security of a day job is that it keeps some of the pressure off. There's a big difference between writing because you love it, and writing to pay the mortgage. That kind of pressure can put a real crimp in your creative output. Of course, for some people, nothing is more inspiring than the knowledge that there are bills to pay. If you don't need a weekly paycheck for security, then kiss the day job goodbye at your earliest opportunity.

"It's a damn good story. If you have any comments, write them on the back of a check."
Erle Stanley Gardner
Writing to an editor
* * *

"As a newly published author, I've known the fear of failure, the fear of looking at the empty pages, and all the troublesome emotions that can lurk in your head at the start of your creative work."

How to Prepare Psychologically
For a Literary Adventure

By Gay G. Gunn

*What has been will be again,
What has been done will be done again;
there is nothing new under the sun.*
Ecclesiastes 1:9

The Bible spoke of there being "nothing new under the sun" centuries ago, so all we modern-day mortals can hope to do is tell the story a little more interestingly than the last time.

Fear—that four-letter word—keeps us all from achieving our full potential in many areas of life, but especially in writing. Once we realize we don't have to pen the "Great American Novel," our goal should be to write the best novel that is within our human purview to accomplish. Ahaaa . . . feel the pressure being relieved and the creativity raining down like manna from heaven?

If you picked up this book then you are ready to begin. You have prepared for this literary adventure all your life. Writing is like taking those dreaded SAT's; you can't really study for them, *per se*, because your success with them (barring the courses on how to take a standardized test) depends upon all your life experiences. Before you even sit down with your yellow pad or at your computer, prior preparedness is 90% of the effort.

You have an idea for a great story in your head. You have read a copious amount of literature: the classics, your favorite fiction and romance writers, newspapers, magazines—any printed word that can help you expand your world view and give you a sense of, or even a need for, your novel's place in it.

You have listened (eavesdropped) on the society around you. While riding the bus, standing in movie lines, finger-popping to music lyrics, you have heard the issues and developed a feel for language and dialogue that rings true and has a believable rhythm and cadence.

Now, armed with your notes, tape recorder, or outline, you are ready to organize and write your novel. This remaining 10% is crucial to the success of completing the task—producing the manuscript. It takes discipline and commitment to give your craft the time it requires. Don't worry that the first line, first paragraph, first page, or even first chapter isn't riveting. Keep writing and get absorbed and lost in the project. Writing is rewriting and you can always go back and redo scenes or flesh out characters, but if you edit yourself every paragraph or page you'll become frustrated and stop. Then there will be nothing to rewrite. Once you get going and your characters grab onto you for dear life and won't let go, you've hit that groove . . . that zone. You don't want to stop—not to eat or answer the phone, and certainly not to go to your "day job."

Congratulations! At that "epiphanic" point you have become a writer.

Writing is like any other all-consuming avocation; the more you do it, the easier the words flow, like those wonderful phrases to describe "her," or the sexy way "he" does that thing with his lip. Then, the ideas will come from everywhere, at any time—in the shower, in the car, waking you up at night. My book, *Everlastin' Love,* was written on the bike trail of Rock Creek Park, and *Nowhere to Run,* came to me in Hampton, Virginia while giving a book discussion on *Everlastin' Love.*

There are no right or wrong ways of approaching a craft as personal as writing. It's all about discovery. As you find your voice, you will also find what works for you. However, what *is* universal if you want to be published, is that you must get serious, become committed, and be disciplined. Believe in yourself and what you are doing. Ignore that nagging fear, use rejection as fuel, and stay focused. Don't deny the world your literary masterpiece any longer. Get started, keep on writing and the rest will come!

<hr />

"Words are, of course, the most powerful drug used by mankind."
Rudyard Kipling
* * *

"It wasn't until I was married and my boys were grown before I got around to writing. I wrote what I wanted to read—bawdy escapes set in England. I've always written the same kind of book. My readers expect a Virginia Henley-type book every time, and they get it—the bawdier, the better. Passion is my business and I hope it becomes yours. Our craft demands it!"

You Must Have that Inner Passion

By Virginia Henley

To become a writer, you must have that inner passion. You must want it so badly you can taste it. You must always say *when* I am published, never *if* I am published. If anything in the world can keep you from your goal, you were never meant to become a writer in the first place.

The single most important ingredient for success is belief in yourself. If I could bottle confidence and hand it out to every unpublished writer, I would do it—but I don't have enough for myself. None of us do. We are riddled with self-doubt and insecurities:

- You write a book, then doubt that you can ever write another.
- You publish a book, then doubt that you will ever publish another.
- You make a best-seller list, then doubt that you will ever do it again.
- You win an award . . . and know it will be your last hurrah!

If you do not believe in yourself, *pretend* that you believe in yourself. People will see your confidence, it will show in your work, and lo and behold you gradually become more confident. Let me tell you that I am an average woman, and if I can do it, you can do it!

I honestly believe you have to have a natural talent for storytelling; you should have a basic knowledge of English grammar; and you must have tenacity. If you have these three basics, sooner or later you *will* be published.

I cannot tell you how to write, I can only tell you how *I* write. I begin with a map, and then I select the period in which I want to set the story. As soon as I have where and when, my juices start to bubble and I create my hero and heroine. My stories are character-driven and it helps if I flesh out whole lives for these people, with a past and a future, as if they were real. I see them, hear them, and even smell them. I know their taste in clothes and food and exactly what they are like in bed. Names are important; they have to be perfect, and are usually authentic names of people living in the area about which I'm writing.

I then do about two months of meticulous research. I never ever use a work of fiction for my research, but only the work of historians. I research who was on the throne and which palaces and castles they used. I research the clothes, food, and morals of the time. The one rule I set for myself is to give the story an authentic flavor of the time period. For instance, a restoration or a regency romp can be filled with risqué incidents and laughter, but in a medieval the tone has to be richer and darker, where the villains are not simply wicked, they are evil.

I open with something that grabs the attention. If I can get "naked" and "virgin" in the first sentence, I'm happy. Early on I try to get the reader's sympathy for my heroine. I open her mind and show some of her thoughts and emotions so the reader will identify with her. The hero is just as important; I try to make my reader fall in love with him. I make him dark, dominant, and dangerous (there is a lurking bastard inside of him), and then I create a heroine who is a match for him, or perhaps *more* than a match for him. I believe these heroines empower women to solve their own problems, without waiting for a man.

I make the chapters short and try to make the story move from place to place instead of keeping it all in one spot. I want to write an adventure that will sweep the reader away, and to do that I know I have to make it move. I don't overuse arcane language. I select period words and phrases and drop them in sparingly for that authentic flavor.

My dialogue is probably the most important thing in my books. Whether they are kings, queens, or servants, they should speak naturally and not in a stilted manner. My dialogue shows that my characters do everything with passion and great emotion. In order to make them jump off the page, I *become* my characters. I not only become the heroine, I become the hero and feel his driving lust. I become the villain and think very evil thoughts. I become all my minor characters . . . from the whore to the over-worked servant with the aching back. I love and adore my minor characters and truly believe they make the difference between a good book and a great book.

When I write, I am always dramatic and often melodramatic. Any time I can shock the reader, I do so. I want to make my reader gasp whether I'm describing the heroine's gown or the hero's sex organ. In my stories I use a lot of humor and a great deal of sex. However, both of these things are very subjective, so I can only write what appeals to me.

My rule of thumb is, the stronger the history, the stronger the sensuality, in order to give the story balance. However, I never forget that I am, first and last, writing a love story. A man and woman meet, and as they resolve their difficulties and conflicts, the romantic relationship develops between them. It ends happily because they form a permanent and exclusive bond and fall in love!

Write this story from the heart, for if you truly care about your characters, it shows, and your readers too will love them and, ultimately, the wonderful book you have written.

Rosemarie, Jade and Sierra
San Francisco

Dear Kathryn,

We are so thrilled that you are helping us!! When your package was delivered by the cute man in brown (our UPS driver), Sierra and I were so excited we ripped it open immediately, without even waiting for Jade to get home from her job. (She's currently in charge of PR for two dance clubs.)

How inspiring these wonderful articles were! What joy to read words of wisdom from the great Harlequin writer Emma Darcy, who shows in her books that she truly understands that souls bond in a great romance. She is one of my all-time favorites.

Sierra rushed to the essay by Catherine Palmer and read, and then re-read it.

When Jade finally did get home and got over being peeved with us for starting without her, she went crazy trying to absorb all the articles in one sitting.

Each article was so different from the rest and yet each showed skillfully the beauty of genre romance . . . and the many challenges we face on the road to writing one!

We now know we must do the following: think of our readers before all else; take genre romance seriously and commit to writing *great* books within the genre (because our writing will be a gift that will touch others); use caution when beginning; don't quit our day jobs quite yet; learn all that we can about the genre and writing in general; and always be passionate about what we write—and about *wanting* to write.

Jade had been the only one of us with a work in progress, but after your emphatic, "Don't start without an outline," and after studying all the articles, she realized the magnitude of what lies ahead and stopped. She had been writing a romantic suspense novel—had even completed three chapters, but she agrees that she needs more help and promises not to write another word until you say go.

That goes for Sierra and me, too!

One thing I know for sure from years of watching my mom struggle to put words to paper—there's more to the process than just spewing words onto the page. Night after night, she worked and re-worked a manuscript until she felt all the words were exactly right and "it sang." She wrote beautiful historicals with complicated plots. Now, though, she urges me to use caution if those are the kinds of books I want to write. (And I do, Kathryn, for I love big historicals!) She says, "Things have changed."

How have things changed? A romance is a romance is a romance ... right? I mean ... boy meets girl; boy loses girl; boy and girl end up living happily-ever-after. Period. What's so different about that?

From reading your first book, *How to Write a Romance and Get it Published,* we know there is a difference between a historical romance and a contemporary romance, that both kinds of romances have been around just about forever, and that these sub-genres of romance already portray love stories in all kinds of different ways. So, what's out there today that's really different? Moreover, what will be different ... popular ... trendy ... tomorrow, and the tomorrow after that? Do we look to the past for these answers, or to what's happening in the present?

We love the genre; we're excited about writing, but ... now what? Could you please give us some insight into the romance genre as it has been, and as you feel it might be? We know it is critically important to know your market and we need some direction here! Help!

Your grateful pupils,
Rosemarie, Jade and Sierra

Kathryn Falk, Lady of Barrow
Romantic Times Magazine
Brooklyn, New York

Dear Girls:

You are so right about the importance of knowing your markets. There have indeed been major changes in the past several years. New avenues are opening up and trends appear. Here's my general outline of the romance genre and a take on where it's heading. Of course, to have *all* the answers, I would have to be a seer or a fortune-teller.

[signature: Kathryn]

With a Fillip and a Twist . . . It's New

By Kathryn Falk

If you've been around long enough, you've probably heard the popular prediction: "The pendulum always swings." You can see that occurrence for yourself in every cultural media. Fashion, music, films, and books go through cycles only to be resurrected with new twists or innovative blending. Did John Grisham really start the legal thriller category? Of course not! My mother read Perry Mason when I was a kid, and in the 1980's it was Scott Turow who made that sub-genre fashionable and launched the latest career move—attorney today, author tomorrow. (At least they don't have to hire anyone to read their contracts!)

Who would have dreamed that ages-old Celtic dancing, combined with new age music and staging borrowed from that master of female sensuality, Busby Berkley, would end up being the phenomenon known as *River Dance*, which spawned *Lord of the Dance*.

If you watched *film noir* in the days of Mickey Spillane and Peter Gunn, you weren't too surprised by *LA Confidential*, were you? Wasn't it the same, with a new twist? Kim Basinger wore the hairstyle that Veronica Lake originated . . . and so on, and so on.

What has gone before in the romance genre sometimes returns again in new guises and with new twists. Knowledge of the classics of romance will provide you with a firm foundation on which to build your writing career.

Only a few sub-genres of romance flourished in the 1970's and early 1980's. Series readers had only Harlequins and the now-defunct MacFadden romances. Silhouette arrived on the scene in the early 80's. Georgette Heyer and Barbara Cartland were the queens of the Regency genre. The Avon Ladies, particularly Kathleen Woodiwiss, Rosemary Rogers, Johanna Lindsey, Bertrice Small, and Shirlee Busbee, along with Warner's lovable Jennifer Wilde (the late Tom E. Huff) were the pioneers of historical romance with sensuous love scenes. Zebra romances arrived in the early 80's, spearheaded by Janelle Taylor and Sylvie Summerfield, and established a lively following for Indian and western settings with more romance than history. Gothic writers were few, but Mary Stewart and Jennifer Blake had many fans in the 1970's. Some male writers made a living for a while in the late 70's, but couldn't "cut the mustard" in the burgeoning romance field. Readers resented their "rape sagas."

Here's a breakdown of romance into the sub-genres we know today:

HISTORICAL: Medium-length or long novels set in any period prior to World War II, often referred to by male detractors as "sex in hoop-skirts" or "bodice rippers"!

SERIES/CATEGORY ROMANCE: Short contemporaries published by Harlequin and Silhouette, numbered in a particular series to be easily collectible, translated worldwide into more than 25 languages, and accounting for astounding book club sales.

REGENCY: Short-to-medium length novels of manners, set during the Regency period in England (1811-1820).

GOTHIC: Medium-length romantic suspense novels involving a mystery and an historical setting.

LONG CONTEMPORARY: These came into vogue in the late 1980's when a handful of series romance authors, particularly LaVyrle Spencer, Sandra Brown, Nora Roberts, and Judith McNaught wanted to write longer books with more sub-plots. Because they had already established strong followings, their publishers allowed them to break out. This sub-genre does follow the romance format of more romance and development of the relationship than other plot points.

INTRIGUE/ROMANTIC SUSPENSE/MYSTERY: These romances are the most flourishing of the new markets. They are wildly popular with both women and men readers, as well as with writers. They're easy for agents and publishers to option for TV, film, and video markets. In addition, they have hardcover (think big-buck) potential because the mystery elements attract an upscale crowd of buyers. The most popular plots can be examined as incorporating the old-fashioned gothic (*frissons* of terror up the spine) and the romantic suspense elements of the genre, particularly if the heroine of the late 90's, the female sleuth, is featured.

HUMOR: These are much appreciated and give a fresh layer to all sub-genres. A new author with a talent for "making 'em laugh" should hitch her wagon, or computer, to this star!

ETHNIC OR MULTICULTURAL: Romances in this category are satisfying an ever-widening circle of readers. To date, the ethnic romances being published or sought are:

AFRICAN-AMERICAN: Romances, which have taken quite a few years (much longer than I expected) to find a niche. However, now they're starting to hit their stride and attracting better distribution and a loyal readership, primarily within the ethnic group written about. There are two African-American series—Arabesque and Indigo—being published. Every romance publisher is open to single title, mainstream books with multicultural characters, particularly in contemporary settings.

LATINO/HISPANIC: Romance is in its infancy, but Genesis has a line, Tango 2, and BET Books/Arabesque line is testing the size of the readership and will gauge any crossover interest from other ethnic groups. Publishers investing in ethnic markets see the demographics of a growing and ever wealthier Hispanic/Latino population and, as a result of the projected markets, are relentlessly searching for manuscripts.

ASIAN: Nearly impossible for editors to find, and there's some question as to whether the second generation Asian readership as a romance market even exists. The problem seems to be with the eastern hero who, culturally/traditionally, was not typically romantic, which may explain why multi-culture/multi-racial Asian romances may establish the first toehold. Historicals (such as Tai-Pan) with Asian settings have always been enormously successful, but until readers exist for Asian romance, there will not be writers of Asian romance. Mainstream publishers are putting out a large number of novels written by Asian authors, but few focus on romance. Nevertheless, Genesis Press is launching its Red Slipper imprint devoted to Asian/Asian-American love stories in 1999.

INSPIRATIONAL: Romances exploded on the market in 1997/98 and readers of *Romantic Times* demanded we include their reviews and ratings in our pages. Of course, we agreed. These are not like any other sub-genre, and are quite different from the inspirational romances that had a brief run in the early 1980's with several romance publishers. This market has a tendency to swing back and forth, depending upon the popularity of the authors. The books reflect a return to traditional religious values, offer comfort, and are written with more sweetness than most romance novels in recent years.

Many romance authors, such as Francine Rivers, are now writing for this sub-genre. Because of the upsurge in publishing opportunities here, and an intuition that these novels could help them make the leap into the mainstream inspirational/spiritual market, more romance authors are crossing over.

If you study *Romantic Times'* reviews and features on this sub-genre, you may eventually notice the proliferation of more "series" inspirationals. There appears to be great potential for inspirational romance to evolve into structured delineations similar to Harlequin/Silhouette. (Both Harlequin and Bantam have already established inspirational romance imprints to compete with the various Christian publishing houses.)

EROTIC: These romances go by many guises in American publishing and always have, from the early days of Rosemary Rogers'

Sweet Savage Love up to the currently available and more graphic British imports.

Unlike traditional "sexy" American romances, the British erotic imports have relationships that are neither monogamous, nor guaranteed to have a happy commitment at the end. Written by women, for women, they express female fantasies, not male, and that's new! Genesis Press has thus far brought two such titles, *Arousing Anna* and *The Women's Club*, to the U.S. in their "Secret Library" anthology series published under its *THERION* imprint.

ALTERNATIVE REALITY: These are romances that encompass all the categories of the paranormal including time travel, fairy, ghost, witch, magic, shape-changing, angel, vampire, and werewolf. Readers wish publishers would produce more selections each month and booksellers say they are the most popular of all the new categories.

MAINSTREAM ROMANCE: To have the qualification "Romance" on the spine, a book should be at least 50-75% romance. If a romance author puts a strong romance into a mainstream plot, the strict parameters of romance will be violated if there's more intrigue, history, or fantasy than romance. Of course, that doesn't keep romance readers from following the author to the mainstream book section!

"The profession of writing makes horse racing seem like a solid, stable business."
John Steinbeck
* * *

Rosemarie Kelly,
San Francisco, CA

Dear Kathryn:

So much for lumping romance into strictly "contemporary" and "historical" categories! I knew a great deal of what you wrote, but Sierra and Jade had no idea that the industry encompassed so many sub-genres and categories. (They don't read *Romantic Times* as carefully as I do, I guess!)

We are going to go back and read some of the classics as you suggest.

At this point we realize this is going to be a far more difficult journey than we envisioned. Maybe we even need to "get back to the basics." Can you help us with this before we go much further? We really don't want to end up simply "spinning those wheels" without direction.

Should we continue to take some writing courses offered through the community college at the same time? What do you think?

Hoping to hear from you soon,
Rosemarie

CHAPTER II

CRAFT AND TECHNIQUE

REVIEWING THE BASICS

Kathryn Falk, Lady of Barrow
Romantic Times Magazine
Brooklyn, New York

Dear Rosemarie, Jade and Sierra,

Rome wasn't built in a day and the writing process won't happen quickly either. So yes, it will certainly help if you can continue to take some writing courses locally. However, if you can't, here's some sound advice from my pal Sylvia Halliday who is one of the best writing instructors. I agree with her completely when she tells you that the most important thing you can do if you want to *write* romance is to *read* romance.

Then, to save you time and frustration, I want you to study one of the all-time-favorite writing tomes. Although it's a guide for creating a mainstream novel, *Writing the Blockbuster Novel*, written by agent Al Zuckerman, is a must for your reference shelf. Al's stable of clients includes Ken Follett, Stephen Hawkins, Nora Roberts,

Eileen Goudge, and Ann Martin, the creator of the phenomenal series, "The Babysitter's Club." (To give just a sample of the authors this dynamite agent represents.)

If more first-time writers read Zuckerman's book before typing even one word, they would be saved hours and hours of wasted effort. I love his book, not only for the advice, which is superb, but also because he shows you how to outline, using as an example Ken Follett's wonderful thriller, *The Man from St. Petersburg*. If you read Follett's book in tandem with *Writing the Blockbuster Novel*, you'll enjoy some amazing observations. If you can't find a copy of *The Man From St. Petersburg*, try one of RT's "Bookstores That Care" (BTC).

Best Wishes,

Kathryn

P.S. Regarding the "Bookstores that Care" . . . these bookstores, located in every state and several countries, are *Romantic Times'* network of romance-friendly new-and-used-books bookstores that sell and trade out-of-print and classic romances. Each store has friendly knowledgeable owners and sales staff, and I assure you these bookstores are the best source for finding any out-of-print books that are not available for purchase on *Romantic Times'* web site: *RomanticTimes.com*.

"A healthy study of the classics, and dedication to your craft will see you through to a successful writing career. It worked for me."

Learning the Basic Skills on Your Own

By Sylvia Halliday

I wrote my first book, *Marielle,* a historical romance, under the name Ena Halliday. I wrote it without knowing "diddly-squat" about writing. How did I do it? I was a reader—a lifelong reader who had devoured Shakespeare, the classics, current fiction, and biographies. I had delighted in the old swashbucklers, mysteries, adventure tales—anything I could get my hands on. Because they were written at a time when writing and grammar were still vital school subjects, even classic "fluff" could subconsciously teach me about the elements and structure that went into making a readable book.

So my first piece of advice is, visit your library. Take out novels written 30 and 40 years ago or earlier—novels such as those written by Du Maurier, Sabatini, Yerby and Anthony Hope. (His *Prisoner of Zenda* is marvelous!) Notice the clean prose, the use of colorful words, the strong narrative line.

For heaven's sake, don't just read current romances! When I'm reading someone's manuscript, I can always tell if the writer has nourished her/himself solely on current fare. The book is filled with "purple prose," too many adverbs and adjectives, garbled grammar, shifting points of view, and tired "romantic" clichés. (Till the day I die, my characters will never "maintain" or "aver." Nor will they "spasm" in the throes of passion!) Reading only current romances makes your work sound tired and derivative. Paradoxically, old books will spur you on to freshness and originality.

My next bit of advice involves adverbs and adjectives. Using too many indicates the writer is not thinking about what is truly vital to make a book come alive—strong action and dialogue. Think of a play or movie. We count on the actor's physical movements, his facial expressions and his words, to understand what he is thinking and feeling. We don't have an interior monologue or a bunch of "-ly" words to give us clues. "'Come here,' he said angrily," is lazy writing. "He pounded the table. 'I order you to come here!'" makes the scene vivid. Don't fall back on easy clichés for your actions, which is a common failing for writers who seem to be on automatic pilot, parroting someone else's book. If she "raises her head" or "clears her throat," ask yourself *why*? Does that action convey an emotion, or is it merely "filler?"

If grammar is your weak point, get a good book on the subject. *The Elements of Style* by William Strunk and E. B. White is probably the best. (And please, if you're writing a romance, learn the difference between "lie" and "lay!" There's far too much reclining in a romance to mix up the usage of these two words! Any dictionary will tell you the difference.)

This thought leads me to word usage. Lately, I'm finding that too many writers are relying on the thesaurus of their computers to give them original words. After you check the thesaurus, you should use a dictionary! The English language has far too many subtleties to make words automatically interchangeable with one another.

Point of view. How do you deal with it? Are you going to head-hop? That's lazy writing. Instead, get yourself into the head of one character and see the scene entirely from his/her perspective. If you're in the heroine's head and you suddenly find it necessary to convey what the hero is thinking, remember that play or movie again. Let your hero's actions or dialogue tell the reader what he is thinking. The heroine can even guess at his emotions, interpreting what she sees. (If you really want to play games with your reader, have her misinterpret his words or actions.)

If you are dealing with topics you have little knowledge about, do proper research. A reader will pick up a glaring inaccuracy and hold it against you. You must be trustworthy and believable to draw the reader into your story.

Every scene has a purpose. The action and dialogue should be meaningful—to advance the plot, to set a mood, to illuminate a character. You can't just say, "Gee, I think I'll write a book," and then let the words pour out in a jumble. A wealth of thinking, planning and analyzing goes into writing. The more you are aware of every word you write, the stronger your book will be.

"When you write, you lay out a line of words.
The line of words is a miner's pick,
a woodcarver's gouge, a surgeon's probe.
You wield it, and it digs a path you follow.
Soon you find yourself deep in new territory.
Is it a dead-end, or have you located
the real subject? You will know tomorrow,
or this time next year.

. . .

You make the path boldly and follow it fearfully.
You go where the path leads.
Annie Dillard
The Writing Life
Pub by Harper Collins

"Very few people can give this kind of advice, no one does it as well as Al Zuckerman...Enjoy him...Learn from him. He's the best."
—from the introduction by

KEN FOLLETT

WRITING
the
BLOCK BUSTER NOVEL

ALBERT ZUCKERMAN

"This is only a short exerpt from my book, but this advice should help you on your way."

Excerpts from Writing the Blockbuster Novel

By Al Zuckerman

The Outline Process

No sane person would think of setting out to construct a sky-scraper or even a one-family home without a detailed set of plans. A big novel must have the literary equivalents of beams and joists strong enough to sustain it excitingly from beginning to end, and it also must contain myriad interlocking parts fully as complex as those in any building type. Yet there are authors who commence a novel without first working up an outline. Outlines, they say, cramp their creativity, inhibit their characters from roaming free and becoming interesting, and take the joy out of writing because this planning process denies them the possibility of making wonderful discoveries that come to them only while they're setting down the novel it-self.

My surmise is that few writers who talk this way ever see their books on the bestseller list. Every mega-book with which I've been involved was planned and re-planned and planned again, much the way architectural drawings are continually revised. Some major authors must write the full text for a number of scenes as a way of getting to know their characters before they put together their outlines, while others can start cold with a first draft synopsis.

Margaret Mitchell, an exception, appears not to have used a written outline for *Gone with the Wind.* What she did do, though, to ensure a plot that would build inexorably to the climax she envisaged was to write her last chapter first and then work her way from back to front, chapter by chapter.

The outlining process, like the writing of the book itself, is almost a matter of layering. No writer, I believe, comes up with a wholly satisfying outline on his first attempt. Through four drafts of outlines for *The Man From St. Petersburg* written over an eight-month period, Ken Follett step by step consciously set out to build a story that contains high stakes, larger-than-life characters, a strong dramatic question, a high concept, farfetched plot premise, intense emotional involvement between several point-of-view characters, and an exotic and interesting setting.

Follett's novel (and those of most best-selling mainstream authors) begins with the plot. At the outset, it's often no more than a strong situation that can be summarized in a sentence or two.

You'll see how Follett uses the outline form gradually to enrich and complicate his plot while at the same time to narrow and sharpen its focus. But character is equally crucial. And Follett, from outline to outline, adds and eliminates *dramatis personae*, as well as their past histories and unique idiosyncrasies—all with a view toward building up the stature of his people, making them interesting, exciting, and enhancing our feelings for them.

Larger Than Life Characters

Your own book will probably need only one larger-than-life character. In fact, it's unlikely that it could easily accommodate more than one. Give him/her an aim, goal, longing or ambition with which you (and the reader) can empathize. It should be something that, if you were in his shoes, you too would desperately want and that you would do anything in your power to bring to fruition. Keep in mind, too, that this goal can be reactive as well as active.

In most of the popular books by Mary Higgins Clark, and in novels such as *Rosemary's Baby* by Ira Levin and, to some extent, in *The Godfather*, the main thrusts of their protagonists are attempts to achieve security, fight off outside threats, escape fearful dangers, or gain relief from adversity. Your major characters (most of whom should not be larger-than-life), will also need to be given an inner desire of their own, a yearning for something or someone that motivates and defines them as a distinctive if not unique being. That drive may be tied totally into the main action.

Your characters could have to cope with a seriously ailing mother, a retarded sister, a semi-delinquent teenage son or a problematic but beloved dog or cat. These or a hundred other situations you might devise will complicate her life (and the plot), freeing her momentarily from the constraints of a fast moving plot and illuminating her humanity. In Michael Crichton's *Rising Sun*, the hero's two-year-old daughter, whom he is struggling to raise as a single parent, serves exactly this function.

Introducing Your Characters

Once you have fixed upon the thrusts or goals of each of your main characters, you must decide how to introduce them and at what points in the story. Try to bring them on one at a time, separately, giving each at least a page before you introduce another character. That way you can solidly establish each one's identity, and the reader is more likely to remember and recognize that character in subsequent scenes. Think of a cocktail party where you try to introduce five or ten people at once, and how difficult it is even to remember their names. In your novel, you don't want to subject your readers to something this difficult.

Your protagonist should be brought on in the first chapter and no later than the second. The readers want to know whom the story essentially is about. If you keep your reader waiting longer than this, he may be disoriented, believing that the seemingly important character he first met is your chief subject. Avoid forcing the reader to make this awkward adjustment. It's also good to introduce all your major characters fairly early in your novel and to keep involving them all the way through, as opposed to bringing on a new character with each new plot complication or a new major character as you approach your ending.

Building Your Characters

Usually it's best to create a protagonist who is loved, admired, and respected—if not universally, then at least by one or two of the characters around him. And your hero in turn should give back some of that good feeling or love to one or more of the people with whom she's involved.

To help you build a big commercial novel, I recommend two specific qualities over and above the ones already discussed: your principal characters' frailties or weaknesses and their levels of self-awareness. Think hard about them as you create your characters. People we think of as "perfect" we usually think of as boring. The individuals we delight in are most often ones with some uncontrollable tendency, less-than-wonderful habit, or off-key idiosyncrasy. As to self-awareness, in real life most of us are pretty blind to our shortcomings. So, the literary character to whom you give at least a glimmer of awareness of his own faults, and who deplores or feels guilty about them, takes on added stature in our estimation. Since you want to endow your characters with stature, cause them at least some of the time to do things that we'll admire and that may even take our breath away.

Rosemarie, Jade & Sierra
San Francisco

Dear Kathryn,

Thank Sylvia for her wonderful words of wisdom.

We rushed out and bought a copy of Al's book, read it—then had to go back out for two more copies. Now we each have a copy beside our beds. What a man! What a book!

Like you said, we may not end up writing a Ken Follett-type book, but now we certainly understand the brilliance of working on nearly a dozen drafts to get the right balance in the outline!

By the way, is Al married?

The Grateful Girls in SF

Kathryn Falk, Lady of Barrow
Romantic Times Magazine
Brooklyn, New York

Dear Ladies,

Al is definitely taken, but join a long line of fans that want him to be their agent. I knew you'd feel that way about his book.

While he has you thinking mainstream, look over Donna Julian's advice on romancing a mainstream story. This next batch of articles also includes priceless guidance from a wondrous author, Pamela Morsi, who writes so sensitively about women's emotions. Her first novel, *Courting Miss Hattie*, is an all-time reader favorite. In addition, take to heart the recommendations of Teresa Medeiros, Sara Orwig, Evelyn Rogers, and Mary Kirk, all of whom have been writing since the 1980's and really know their stuff. I've added a few other articles that should prove helpful, from a group of newcomers who bring fresh insight to writing for tomorrow's markets.

Best Wishes,

Kathryn

P.S. Al wishes you a lot of luck. I think he'll look at your manuscripts the day you finish!

"I understand you've had a discourse on mainstream plotting from the master, Al Zuckerman, so this is a good time to discuss putting romance into a mainstream plot – or vice versa."

Putting Romance in Your Mainstream Novel

By Donna Julian

No two authors, editors, or agents would agree completely about what constitutes a mainstream romance—and with good reason. It's not simple to define. Is it mainstream or romance? If the core of the plot is romance, the book's a romance. If the story can stand on its own without the added romance element, it's a mainstream.

Gone with the Wind is an excellent example of a mainstream novel often referred to as a romance. Test it yourself. If Scarlett and Rhett had never met, would there still have been a book? Absolutely. Margaret Mitchell's story was centered on a spoiled vain woman who discovered her strengths through adversity. Of course, that mainstream novel wouldn't have been as compelling had Rhett never walked onto the pages and crawled under Scarlett's skin.

My book *Slow Dance* is another example of a story that could have worked successfully without the romance element. The passion between Lily and Sash is not critical to the plot. (However, it was too great for this author to ignore.) *A Kiss in the Dark* by Tiffany White is a book that epitomizes the romance novel. The love story not only drives the plot; it *is* the plot! It's sensual, funny, heartwarming, and deliciously enticing.

So, you've determined that your book is more "mainstream," but still want to appeal to the romance reader. What do you do? First off, count your blessings. Readers expect romance novels to adhere to a fairly strict set of rules but they give mainstream writers more leeway. In a mainstream, your hero and heroine don't have to be together in every chapter. Their relationship can develop subtly and softly like a Renoir (as in Anne Rivers Siddon's *Up Island)* or boldly and richly like a Peter Max illustration (a la Sandra Brown). They don't even have to have a happy-ever-after ending. (But trust me when I tell you, most readers prefer/demand a fairytale resolution—regardless of genre.)

Choosing your setting carefully can also create an ambience of romance. *The Blue Lagoon* by Henry D. Stacpoole has an exotic and romantic setting, which is pivotal for the romance part of the book. Although the book is strongly a romance, it qualifies for mainstream status because the book is first a story of survival. This book could have taken place nowhere else other than the exotic island that surrounds the lagoon, and the lagoon itself.

Meryl Sawyer selected the ultimate stage for romance in her erotic mainstream thriller *Last Night* set in Maui, Hawaii. Romance and seduction are as indigenous to Maui as the heady redolence of island flowers and the chilling threat of dormant volcanoes.

Michael Crichton, one of the most savvy authors in the biz (and undoubtedly the one with the most divergent list of bestsellers to his credit), recognized that the core of his dynamic mainstream novel, *Disclosure*—the complex and devious machinations at work in a corporate merger—wasn't enough book to drag readers into his plot. With his usual flawless instinct, he introduced a past relationship and he tossed in a sex scene so daring and explicit the book should have come with a warning: Avoid if celibate.

Mainstream allows for elements of suspense, horror, mystery, and romance to be enfolded into a novel like ingredients that enhance a recipe. Romance is not a requirement in mainstream novels, nor is it in life. Monks live without it. So do my neutered cat and spayed dog. However, most of the population in general finds it a yummy essential.

I enjoy penning novels that overflow the confines of genre fiction, yet still include a romance. Why? Like my readers, I just can't get past the most fundamental of all of life's influences: LOVE.

"Write fast, write close to the bone, write for ten hours straight until you're not thinking in words anymore but in colors, in smells, in waves of memory.
Write what you care about."
Bonnie Friedman
From, *Writing Past Dark*
Pub, Harper Collins
* * *

"I haven't always been a writer. In fact, writing is a skill that has come to me late in life, but I love my work and I hope all your dreams of becoming storytellers will come true too."

Making up Stories

By Pamela Morsi

I began writing, seriously, for the first time in 1988. Since then I've had twelve novels published. I've won a dozen awards, some for writing, some for selling. There are nearly two million copies of my books in print. But, I'm not a natural writer.

I don't love language, nor am I in awe of the written word. I just like *making up stories*. I've been doing that in my head since long before I knew my ABCs. This, I am convinced, is a common malady.

As a professional writer, I can't begin to tell you how many times someone has come up to me and said, "Have I got a story for you!" Almost like Pavlov's dog, this statement now invariably causes me to slip into a semi-hypnotic trance where I nod politely and maintain a pretense of listening. The writer who said that there is nothing new under the sun was undoubtedly speaking of these ideas.

I believe a writer's ideas are neither the property nor the creation of the writer. They are universal, as in nature. It's almost as if there is a great storehouse somewhere that we, as writers, can tap into. Or maybe these ideas are carried on our DNA codes or reside in the darkest depths of our brain stem where our ancestors revered them a billion generations ago.

There is never a shortage of ideas. You never need anyone to give you any. Nor is there ever a surplus. None are ever in excess. A constant supply is always available for the taking. All the writer must do is transform an idea into a story, a seemingly very simple proposition. Without the story, the idea returns to the vast mental wasteland from whence it came. We can't let that happen to some of the wonderful ideas that come our way. We must write the story.

Not all story ideas are meant to be novels. Some ideas are just not sufficient to create novels. That is why the short story, poem, even the song lyric continue to exist. (I bet you were wondering about that.) The "Achy Breaky Heart" or "Whoomp! (There It Is)" are ideas that come from the same omnipotent mass of knowledge that sent us *Ulysses*, but the parameters of the stories in these songs are simply narrower than the boundaries of the James Joyce novel.

Even a very good idea will not necessarily make a good novel. All of us have had the sad experience of eagerly picking up a likely story that starts out with a marvelous premise then falls so flat by page 100 we can only barely drag ourselves through the remaining 300 pages.

Like seeds scattered on a rock, ideas blossom quickly and hopefully take root. However, if they don't have enough depth to reach down to the moisture that gives them sustenance, they inevitably whither away.

Some ideas are problematic by their very nature. Ideas heavily laden with intricate subplots and unlikely motivations frequently get tangled in their own complexity. The luckless writer who labors twenty years upon some weighty tome that never quite works out is a cliché. I am not saying complexity is bad, but I do think simplicity is better. Please don't make the mistake of thinking that this is limiting. You don't have to use a lot of words to make a statement.

Another test of whether an idea is a good one is whether or not you can really live with it. Aside from the tastes or interests of any reader or editor, you as the writer will have to spend more time with this idea than you do with your children, your parents, or your spouse. This idea will be a constant floater on the back of your everyday life for months, maybe even years. Even after the work is complete, it lingers as a tie to a period of your life as clearly and unshakably as memories of, for example, your high school years.

A dear friend, whom I think is constantly trying to ease me into more literary pursuits, once asked me why I didn't try to write something around the theme of the futility of life and the irony of the survival instinct. Now that is an interesting concept, that life is so meaningless that nature had to code in an instinct to make us put up with it. There are lots of people who could really make a go of that idea. I cannot, however, imagine voluntarily putting myself—perky Pollyanna that I am—into a grand funk for a year. It's just not something my peculiar personality can be happy with. An interviewer asked me one time why there are never any villains in my writing. I told her I have the luxury of creating a whole world of my choosing, and why wouldn't I want to fill it with people who are basically decent and trying to do the right thing? As a writer, I can live with that scenario.

Be sure that for the long haul—and novel writing is a long haul—you can hang in there and cope. If you are creating a sociopath stalker/slayer, be aware that person is going to live in your house for the next year. Don't push yourself into paranoid agoraphobia.

Occasionally, when the moon is right, and the stars are aligned, the ideas that come to you are the perfect blend of passion, lucidity, and entertainment. When that happens, all you as a writer have to do is pray, hold your mouth just right, and work until your fingers are ready to fall off. Plant your fanny in the chair and write. That's not just your vocation, it's your duty. Why else would you have been granted this gift?

There are really two kinds or writers. Actually, there may be a hundred types, but as I said I go for simplicity so I'll divide them merely into two. There are those who just love to write. They love letters and language and the written word. They look at parts of speech as truths evoking reverence. English, Spanish, or whatever their language is as important to them as what they use it for. Then there are those who use writing as the medium to convey stories. These are storytellers first. Their tradition is a different one from the language lover, but one in which they can feel just as much pride. That's the group from which I come. If I could just tell my stories, make movies of them, sing them, I would do that and I would be just as content with that outcome as I am now to see them on the printed page. I chose writing because no other medium was readily available to me. I hate to bastardize ol' Marshall McLuhan, but the medium is not *my* message. I only use it.

That is not always easy. What I envision in my mind is sometimes very hard to get down on paper. The act of making the evanescent into the tangible forces the idea to evolve—most frequently in ways unexpected. Often it's hard to really get a handle on it.

There is a process that turns these stories in our heads into written words on the page. My personal take on that process can be summed up this way:

- Don't begin at the beginning.
- Don't write what you know.
- Never rewrite when you can move forward.
- Enjoy yourself.

I did say this was my personal take on this process.

As a writer, you must have a routine. It can be an amount of time devoted to writing, a number of pages or words completed, or whatever. But it has to be an absolute. I once sat on a panel where writers were telling about their daily schedules. Most were saying that they worked six to eight hours per day every day. More than a few admitted to 10 years with no time off on weekends. One author said that she had written 2500 words every day in the previous 10 years including every Christmas day and the day of her wedding.

By comparison, I am a slug. When it was my turn, I was a little bit sheepish to admit that my routine, my absolute, is that every day (well not every day—Monday through Fridays only) I turn on the computer. That's it. That's all I have to do. Somehow, just that much gives me the impetus to write a couple of books every year.

Okay, let's have a look at this little recipe that I've put together for you. I'm sure that most of you have looked at a million "how to write" books which break a novel down into its components and then tell you all the specifics on what goes where. I think these good books are useful. However, writing, like sewing or painting or auto mechanics, is something that's best learned hands-on.

There is writing, and there is rewriting. Writing is creating. Spilling out the idea in your head and translating it into meaningful little black squiggles on a page. This is magic. You think you're in control one minute, plodding one word after another and the next you're typing for all you are worth and whole scenes are pouring out on the pages as bright and as visual as paints on a canvas. There is nothing quite like the feeling of halting in mid-paragraph, gazing at the words you've just written and whispering in awe, "This is good. This is really good."

Rewriting is looking back over that same work and making sure every subject has a predicate, the tenses agree, the voice isn't passive and the adverbs are actually part of the English language. Rewriting is a skill entirely different from the writing. If you can only be good at one, be good at writing. There's a story about an author who didn't know where to put his commas. His editor told him to just leave them out completely. There are lots of people at the publishing house who know where to put them.

I am fortunate. My work comes out pretty clean. My first draft looks pretty good. However, everybody needs rewrites. It is a shame to waste what knowledge you have about grammar and punctuation by ignoring the contribution of both to making what you say understandable to your reader. You must write and rewrite, just please don't try to do them at the same time.

Some authors talk about waiting for the "Muse." Other authors scoff at that and tell you that the Muse is an excuse for lazy writers to be lazy. I have already confessed to you that I am a lazy writer. Although I don't call it "waiting for the Muse," there are times when I just stare at a blank screen and can't think of what to say next. Being "blocked" is another "author-ish" term that the more prolific sneer at. It is a common affliction and is—as far as I know—almost always temporary. Don't worry about it or it *will* make you crazy. You can't make it go away, so don't even try. There are those who say that Papa Hemingway blew his head off trying to make it go away. Whether he is unblocked in the afterlife, I couldn't say. For sure he's no longer writing anything for us to read.

This "blocked" time, if you suffer with it, is rewrite time. As I said in my little Pam-rule, never rewrite when you can move forward. As long as things are flowing, keep flowing with them. The spigot will slow to a trickle soon enough, and it may shut off completely. When it does, don't sit and stare blankly, rewrite. Polish, perfect, and review what you've already written. For me, at least, this invariably gets the idea back on track and the creative part going again.

Okay, you've got your idea; you're ready to roll. You've agreed to a schedule. You've got your page set up. Inch margins all around should leave you 25 to 27 lines per page. Ten words to a line is 250 words to a page. For a 100,000-word novel that means 400 pages.

I try to make my chapters 20 pages long, two scenes to a chapter, so I know the book should consist of about 40 scenes. I use this as a guide. Hard and fast rules are for accountants and physicists; writers just need a ballpark of parameters to move around in.

Let's divide those 400 pages or 40 scenes into beginning middle and end. Don't divide them equally. The end should be shortest and the middle longer than the beginning. Perhaps use 100 pages for the beginning, 250 for the middle and 50 for the end. Try to be aware of where you are, but don't get obsessive about it. You want to get things set up without too much dawdling around and you want enough substance in the middle so that people will be eager for the ending resolution. If your storyline is too short, you'll have to add scenes or maybe a subplot. I don't get frantic if I haven't got the set-up down and I'm on page 155, nor do I start throwing extraneous stuff into the story when I find I'm already set up on page 30. I'm just cognizant that if the beginning is long, the middle may need to move a little faster. Anything can be fixed later, but being aware of these numbers helps you to keep at a workable pace. They don't mean you lose anything in spontaneity.

Ultimately, your publisher will have a set length that they want it to be; pages are money and they've got that down to a science. If it's too short, the publisher will make the print bigger and if it's too long they'll make the print smaller.

The beginning of your novel needs a compelling hook. This is not some affectation, and it doesn't have to be integral to your plot; it just has to be there. This fits perfectly with my rule about not beginning at the beginning. The hook is vital to get your book read— by the reader ultimately, but first by an editor.

A friend asked me to read a manuscript of hers. I got to about page 25 and quit. I told her that I thought it needed work. She pleaded with me to continue to read it. "It gets really good on about page 80," she assured me. Well, I can assure you that no busy editor is going to slog through 70 pages of an across-the-transom manuscript waiting for it to get good. Most editors say they know by page ten if they want to buy a manuscript. An editor who's a good friend of mine tells me that *by page three* she's sold on it or uninterested.

You have got to give the entire feel and rhythm of your book right at the jump go. Frequently, I find I don't really understand that feel and rhythm until the book I am writing is complete so I wait until I'm done to write the beginning.

After hooking your reader's interest (by fair means or foul) take your good idea—the one that you've snatched from that great fount of ideas in the sky—and put it in a setting. The setting can be a background with time, weather, and all that. Alternatively, it can be pivoting forces within your plot, if you set them up like steamy Cajun swamps or drought stricken farmlands. These forces can be as integral to your story as characters.

Characters. Some people call them protagonists and antagonists. In romance we call them hero and heroine, and they drive the story in a way plot alone cannot. Characters have motivations and they have histories. They have their own agendas and their own conflicts. Characters will have impressions of each other. The circumstances of the plot are going to change these characters. Characters resist change and try to resolve their own conflicts without involving themselves in the plot conflict or the conflict of the other character. They will not be successful because only you, the writer, can resolve their conflicts.

Weave fact and fiction together. The more anchors in reality the reader can hang on to, the more credible your tale. When you're doing research, the things that stick in your mind will be the same things that catch your readers' attention. Which is why you shouldn't write what you know. The reader is a foreigner in this place and time; you need to be able to feel that sense of strangeness first yourself.

Pace yourself carefully. You cannot fill the first fifty pages with just characters, setting or conflict. Everything about these people, this place and their problems must be presented gradually around the structure of evolving plot.

By the end of the beginning, your reader should be able to visualize your setting. He/she should be knowledgeable about your characters and their histories, empathetic with their situation. The reader should be acquainted with the plot.

When you get to the middle you should be actively engaged in the plot. There should be strong contrast between the characters. Characters can begin to grow. Think of it like this: In the beginning of the book you met and hit it off with these characters at a dinner party; by the middle of the book, these people have been hour-long guests/victims of the *Jenny Jones Show*.

The plot continues to come together. Exciting events take place. Each one, like raindrops on the windshield, slowly converges with other drops. As they come together, creating what some writers call the "red string," the pace increases. The "red string" links up all elements of the story. Once it is pulled, all hell breaks loose.

Keep the tension ascending and descending. The reader will release pent-up tension held in too long. Release that tension by interspersing quiet scenes. Don't allow the reader to release it by putting down the book.

By the end of the middle, start wrapping up the internal conflicts of the hero and heroine, or better yet, allow them to mesh with the external plot conflict. Close any options for resolution that you are not going to use. If there are escape routes from the island by both helicopter or boat, either the gas must leak out of the helicopter or the boat must get a hole in it. This is the time to have betrayals, ticking clocks, unanticipated disasters and amnesiac revelations. By this point in the story, subplots should be resolved, the truth is ready to be, or has been, revealed; the pace is intense and dramatic.

The final pages of the book move faster and faster as time becomes a factor. Disaster lurks around every corner and it is dark, darker, darkest—but only just before the dawn. As a writer, you should be so caught up in the book during this phase that eating, sleeping, and working are all done on automatic pilot. The book should be the only thing that holds your concentration. This should be fun. If you're not enjoying this heart pounding and squirming in your seat, your readers won't either.

The resolution, when it comes, will affect everybody, including you. At this point nothing should be gradual. Don't wait for the ship to come in, swim for it. Once the plot conflict is resolved, don't linger. Any tie-in, afterthought or epilogue should be less than ten pages.

Don't come all this way and then blow it. Leave them wishing there were a hundred pages more.

<hr />

"The fundamental fantasy of the romance novel isn't a sexual fantasy. These are novels of female empowerment—stories in which women emerge victorious from every obstacle that life throws their way."
Susan Elizabeth Phillips

* * *

"Here's an exercise to help you on the road to publication. Pin the following quote on your bulletin board: 'If you were an actor, Chapter One would be your audition.'"

Welcome to Short Attention Span Theatre

By Teresa Medeiros

Welcome to "Short Attention Span Theater!"

Most readers will generously allow you three to five pages at the most to lure their attention away from the demands of home and career. Thus, it's no accident that many romance authors are former journalists. You should always strive to answer the Five W's in your first chapter: Who? When? Where? Why? And What? Answering the "Who?" introduces the reader to your characters. Answering "When?" and "Where?" provides them with a vibrant sense of time and place. Answering "What?" should involve action of some kind and answering "Why?" sets the stage for those twin essentials of any dynamic fiction—conflict and motivation.

The trick is to answer all of those questions without over-saturating the reader and bogging down the storyline. You don't have to introduce them to every character, nor do you have to set up every subplot or every motivation in the first chapter. If your hero has been imprisoned unjustly for a number of years, as Gerard was in my novel *Thief of Hearts* (September, 1994), isn't it enough to have him light a lamp because he hates the dark? The reader may not learn why he hates the dark until he confesses all to the heroine in Chapter Seventeen.

The number one flaw beginning writers make is trying to cram too much background information into the beginning chapters. If it makes the process easier, you can overwrite the first few chapters because *you* need to know the information. However, you should always go back later, cut the overkill, and sprinkle the pertinent information throughout the manuscript.

Chapter One should be a seduction, a gentle tease promising pleasures to come. It's not Demi Moore in the movie *Striptease,* peeling off her clothes at the slightest provocation. It's Kelly McGillis in *Witness*, blushing to her hairline when Harrison Ford accidentally witnesses her bathing. You want to hint and tantalize and coax the reader into continuing to turn the page. Even in a romance, an aura of mystery is essential. If everything is neatly laid out and predictable, the reader has no motivation to keep reading.

There is no set formula for picking the choice scene to begin your story. I've used snippets of dialogue, adventure sequences, conflicts between key characters. Conflict is the cornerstone. You must communicate to the reader that you're on the verge of taking your hero and heroine on a roller-coaster ride that will change their lives forever. In my April, 1998 release, *Nobody's Darling*, Esmerelda arrives in a sleepy western town to bring her brother's killer to justice. *In Breath of Magic*, Arian is arrested and charged with witchcraft. In *Fairest of Them All,* Holly's father announces that he has arranged a tournament in which she will be the prize. *In Thief of Hearts*, Lucy sees a pirate ship emerging from the mist. In all of these first chapters, SOMETHING HAPPENS. Try putting your first chapter to this test: Can you visualize it as a movie scene? If so, would you be willing to plop down seven dollars at the ticket booth to find out what happens next?

You should also establish empathy for your characters in these opening shots. Horror writers use this technique all the time. When the Frankenstein monster kills the little blonde girl who's been picking flowers in the forest, we're much more deeply moved than if he'd simply torn off the head of a stranger.

Get into your characters' heads and use their senses to show the reader how they feel. Are they exhilarated? Afraid? Aroused? Does sweat trickle down their cheeks? Do they smell gunpowder or the salty tang of the sea? Do they hear the crash of distant thunder? Instead of telling your reader about your characters' traits, use action to reveal their quirks.

In the opening paragraph of *Heather and Velvet* . . .

"Prudence plunged through the slick underbrush. The coil of hair at her nape unrolled and fell around her shoulders in sodden ropes. She paused in her mad flight to pluck out her pearl-tipped hairpins with methodical fingers. She tucked them in her deep pocket with a tidy pat so none would be lost, though she suspected the caution was unwarranted. Although her aunt would never admit it, she would not waste genuine pearls on her homely niece."

What did we learn in that single paragraph? That Prudence is in a terrible hurry, perhaps even in a life and death situation, yet she stopped long enough to pick out her hairpins and secure them in her pocket, even though she knows they probably don't have much value. We've also learned that her relationship with her aunt is not a warm one. Prudence perceives herself as homely and her aunt's attitude has contributed to this perception. Yet there's no hint of self-pity in her thoughts, just wry humor. Prudence's plainness is simply a fact of life and that perhaps, more than anything makes her admirable and intriguing to the reader.

The two most important sentences in chapter one are the first and the last. Most of us can remember the lines that began classic romantic novels like *Gone with the Wind* and *Rebecca*. Try thumbing through some more recent romances and analyzing the authors' word choices.

57

The first sentence should read like music, striking a chord of excitement and empathy in the reader.

The second most important sentence in Chapter One is the last one. You don't have to end <u>every</u> chapter of your romance with a cliffhanger, but you should definitely end Chapter One that way. If you've written an incredible slam-bang beginning that runs thirty pages, try stopping at a crucial moment and dividing it into two chapters. Remember, this is your audition—the only one you may ever get—and you want to leave the reader applauding and eager for more.

If you can hook your reader in Chapter One, I can promise you that when the curtain falls and the footlights go down, you'll hear those magical words emerging from the darkened theater: "Congratulations! You've got the part!"

"You have probably got about three pages to hook a reader—and more importantly, an editor—into buying your book."

Hook Your Reader:
The First Page is the Best

By Sara Orwig

She never saw it coming. Laura stepped outside . . . locking the door and hurrying to her car as fog swirled beneath the tall yard light. As she twisted the key in the lock of her car door, she heard a footfall behind her . . .

Hopefully, you have read this far. If you have, it was because the opening grabbed your attention. This is what you want to do with your novel. Hook your reader into your story—and, if possible, do it on the first page. The first *paragraph* is better. The first *line* is best.

How do you grab and hold your reader's interest?

Begin with <u>characterization</u>. Introduce your main character and give the reader a reason to identify or sympathize with her or him. Then immediately throw this character into a dilemma. If you write humor, involve your character in an unexpected situation that might bring a chuckle. For example, I once had a book open with a patent attorney calling on a toy maker. My heroine rings the doorbell and when the door opens she is facing a gorilla—my toy maker dressed in a gorilla costume and hopelessly stuck in it because the zipper is caught (*Beware the Wizard*, Loveswept, Bantam Books) . By the end of your first scene the reader should be hooked into wanting to know what will happen next to this character.

Start your novel with <u>emotion</u>. Readers identify swiftly with emotion because emotion is universal. Everyone identifies with sorrow, joy, agony, etc. Open with a character caught in the throes of a strong emotion. Show your character grappling with this emotion. You will likely hook your reader into that emotional struggle and thus your story.

Open with <u>dialogue</u>. When you open with dialogue, your reader becomes an eavesdropper, avidly listening to a conversation and caught up in what is unfolding. Dialogue speeds up the story and makes it a page-turner. You can move from the opening right into your story, and your reader will be swept along by this conversation between your characters.

Open dialogue with a <u>question</u>. *("My God, Jeremy, what have you done to her?")* Raise this question in the reader's mind along with the question posed in your story. We are all curious enough creatures to want to know the answer to the question or to see why it was being asked.

Begin with <u>conflict</u> . . . the heart of stories. This does not have to be a physical fight, but can be some kind of problem, threat, or a struggle between your hero and heroine. Open with conflict and your reader's curiosity will hold and she/he will keep turning pages, needing to see the outcome of the conflict.

Now *heighten* the conflict, increase what is at stake and move on to the next big scene.

Action **will carry your reader along.** Open with something happening, someone doing something. The reader watches this scene unfold and if it is compelling enough, will be caught up in the action and drama of the crisis.

Set the stage. Open with the setting or sensory details. Bring a vivid picture to the mind of your reader with details of where this story is taking place. This mustn't go on too long before the introduction of a character or dilemma, but setting can give an important foundational backdrop. Get in how something smells, feels, sounds, etc. Use specific words so your reader gets a clear image. (The sharp tang of sea breezes dancing through forests of pine, the satin smoothness of a baby's back, the clang and clatter of tumbling trash bins.)

However you open, start with the moment of *irrevocable change* in your character's life. After this moment, your character's life will never go back to the way it was.

To really hook your reader, in the first scene:

Introduce your hero and/or heroine.

Let the reader know where and when this scene is taking place and who is involved.

Show your reader what is happening and why.

Something interesting has to happen in that critically important first scene. Before I buy a book or decide to read one, I pick it up and open it and read the first page. If it does not interest me, sometimes I thumb through a little, but most of the time, I set the book down and go on to the next one.

Unless there is a fantastic reason, this is not the time for the family history of your characters. Just like the movies, jump into the story, hook your reader and then, later in the story, your reader will be ready and want to know the character's family history.

Hook the reader with the kind of opening *you* like to read, with words that carry *you* right into the heart of a story and show characters you would pull for and care about. *You* have to care if your *reader* is going to care.

Don't worry about trying to be clever as much as pouring out *your* story from *your* heart. That's what is most important. Be true to your own feelings and let those emotions shine through your story. Then your characters are certain to come alive, reach out and hook your reader.

"Beware of the perfect characters. Always write as if the good have weaknesses and the evil have reasons."
Mona Sizer
* * *

Aside from characters, plot is everything. John Irving said it best for me. I keep his quote handy with each new book I plot and it inspires me again and again.

Plotting—It's the Skeleton

By Linda Castle

"Plot isn't what compels many novelists to write, or some readers to read. However, if you choose to write a novel without a plot, I would hope three things for you: that your prose is gorgeous, that your insights into the human condition are inspirational, and that your book is short. I am directing my remarks, of course, to those writers (and readers) of long novels."
John Irving

It is said there are only three plots: 1. Man against man. 2. Man against himself. 3. Man against nature.

What are you writing? Which one of these three comes closest to describing *your* book?

Novels are either *plot*-driven, or *character*-driven. It's extremely important you know the difference. If your characters' inner turmoil, background, circumstance and/or belief systems are what move the story forward, you are most likely writing a *character*-driven novel. If outside events, such as politics, weather, or natural disasters (external conflicts) are what move your story forward, then you are definitely writing a *plot*-driven novel. The trend now is for character-driven novels. However, there are still many popular novels published each year that are primarily plot-driven.

Once you understand what the driving force is behind your novel, then take a look at *sub-plot*. Plot is like the sound of the main singer's voice—sub-plot is the back-up singers doing the "doo-wop."

In a romance novel the plot consists of attractions, conflict, and ultimate resolution-leading-to-a-happy-ending between the hero and the heroine. The sub-plot is the side-story woven through their quest, which keeps them interesting and off balance. If it is not a romance that you are writing, then the sub-plot/plot could be exactly the reverse. Let me give you some examples:

The hero is fighting in the Civil War and his attraction/conflict is with a heroine on the opposing side. Their improbable romance is the plot, and the Civil War as a whole, and the specific battles going on around them while they reach a happy resolution, is the sub-plot.

The hero is a private detective looking for stolen gems and he falls in love with the victim. The plot is their developing relationship—solving the crime and recovering the jewels is the sub-plot.

The hero returns from war to find his father dead, his fortune lost. He is attracted to a girl who knew him in his youth and found him to be selfish, spoiled and wholly unsuitable. Their budding romance and the conflicts between them is the plot. His quest to restore his name, land and foil the villain responsible for the murder of his father is the sub-plot.

The plot runs the entire length of the story, while the sub-plot bobs and weaves through it. Adding additional sub-plots can create longer and more involved novels.

Do your characters become complacent and comfortable in the middle of your book? Use the sub-plot to knock the wind out of them. Every hero should be brought to his knees at least once in the middle of your story by a sharp-edged sub-plot.

If you want a secondary love story, craft a developing relationship of lesser characters to become your sub-plot.

Sub-plot is the easiest way to keep a story moving rapidly. A sub-plot will always provide a handy incident to keep your hero and heroine progressing toward the end of their separate story.

Good sub-plotting will rescue you from writer's block and the "What are they going to do now?" syndrome. The side story will have nooks, crannies and deep ravines for your characters to fall into. Each twist and turn of sub-plotting forces the hero and heroine to react and thereby generate your main plot.

A well-developed sub-plot is also the perfect vehicle to set the tonal quality of your manuscript. By using a sub-plot involving conspiracy or intrigue, you will have mystery. Creating a comedic secondary couple who experience one pit-fall after another through their bid for love will enable you to write a light, entertaining book without forcing your main romance to be funny. The hero and heroine can be serious people, but your sub-plot will flavor the book with humor and satire. Conversely, the main romance may be light while the sub-plot is filled with dark deceptions to keep your work from becoming slap-stick and foolish.

By honing your skills in creating sub-plots, you can quickly and more easily write a book with additional depth. That's what will keep your reader turning each page until the satisfying climax.

Imagine a long horizontal line. Better yet, actually draw one on a sheet of paper. This long line is your story. Put one, short, intersecting vertical line at the very middle—this is your "point of no return." This centerline symbolizes the point in your story when your hero or heroine would really like to go back to the point at which we met them. However, the character is no longer the same person because of all the pressures and changes. He or she cannot go back, no matter how much they wish it to happen.

Begin to intersect the long horizontal line with shorter vertical lines—only a few—don't do more than two or three to begin with. Each time you add a short vertical line, it stands for a new sub-plot in your novel.

Here is the really important part: The first sub-plot introduced will be the next-to-the-last element solved in your story. The main plot must be *the last thing solved*. This is not a variable; it is an absolute. *The last element of your story to be solved must be the main plot.* If it is a romance, the story ends when the couple is together and happy. You absolutely cannot have another sub-plot solved after they are together. *You can't.* This is such a simple concept, but one that takes writers a while to realize. Once that couple is together and the conflict is solved, you are at the end of your book. Period.

If you have managed to keep up with me you have already figured out that each sub-plot has a rigid place in the second half of the book when it must be solved. The last sub-plot introduced is the first sub-plot solved and so on.

When you finish drawing this out on a piece of paper it will be symmetrical and even. That is how a novel must be plotted: symmetrical, even, balanced. If you do this, your reader will have a sense of satisfaction that everything fell effortlessly into place, and the story flowed.

As your skill level increases, you will be able to introduce more and more sub-plots and begin writing longer and longer novels—but they will always have balance and will never overwhelm you. Once you learn this, then sub-plot and plotting will become a joy and a wonderful tool to help create worlds of fantasy.

"Writing is so difficult that I feel that writers having had their hell on earth will escape all punishment in the hereafter."
Jessamyn West
* * *

"Kathryn called and asked me to give you some tips on that all-so important "writer's voice." This is a hard one, but I'll try..."

The Writer's Voice

By Haywood Smith

Voice is literally what it sounds like.

Let's say you hear someone talking in the next room. If it's your mother or your sister or your best friend, you'll recognize the voice right away.

Or, you're in the kitchen and your TV's blaring away in the den. You don't have to see the screen to recognize Bugs Bunny—or Elmer Fudd, or Donald Duck, or Mickey Mouse, or (shudder) Barney. Each of those fictional creations has a unique, identifiable voice.

Another way of describing it would be to say that voice is the flavor of your writing. I've eaten a hundred different kinds of spaghetti sauce in my lifetime, but no two cooks make it exactly alike. Some batches are memorable, some not, and I can tell with one bite if it's canned. There are as many variations on spaghetti sauce as there are cooks. Ditto for potato salad. Even though the basic ingredients are all the same, every recipe is different, so the flavors vary. If your potato salad is bland or forgettable, nobody will ask you to bring any to the picnic. Good writing has its own memorable flavor, too. If it doesn't, nobody will want to publish it, much less read it.

An author's voice is the unique pattern and inflection of his/her writing. It's the subtle (or not so subtle) combination of style, mood, rhythm, vocabulary, and technique that together produce a unique literary "fingerprint."

Diana Gabaldon fans know exactly how a Diana Gabaldon book is supposed to read. Diana's literary fingerprint, unlike any other author's, is her own voice and hers alone. The same applies to

Deborah Smith, Ernest Hemingway, Mark Twain, Meryl Sawyer, Julie Garwood, Stephen King, and Danielle Steel. I could go on and on.

I'm often asked if voice can be learned. I don't think it can. As far as I am concerned, a writer either has a voice or doesn't. I could no more teach someone to have a voice than I could teach him or her to have fingerprints. However, there are wonderful writers and teachers who disagree with me.

Voice has little or nothing to do with technical elements like grammar or syntax. A writer can be very skilled, yet lack an individual voice. Many newspaper articles and textbooks are voiceless. They're deliberately written in generic style—just-the-facts-ma'am, "Brand-X" prose—technically perfect, but lacking personality. Good fiction is another matter; it must have a memorable personality. If you read a book or a manuscript that could have been written by anybody (or nobody in particular), that writer lacks voice. My editor, Jennifer Enderlin, has often said most of the manuscripts she rejects aren't bad, they're just fine—but they don't have that unselfconscious spark of individual style that is voice.

When I write a sentence, I know whether or not that sentence "sounds" right to me. If it doesn't, I change it, adjust the cadence (rhythm and alliteration are very important to me) or the words, or the structure of the sentence until it "sounds" right. I can't describe exactly what my voice is, but I do know what it isn't.

As long as your writing has even an inkling of individuality, there's hope. A weak voice can be strengthened. It's simply a question of identifying the unique elements of your particular style and reinforcing those elements. Pay attention to your instinct. "Listen" to your prose. Read it out aloud. Ask yourself what makes your style different, and then polish those differences until they glow with the subtle patina of your grandmother's silver.

If you determine that you indeed do not have a "voice," but you still have the writing bug, find somebody who thinks voice can be taught and get busy learning. I'd never want to be the one to tell any writer to hang it up. After all, every published author I know—and that includes me—is somebody who was too stubborn to give up, and too ignorant to take "no," "no," "no," and "NO!" for an answer. So keep dreaming, and keep writing.

"For just when ideas fail, a word comes in to save the situation."
Goethe
* * *

"Antoinette Stockenberg's advice for how to shore up a sagging middle is pithy and memorable: 'Drop a body through the roof.'"In lieu of that, read on for some preparatory instruction."

Avoiding the Sagging Middle

By Evelyn Rogers

Whether or not to write from an outline is a contentious issue in the romance genre. Some can, and some just can't. It's rather on a par with whether to have toilet paper coming over the top of the holder or from underneath. In either situation, practitioners on opposite sides are not inclined to compromise.

I'm in the use-an-outline and over-the-top camps.

In approaching the creation of a book, I have to know where I'm starting and where I'm heading with at least a skeletal idea of how I am going to get from beginning to end. I feel very strongly that you should too. Only in this way can you avoid that all-too-common hazard in the crafting of a book: the sagging middle.

In the beginning, establish the setting, primary and secondary characters, their personalities and goals, and the conflict that keeps them from getting where they want to go. Put in a change that spurs them to action, a motivational occurrence that gets them up and running toward their respective goals. In the case of the hero and heroine, give them opposite objectives that will inevitably throw them into battle with one another. In the end, settle the conflict with the characters either reaching their initial goals or attaining new goals that have come about as they changed during the course of the story.

And in the middle? Ahhh, here's the tricky part, and not just because it occupies about half the book. If you've come up with a solid story line, sympathetic protagonists facing conflicts with suitably hard-to-attain objectives, your readers will pounce on your book at the beginning. Likewise, at the end they will want to know how your characters have overcome seemingly insurmountable odds. But will they turn the pages with equal avidity to see how you get from Point A to Point Z? Or will your fast-paced start and your thrilling conclusion be separated by the literary equivalent of Death Valley?

Here's where a good outline helps. Too rigid and it's like the old-fashioned teacher standing over her students with ruler in hand, more often than not stifling creativity. Too loose, you have the anything-goes sort who can't keep her students in their seats. In this latter situation, you can easily wander down paths away from your desired destination and thus lose the dynamic forward movement of your tale.

An admirer of tightly-plotted books, I prefer an outline that lays out two to five plot twists/changes/complications to the basic story, the number depending on the length of the book, each complication arising from what has gone before. As you structure your book, it's not necessary to spell out how you get from complication to complication. By its nature, an outline is not long or wordy or stuffed with detail. However, it does lead you along the right path.

Here are a few suggestions as to how these complications can be created to thicken the plot and make life suitably tough for the hero and/or heroine:

a. An action by the one or both of your protagonists backfires, throwing him/her further away from the goal, e.g., Jane is running from Dick because she thinks he wants only her newly inherited money, but as her London-bound plane takes off, he settles into the adjoining first-class seat and orders champagne for them both.

b. A secondary character proves to be other than he/she seems.

c. The aforementioned Jane depends upon a maiden aunt to provide her refuge in a deserted mountain cabin, but when she shows up, Dick, having won over the aunt, is waiting for her with a chilled bottle of champagne.

d. The protagonist undergoes a change that threatens the attainment of her goal.

e. Believing Dick to be a self-serving hustler, Jane finds herself falling under the spell of his charms; fighting herself as well as him, she takes off from the cabin and finds herself in the midst of a training camp for a secret militia threatening the overthrow of the state.

A warning here: If you plan to throw in a secret militia, hint early on that uniformed men and women have been seen in the area near the cabin. Such foreshadowing can make far-out complications believable. What you want to do is surprise your readers with a twist they should have seen coming. This is not an easy accomplishment. It takes not only careful writing, but oftentimes much rewriting. In *The Forever Bride,* at a point in the middle of the book I had need of a diamond ring; I had to rewrite a portion of an early chapter to put it in. The ring proved useful at several junctures in the unfolding of the plot.

The following devices may seem useful/desirable/interesting to the writer, but can have the reader tossing your novel aside for a brief nap. Hence, they are to be avoided:

1. **Lumps of background material.** Feather in details where they matter, a little at a time. Your readers are intelligent; otherwise they wouldn't be reading your book. Give them credit. Put in as few details of past action as necessary; they will be able to string these details together for an overall grasp of what has gone before.

2. **An oversupply of research data.** I do a great deal of note taking for each book, whether it's contemporary or historical, but I use only a fraction of what I learn. Maybe the food Jane would have been served in first-class is interesting to you, but it doesn't further her story unless she dumps her paté with truffles in Dick's lap, along with her untouched champagne. Here's an aphorism to keep in mind: Concerning the material turned up in your research, use as much as necessary and as little as possible.

3. **Flashbacks.** Sometimes retelling a scene from the past is the only way to get across a point important to the plot. If this is so, don't insert the scene while Jane is in the midst of a rousing argument with Dick, or while they are sharing their first kiss, or he's unbuttoning her blouse, or . . . you get the idea. Insert any essential flashbacks between such scenes. Make sure the flashback fits, either as a result of the previous scene or as a foreshadowing of the one coming up— and keep it short.

4. **Extended action scenes.** Yes, you can have a fight scene that's too long, or a battle sequence, or a chase. How long should you make such scenes? Instinct helps here, reading over what you've written, and asking someone to read it for you. Pick someone whose opinion you trust, possibly another writer or someone in your critique group if you're fortunate enough to get a good one going.

5. **The introduction of new major characters.** Minor players in your story are essential to flesh out the overall picture you are presenting. However, by the middle of the book, it's too late to throw in a vital villain or a vamp to tempt the hero, unless you have hinted early on that such characters are waiting their turn on the stage.

6. **Excessive emphasis on secondary plots.** Throughout the middle of the book, tie up the complications involving secondary characters, leaving to the end of the book the climax and resolution of the primary plot. Make the settling of these secondary plots influence the conflict between your hero and heroine. Jane's maiden aunt, having foresworn romantic entanglements because of her cynical view of men, has been a major persuasive force in her life. Not only does she set up her niece with Dick, she runs off with the head of the militia, who tosses aside his uniform and weapons in the pursuit of true love.

7. **Excessive dialogue.** Usually conversation quickens the pace of a book, but only if it is inserted in the right amounts. Avoid having your characters maunder on about a given topic. They might do so in real life, but in a book you want to be selective. My favorite definition of dialogue is that it's what characters do to one another. What they say should be for a purpose, e.g., to persuade, confront, seduce. Through dialogue, characters can charm, wheedle, lie and antagonize, but they should never bore.

Whatever you insert in the middle of your book, make sure it moves your hero and heroine toward the settling of their conflicts, at the same time it throws up barriers that test their determination and strength of character. The higher the barrier, the stronger the character. It is in strong characters that must strive hard for their happy ending that readers find their greatest satisfaction.

"My best advice is to keep one question in your mind: "What happens next?" This is what every author wants readers to be asking as they turn each and every page."

Abuse of the Past Perfect Verb Tense

By Mary Kirk

I've developed a particularly strong knee-jerk reaction to the use—or rather, the abuse—of the past-perfect verb tense. For example, here's the hero, waiting in his car in the heroine's driveway for her to come home from work. As he waits, he recalls—for two or three pages—the past 48 hours which we, the readers, didn't see from his point of view, because we were in the heroine's point-of-view.

> *Joe waited impatiently for Sally's arrival. It had been too long since he'd seen her, too long since he'd held her and felt her tenderness and warmth.*
>
> *The past two days had been hell. First, he'd had a terrible fight with Lou. Lou thought Sally was bad for him, and he hadn't held back in speaking his mind on the subject; it had taken all of Joe's self-restraint not to knock his best friend flat for the things he'd said. In the end, Lou had apologized, but Joe had still felt angry and, frankly, a little depressed; added to all the other arguments he and Lou had been through lately, it seemed as if he and his life-long friend were drifting apart.*
>
> *In that state of mind, he'd left Lou's house and gone to work, where he had discovered that they had lost the Dawson account . . . etc., etc.*

You get the idea. It gets even worse when you're trying to relate an event in a character's past that also contains a past event. To the best of my knowledge, there is no past-past-perfect tense. However, I've seen writers fumble around trying to create one.

A scene such as the one above might very well be necessary and the only way to convey important information. Then again, it might be deadly to the pacing of the story. Why? Because hearing about something that's already happened isn't nearly as interesting as seeing it happen. However, you can't include every scene, or the manuscript would be 1,000 pages, right?

Okay, sometimes it's appropriate to tell about a phone call the hero got the previous morning or about the trip to the store the heroine made that afternoon. And sometimes it's even more appropriate simply to eliminate unnecessary details—things you put in a first draft when your right brain is cooking and you (correctly) aren't censuring it, but upon second thought you realize the reader doesn't really need to know.

The point is, be careful about how often you use the past perfect tense—or rather, be aware of how often you use it.

Also, be aware of how long the sections are that are told in the past perfect. A sentence or two isn't usually a problem; a page now and then may be all right. When you realize you've started every chapter in a book with a past-perfect recap, or that the main characters can't have a single conversation without recalling things that happened to them in their respective pasts that helped to create the present conflict, it's safe to say you're in trouble.

The old adage "show, don't tell" applies equally to events and circumstances of the past as well as of the present. In other words, it's no more effective—perhaps even less so—to tell a reader about a traumatic childhood incident in your heroine's life than it is to tell about a traumatic incident that happens during the course of the present story. It's usually much more effective to show the reader the incident through a dream or flashback, perhaps. If you must tell the incident, then doing so in dialogue usually works better than in narrative. In other words, most readers would rather hear the heroine tell the hero what happened to her than to learn about it as she agonizes over whether or not to tell him.

Books that rely heavily on back-story present more of a challenge than most, vis-a-vis verb tense. In my fourth book, *Promises* (Silhouette *Special Edition*), hero and heroine have known each other since childhood, were married for ten years, and have been divorced for three years when the book begins. Judicious use of flashbacks, told in straight past-tense didn't entirely eliminate the need for the past-perfect, but did help give immediacy to the years of the characters' marriage and their past conflict.

Author Diane Chamberlain, in her book *Secret Lives* (Harper Collins), solved the past-perfect problem she faced creatively and effectively. She needed the heroine to gradually learn secrets about her deceased mother, so she told the mother's story in journals that the heroine is given at the beginning of the book. The journals comprise about half of the novel and are, by themselves, every bit as compelling a story as the one related in the present, which they are designed to illuminate.

I'm sure we can all think of books we've read which needed a complex back-story to develop the plot. Even if the story you're writing doesn't need this back-story you might get hints from one that does, about handling the past-perfect or alternatives to its use.

The bottom line on the past perfect is this: It's a necessary and useful tool; used well, it can be made compelling. However, by itself, it has no urgency, no tension. Something has happened. It's over. The character through whose point of view the reader is learning about the event has survived. Chances are, whoever didn't survive is long-since dead and the reader never knew him or her anyway, so who cares? Your job as a writer is to make the reader care. Your job is to make that reader keep asking, "What happens next?"

"If your readers don't want to read on at the end of each page, you've lost them and your book will fail miserably."

Writing a Page-Turner

By Tess Mallory

Writing a romance that is also a page-turner is relatively easy. Everything in your book must relate either to the storyline or the characters. Now, this may seem to be a rather silly statement. <u>Of course</u> everything relates to one or the other, doesn't it? You'd be surprised at how easy it is to write dialogue or action that has nothing to do with the rest of the story.

Is a passage of your writing superfluous or important? Ask yourself:

1) Does it (the passage) further the plot?
2) Does it further the reader's understanding of the characters?
3) Does it slow down the action?

If you answer "yes" to either of the first two questions, or "no" to the third, then you can assume that your passage is important and necessary to the story.

Now ask, does the last line in each chapter make me want to turn the page? In order for your book to be a page-turner, the answer to this question must be a resounding YES!

Descriptive paragraphs can bring us to a deeper understanding of the characters and, thus, also further the plot. A description of the heroine's ball gown may be simply a description, or it can be a way to alert the reader to a different facet of your character's personality. If the heroine has always been shy and suddenly decides to wear red, doesn't this tell us something has changed?

Descriptions of the hero and heroine are part of the mystique . . . the thrill of the genre. If you describe your hero and heroine in a way that makes your reader take them into her/his heart, you will have fulfilled your reader's every expectation and the answer to question two will be yes.

What about descriptions of places; how do they move forward or slow down your story?

While your reader wants to know how the world in which she finds herself looks, smells, and feels, if your description bogs down the flow of your story—the rhythm, the cadence of your thoughts— beware. Your reader won't keep turning the pages if she encounters page after page of long descriptive narrative when what she wants is to get back to the action of the story. Never interrupt the action of your story with long description. If your heroine is running from outlaws and she stops to admire the countryside for two pages, you've lost your audience.

What if you've asked the above questions, get all the answers correct and your novel *still* seems to fall flat? Examine your dialogue. If your characters are having a conversation about whether or not it is going to rain that day, it had better be important to the story. They had better be discussing such a mundane thing because they are wondering if their getaway from the sultan's palace will be made more difficult by the change in the weather—not because the writer is stumped for pertinent dialogue. There is no such thing as small talk in a novel.

Dialogue is a great way for the reader to learn about the personalities of the characters, important plot points and vital information, without the author having to come right out and tell it in an omniscient fashion. It works like this:

Lenore had been raised on a small farm near London and had only now, at the age of seventeen, found the courage to run away from her aunt and uncle and start a new life. Her aunt and uncle would be happy that they no longer had to feed and clothe her. Now she was virtually alone in the world.

This is not terrible but the author is *telling*, not showing. Most romances today are not written in an omniscient, third-person viewpoint. See how much better this passage flows through dialogue:

"You don't act like a girl raised in the city," Robert Princeton said, leaning back in his chair, his gaze raking over the young woman sitting

stiffly in front of him. "You're too nervous, too naive."

Lenore lifted her chin slightly. "I was raised on a small farm by my aunt and uncle."

One brow rose. "What brings you to London?"

She swallowed hard. "I—I— ran away. I couldn't stand it any longer."

His dark brown eyes held her nervous gaze for a long moment. "How old are you?"

"Seventeen." She whispered the word.

"And will your aunt and uncle come looking for you?"

Lenore hesitated, then shrugged. "I doubt it. I think they will be very glad they do not have to feed and clothe me any longer."

Robert smiled, the gesture sending a sudden chill through Lenore's soul. "Well, then, it would seem you are all alone in the world."

You can see—and feel—the difference. We learned so much more about both Lenore and Robert through this little exchange. This passage touches your emotions so much more than the "telling" passage.

As long as what the characters are talking about furthers the plot or your understanding of the characters as people, your novel will be a page-turner. However, if Robert and Lenore's conversation centers about whether or not she wants cream or lemon in her tea, it becomes a superfluous and wasted piece of dialogue.

Suppose you've hooked your reader through one exciting chapter. When you write the last page of that chapter, you may follow the natural inclination of many authors and finish with some kind of resolution: The heroine's been running from the outlaws and she finds a cave where she curls up and goes to sleep, feeling safe. This might be the "normal" progression of a storyline, but does this make your reader want to turn the page? No, this makes your reader feel "satisfied." Now she can put the book down on the nightstand and turn off the light. Maybe tomorrow she'll pick up your book again . . . or maybe she won't.

How do you keep her turning the pages?

End each chapter with a "cliff-hanger." In the last few lines, introduce a new conflict. Using the example above: Does she hear something in the cave? Does someone come to the entrance of the cave? A cliffhanger can be something as simple as someone making a startling statement or asking a damning question. Don't leave the end of a chapter all neatly sewn up, leave a thread that leads your reader to the beginning of the next chapter.

Ultimately, you must cut anything that doesn't meet the criteria determined by the first three questions. And you *must* leave your reader hungry for more. It's as simple as that.

Then your reader will turn the page . . . and keep reading.

"*Try sitting at your typewriter and without thinking begin to write Russell Edson-type pieces. This means letting go and allowing the elm in your front yard to pick itself up and walk over to Iowa. Try for good, strong first sentences. You might want to take the first half of your sentence from a newspaper article and finish the sentence with an ingredient listed in a cookbook. Play around. Dive into absurdity and write. Take chances. You will succeed if you are fearless of failure.*"
Natalie Goldberg
Writing Down the Bones
* * *

Jade Ling,
The Writers Colony, San Francisco

Dear Kathryn,

Rosemarie is planning to drop you a note of thanks for the wonderful articles that you sent to us, but I could not wait to say a grateful thank you of my own. (People do say I'm impatient.)

I know Rosemarie told you that I had begun to write a romance. I had a wonderful idea for a heroine and hero; he was tall and sleek with golden hair (I'm a pushover for blondes) and my heroine was Chinese, funny and impulsive, with shiny, midnight black hair she could sit on. Hmmm. Sounds a bit like me!

The contemporary story I thought up seemed great too. I could envision the beginning without any trouble at all, and had a super-suspenseful ending. So, I started to type and words just seemed to fly off my fingers and onto the computer screen. In the opening scene, they bump into each other (literally) on a crowded street corner in Chinatown because, as usual, my heroine is rushing to and fro' without watching where she is going on her way to her job as a publicist for ... Whoops! I just realized that I *was* writing myself and my own personal stuff into that story. Am I allowed to do that?

Anyway, I got several chapters into the thing and ... POOF! It just disappeared out from under me. I hit a stage where my story dried up and I could not think of one more scene to write. Actually, I could think of dozens, but none that seemed to <u>lead</u> anywhere. My characters were nice to each other, but nothing interesting was happening and suddenly it was booorrring.

Right about the time I was despairing over my writing attempt, your second box of articles arrived and, lo and behold, there was

Evelyn Rogers telling me how to shore up a sagging middle, and Tess Mallory telling me to "Write a Page-Turner." (I'm certainly going to try to do both of those things next time!)

Linda Castle talked about plotting and after reading her article, I realized plot was something I hadn't even_thought_ about and certainly didn't HAVE for my book. And, of course . . . wonderful Al Zuckerman. Oh, if only I had read him before wasting all those evenings at the computer.

I know I have a lot to learn before I start again. For instance, several of the authors who wrote to us talk about the importance of wonderful characters. Well, remember how I said my characters were nice and boring? I need to know what to do to make them come alive.

Writing boring characters stopped me in my tracks, so I can well imagine it will do exactly that to my _readers_, too! If characterization is this critical, I—we all—need further help understanding the process. What are the secrets to writing great characters, Kathryn? Please help!

(Just call me "Stymied in San Francisco")
Jade

CHAPTER 2

CHARACTER AND EMOTION

Kathryn Falk, Lady of Barrow
Romantic Times Magazine
Brooklyn, New York

Dear "Stymied,"

You're going through a very normal anxiety period for novice writers. You don't become a concert pianist after a few months of lessons. You don't just sit down and a novel pours out of you either!

In answer to your first question about personal experiences: For your first book it will help to write about what you know in the way of settings, careers, family backgrounds and socio-economics. If you've never played polo, then you shouldn't write about polo players in your first book. If you're not accustomed to hanging out with models and attending New York parties, don't make this group the center of your first novel.

You have San Francisco at your feet; start there and paint your book with details that are already familiar to you. Your characters could meet under the Golden Gate Bridge, or on a cable car. They could get each other's meals by mistake at Fisherman's Wharf or ...? See how you paint a book with familiar details?

Never make your characters exactly like yourself. Major characters need to be memorable, and the way to do this is to write them "larger than life." Those characters are the most important element of your story. (Re-read that part in Zuckerman's book!)

Another tip: Read biographies, both historical and contemporary and study the motivations and choices these people make/have made.

When you join a writers' group, or take a writing course, you will often hear this expression: "Today's romance novels are character-driven." It's true. You read a wonderful romance, full and rich and it touches your heart. When you put down that book what do you remember most? The man and the woman in the story, of course. You close the book and their faces linger in your memory for a very long time.

Whether the setting is the Civil War or World War II doesn't matter half as much as the characters do. You will always remember:

Rhett and Scarlett (Margaret Mitchell's *Gone With the Wind*)

Steve and Ginny (*Sweet Savage Love* by Rosemary Rogers)

Skye and Niall (Bertrice Small for the Skye O'Malley series)

Angelique and Joffrey, Comte de Peyrac (the Angelique series by Sergeanne Golon)

Katherine and John of Gaunt (Anya Seton's wonderful *Katherine*).

These characters let you escape into their lives and share their love, their pain, and their destinies. And, for a few (too few) hours they enable you to forget everything as you are swept along with these star-crossed lovers.

Here's a trick that might be a good exercise. Write—when the time has come and you are ready—in the first person. Then *rewrite* the whole story in the third person. More than one published author uses this method to tap emotionally into her characters.

Before you begin writing romances, it's imperative that you understand that romance writing is a "science." There's a reason why women become addicted to, and crave, them. Chris Peirson, whose specialty is "why romances are socio-biologically—not politically—

correct," has contributed an article. Before you mentally argue with her thesis, remember this: how else can you explain why all types of women around the world can read the same romances, in any language, understand them, and take them to heart. You may be too much of a feminist to want to hear what she has to say, but in romance publishing her brand of "Darwinism" works. You don't have to look further than Jane Austen for confirmation of this. She was the most socio-biologically "correct" romance writer of all, which is why her books and movies are still enjoyed. She thoroughly understood a woman's need for status and resources in a man. If you want to touch all your readers' emotions, don't waste your time being politically correct. It all boils down to "Getting the alpha male to commit, " and *that* is the psychology of a romance."

Another proponent of the "tame-the-alpha-male" school is Barbara Cartland, born in 1901. She still sells four million books a year based on the premise of "two souls touching," and is 100% "socio-biologically correct" in her stories.

I have also called upon half a dozen romance writers—including the new queen of the Regency Historical, Mary Balogh—to help you. Each one understands the building blocks of character development and emotion in a romance novel. I hope you will take it all to heart and allow their advice and philosophy to sink in slowly and deeply. Without great characters you will never have a great story.

Kathryn

"Everything is truly possible as long as you help your reader understand why your characters do what they do."

Debra Dixon

* * *

"In studying men and women and romance, I have come to some deep convictions about how much easier romance writers could make their work, if they'd just realize how close to the cave we still are."

Make Your Characters Socio-Biologically Correct

By Chris Peirson

If you want to write a well-loved best-selling romance, keep one thing in mind, and one thing only: Romance readers are looking for an emotional and sexual experience. And, they want it to be the "re-creation," to a large extent, of the emotional experience that occurs when the "female reproductive strategy" triumphs over the "male reproductive strategy." Translated that means: She gets the male to commit to her and her offspring but he does not get her to commit sexually without having to first commit himself! (This is what we recall when we're older, which is why older women love "first love" stories.)

To fully understand this truism, you have to look back centuries, to the survival of the human species on the savannas and hillsides of an earlier epoch when only the strongest survived. The powerful male beat out all his opponents and won the female; his seed impregnated her and his line survived. The powerful female attracted the powerful male and his seed impregnated her and her line survived.

His power came from his strength.

Her power came from her ability to attract.

So what has really changed?

Nada.

Look at films. We have leading men—powerful males—like Mel Gibson, Warren Beatty, Michael Douglas, and Harrison Ford. All are at the height of their social and (perceived) sexual power. And who are they paired with?

Women under 40.

This makes sense only when we look at the centuries of biological programming that have gone on before. Those stars, in their 50's and 60's, having bested all the other (cavemen, male lions, etc.), are at the height of their social and financial resources and have won the right to the female. A woman's power, on the other hand, is tied to her reproductive cycle. And women are at the height of their reproductive cycle when they are in their early-to-late twenties.

Writers, your older readers may not want to hear this, but if you write a romance with a 40 or 50-year-old heroine, you will probably have most likely written a difficult—if not impossible—book to sell. Maybe things will gradually change for heroines as medicine allows women to reproduce at later and later ages, but it's not happening in fiction yet.

Women still like to read about a recreation of their earlier reproductive power. Maximum sexual struggle occurs when a woman is at the height of that power. If she has this power, she triumphs; she bends the male to her will.

How do you, as a writer of romance, show that your heroine is biologically powerful? You create one who is healthy, with good skin and a lush—translate that as being able to produce great offspring— body. To describe her as "beautiful" is to use a code word for biological power.

To put it another way: waist and hip definition.

This may be a difficult premise for feminist writers to concede. I am a feminist myself, an attorney, but in this matter I have to agree that we have to look to our biological roots to write a compelling romance novel.

My advice is, try not to edit yourself to be too politically correct. Feed the readers' fantasies. They love incredible uncontrolled passion—like that shown when a hero, who is usually very controlled, loses control with the heroine.

Readers love male sexual dominance. Jung said women need to fear their men a little. Aggression and sex are right next to each other in the brain and that is exciting. A strong sexual commitment to the female is very exciting to her, and the writer who can recreate that strong sexual commitment from the male to the female will succeed every time.

One of the best books that Judith McNaught ever wrote (*Double Standard*) is not at all politically correct. It shows a double standard where the boss harasses the female, yet it works. In this story, as in all successful romance writing, the story works because we have a coy, choosy, careful female versus an aggressive, powerful, determined hero. If you have a female who is too high in masculine energy and a hero high in female energy, where is the triumph in getting the already-warm, nurturing male to commit to fatherhood?

The Horse Whisperer, an immensely popular novel and movie, is a good example of what happens to a female who is high in masculine energy. She is ruthless, powerful, and goal-oriented, and has a husband who is kind and sensitive. The heroine becomes involved with another man who brings her back to her feminine side—to the root of her feminine values—bringing her closer to her child.

I am a big believer in feminine values. I like to see heroines who are sweet and kind and moral and understanding and loving with children. A great many other readers seem to feel the same. As women adopt masculine values and compete with men in the workplace and in boardrooms, they lose some of the protection that society used to afford women. Men are aggressive to men, and if men perceive women as being "men" they will attack women too.

I hate to think we are puppets of our hormones and our genes, but to some extent, we are. The brain evolved to human psychology two or three million years ago. People still need a jolt to that two-or-three-million-year psychology because it causes an endomorphic rush that is addictive. A well-written romance gives this jolt. Some readers are so addicted to this deep primal jolt they read one or more romances a week, maybe even one a day.

I got into the study of the romance genre because I had heard this was true and wanted to know why. I have since discovered that the jolt is akin to the prehistoric paragon of hitting her over the head and carrying her off to the cave.

There is a hormone-driven phenomenon in male and female behavior that is interesting from a biological standpoint. Once the female has sex with the male, she produces the hormone oxytocin and this causes her to bond with the male. She becomes emotionally bound. Perhaps this explains why a lot of arranged marriages eventually work.

In romance novels, the heroine is a "place holder" for the female reader. Through the heroine, the reader feels the power of the dark, dangerous, and ultimately devoted male, and will bond with the hero. How thrilling!

The danger/sexual dominance of the male is thinly veiled in many of our traditions. Take marriage, for example. Do you know why the bride stands to the left of the groom in a wedding ceremony? It was originally done so that he could keep his right (sword arm) free in case of attack. The best man was there to fight by his side.

Why are we so attracted to the "Mondo" male who is angry at his own attraction to the female, maybe even a little mean? Eventually, the female tames him and turns him into father material and he actually modifies his behavior and becomes capable of bonding with her. That proves she is powerful.

In some romance novels the hero and heroine bond early and then work against an outside evil toward a common goal. The male is already there for the female. They are a "survival reproductive pair."

These romances are not as powerful as books where the female has to first tame the male beast. (Possibly he is a brain surgeon, knight in shining armor, paratrooper, etc., who refuses to commit.) When the female gets commitment, she is triumphant. It is the ultimate female fantasy.

For males, however, their favorite fantasy is for the female who will give them sex without expecting commitment. Male "tough guy" movies are good examples. If the male does succumb and commits to the female after having sex with her, chances are by the end of the movie she will be killed off or will have gone to jail.

However, the movies that are enormously popular are those which get the biological "formula" correct. *Titanic* was just such a movie. Pure, classic romance, a young seventeen-year-old female at the height of her female reproductive power and two men—one with resources, the other of good breeding stock—who make a commitment to the female. We all know which one she chose.

The formula also worked well in the film *The Last of the Mohicans*. The heroine had a choice between a high-status guy and one of very good breeding stock, and she chose the Mohican over the Englishman. Love conquers all, or should we say good breeding stock counts too! Survival of the species becomes the ultimate criteria for sexual commitment.

In romance novels that sell really well, the heroines tend to be virgins (often found more and more frequently only in historicals). Sales figures are highest for the younger heroine; the older your heroine is over 28, the more power she—and, in the end, your book— loses.

Remember those movies where the heroine is always under 40? There's that biological conditioning. It affects everything we do.

Monkeys will eat fruit that isn't ripe, but we won't; we evolved to like the taste of ripe fruit because ripe fruit is easier for our systems to digest. When men get stressed out, they'll eat a steak (needing the protein before battle) even though, with modern information about cholesterol, their reasoning should override that urge. You can't intellectually force yourself not to respond. You are responding because of things that made a difference "back then on the savanna."

Centuries ago, if the male chose a female who was past reproduction, his genes died out, so the male was not about to commit to a female who didn't make him feel "paternal confidence." If a female chose a warm, loving kind male who couldn't protect her, her genes didn't make it into the next generation either. If you are out on the savanna, you are going to die if the male is not strong enough to protect you.

I have a friend who divorced her husband after she heard a noise in the basement. Instead of leaping out of bed to protect her, he handed her the flashlight. He no longer made her feel that primal sense of protection—and as a result, she never again felt that all-important biological jolt.

Make your readers feel that jolt and they'll love you forever.

"I heard you are very interested in becoming romance writers. Getting published is the ultimate thrill, but what you'll learn about yourself and your craft along the way is immeasurable. Good luck."

Where Lies the Magic?

By Mary Balogh

As *readers* of romance, we can simply enjoy—or not enjoy—the books we read, without pausing to ask ourselves what it is that makes one book more "readable" than another. However, as *writers*, we *must* ask the question—and answer it too.

A suspenseful action-packed plot will certainly impel the reader forward. It is human nature to have a weakness for a good story. Vividly described, exotic settings, often from the past, transport us away from our humdrum lives into a dream world. Realistic multi-dimensional characters caught up in a seemingly insurmountable conflict grab and hold our sympathies . . . or antipathies. Love scenes, well done, can satisfy our deepest belief in the wonder of romantic love. All are necessary elements of a romantic novel. But what exactly is it that makes some of these books affect us so deeply that they find their way onto that coveted "keeper" shelf, to be read over and over again? Where lies the magic?

There is no single answer, of course. Every writer is unique. Every great writer brings her/his unique magic to the craft of writing. What makes *my* imagination take wing is the compulsion to create heroes and heroines from deep within their psyches. My plots are only necessary vehicles for the development of two real people fighting the odds in order to achieve their happily-ever-after. I become them. I feel less that I have created them than that they have possessed me.

Let me try to explain more clearly, and step-by-step, how this might be accomplished.

First, one has to create two characters who will be *accepted* as hero and heroine. This does not mean they must be "heroic" in any stereotypical sense—either in looks or behavior. It does mean that they must be people with whom the reader can identify and sympathize, about whom the reader can care deeply. When they are handled by a skilled writer, often the most ordinary, most flawed individuals become very dear indeed to a reader in the course of a book. Readers don't need characters drastically different from themselves. We all need to believe that a storybook love could happen to us.

Secondly, the hero and heroine must be *worthy* of one another. This does not mean that they have to be "heroic" characters right from the start. It does not mean that they must be obviously compatible. Indeed, very often when I have created a heroine in my mind and am about to create the hero (or vice versa), I ask myself what type of man would she be *least* likely to end up with. When I have the answer, I have my hero. If I have a sensible, rather straitlaced bluestocking for a Regency heroine, for example, what could be more obvious than that I need a sleazy rake for a hero? (*The Notorious Rake*, Signet Regency.)

What being worthy of each other does mean is . . . they must each be equally interesting and equally complex. Sometimes the temptation when one has a great idea for one character is to create another whose only real function is to provide the romantic interest. But a complex hero needs a complex heroine. Doing half a job of creation will not produce a great book.

Heroes and heroines who are independently complex will probably be in conflict with each other. Here are two worlds destined to meld into one through the power of love—but not without a few storms! The conflict must be real enough and powerful enough to seem insoluble. It must keep these two characters apart for almost the whole of the book.

If the hero and heroine confess their love for each other halfway through the book, but have to solve a few plot conflicts before the end, the reader's interest will wane quite sharply. When one reads romance it is not the story itself that keeps one riveted. It is the *romance*. Therefore, the resolution of the conflict should come very gradually and must be believable. A simple kiss or even a full sexual experience is not enough to solve a conflict worthy of the name—indeed it may only further complicate matters.

An absolutely essential aspect of developing characters—but one much neglected—is an attention to their pasts. We are all products of everything that has happened to us in our lives. Most of us carry around a great deal of emotional baggage that colors the way we behave and react to life and other people. Many of us carry about a great deal of pain, often repressed or incompletely dealt with. Before any of us can live peaceful fulfilled lives, and certainly before we can have joyful meaningful love relationships, we need to deal with all these unresolved problems of the past.

In order to create multi-dimensional characters, we have to be aware of everything that has had an impact on their lives. The way the past shapes the plot and the development of the love relationship can become the main focus of the reader's interest especially when the past is only gradually revealed in the course of the book. People—we, ourselves—frequently say and do things we do not mean or even intend to say or do. Why? We often hurt those nearest and dearest to us. Why? Why do these contradictions exist in human nature? To say people are just *bad* is far too simplistic an explanation. The answers often lie in the past. What a mine of possibilities for the perceptive writer!

By this point, the writer has two very real, very complex, characters that come into conflict with each other in the course of the plot, until eventually they make a rich love commitment to each other—though I am fond of making it clear that eternal happiness is never guaranteed. Even the happiest of love relationships have to be worked on every day of the lovers' lives.

The ingredients of a good romance are now in place. How can the writer make magic of them? We come to the all-important question of *point of view*. My stories are written episode-by-episode from the alternating points of view of the hero and heroine . . . one at a time. (Sometimes it is necessary to use someone else's point of view, but it is wise to do this sparingly as it dilutes the emotional impact of the love story.) The reader lives that episode from deep within the mind of either the hero or the heroine. We see the events of the plot and react to them with that character, and it can seem a little restrictive. What if that character is misinterpreting events? What if we do not know how the other one is interpreting them or reacting to them? What if, locked in the mind of the hero, the reader can see there are certain things he is not revealing to the heroine? What if he is rejecting her while inwardly he is crying out for her acceptance? The temptation as a writer is to jump over to the other character in order to give the reader more information. But real life is lived in this restrictive way. And being locked into one character's point of view for a whole episode can be emotionally powerful. We feel as trapped in the life, mind and emotions of the hero (or heroine) as he is himself. Sometimes we could *shake* him—but that is the sort of emotional involvement we want our readers to have in our book.

But, of course, it is a book we are writing. As authors we are omniscient. We can give the reader this deep inner awareness of both the hero and the heroine, but separately, not all mixed up together. If there is a real need to know how each is feeling on a certain occasion, the episode can be retold from the other's point of view, or relived through memory.

We all know that if two people give an account of the same series of events, the accounts will be very different, even if both are earnestly trying to be honest. Much can be made of this fact when the writer switches point of view. The first chapter of my novel, *The First Snowdrop* (Signet Regency), for example, consists of two episodes. Actually, it is the identical series of events shown first through the hero's eyes and then through the heroine's. They see the events so differently that one would hardly know they had lived through the same experience.

The trick is always to be inside the mind of one of the characters, not simply to tell what happens in an impersonal, narrative way with an occasional reference to how the characters are feeling. It is effective as a general rule to alternate between the two points of view, but at the start of each episode one must ask oneself what plot element needs to happen next and through whose eyes it will be most effective to see it.

I have found from experience that a story feels "flat" when I am simply narrating it. I have to go back and rewrite, getting myself into the mind of one of my characters. You see, we rarely, if ever, simply observe what is happening to us. We react emotionally to almost all the events of our lives. As writers, we can make this happen in a good book. It must constantly have emotion, what I think of as passion, though that does not necessarily mean sexual passion.

Writing in this way—that is, not simply narrating a story, but *living* it deeply with both the hero and the heroine—has its dangers. One can be swept along by emotion and lose touch with "reality." One needs frequently to pause to check out certain things. Would the characters *really* do that or say that? If one looks at them from the outside, one is often not certain. After all, we do not always understand ourselves, so how can we possibly understand others? But when one is living the life of a character from within, one is better able to answer with confidence: "Yes, he really would do something this stupid or say something this vicious . . . but not necessarily because he is either stupid or vicious."

Sometimes, because past experiences are repressed, even the character is not sure why he has done something. But when the writer is deep inside his mind and emotions, the truth can come out gradually and subtly and convincingly.

Another check I frequently impose upon myself as I write is this: Am I writing a romance? It is easy to get carried away with an intricate plot. It is easy to become so fascinated by a character that the book becomes a psychological study. Readers of romance don't want just that. They want a *love story.*

A wise editor once told me the hero and heroine should not be apart for longer than ten pages at a time. It is a good rule of thumb. Keep them together. Contrive believable ways of bringing them together. Let them hammer out their differences. Let love grow and have passion explode all over the place. I will not say that everything else should be subordinate to the romance, but certainly everything should add up to romance. Romance is the *raison d'être* of the book.

There is a final check I keep doing as I am writing—and it is perhaps the most important. Is this a book I am passionately involved in? If it has become simply something I am moving along from point A to point B, I know that I have gone drastically wrong somewhere. I am telling the story from the outside and have lost that depth of involvement that I know my books need. Is what I am writing a book I cannot *stop* writing, or at least one I cannot stop *living* when I do leave my computer? Is this story, and are these characters, *haunting* me? If the answer is no to any of these questions—and I must be brutally honest here—then something is wrong. I must find out what it is.

If *I, the author*, am not passionately involved in my own book, and if it is possible for *me* to take it up or set it down at will, it would be foolish of me to expect the book to keep a *reader* up until those wee, small hours. If I want to write a book *someone else* will not be able to put down, then I have to write one that *I* can't put down. And what better way to accomplish that than to enter so deeply into two characters' lives that they take on reality in my own life.

"Take a pen; dip quill in motivation;
underline faults, reason, desire
. . . and make fiction of us all."
Ann Peach

* * *

"When beginning to paint a hero, remember . . . dark is dangerous and more. We may not be able to live with them, but the bad boys are the ones we remember."

The Dark and the Light

By Anne Stuart

What is the appeal of the dark and dangerous male, and when do things become too dark? Why can't we have nice, normal, caring heroes in our books? Why do people respond to brooding, tormented, cynical heroes who seem to hate themselves almost as much as they hate the heroine?

I'm deliberately putting it as harshly as I can, despite the fact that I write dark heroes almost exclusively, books so dark that most of my reviews carry the warning that "this isn't for every reader." The desire for dark dangerous men isn't something new. Think of the famous romantic heroes of the past: Mr. Rochester in *Jane Eyre,* Heathcliff in *Wuthering Heights,* even over-bred Mr. Darcy in *Pride and Prejudice* has his difficult moments. Dark heroes don't usually belong in a comedy of manners. Sixty years ago, Scarlett O'Hara kept making the mistake of pining after pale, civilized Ashley Wilkes and resisting the decidedly dangerous Rhett Butler, but Rhett was the one all the sensible women readers wanted. All matchmaking Regency mamas have a soft spot for a rake, and burned-out spies, soldiers, cops, and cowboys are a staple of modern romance novels. Why?

For one thing, women love a challenge. A handsome, well-adjusted, sensible man, capable of commitment and sustaining a long-term relationship will have enough conflict to sustain a full-length novel, but he probably belongs in a science fiction novel along with other alien creatures. The one way around it would be to have a dark and dangerous heroine, reversing the roles, but while that makes an interesting story, it's hard to make it a compelling romance. In a novel there is always a quest, and in a romance it's the quest for fulfilling love. If the hero is for it and the heroine dead-set against it, the readers could have trouble identifying.

Women know that love is strength, but quite often men see it as weakness. It's the hero's quest to overcome his isolation and bond with a worthy female, and the more he resists, the more external and internal complications get in the way, the more compelling a story.

Darkness and light are an essential part of the world. Night and day, winter and summer. The most universally celebrated holidays occur around the solstices, where light returns to the darkness in the form of a savior, the miracle of Hanukkah, or the beneficent sun. Bringing light to the wounded soul of a dark man brings the same kind of emotional resonance to the reader.

The question is, how dark can you reasonably go without losing your readers? Can he rape or beat the heroine? Probably not anymore, though such were staples of earlier historical romances, along with kidnapping (which is still a viable alternative). Can he kill other people, either justifiably or without qualm? Does he have a recognizable code of honor, his own sense of honor, or no honor at all? How bad can he possibly be?

I personally like pushing things to the very edge, though this is much too far for many readers. I like the sense that sometimes the greatest threat to the heroine is not the serial killer lurking in the woods but the enigmatic hero himself. I want a love so extreme that it goes beyond time and space, beyond honor and ethics, beyond reality and fantasy into a realm that few people could comprehend. And you have to have characters who are willing to take it to the very edge and beyond.

You need men who are capable of killing, of losing everything, sacrificing everything for their sense of rightness, women who are willing to make that same sacrifice, not to be absorbed by the hero, but to bond. I want to read about the love that's stronger than death and taxes, because real life is far too full of the last two "bummers."

That doesn't mean I don't adore comedies, light romances, stories of suburban disaster and blind dates gone awry. It doesn't mean that I can't fall in love with one of Jennifer Greene's or Judith Arnold's decent heroes, or laugh till I cry over Jennifer Crusie's conflicted nineties woman. It doesn't mean that darkness is devoid of humor or light, either. Unrelenting darkness gets to be a little depressing after a while, and a humorless hero, no matter how wounded, can become annoying.

In a dark, larger-than-life story it all comes down to what's at stake. If it's release from an apartment and a job as a secretary, then I'm not that interested. Chances are I'd rather have my own apartment and job than marry some boring businessman. If the stakes are life and death, then things get a little more exciting. I'd much rather read about a woman trying to survive being stranded in a war-torn city with a cocky cynical pilot than someone finding a father for the baby left in her care. Of course, the great writers like Linda Howard can do both in the same book.

The trick to writing dark and dangerous men is to know how far you can go without losing your readers. I'm usually lost when it comes to severed body parts or abused children, but other people are less (or more) squeamish. You need to keep your readers in mind, but also be true to your book and your characters. Taking chances is dangerous, but it's the only way to truly live.

And one thing more . . . you need to ground your characters in reality before you let them fly into the darkness. Give them a life, a family, a reason for being who they are. If you've given them that much, you know they'll land safely.

"When I was a child, I read Zane Grey. He wrote about the Wild West and the men who lived it. He wrote about men who were willing to die for a cause... or for the love of a good woman. He wrote about men who knew the meaning of sacrifice. I loved Zane Grey's stories . . . and I loved the men he wrote. Why? Because I lived within the pages of those books."

Infuse Your Writing with Emotion

By Sharon Sala

Zane Grey knew how to make his readers feel pain and smell dust. Although my family did not own a horse, I rode with his heroes through stark, untamed lands and learned to appreciate a different kind of beauty than the world with which I was familiar. The author captured my imagination by capturing my emotions. I cried. I cheered. I angered. I feared. And did it all between the pages of books.

Even though I might not have been able to identify with the pain of a gunshot, I could identify with pain. Even though I did not know what it felt like to be torn to pieces by Cholla cactus or lost in the badlands, I knew what it felt like to hurt . . . and I knew the fear of being lost. I identified. And because I did so, the characters became real to me.

When I first began writing, my instinct was to recreate that magical link between book and reader, and the only way I knew how was by using emotion. I once had a beginning writer ask me why emotion is so important to a story. I told her it is simple: Emotion is to a story, what breath is to a body. Without it, neither will live.

The most remarkable characters in books are nothing more than words on paper unless the reader *cares* about them. The question then must be asked, how does a writer make characters believable? How do we bring them to life so that the reader keeps turning the pages of the book? Again, the answer is simple. Give them a life in which to live.

Think about those words. How does one go about bringing flat, one-dimensional characters to life with nothing more than a series of connecting words? Emotion.

To evoke emotion within a reader, in essence, I tap into my reader's own memories. When a reader can identify with a character through similar experiences, then the characters are easier to understand. That, in turn, makes the story more believable. For the time a reader is turning the pages of a book, he/she is in another place. It's your duty as a writer to bring that place to life.

Use commonplace things as identifiable fears. Although he doesn't write romance, Stephen King is a master at this. He takes the simplest bits of our everyday lives and adds horrifying twists. This accomplishes two things at once. Because of the ordinary situations in which his characters find themselves, we, the readers, identify. Then he takes our innermost fears and adds them into the ordinary, thereby turning the story into something easily relate-able and unforgettable. As a writer, he's accomplished his job. We see ourselves between the pages of his books with all of our hang-ups and hidden fears. For a fiction writer within the horror genre, he's a master of suspense.

While I have no desire to frighten my readers, I do strive to make my story relate to the real world, but at the same time, be an unforgettable piece of fiction. To do this, I put myself in my characters' situations. If I were there, what would I be seeing? What would it take to make me afraid? How would I react in a specific situation? Would

I laugh? Would I cry? What would I see? What would I smell? How would the geography as well as the weather affect what was going on in my world?

For example: There is nothing more frightening to a parent than a missing child. Imagine a mother walking into a kitchen and finding her child has disappeared. The half-eaten cookie the child had been eating is still on the table and a glass of milk has been spilled on the floor. The only sound she can hear is the steady ticking of the kitchen clock.

This scene creates an instant panic for the mother as well as the reader.

Your characters, both lead and secondary, must have strengths as well as weaknesses. Even the best hero must have flaws—but not moral flaws that would turn people off. A hero can stand against the majority on any given issue if his reasoning is sound. The same must be said for the heroine. Give her spirit. Give her grace. And for goodness sake, give her a good dose of common sense.

By the same rule, a truly evil character must also have at least one human, redeeming trait. If the reader can identify with a bad man's childhood, or if the villain happens to have a sweet tooth or a personality trait that even a pastor might share, then so much the better.

I saw a movie once with the stereotypical bad guy. He was bad with a capital B, but he had a strange, compulsive habit that I could relate to. He was constantly flossing his teeth. In fact, he was obsessed with dental hygiene in general. He couldn't pass a mirror without testing his grin and he would stop and floss at the most bizarre moments during the film. It was comical, but his fanaticism about it only added to his evil persona. Because of that, in my mind, he became real, not just an actor doing a job.

Lesson to be learned: We don't have to like the villain, but it helps if we understand him.

Conflict is an all-important part of any good book no matter what the genre, and emotional conflict is quite often the most difficult to conquer. You are the writer. Pull out all the stops and take your reader on an emotional roller-coaster ride through the pages of your story. Within a few well-chosen words, your book can become an impossible-to-put-down page-turner. The highest compliment a writer can receive is when a reader claims to have stayed up until all hours to get to the very last page, then expresses sorrow that there were no more pages to read.

That, my friends, is what a book is all about. It's memorable stories with memorable characters that stay with you long after the last page was read and the book was closed.

Sometimes emotion so overtakes a book that it almost becomes its own character. If a book is driven by dark deeds and one life-threatening scene after another, emotion alone will keep a reader turning the pages. As a writer, if you can achieve this, you have tapped into your own Mother Lode. It will lift your story out of the mundane and make it memorable.

If you do it right, adding emotion to your story can become the truest form of empathy for your reader. Webster says it best with the definition of empathy, stating that it is "the identification with, or vicarious experiencing of the feelings or thoughts of others."

Remember what I said before: To bring your characters to life, give them a life in which to live. Make the following your new phrase to write by:

DON'T JUST DO IT . . . DO IT WITH EMOTION.

"There is no way of writing well and also of writing easily."
Anthony Trollope
* * *

"Next to a good cry, there's nothing quite like laughing out loud. And when I find myself doing both while reading a book, then I know the author has mined my emotions for all they're worth and written a book that is a winner."

Use Humor to Mine Those Emotions

By Millie Criswell

Injecting humor into writing is tricky. There's a subtlety involved so that the result is not slapstick comedy—the type the Three Stooges used so effectively. Instead, the result should be believable situations that amuse, that leave us smiling or chuckling with delight.

The easiest way to add humor to your novel is to give your hero and heroine opposite character traits. Opposites not only attract; they make for rather funny moments. Remember Shakespeare's *The Taming of the Shrew*?

If your hero is obsessively neat and your heroine has always been a slob, or your heroine is a stiff-necked spinster who abhors laziness and alcohol and your hero's a womanizing drifter who likes to imbibe, you're going to have humorous situations right from their first meeting.

In my novel *Prim Rose*, farm girl Rose Elizabeth Martin earned her living by the sweat of her brow. Alexander Warrick was a cultured, privileged English duke. Their widely diverse backgrounds made for some truly memorable and humorous moments.

Setting up embarrassing situations for your hero and heroine to overcome is a great way to inject humor into the story. If your hero has never milked a cow or castrated a pig, you've instantly got the perfect vehicle to illustrate his ineptness. The same is true if your heroine has few social graces and must learn them overnight, or if she's a terrible cook and has to host an important dinner party for twelve.

Perhaps she's a witch but is awful at performing incantations, as is the delightful heroine in Jill Barnett's *Bewitching*.

Sprinkle large doses of humor in the dialogue. A character's wry wit shines through in the words he/she speaks.

In *Prim Rose*, Alexander learns firsthand that castrating pigs is far from fun, but the reader finds much to enjoy in his abhorrence of the situation:

> *"Soon we'll have to castrate this little fellow," she explained.*
>
> *Rose's words sent chills rushing through Alexander. He crossed his legs against the unwelcome image she evoked, feeling nothing but pity and a large measure of male empathy for the poor little creature. "Is that really necessary? It seems rather a drastic measure." It wasn't difficult to imagine her castrating any male that didn't meet her rigid specifications, and it made the area between his legs ache. "I don't see you castrating the girl pigs. I don't think it's quite fair."*
>
> *"Castration without representation, your grace? Is that what you're saying?"*
>
> *He ignored her laughter. "Your Patrick Henry would no doubt agree with me."*
>
> *"I doubt Patrick Henry would have agreed with anything you English had to say, your dukeness."*

Witty repartee between the hero and heroine can also lighten a dramatic moment or add spice to a love scene.

Oftentimes, secondary characters can be used quite effectively to add a little comic relief, through dialogue, or in the way the individual is characterized. Children really do say the "darndest" things, as Art Linkletter once pointed out, and can be used very effectively to contribute lighter moments.

Even animals can add an unusual flavor to a story.

Chance Rafferty, gambler and saloon-owner in Sweet Laurel, had an incorrigible parrot named Percy who, more often than not, said some pretty outrageous things at the most inappropriate times, like when temperance worker Laurel Martin came to visit:

> *"How about a poke, sweetie?" Squawk. "Fire in the hole."*

Shocked by the outrageous comments, Laurel spun around to find a large green parrot perched on the end of the bar.

Chance swallowed his smile at her outraged expression. "You'll have to excuse Percy, Miss Martin. He's definitely lacking in manners."

Considering his owner, Laurel wasn't at all surprised by that.

"Percy wants a kiss." Squawk. "Give me some tongue, sweetie."

I think you get the picture. But keep in mind that a little bit of that type of humorous dialogue goes a loooong way. Even humor can get tedious if used in over-abundance.

You might think portraying humor during a love scene is strictly taboo. Not true, if you don't mind adding to your hero and heroine's frustration level, as I did in *Prim Rose*:

Their kiss was sweet and hot, and Rose lost herself in the sheer ecstasy of it.

Ribet ... ribet ... ribet ...

Alexander stopped and turned his head, looking none too pleased by the interruption. "What the hell was that?"

A huge smile of relief lit Rose Elizabeth's face. Lester had survived! He was back. "Just Lester. He sleeps under the bed."

Ribet ... ribet ... ribet ... The croaking sound grew louder.

The duke's eyes widened. "Has that damned frog been sleeping under this bed all the while?"

Rose smiled impishly, happy to be back in control of her emotions, her body, if only for a moment. "Lester disappeared during the tornado, and now he's back. And he's always slept under the bed. He's usually quiet and hardly ever croaks at night, but I guess our activity disturbed him."

"Well, isn't that just too damned bad!" Alexander leaned over the side of the bed and peered beneath it, scowling. A bloat-faced frog with bulging eyes stared back at him.

"Ribet ... ribet ... ribet ... "

"Oh my God!"

If you can't tell a joke without ruining the punchline, think you're not a particularly funny person, and are worried that you can't write humor, don't despair. There are plenty of things you can do to learn. Read authors who are particularly good at writing humor. Study their scenes, dialogue, and note what makes them work. View romantic comedies. Some of the best situations and dialogue have been filmed for the silver screen. Study some of the memorable ones such as: *Steel Magnolias* (excellent dialogue), *When Harry Met Sally* (witty repartee), *Sleepless in Seattle* (wry humor), *It Happened One Night*, and many of the classic Kathryn Hepburn/ Spencer Tracy movies (which are wonderful examples of witty repartee.)

Life would be pretty dull if the people we encountered didn't have senses of humor and didn't laugh or do any of the dozens of other silly things people do. Likewise, the characters in your book are going to seem pretty dull if they don't possess the same traits and emotions "real" people do.

Interjecting humor into a novel brings characters to life. Through humor we can illustrate frailties, faults, intelligence, and countless other attributes.

Humor means different things to different people. I don't find the Three Stooges to be the least bit funny, yet millions of other people obviously do. Develop and refine your own brand of humor, drawing on your life experiences, what you deem humorous . . . and what is suitable for your characters.

Love might make the world go round, but laughter makes the circumvention a lot more enjoyable.

Ribbet . . .

"I hear there's a trio of aspiring romance writers living together and studying the craft. Here's my note for your bulletin board: Emotion—tears, laughter, grief, joy—the heart of romance."

The Heart of Romance

By Lorraine Heath

I wish I could tell you that you simply plug emotion into a scene, into a chapter, into a story. But as with all things in writing, nothing is simple, nothing is easy; if it were, everyone would be doing it.

I'm certain you are aware that emotion is extremely complex—not only in life, but also in writing. To have emotion in a story, a writer must have: a compelling voice, plot and conflict along with dynamic characters, realistic dialogue and interesting setting.

When woven together, all these things help to create a tapestry of emotion. However, the greatest of these is compelling characters; they are the key to bringing depth of emotion to the story.

I have never had a reader write and tell me she loved my plot or she loved my setting or she loved my conflict. I have had *many* readers write to tell me that they will never forget Clay or Meg or Jake or any of the other characters in my books.

This is where we, as writers, must begin. In order to touch a chord of emotion in our readers, in order to make them care about the characters, we must bring the characters to life. We must think of them as people. We must let the readers come to know the characters.

Sometimes we have the misconception that if we bring tragedy to our characters our readers will grieve. If we give our characters heartfelt desires, our readers will rejoice. The level of that emotion we elicit in our readers is dependent upon how well we let our readers come to know the characters. If readers feel the characters have become their friends, readers' emotions will run more deeply.

To bring emotion to your stories: *Think of your characters as people and give the reader the opportunity to come to know them.*

As a writer, I am most concerned with the internal structure of my characters, rather than the outer shell—unless an aspect of the appearance has a bearing on the conflict or plays a role in the plot. I don't mean to diminish the importance of physical appearance. It is important, particularly in a romance, but the heart of the story resides with the characters and it is their *hearts* I must reveal to the reader.

My hero and heroine usually come to me fully grown within my imagination. I must come to know them, to understand them, in order to see them as people. I truly believe that in writing our stories we can create any scenario and make it believable if we develop a background for our characters that explains their motivation. Unlikely scenarios become stirring or heart-rending with the right motivation.

In writing a novel, we don't want to give the reader a clinical dissertation on a person's behavior—what we want, as writers, is to show that person's motivation. We do that by revealing the character's personality through his actions and through his mannerisms. The reader then not only comes to feel as though she has discovered a new friend, but also comes away from the story with a feeling of satisfaction. Keep the story close to the character.

Example: *It was a blistering hot day.*

This is an example of a passive description. What have I shown the reader? Nothing. I've told the reader that it was very hot—but where is the character?

Example: *John Stetson removed his hat and wiped his sweating brow. He'd never known a hotter day.*

This example reflects an active description. I've shown the reader that the day was hot—but I've placed the character in the middle of the heat, given his perspective on it.

Neither example is wrong, but I think the second example brings the reader closer to the character.

Example: *A thousand gnarled and crooked posts served as anchors for his barbed wire fence.*

The character is a little closer in this example. We refer to *his* fence. But how can we use the character to show the reader that the land is fenced in? How can we keep the character close to the reader? Would this work?

Example: *He worked the ridge of his spine into a comfortable position against the gnarled and crooked post that served as one of a thousand anchors for his barbed wire fence.*

Keeping the character close to the reader does not mean a writer must include the character or a reference to the character in every sentence, particularly when describing things outside the character—but a writer can keep the character close by bringing the character back into play.

Example: *The nearby river flowed to the rhythm of Nature's lullaby: the mating calls of insects mingled with the occasional swoosh of an owl's wings and the howl of a stalking coyote. Dallas wanted his son to hear that song, to appreciate the magnificence of nature, to tame it, to own it.* (*Texas Glory*, 1998.)

Momentarily, I left the character to describe the sounds of the night . . . but then I returned to let the reader know why these sounds were important to the character.

Lengthy descriptions that never bring the character into play can cause the reader to lose sight of the character. If we keep the character close to the story, the scenes, and the descriptions, we are more likely to keep the character close to the reader.

Whenever possible, avoid descriptions that read like a grocery list:

He was tall, with black hair and brown eyes. He had broad shoulders and a wide chest that tapered down to a narrow waist and even narrower hips.

It is better to combine physical description with action:

Cordelia had only seen Dallas Leigh once, and then only from a distance. He was taller than she was, broader than she was, and when he'd announced that the land he'd roped off was to be used for a town, the wind had been gracious enough to carry his deep voice to everyone who had gathered around him. She didn't think he was a man who would have accepted less. (*Texas Glory*, 1998)

Hopefully with this passage, I've given you a better feel for the character, even though I have not told you much about his appearance.

In your opinion, which of these examples bring the character closer to the reader?

A. *Someone nudged his shoulder.*
B. *He felt someone nudge his shoulder.*

A. *The stars sparkled like diamonds thrown on black velvet.*
B. *He gazed at the stars that sparkled like diamonds thrown on black velvet.*

A. *The water rushed over the falls.*
B. *He heard the water rushing over the falls.*

A. *Gently, she touched him.*
B. *In all his life, he'd never known a touch as gentle as the one she gave him.*

I think in each instance, Example B brings the character closer to the reader.

There isn't any rule—as far as I know—for how often you should bring the character into the story, or how often you should mention him. But we must remember that it is the character's story, and the reader must have his/her perspective if she is to understand that character.

If we keep the character close to the reader, we are more likely to reveal the heart of the story—and the heart of our characters—to the reader.

"I believe that the most compelling trait to consider about your characters is motivation. Start by looking at yourselves. Do you know, down deep, why you want to write a romance? What motivates you? Before writing a sentence of your novel, you must know what makes your characters 'tick.' "

"Why? Why? Why?"

By Martha Hix

Motivation is the reason WHY a character behaves in any particular fashion, in any given situation. Be it joy, despair, anger, or whatever, these are the feelings that say a lot about the hero and heroine, and the other people in their love story, and provide the motivation for what they do. Motivation adds layers to a character, and ensures that the reader will be interested in story-book people.

Readers like to identify with "their" fictional folks. Thus, it's the writer's job to make these characters come alive with needs and desires that make sense.

• Your hero and heroine should each have a main goal, and smaller ones.

• Before the end of your book, these goals must be met, set aside, or sacrificed.

All goals—believe it or not—boil down to escape, possession, or revenge. Set goals, and then figure out WHY each goal is important to the character.

Let's take your heroine. She wants or needs something, and it could be big or small. Whatever she wants, give her enough believable background so her wants or needs seem reasonable.

Take the "escape" route. If your heroine enters a marriage of convenience just so she can move into the hero's great house and get away from her bossy neighbor, that's not a good enough reason. If she's lost her job, has no one to turn to, her rent's overdue, and that neighbor is a convicted child molester, that's a better reason. If she's lost her job, has no one to turn to, and has a young child, that's a far better reason. However! You must make the reader understand WHY she can't take in ironing or get a job at the grocery store, or do any one of a million things modern women can do to keep their independence.

Don't make your people too good . . . or too bad. Even villains have admirable traits. Heroes and heroines should have more good traits than "cruddy" ones, but don't make them too perfect. Create characters that have a multitude of wants and needs, exemplary attributes and picayune eccentricities. Humanize them. Have them love, despise, fear, and/or face obstacles, with their unique way of looking at the world. Let the hero know WHY he loves the heroine. The same goes for her. Make their goals laudable, or at least understandable.

The best way to give your characters motivation is to breathe life into their psyches. Decide the relevant events in your hero and heroine's lives, and in the lives of the people who influence them. Know how each has reacted to pertinent events in their background—pertinent being those events that mean something in the story.

Grow to know your characters, either by writing their life stories or by a time line. Create one for the hero and another for his heroine. Start with the year of their birth, or earlier, if something happened in their family, or situation, that still has relevance to the love story. Afterward, as you understand more about their lives, fill in other occurrences.

Pay close attention to the date leading up to the start of their story. If you understand what makes these people tick on page one, you'll find it easier to write your book. Time lines are also a great way to keep track of ages and dates. More than anything, they will help you understand WHY your fictional folks behave as they do.

Think *plausible*. The main thing to keep in mind as you're writing is to ask yourself, "WHY is my hero/heroine doing this? Is he/she behaving in a reasonable manner? Will the woman I've never met, but who'll pay good money for my book, understand this behavior?" Always ask yourself WHY all your fictional folks are doing everything and whether you've explained their actions without going on too long about it. Explain briefly and clearly.

Motivation really isn't hard. Just make your people human.

"Here are some work sheets that I hand out on characterization when I lecture on writing romances. Hope they help you as well."

Heroes and Antiheroes

By Suzanne Forster

THREE RULES OF THUMB FOR THE HERO

1. The hero makes or breaks the story. He is the object of the fantasy. The catalyst. He embodies the heroine's fear of, and desire for, intimacy on every level.
2. To be a great hero, he must also be a villain. Don't be afraid of your hero's dark tendencies. Internal conflicts give a hero dimension and complexity. It's whether or not we ACT on dark impulses that determines our character, and ultimately builds it.
3. Nobility—The hero must have some, no matter how deeply buried. Selflessness can ennoble a man, as can doing the right thing for the wrong reason.

SEVEN CHARACTERISTICS THAT EMPOWER HEROES

1. Autonomy
2. Action

3. Leadership
4. Expertise
5. Success
6. Perceptiveness (a man who can read people)
7. Intelligence

NICE GUY HEROES—
HOW TO KEEP THE STORY EXCITING

1. **Internal Conflict**: Create characters whose worlds are in conflict. Create characters that have a fundamental clash of beliefs, attitudes, or values.
2. **External Conflict**: Raise the stakes of your story. Create bigger roadblocks to your characters getting together. Go for broke. Make it look impossible.
3. **Characterization**: Empower your hero. Create situations and scenes that allow him to demonstrate both his physical strength and his strength of character.
4. **Description**: Give lots of loving detail.
5. **Humor**: Great device to keep story fast-paced, interesting, and hero appealing.

ANTIHEROES—WHY SO EXCITING?

1. Built-in image. All the "R" words: rakes, rogues, rebels, and renegades.
2. They tap into the unexpressed rebel in each of us.
3. They're mysterious and often dangerous.
4. They arouse sexual curiosity.
5. They trigger fantasies—seduction and ravishment—perhaps because they seem to have an ability to take over a woman's will. (For example, classic dark heroes like Dracula and the Phantom of the Opera.)

CHARACTERIZING THE DARK HERO

There's no one personality type that can define him, but there are some characteristics that distinguish him:

1. **Insularity:** He has the appearance of inaccessibility and emotional invulnerability.
2. **Volatility:** There's a ticking bomb quality about him.
3. **Passionate idealism.**
4. **Cynical disillusionment:** The implication is he has "seen too much of the world" or has somehow had his illusions shattered.
5. **Unpredictability.**

FURTHER METHODS OF CHARACTERIZING A DARK HERO

1. **Language/dialogue:** Provocative, challenging dialogue will make the heroine—and the reader—catch her breath.
2. **Physicality:** Physique, posture that conveys self-possession, confidence, and even some arrogance if that's appropriate.
3. **Dangerous trappings:** The antihero's clothing and gear, his mode of transportation, his weapons (if any) and his environment should all be appropriate and authentic, but distinctive enough to set him apart from the pack.
4. **Vulnerability:** Find ways to reveal the inner man without compromising the antihero image. We need to know what forces have shaped him. His pain/losses. Also, hints of his gentle tender side.

OUTER CLUES TO THE INNER MAN

1. **The Visual Man:** Logical and rational. Tends to be overly intellectual and overly critical. Experiences the world mainly through his own eyes. Prides himself on ability to read others' points of view. Typical dialogue: "I SEE what you mean". "Our VIEWPOINTS differ."
2. **The Auditory Man:** Learns and retains knowledge by hearing. Fast, bright, impatient and logical. Turned on by sexy breathing. Typical dialogue: "How does Sunday SOUND?" "I HEAR what you're saying."
3. **The Olfactory Man:** Perceives things primarily through his sense of smell. Personality wise, he's mercurial. He hates being pinned down and is annoyed when his conclusions are questioned. He's

impulsive and intuitive. Typical dialogue: "I love the way you SMELL." "Something about this deal STINKS."

4. **The Tactile Man:** Perceives things through his body and sense of touch. Contact is basic requirement. Needs to touch and be touched. Typical dialogue: "You FEEL wonderful." "I love the way this car HUGS the road."

COLORS REVEAL CLUES TO THE INNER MAN

BROWN: He's methodical, practical, and prefers security to risk taking. BUT, he also enjoys lovemaking. May even have a prodigious appetite in this regard.

GRAY: No surprises in store here. He is basic, conservative, traditional, proud, responsible, and serious.

PINK: If he's head to toe in pink lock your closet. If he wears the occasional pink polo shirt, he's sentimental, warm, friendly, idealistic, and nonjudgmental.

RED: Implies passion. Occasional use indicates liveliness and vitality. Habitual use indicates aggression. Also indicates ardor, courage, competitiveness, impulsiveness, and possessiveness. Short fuse.

BLUE: Quiet, tranquil, peaceable, but may also be introverted and detached.

YELLOW: Intelligent, spiritual, and optimistic.

GREEN: Nurturing, caring, but very principled and stubborn.

BLACK: Intense, sophisticated, individualistic, a loner. Prefers a mysterious woman and enjoys discovering everything about her, but he will reveal very little of himself. If his apartment is black, don't fool around with his emotions. If his sheets are black, watch your neck!

THINGS (SOME) WOMEN FIND IRRESISTIBLE ABOUT MEN

- Curls at the nape of a man's neck.
- The size and shape of a man's hands.
- The sight of a man asleep, especially if he's looking all tousled and sexy.
- Tattoos, especially if they're on the biceps or some muscular part of the body.

- Bikini underwear on a man.
- No underwear at all.

"I hate writing, but I love having written."
Dorothy Parker
* * *

As soon as we heard you needed tips on writing fascinating characters, we came up with a mix-and-match exercise. Hope this helps the process.

Ann

Judith

Make Mine Heroic

By Ann Peach with Judith Kohnen

MAKE HER	MAKE HIM
Adorable, amiable, alluring, ambitious	Authoritative, angry, august adventurous
Beautiful, biddable, brazen, beguiling	Bad, breathtaking, bold, brave
Cuddly, content, creative, curvaceous	Coarse, crafty, captivating, cautious
Dizzy, delightful, dazzling, daring	Debonair, dashing, devastating determined
Electrifying, eager, enchanting, enticing,	Elegant, exemplary, energetic, enthralling
Feminine, feline, fearless, feisty	Funny, forthright, fabulous, faithful
Gorgeous, gracious, gregarious, graceful	Gentle, gruff, grand, gallant
Happy, healthy, hopeful, hot-blooded	Hovering, handsome, hell-bent, honorable
Irrepressible, individual, impish, independent	Individual, irritating, intriguing, intoxicating
Joyful, jubilant, jinxed, jaunty	Jaded, just, jealous, jovial
Kooky, knowledgeable, keen, kittenish	Kind-hearted, kingly, knightly, kiss-able
Loveable, lively, lovely, lady-like	Lusty, lordly, lucky, legendary,

Misty-eyed, mischievous, mysterious, moral

Mighty, merciful, masculine, muscular

Naughty, needy, near-sighted, neat

Noble, naive, nurturing, notorious

Openly-flirtatious, optimistic, outragious, obliging

Open-minded, obstinate, outdoorsy, bliging, overwhelming

Pretty, pliant, pouting, passionate

Proud, powerful, prosperous, possessive

Quick-witted, queenly, quizzical, quaint

Quick. quiet, quality, questionable

Righteous, ravishing, reluctant, reckless

Riveting, rapacious, romantic, roguish

Sexy, sweet, sensational, strong-willed

Sexy, soulful, sinful, sophisticated

Tall, tiny, talented, tantalizing

Tall, torn, troubled, trustworthy

Understanding, unavailable, uproarious, uncommon

Unapproachable, unkempt, unforgettable, unfailing

Vivacious, voluptuous, vital, venturesome

Vulnerable, valiant, virtuous, vain

Wistful, warm, watchful, winsome

Worried, wry, wonderful, well-built

X-traordinary

X-ceptional

Yielding

Yummy

Zany

Zealous

It's fun to mix and match these traits as a way of easily creating terrific, memorable characters. Try this exercise: Close your eyes and point to any three of the heroines' characteristics listed above. She's, hmmm . . . "jinxed, fearless, and tiny." Can you picture her? Give her a name, clothe her with the finest garments and drop her into an era. Got her now? See how easy this is? Now try the hero. Close those eyes, point to the page again and . . . "unkempt, authoritative, worried." Aha! We have the beginnings of a terrific romance here. Who is he? Why is such an authoritative, commanding man worried? And why is his hair wind-tossed and down around his shoulders? Why are his clothes torn? What mishap has his shirt half undone?

Let's try again. She's . . . "gorgeous, mysterious, watchful." He's . . . "bad, questionable, breathtaking." Do you have them fixed firmly in your mind already? We do—and here's a part of their story . . .

Lacey waited nearly twenty minutes after Ryan—bundled heavily against the snow—had left his Gramercy Park brownstone, before breaking into the building.

Getting in was easy. Surprisingly easy. She didn't even need the set of lock picks in her Vuitton bag, but instead jimmied the main door lock with just a credit card.

"Such a cautious man, and you forgot to lock the deadbolt"! Lacey murmered in surprise as the door swung open. Not like you at all Ryan, she thought, certain in her assessment of him after almost two weeks of close surveillance.

Once inside, she quietly shut the heavy door and then froze, head tilted straining to hear even the slightest sound. Silence.

With rapid strides of her long, slender legs, Lacey crossed the marble-floored foyer and ran up the curving flight of stairs. She headed straight for Ryan's bedroom door. It was closed.

Taking a deep, steadying breath, Lacey wrapped tentative fingers around the brass handle and slowly, silently, eased the door open.

Ryan stood not five feet in front of her . . . naked.

Lacey's barely muffled gasp of surprise spun him around to face her

Willing the pounding of her heart to slow, she took in every magnificent inch of him with a leisurely sweep of her olive green eyes.

"Not bad for a thief," she finally purred as her eyes drifted back up to his face.

This is how characters direct your stories all by themselves. If you fix them in your mind and give motivation as wings for their emotions, you'll have your best-selling book up and running before you know it.

Rosemarie, Jade and Sierra
Excited in San Francisco

Dear Kathryn,
"We think we got it!" (Again.) Sharon Sala was so right when she said, "The most remarkable characters in books are nothing more than words on paper unless the reader CARES about them." Every great book that any of us remembers has had truly *memorable* characters. It's true that a great romance *is* its characters.

As I write this, Jade is standing over my shoulder making sure that I thank you "profoundly" for all the help you are giving. So, from all of us, thank you SO VERY MUCH!

We are now going to read all the books by Balogh, Stuart, Sala, Heath, Hix, and Forster. What a savvy group! They have convinced us that wonderful characters, artfully portrayed, are what will make or break any book.

After we digested the latest batch of articles on character and emotion, we spent the past week doing something new...a bit of a "writing-exercise-without-actually-writing" that we thought up. Well, we didn't really think it up; we simply expanded upon Ann Peach's and Judith Kohnen's suggestions about character characteristics. This is the result:

All week, when we looked at people and the situations they got themselves into, we looked at those encounters in terms of what emotions the people involved were actually feeling...and showing. We then wrote down "buzzwords" for those feelings. We had thought that this would be a cinch! How wrong we were. Emotions are not always so easy to describe—even in the first person!

Thursday, Sierra was walking her dog, Shawnie, in Golden Gate Park when a small boy lost hold of his mother's hand and tumbled to the ground. He started to wail, and didn't stop even after mom picked him up and dusted him off. She reassured him that he was fine, but he continued to cry. Sierra reached for her pink, spiral-bound notebook (each of us has taken to carrying one everywhere), described the incident and wrote down "sad." But when she came alongside the little fellow, she had to scratch out that word. He wasn't "sad," he was "furious." When he had fallen, tripping over one of the long laces that had come undone on his tiny tennis shoes, he had dropped his ice cream cone and was wailing because his mother wouldn't let him pick it up and eat it again.

Sierra came up with several new descriptive terms and before she knew it, she had actually written a small scene about the incident. When she showed it to me later, I could actually feel that little boy's anger as though I'd been there!

The second exercise (in the same pink notebooks) was to write down the character traits of the more colorful and exciting personalities that we encountered day-to-day. This has been fun!

There is a gorgeous new waiter in a restaurant I frequent near the school where I teach, and the first time I saw him I thought "heather and kilts!" He has shoulder-length auburn hair (which he wears pulled back by a strip of leather) and the broadest shoulders I have ever seen outside the movies. (Sigh!) But telling you that is describing his looks—and my exercise was supposed to be describing his character. Here goes: In the restaurant two nights ago, he swooped down to pick up a napkin a lady had dropped and presented it to her with a flourish. His character word: "gallant." When he did finally get to my table, our eyes locked over my menu and oooh, that rascal; the look was definitely smoldering. As a result of that, I wrote down, "sensuous" and...whew! I stopped writing after that; but you get the picture.

We know you don't want us to start writing a whole book yet, but what do you think about these exercises?

By the way, I have a date tonight with the waiter.

Rosemarie

CHAPTER IV

WRITE THE SENSUAL ROMANCE

Kathryn Falk, Lady of Barrow
Romantic Times Magazine
Brooklyn, New York

Dear Ladies in the Shadow of the Golden Gate Bridge:

Now you have me painting pictures with words! Exercising your powers of observation is paramount. You need to use all of your senses (sight, sound, smell, taste, and touch) with your writing. You might want to organize your notebooks completely, though. Some writers take copious notes and put them under headings such as "descriptions of the weather" or "the smell of food" to have on hand when they're actually at the writing stage.

To help start you out collecting a variety of phrases and descriptive words, look over *The Romance Writers Phrase Book* by Jean Kent and Candace Shelton.

It seems like you are primed for the next batch of articles. It's time to get you thinking about a critically important component of your characters' lives and the romance novel craft—passionate and sensual scenes. Since I wrote my first "How to Write" book, the romance market has certainly "heated up." What might in the past have bordered on risqué is now "the norm." Sexual encounters are more graphically portrayed and more frequent in books written for today's markets. (The exception to this is the Inspirational market.)

Some mainstream authors, like Danielle Steel (who swears she is not a romance writer, by the way), aren't comfortable writing graphic sensual scenes. As thriller writer Alistair MacLean always said, perhaps it "slows down the action."

However, you're going for the *romance* novel and it must be passionate and more. Today's readers are about equally divided into three camps: one desiring books that keep the actual sex scenes off the page (so the readers' imaginations fill in the "good parts"); a second enthralled by the writer's most erotic descriptions; and the third preferring a spicy-type read that falls somewhere in between the others.

To fulfil the needs of these three groups of readers, today's romances are written by three categories of writers:

Category #1: Authors of "sweet" romances, especially those writing for the new inspirational market, such as Janette Oke and Francine Rivers, who manage to create sensual tension without graphic description of the actual sexual act.

Category #2: Authors like Heather Graham, Pamela Morsi, LaVyrle Spencer, and Diana Gabaldon who write sensuous scenes but who sprinkle them moderately throughout the books they write.

Category #3: Authors like Bertrice Small, Susan Johnson, and Virginia Henley who know their readers expect hotter-than-hot in the lovemaking department, and deliver it.

I wish I could say you can pick or choose your level of writing-sensuality but it never has worked that way. Either you *can* write hot love scenes or you *cannot*.

If you find writing sensual scenes difficult, a solution to this is to add lovemaking scenes *after* finishing the first draft. This is a writing trick used by Judith McNaught and others. If you find describing sensuality easy—overdo it. If not, get a friend to work with you on the "juicy bits." There's certainly an art to writing passionate love scenes.

Getting yourself into the mood might help considerably. Take a cue from Bertrice Small, known as "Lust's Leading Lady," who reads *The Story of O* and some of Roberta Latow's books to further inflame her erotic fantasies when she's about to embark on writing a new, luscious adventure!

Writing your own erotic "reference book" is another possibility. The Fern Michaels team, when starting out in the late 1970's, created a book of their wildest fantasies and then "borrowed" from it for several of their pirate historicals. This might be a terrific late-night pajama party project for the three of you! Release your inhibitions and let them run wild on paper!

By the way, the hottest article I'm sending to you is by English writer Jeanne Montague, who is a *great-grandmother*!

P.S. For Rosemarie: How did the date with the longhaired waiter turn out?

"I'm always prepared to write super sensual romance. But sometimes I like to stroke some silk or velvet, or sniff one of my favorite perfumes just to inspire me to find the right descriptive words. A good read and some wine will get my imagination going, too, as well as the prospect of an early night with my partner —or memories of previous ones!"
Margaret Melrose
One of Britain's Most Prolific Super-Sensuous Writers
* * *

"I'm told that you might be interested in writing passionate historical romances. Watch out! I've always said that anyone who actually lived the lives of my heroines would be dead by thirty! I wish you as much success with your 'sexual fantasies' as I've had with mine!"

I Write the Passionate Love Scene

By Bertrice Small

Imagination is exactly what a writer needs to create steamy love scenes, for fantasy—that stuff of dreams—is fed by imagination.

But, you ask, what about personal experience?

Listen, honey, personal experience will get you just so far. After that you need a *vivid* imagination—and a whole library of good research books. Sorry to disappoint you, but that's the truth.

When people refer to "sex" scenes in my novels, I always correct them. They are not "sex" scenes; they are sensual and erotic *love* scenes. Pure, raw sex, by itself, lacks the ingredients necessary to create a good love scene. To make a good scene work, you need strong emotions—love, hate, etc.—as well as all the right moves. Those emotions come from developing your characters *before* you co-join them, not after.

One little trick I like to employ is moving back and forth between the two lovers' thoughts. He feels, she feels. (No pun intended!) In order to do this successfully, you must *become* each character in your head.

As an example, let's use fictional characters in a historical romance: Perhaps she's young and inexperienced. She's nervous, maybe even a bit frightened. She doesn't have the wealth of knowledge regarding sexual matters, as do today's young women. She's been given the barest of details for the most part by an embarrassed mother, or guardian. (Yet sex in the historical eras in which I write, was pretty matter-of-fact for all that.)

Her partner is always experienced, older. He desires her physically, and is already in love, or falling in love with this girl. He struggles to keep his overwhelming lust in check because he wants her to enjoy his attentions, not be afraid of him.

Think hard about how each one of them feels at this time. Turn it over and over in your mind until you are squirming in your typing chair, and ready to jump your own significant other!

With a heroine who is more experienced, you can have more fun. Perhaps she's the aggressor. Perhaps they enjoy playing a game of cat and mouse before consummating their union. Here dialogue plays a great part. I like to interject humor in scenes like this.

Now we come to the difficult part. The actual sex act itself, and the foreplay leading up to it. Most of us have already had sex ourselves, and some of us have had more interesting sex than other people, but all of us secretly long for a wild, erotic time in which we attain multiple orgasms with a passionate, well-buffed, tender, and humorous guy. Few of us ever reach that point, and ninety percent of the women who claim to have, are patent liars. *But anyone can imagine.*

Get out your research books, and start thinking about your own secret fantasies. Let your imagination run free to feed these fantasies. Perhaps this is stuff that in reality you wouldn't want to do, or are even afraid of doing, but you think it nonetheless. Do you want to dominate, or be dominated? Spanked? Service two men at the same time? Be serviced? Your imagination should be boundary-free at this point.

Let your imagination roam, and write it all down, but once you begin writing it, become a choreographer who moves slowly and carefully. Each action must be preceded and followed by the correct act. Arc noses, and other salient parts where they should be? When he carried her across the room, did you remember to have him put her down?

(If you are really adventurous, you might even try out some of the more interesting love-play on your own partner. You could be well rewarded for your efforts!)

So, there it is. Writing passion is part experience, part research, good choreography, plus smoke and mirrors.

"Get on the super sensuous bandwagon, if you dare. Tap into your—and your readers'—DEEPEST fantasies, it's a challenge, but like eating chocolate, it's addictive!"

Infuse it With Passion

By Susan Paul

"Passion" has definitely increased between the (romance) covers. Sexual encounters are more numerous and more graphically portrayed than in the past. No more does the director/writer "fade-to-black." But how much sex is *too* much? When does a romance stop being a romance and become, well, almost pornography?

One pundit said there's only one difference between super-sensual romance and erotica—COMMITMENT. In lay terms, acrobatics, experimentation and, exploration of fantasies are permissible in a romance if done strictly with Mr. Right.

A super sensual romance novel should have a fairly traditional structure. But whereas, in a more traditional romance, a chapter might end with a passionate kiss and a promise of shuddering delights to come, in the sensual romance the chapter will also end with a kiss—only the kiss is one of blissful contentment that takes place . . . afterward.

Hot and spicy is great, but don't ever be crass. Mix passion with love. Use poetic words for body parts and physical exploration. Avoid vulgar language. In our reading material, as in life, we (women of the world) don't need to be shocked; we need to be caressed, titillated, teased and have our senses aroused.

The romantic *story* must be the center of the super sensual romance—not just filler that takes the reader bed hopping from one love scene to the next. The key to writing good super sensual romance is to make it a "real" story that is also sizzling, genuinely thrilling, fast paced, fantastically written and sexually satisfying. Just like real-life. We wish . . .

"The South and its Southern Belles have always fascinated me."
He shot Kaki a wicked grin. "I am just dying to eat a Georgia
Peach." Kaki tried to smother a chuckle and failed. "What if I
told you that I know where you could find one right here in San
Tropez?" James lifted an eyebrow. "I'd say show me." "Just walk
this way . . ."
From The Bodyguard by Susan Paul and Betsy Morgan
in Secrets *Vol. 4*
* * *

"I'm sure you know by now that the expression 'Sex Sells!' has been the preeminent merchandising battle cry for almost any product across numerous decades."

"Sex Sells!"

By Stella Cameron

In the field of contemporary mainstream romance writing, "sex sells" is a frequent, and accurate, statement. However, sex is only one ingredient in a successful novel in this complex genre—a genre which is expanding, reaching readers who have never before read romance, because now it folds mainstream elements such as mystery, suspense, action/adventure, paranormal, horror, medical thriller, and legal thriller into the sensuous romance.

As a writer, your voice, natural strengths, and interests will lead you to your chosen, trademark-story type. Once you've arrived at this destination, the true thrill and challenge lie open before you. The thrill lies in the freedom to go as far and as daringly as you choose. The challenge is the delicate and absolutely essential integration of a powerful, sensuous romance with a powerful plot. Never become so enthralled with your magnificent *plot* that you forget the magnificent *romance* to which you must yield center stage. The magic of a winning combination is teased from a skillful balance among all elements of your novel: characterization (both protagonist and secondary), unfolding love story, motivation, plot, subsidiary plots, and background. Layering in numerous explicit or graphic sex scenes will not overcome shortcomings in the overall richness of construction in your novel.

The argument that my comments on the contemporary mainstream romance are also applicable to the historical romance is predictable. Since I write both, I feel confident in making the simple rebuttal that whereas historical romance is, at least to some degree, always confined by the conventions of the historical period, contemporary mainstream romance has no such restraints. Reading the work of other writers currently working on mainstream romances is essential to understanding the market.

I must tip my hat to the contemporary category lines and their contribution to the emergence of sensuous mainstream romance. Harlequin, and Silhouette continue to publish extraordinarily well-crafted contemporary romances. No contemporary (or, in my opinion, historical) romance writer's study of the genre would be complete without reading some of these fine books.

Sensuous contemporary romance is a genre that continues to grow in popularity. If you have a strong, individual writing style, a "nose" for fresh, compelling stories, and a love affair with no-holds-barred romance, you may be at that dream destination: the right place at the right time!

"Here's my philosophy: Life should be enjoyed . . . every day, every hour, every minute. That means using all our senses: taste, touch, smell and sight. If we're not doing that, we're missing out on a lot."

Why Not Write Sensual Romance?

By Lori Foster

Our bodies were created with the instinctive need to indulge our senses, and the most intense, explosive feeling of sensual pleasure comes through sex. Why shouldn't that carry through in our writing?

People say money makes the world go 'round. They're wrong. It's sex. Or sex appeal, or sensuality, or that little touch and look that make your heart pound and your body heat. It's a vital, fundamental part of basic nature. When all is said and done, we're animals—human animals, with refined senses.

To write about romance—any romance—without sex, isn't honest. To create a hero and heroine who aren't driven to touch and explore each other is cowardly and a cop-out. Why do so many romance writers shy away from the realities of the bedroom?

In today's real world, caution rules. Safe sex is the order of the day. This serves to make the romance novel enthralling. Readers can experience hot, sizzling, (safe) romantic sex through the experiences of their favorite characters. It's fantasy, sure, but it is important all the same.

Real romance isn't centered solely on emotions or mechanics. The two must work together and become intertwined to establish uncompromising love. This is true of life, and it should be true of written romance.

As a writer, I want my readers deeply involved in my love stories. I want them anxious to see my hero and heroine sharing every aspect of love, feeling the passionate anger of an argument or the whisper of the hero's breath on her cheek during sex. Readers should "experience" the warmth of aroused skin, hot looks, and passionate kisses.

This is fiction, so the hero can be the perfect lover.

Eye contact is a must. In many ways it's more intimate than a physical stroke, and can be used with devastating effect, both on the written page and in real life. Eyes reflect fears and hope, pathos and passion. What hero doesn't want to see into his heroine's soul?

Sex in the dark is out, unless the dark can be used to enhance other senses. Today's romances are seldom shy and sweet. This is not an age of innocence; it's an age of intelligence, and women's freedom. Women deserve to be seen. If the hero can see the heroine, she can see him, too. I enjoy showing the thrill of their discovery and their resulting excitement.

Sex between our heroes and heroines (above average, fascinating people) should never be dull or merely perfunctory. Rich or poor, pretty or plain, dynamic or withdrawn, the hero and heroine have to be sexually attracted to each other. That's too important to skimp on. Beyond that, our characters love each other, so they should be able to share that love in the most elemental way possible. It's not nasty, or embarrassing; it's erotic and enveloping and all encompassing. It's lovemaking. Why pull back, or rely upon ridiculous euphemisms to describe a natural physical response? An erection is just that. An orgasm is even more. You can't be struck down for being accurate.

Never leave your readers guessing. Be explicit and allow your characters good wholesome sex—and plenty of reasons and opportunities to indulge. Ultimately, if you grant them this, your characters will be very happy. Which leads to what is, after all, the most basic criteria for a romance: the happy ending.

"The reader should be able to experience what the characters feel, get under their skin. Sex scenes should not be hurried. It takes a while to establish a mood, to describe fully what is stimulating the characters. It's even more important in this type of fiction that all the senses are aroused through the writing."
Margaret Melrose
* * *

"Aspiring to erotica? Look for the first American erotic romance anthology that was published in the fall of 1998 by Kensington. It was a major breakthrough in "our" category. We have put together a collection that pushes the envelope on this popular sub-genre of super sensual/erotica."

How to Write Sexy

By Thea Devine

Writing about sex is hot, hard, sweaty work. In writing about it, or in doing it, the secret to good sex is conflict, motivation, tension . . . explosion.

Romances, as we write them today, contain a certain structure, or framework, as I prefer to call it:

a. Get the characters together.

b. Define the conflict that pushes them apart.

c. Give them "baggage" to create complications.

Then add this crucial component: an "oppositeness," a polarity, a contradiction between them that will spark like flint on stone. Immovable object vs. irresistible force. The thing I call the pull-tug. She pulls one way; he tugs the other. They are going the same way in opposite directions. This wonderful defining device serves the characterization, the story and the sex. This contradiction feeds the movement of the story, the conflict, the motivation and the characters' reactions to each other. In essence, they sniff around each other for the length of the book. And when they finally come together, they are Adam and Eve, the only people in the world who ever discovered sex.

You want to make your love scenes as intimate as possible. Use pronouns. No one will forget who is making love. Don't use negative visual images. She is not "on fire." He does not "impale her with his molten rod." Show all facets of their sensuality—what they do for each other as well as to each other—and not necessarily during sex.

Make your heroine active. Things don't happen *to* her, they happen because she *wants* them to. The reader must always feel the heroine has some control and that she is a participant and not an object.

Find new ways to express and articulate what your characters are doing in bed. Don't resort to cliché phrasing or describe the act bluntly.

Focus on foreplay. You have to dig into yourself and imagine what it looks like and feels like. Then describe it. Use chewy words. Collect them so you can refer to them. I promise you won't be able to think of one when you're in the midst of writing a love scene.

Keep a list of adjectives (no matter how far-fetched) to describe him in all his masculine glory and her in all her ripe femininity.

Do not backtrack during the love scene. If they are going at it hot and heavy, don't intrude and remind your reader that your hero is so experienced he's sure to please the heroine. SHE sure doesn't want to know that—and neither, I think, does your reader.

The way you write sex scenes comes out of who you are, what turns you on, what you like to do, to watch, to try, what you fantasize about, what you saw on TV, in the movies, in a magazine or book, what your best friend told you or what you think you could do better. The key to making these scenes work is don't hold back. You can always decide later how much or how little to cut. No one ever has to know if it's your fantasy or your reality.

Finally, it occurs to me that the book itself is a sex act: You have endless foreplay, climax after climax and, in the end, real satisfaction. Your job is to seduce your reader through this act using great protagonists, a page-turning story, and most importantly, well-written, well-motivated, heart-stopping sex.

"It's important to try and avoid clichés, although you're dealing with some tricky areas as far as vocabulary is concerned. Generally, I think if the writer is comfortable with the words he/she uses, it will come out right. You can't hope to please everyone since different words have different associations for different people. "

Margaret Melrose

* * *

"Beware the curse of the purple prose. None of the writers in my critique group makes a practice of using this technique in their romance manuscripts, and I hope you won't either!"

The Purple Prose Eater

By Deb Stover

Purple Prose. What is it? Where did this term originate, and how did romance authors become the lucky professionals to be slapped with this label? Mr. Webster failed to provide me with a definition, so I felt duty-bound to compose one myself.

Purple prose consists of words and phrases that sound stilted, overly descriptive, or cliché. Now that doesn't mean we should never use beautiful, descriptive language. Not at all. What it means is the overuse of it irritates your reader and can mutate into the dreaded purple prose.

The main area where romance writers in particular are accused of inflicting the reader with purple prose is in love scenes. Why? In the seventies, when authors first threw open the bedroom doors on love scenes in romance novels, writers had to devise creative ways to describe human anatomy. Apparently, the powers-that-be felt the reading public could only handle one shock at a time, so we formulated all sorts of interesting words and phrases to substitute for more clinical terms.

We still use euphemisms in love scenes, though I find them much more realistic than they once were. However, beginning writers will often depend on the euphemisms of the past, rather than simply calling a breast a breast.

Examples? Let's start with clichés.

"Every fiber of her being."

"Slow burn of anger."

"Orbs" for eyes. One book I read used the phrase "sapphire orbs" repeatedly to describe the heroine's eyes. We don't need to be reminded too often what color a character's eyes are. In my early days, I once wrote a hero with emerald eyes. I've learned since then.

A recent survey I conducted has revealed some rather interesting tidbits of the inadvertent use of purple prose. A few brave authors have given their consent for us to study their examples—an incredibly magnanimous gesture.

Author Jo Beverly believes that "physical description only needs to be done once or twice. Any further reference should be indirect. Having told us that the hero has long ebony hair, I don't want it mentioned again, thanks. For me it definitely comes into the purple prose category to not only be constantly repeating physical characteristics, but also using the same flowery phrases that we probably shouldn't have used in the first place!"

A romance reader who wishes to remain anonymous said, "I can't stand breasts being referred to as mounds. Makes me think of a candy bar. And I can't stand anyone bucking. I think of a rodeo."

That's pretty self-explanatory.

Author Patricia Ryan gets right into the euphemism subject with her answer: "Arousal as a euphemism for erection. What's wrong with erection? Ditto on mounds for breasts. Don't mention stallion in reference to your hero. Ick. Now that I'm warmed to my subject, I have to 'fess-up' to a somewhat lavender little phrase of my own. I did, I confess, make reference in a kissing scene to the hero and heroine's tongues being engaged in, well . . . in a primitive mating dance. I actually wrote it and printed it out and sent it to my agent, who called me up and said, 'Primitive mating dance?' And I said, 'Uh

. . .' Thank God for agents with good taste, is all I can say. I view that incident as a slip in my otherwise rather ruthless quest to use real words and normal language as much as possible, especially in my historical stuff. Looking back, I think I was probably just being lazy when I used that phrase instead of putting the old gray matter to work squeezing out something better."

Another anonymous reader also admits to hating the term "mounds" in reference to breasts. She goes on to say: "Also, globes. Can't stand globes. I picture the school type, swirling madly on their stands. Why can't we call 'em what they are?"

Author Sonia Simone believes the phrase "his sex" is a good substitute for penis. She calls this term "raunch literary," whatever that means. It sounds good, and works for me.

Here's an opinion on using graphic slang from one of the masters of the romance genre, Anne Stuart: "Words like 'cock' should be used judiciously. Sometimes the shock value can be very erotic. Sometimes it can be jarring." Anne later commented that she considers the word penis a "whiny, nasal little word." Then she confesses, and I quote, "I once, God help me, called it 'the raging beast of his desire' but I saved my reputation when I saw the galleys and almost barfed." She also admitted that in her novel *Night of the Phantom,* she used the phrase "filled her with the hot wet tumult of his love." When she saw it in print, she wanted to scream.

Now *that* is purple prose! Don't do that. When you're as successful as Anne Stuart is, you can do that. If you want to.

Speaking of male nether-regions . . .

While participating in a Romance Writers' open critique group last year, I ran across an interesting euphemism for erection: "Love tool." I'm not divulging the identity of the writer for fear of life and limb, but I think you all must realize this is not a good euphemism for erection. In fact, all I had to do was read it aloud. The perpetrator perceived my message loud and clear.

A well-known Regency author feels the word "erection" is preferable to "penis" in a love scene. I tend to agree, though I have used the term penis from the male point of view.

Another successful Regency author, Lynn Kerstan, said that the funniest term she ever read was in a contest entry: "...his tumescent tube of fire." An unpublished writer asked me if "raging monster of his lust" would be acceptable. I said, "Sure, go for it. That'll cut down on the competition."

Some of the participants in my research became a little . . . carried away. Example? "The dragon of his desire writhed beneath his tight-stretched trousers." Ahem.

Historical author Susan Wiggs admits that her editor once omitted her reference to the male sex organ as "the bald avenger." Wonder why.

"Manhood" has been overused, but you'll still run across it. It doesn't bother me by itself, but we have to be careful about the adjectives we put with it. "Manroot," on the other hand, is about as purple as they come.

The phrase "his hardness," makes me think of royalty for some reason. I don't think that was the author's intention.

"Throbbing member?" Well...

"Turgid shaft." Even I'm guilty of that one. Sigh.

"Her gaze traveled down his muscular chest and lean hips to his softly swaying promise of future delight." It doesn't do a thing for me.

Robin Williams once used the phrases "throbbing love machine" and "heat-seeking moisture missile" in reference to the male sex organ in its aroused state.

I've seen "sword" used as a euphemism for erection. There seems to be a food and warfare thing relating to gender in romance novels. Have you ever noticed it? You'll see reference to foods with female genitalia and weaponry with male.

Hmm. Freud could've used this stuff.

Now, in all fairness, the responses to my survey didn't net nearly as many colorful substitutions for female body parts. You don't suppose that's because the respondents were all women, do you?

"Hot sleeve of love?"

"Her moist warmth." Think about it.

"Silken warmth." Hmm.

"The heat of her femininity." Well, maybe on occasion. At least that doesn't push the giggle button.

"Nest of desire?" Give me a break.

"Perky, pebbled, and plentiful" are often used to describe breasts and nipples. As one reader pointed out, have you ever seen "upturned nipples?" Think gravity, writers. Gravity.

"Nether lips." Not for me.

"Mound of Venus." Yuck.

In addition to the different nouns we use to depict human anatomy, there are other words which can be overdone until they also become cliché. "Quivering" and "throbbing" come to mind. I always wondered why she does the quivering and he does the throbbing. That doesn't quite seem fair, does it?

One way of identifying purple prose is by your reaction when you read it. Does it make you laugh out loud because it's so ludicrous? Or does it make you shake your head in disgust? If it does, feed it to the Purple Prose-Eater—in other words, lose it. He'll appreciate it a lot more than your readers will.

"In writing sensuous romance as in sex: tease. Tease the readers, make them guess, make them wait . . . then release them in a satisfying way."
Margaret Melrose
* * *

"I have switched from writing historicals, young adults, and gothics to what is known in England as erotic romance. Writing as Zara Devereux, Tesni Morgan and Roxane Beaufort, I am a great-grandmother who is, literally, turning my fantasies into profitable fiction."

Erotic Fiction by Women . . . for Women

By Jeanne Montague

At one time, women's access to erotica was limited, the best being *Delta of Venus* by Anais Nin or *The Story of O,* by Pauline Reage. The rest was porn, written by men . . . for men.

Women found themselves uncomfortable with what was available. Pornographic literature was too aggressive, too phallic, almost intimidating. Women turned instead to other genres, chiefly romantic fiction, for fantasy fulfillment. Now, women's erotic fiction is being recognized in England as a sub-genre in its own right. There are numerous opportunities for women writers in this area as the demand for well-written erotica increases. Unlike that of the male who gets bogged down in anatomical details, the female imagination knows no limits; it is sensual, experimental, and a veritable storehouse of secret treasures.

Valerie Kelly says in her very informative book *How to Write Erotica*, "It is important to distinguish between erotica and pornography. Erotica celebrates sexuality, sex with caring, sex as an expression and communication between lovers, sex as a release of emotions, as a solution to alienation and loneliness. Pornography exploits and often degrades sexuality. It shows sex for the purpose of objectifying it. Sex imposed on one sex by the other, sex with violence and humiliation, and sex performed without feeling."

One of the stipulations made by two British publishers of female erotica, *Black Lace* and *X Libris,* is the books must be written *by women, for women*. If a male author submits a manuscript, it is not even read.

I thought I'd never be able to write anything so explicit because my former novels had been sexy only when needed; the story and its plot were always paramount. Most publishers of erotica, on the other hand, caution the writer about getting too involved with the plot, stating it should never take over the sexual activity, which is the main force of the book. (At the same time, though, they want a believable story line to link the sexy bits together.)

Initiation of the heroine is important; this is an innocent taking part in a kind of rite of passage. New plots are rare, so adapt ones used in romances, but from the heroine's sexual viewpoint.

There is usually a dominating male, probably assisted by his sophisticated mistress, who brings to the fore the submissive sexuality of the heroine. This doesn't mean that she is a lukewarm personality, but that she begins to like the sexually submissive role.

Many fairytales and classic works of literature have domination/submission themes. Think of *Cinderella* and *Jane Eyre*.

Remember what themes gave you a thrill. Think of ways you can combine history and fairytales, or apply these to contemporary scenarios. There's a vast field of opportunity in history in which to set your scene. Choose themes that turn *you* on. This will make your work all the more powerful. However, don't make the mistake of writing a sensual romance novel. Sensual romances are not erotica.

My first reaction on studying the market was one of surprise at the high quality of the writing. I had expected it to be tacky. It wasn't. Other experienced authors were turning their talents to erotica. I decided to give it a shot. The guidelines said these were written and directed at the 30-40 age group of higher-income-bracketed women—educated, intelligent, and probably career-oriented. They like to fantasize about something that could possibly really happen—making love to the gas station man, the guy she meets in the supermarket, or a neighbor.

One of the cardinal rules is *the heroine is in charge*. Nothing is ever done *to* her that she doesn't *want* done. These books are not Mills

& Boon (Harlequin) with a little sex thrown in. These are a whole different ball game.

The heroine is often a career woman who has possibly never been completely sexually fulfilled. The story concerns her "coming out"— finding herself. She has to be reasonably well off, but without any problems with money or relatives. She is independent, has her own business maybe.

I write under different names for this market, though this is a personal choice. As it is, I get enough cracks from those friends to whom I've confessed I'm writing erotica. They want to know if I really do all those things. "No wonder your husband is looking so tired these days," they say, and so on. I treat these remarks with scorn. After all, you don't have to commit a murder in order to write a detective story.

One has to lose one's inhibitions to write erotica. Writing sexually explicit material is very difficult and stretches one's skill to the limit. Writing these books gives one a platform on which to air feminine issues long-neglected, particularly women's sexual needs. These are liberating books to write. I'm not talking physical freedom, but mental. If it helps women to understand themselves and their needs, and to differentiate between love and sex, as men do, then such literature is long overdue.

Sex is energy, a source of life to be enjoyed, used to feed and feel other aspects of our lives—social, intellectual, abstract, and physical. Women realize that the most erogenous zone is the mind. They can appreciate the dazzling reverberations of sexual encounters.

When you write erotica, you can orchestrate all the senses: touch, sound, sight, palate, and all the euphoric accompaniments, background music, moods, atmosphere and variations. Build up your love scenes slowly, using mental foreplay and painting exciting mind-pictures for the reader. As writers, we are free to fuse sexuality and feeling, sensuality and emotion. Within the genre, it is possible to develop an elegant erotic style that is poetic in expression.

The settings are vital as is the use of description of all experiences of the senses: the taste of exquisite food or the lover's body, the touch of silk, velvet, anything tactile, including the lover's skin, the smell of perfume, flowers, the sea and the lover, the sight of glorious, exotic views, gorgeous interiors, lovely women, handsome men, high fashion and again . . . back to the lover's body.

Sound is important, including what is said with a sexy content, the sounds of nature, or a lovely speaking voice.

Ultimately it all boils down to one thing: orgasms, experienced from the heroine's point of view (though there can be separate sections devoted to the men or other female characters).

Above all, have fun with them. At its simplest, erotica means "alive." The more alive we feel, the more awakened to the life force in and around us.

Rosemary,
Une Femme D'érotique,
"Turned on" in San Francisco

Dear Kathryn,

Before I thank you for this latest (thrilling) group of articles, I must fill you in on THE DATE. "My" waiter's name is Alex; he's sweet and tender and strong enough to defend a castle. Which is lucky, because he just happens to own one. Yes, that's right. A castle! Back in Scotland, the country I adore. Seems that darling man isn't strictly a waiter in that restaurant; he is also the _owner_ of the restaurant . . . and the rest of the chain, too. He has been working incognito in several of the restaurants because there has been some problem with missing funds. Yummy doesn't begin to describe this man. Last night he took me to dinner at the glamorous Pacific Restaurant and then to Tango Night at the Top of the Mark Hotel. A Scot who can tango. Wow! I was in heaven!

When we finally got back to the door of my apartment at the end of the evening, he never said a word, just locked eyes with me, moved to within a hairsbreadth of me, threaded his long fingers through my hair, tipped my head back and . . . well . . .

Suffice it to say, the evening gave me a whole new perspective on motivation and choice!

I haven't forgotten my decision to concentrate on being a writer, though. I've just been a little side-tracked along the way . . . Wow! What a challenge this getting-ready-to-write is, Kathryn. Each group of articles you send opens our eyes to new horizons.

None of us had any idea there was so much to writing sensuous romance—so much to consider. We see from the new romances we are reading that the market has definitely changed "sensually," and each of us, as writers, must be prepared to unleash our fantasies (on paper) as well as we can.

This last batch you sent was perfect for us. Jade, Sierra, and I already love super-sensuous romances and so had previously read at least one or two books from the authors who wrote to us. We suspect that makes us great candidates to inject healthy doses of sexuality into the books we will eventually write. We are not sure that we are quite ready to go the erotic route though.

We made an immediate trip to one of our local Bookstores That Care and bought the *Story of O.* Coincidentally, they also happened to have a copy of Roberta Latow's out-of-print book, *Three Rivers.* However, we need a few more suggestions for "super sensuous reads." Help!

Waiting "breathlessly" . . .
Rosemarie

Kathryn Falk, Lady of Barrow
Romantic Times Magazine
Brooklyn, New York

Dear Girls:

Mmmmm. Rosemarie, your waiter sounds intriguing. Are you sure you need even more in the way of sensuous reads? Just kidding. In any event, help is on the way.

You should read *Writing Erotic Fiction* by Derek Parker. It discusses plot and the "explicit" role of the language in this genre. Jeanne Montague was right to mention *How to Write Erotica* by Valerie Kelly. It is a helpful reference book that covers the entire erotic writing world, including short stories.

For a complete reading list of "hot" novels, look over the list of RT-recommended super-sensuous and erotic books on *RomanticTimes.com*. Explore some titles from the British lines *Black Lace, X-Libris,* and *Liaison*. They are written exclusively for women's fantasies, primarily by women writers. Also check out Genesis Press's *Secret Library* series published under their *THERION* imprint. Volume One contains two erotic novels originally published in the UK by X-Libris.

By the way, I hope you are continuing to keep up with current popular titles being published. It's important to read all genres. This way you learn what excites a majority of readers and what are currently popular subjects and themes. However, keep in mind, the books you are reading now were purchased a year or so ago by the editors, and are just hitting the shelves now.

Kathryn

Rosemarie Kelly,
San Francisco

Dear Kathryn,

We are definitely keeping up with "current reads" as you suggested. The *RomanticTimes.com* web site was a fabulous help. We ordered a huge selection of books and since they've arrived we have had little sleep.

On the same web site, I also looked up my favorite type of historical, the Scottish novel, and loved the list compiled for *RT*'s "theme spotlight." There were Scottish titles I'd never heard of. I'm going to read as many of those as I can because I'm thinking of writing a Scottish historical. I know it has been done, done, done, but I love, love, LOVE those kilts! And Bonnie Prince Charlie, too. (Maybe I could make my Scottish romance super-sensuous?!)

There is one aspect of doing this that has me kind of nervous about attempting to write a historical—the incredible amount of effort that goes into research for a historical novel. My mother warned me that readers are right on top of you if you make a mistake—there will always be someone out there who is extremely knowledgeable about when a fork was first used, and whether or not a young girl had to keep her hair covered in Medieval times.

I minored in history, know more than a bit about Scotland and find the historical romances I read present fairly accurate portrayals of Scottish history. This means the authors of these romances have "done their homework." What they know and correctly convey is sometimes so detailed that it's obvious the amount of research they have done has been extensive. When I start to research, I begin with my local library (and the Internet). Is this the way it's done by successful, published authors? Do they have favorite reference books? They all seem to know so much; maybe they have all been reincarnated and are just writing down what they remember. (Just joking ... or am I?) I would appreciate knowing how much research authors actually do, and would be interested in some of their favorite sources.

What about contemporary stories? How much research do they entail? We are quite serious about getting the research part of things down pat. Will you please help with this critically important aspect of the writing process?

By the way, keeping up with the new authors you have introduced, plus all our old favorites, has resulted in a new decorating scheme here in Chinatown. Our shelves runneth over. Our growing collection of romance novels—would you believe we now have more than 500—takes up three floor-to-ceiling bookcases.

Regards, from "ye olde book collector,"
Rosemarie

CHAPTER V

RESEARCHING ROMANCES

Kathryn Falk, Lady of Barrow
Romantic Times Magazine
Brooklyn, New York

Dear "Lady of the Knight" (Rosemarie),

So you want to consider becoming an historical romance author? That means commitment in a *big* way! And yes, it will require considerable time spent on research.

Most historical romance authors become specialists in a particular period. I'm told it takes about five years of concentrated reading and research to absorb an era. The idea is to avoid having to bob into and out of research material while you're writing, in order to deliver authentic customs, language, food, clothing, social issues, historical incidents, etc. You are right that readers have a good handle on these details and will be extremely disappointed if you don't get everything correct. In romance writing, the truth really is in the details.

As you can imagine, contemporary romances require much less research. (This is another good reason for writing what you know.) However, a well-written contemporary romance is as completely thought out and accurate as a historical, and so will still require dedication and research commitment.

I've asked Constance O'Banyon and Tori Phillips, two talented and knowledgeable writers of historical romance to guide you "onward and upward," as the saying goes.

In addition, I sent your questions to quite a few pals who have put on their thinking caps, and will pass on tips about their research methods and sources to you. Even the great Johanna Lindsey has sent along some valuable tips and she says, "Aloha!" (She lives in a house on her own mountaintop in Hawaii!) You are really getting an abundance in this shipment. Jude Deveraux, Bertrice Small, Jill Marie Landis, Dorothy Garlock, and Teresa Medeiros, to name just a few, have all answered your research questions. How lucky can you get?

Finally, as a special treat, I've given you a peek at Pamela Morsi's complete list of research books. It may seem a bit daunting to realize how many sources one author relies upon, but I hope it will serve as inspiration for you to start your own serious research library—a must-have for most writers.

Seeing as how you are so interested in the history of Scotland and love Bonnie Prince Charlie with a passion, I have a real treat for you. HRH Prince Michael, claimant to the throne of Scotland and descendant of that same Bonnie Prince, has written a fascinating book, *The Forgotten Monarchy of Scotland*. It contains a great deal of new genealogical information about the Scots' monarchy. Anyone who is planning to write about Scotland's history needs a copy.

Regards,

Kathryn

"I research for months; I haunt the public library and tear apart my own. I need to know the sounds and the flavors and the scents of an era. I have to know what colors would have been woven and what storms my heroine braved. I need to know what brides wore and what confidences they might have shared. I need a list of occupations, and servants' titles, too. Who would have walked? Who would have ridden? What did they yearn for and purchase and lust after and lose? I need the shape of it and the sense of it. Then I toss it all aside and start with dialogue."

Ann Peach

* * *

"I have a large library. I'm practically married to my research books when I write my novels. I encourage you to be the same."

Research: A Necessary Tool

By Constance O'Banyon

Research: Careful hunting for facts or truth about a subject; to search again or repeatedly, attempt to discover, explore, search and inquire.
—The World Book Dictionary

How important is research when writing good fiction? It's <u>critically</u> important. Imagine that someone in the year 2055 decides to write a historical novel set in 1955. Suppose this author depicts a female character in bell-bottom hip-huggers and clogs, with her hair worn in a shag haircut . . . a popular look in the '70s. The researcher of the future only missed the mark by 20 years, but what an enormous mistake! We know that in 1955 the heroine would have worn bobby socks and cancans, with her hair pulled back in a ponytail. If we don't check our facts, we can miss historical fashion by the same margin.

Remember at the beginning of *Gone with the Wind*, where Scarlett O'Hara wore hoop skirts, and then, toward the end of the book, she wore a bustle? Margaret Mitchell did her research and changed the dress style to go with the times. So must you. Be accurate.

(I admit that I am a chump for every costume book that crosses my path and if you write one, you can be sure I'll buy it. I have two shelves of costume books now and am working on the third. When I am ready to write a book, I stack them on the floor by my desk for easy reference.)

There are many pitfalls you can avoid just by doing the proper research. Imagine putting nylon hose on a woman in the roaring twenties, when in fact, the fabric did not come into use until the next decade. Don't let your Viking hero give his lady an orchid, because those fragile flowers could only be found in tropical climes in his day.

I sometimes become so involved in reading research books that I have to be careful not to dump everything I have learned into my book. While I was writing *Song of the Nightingale*, I became so fascinated by an account of the battle of Waterloo that I had my French and English soldiers tramping across fields of oats, beans, corn, peas and barley. My daughter, who edits for me, shoved the page with the battle scene under my face and said, "Mom, do you really think your reader is going to *care* what crops were grown at Waterloo when Wellington met Napoleon?" Of course, she was right. I had thrown in too many facts and had slowed down the action. Needless to say, I edited out all the food (well, almost all), and got on with the battle.

There is no need to share too much knowledge with your readers or they can easily become overwhelmed. For accuracy and flavor I need to know everything I can learn about a particular era. No one but you will know how diligently you researched your facts. However, the knowledge isn't lost. It's there on every page, it's in every word our characters utter, and it sets the tone for your book and makes it believable.

I once spoke to a reader who was unhappy about a book she had just finished. She complained that the author had said there were greasewood trees in West Texas, but the reader lived there knew there were not. I asked her if she liked the book otherwise, and she said,

"No, because after that mistake, I was unable to believe anything the author wrote."

Get your facts right, because if you don't, someone will know you made a mistake; even the question of greasewood trees in West Texas is important to someone. If you are going to write about Texas, find a book on trees, plants and animal life in Texas. Do the same thing for any locale of which you want to write.

To touch quickly on dialogue (for I consider it an important part of research): be consistent. It stands to reason that a tavern wench of the 1700's would not speak with the same eloquence of a duchess, nor would a barmaid speak with the diction of a schoolmarm. Don't have the tavern wench suddenly become an eloquent orator halfway through your book, unless you're making a point.

Another important point is the use of historical figures in your book. I have no problem with this if it's done properly and, above all, sparingly. For instance, if you have George Washington at home in Mount Vernon at the time when he was actually wintering at Valley Forge, then you did not do your research. By all means, use historical characters, but don't overuse them and make certain that you put them in the right place at the right time.

Researching can be challenging, but it is as necessary as any other tool you will use in creating your book. It is crucial, whether you are writing a contemporary or a historical. It is the glue that holds the book together. One of the thrills I get from writing is making characters come alive on the pages. So, go ahead: explore, discover, have fun—but beware, research can be addictive.

Today's author has so many marvelous research resources to use. The following are just a few:

The Public Library:
Any public library has a trained staff that is willing to help you find what you need. Don't overlook the inter-library loan program, where your local library can find the exact book you need from another city or state.

Travel Books and Videos:
I have found both of these to be helpful. It would be wonderful if we could always visit the places we write about, but that's not al-

ways possible. To me, the next best thing to being there is a travel book with a lot of photographs. Let us say, for instance, that you are writing about Egypt, and for whatever reason you can't travel there. Go to your local bookstore and buy a travel book. My personal favorites are Baedeker's and Fodor's, but the selection is plentiful. These books will give you geography, climate, history, vegetation, animal life, religions, customs and valuable information that will convince your reader that you have actually been to Egypt. Videos are good to visualize your setting and are filled with historical facts of the region. The catalogue "Britannia" has a wide variety of videos from around the world. Their address is:

Britannia Collection,
P.O. Box 64413
St. Paul, MN 55164-0415

Another good resource is:
The Video Catalogue
P.O. Box 64267
St. Paul, MN 55164-0267

I have used both and have never been disappointed.

Children's Book Section
If you haven't discovered this fantastic source of research, you are in for a treat. It's a virtual treasure trove. I have found the most wonderful research books just browsing through the children's book section of my local bookstore. My personal favorites are the "Eyewitness" series by Dorling Kindersley. Take, for example, the book *Castles*. Using color photographs, it details daily life in a medieval castle, depicting every inhabitant from the lowest servant to the lord, showing their manner of dress and their functions. The Eyewitness series has a wide variety of subjects. Prepare to be entertained, as well as informed. So, if you haven't checked out the children's section, do so. You will be amazed by the bounty you'll find there.

The Internet
The new kid on the block is probably the most powerful: the Internet! I confess that I'm a novice on the net, and, personally, I

prefer to do my research from a book. If you have access to the Internet, however, you have a proficient tool at your disposal. One word of caution: Make sure the source you use is reliable.

I just finished a short story for Leisure Books as part of their Celebrations anthology, and needed to know about Aspen, Colorado. I did not have time to make the trip so I keyed "Aspen" into an Internet search engine and out came pages and pages of research material. I pushed it even further. I needed to know about skiing, and soon my printer was churning out volumes on wedge steps, side stepping, and even what clothing to wear. I had the equivalent of an online ski instructor. I now know all the moves it takes to ski down a mountain, in theory, if not in practice. So, if you have access to the Internet, try it out. You may be surprised by the wealth of information you can have via your home computer.

I have touched upon only a few tools at your disposal. Find what is comfortable for you and use it. Never take any fact for granted and you'll be saved a lot of embarrassment.

* * *

Historical Research—it's all in the Details

One of my pet peeves is reading a book about the nobility and finding that the author has her/his titles incorrect. Below is a listing of peerage in order of importance and rank. I will be using the names John and Mary Tilsbury of Chatworth to show the correct usage.

1. King or Queen: His or Her Majesty
2. Crowned Prince or Princess (meaning the heir apparent): His or Her Royal Highness.
3. Prince or Princess not in immediate line for the throne: His or Her Highness
4. Duke or Duchess: His or Her Grace, Duke or Duchess of Chatworth. *Note that Dukes and Duchesses rarely have the same surname as their title. Example: John Tilsbury, Duke of Chatworth. (A word of caution: A Duke or a Duchess is never referred to as "My Lord" or "My Lady.")*

5. The children of a Duke and Duchess: Use first names with title in speaking to them. Example: Lady Sally or Lord Robert. Introducing them is more formal. Example: Lady Sally Tilsbury or Lord Robert Tilsbury.
6. Marquess or Marchioness: His Lordship or Her Ladyship. John Tilsbury, The Marquess of Chatworth. In direct address: Lord or Lady Chatworth.
7. Earl or Countess: His Lord or Her Lady, the Earl or Lady of Chatworth. In direct address: My Lord or My Lady.
8. Viscount or Viscountess: His Lord or Her Lady, Lord or Lady Chatworth. In direct address: My Lord or My Lady.
9. Baron or Baroness: His Lord or Her Lady, Lord or Lady Tilsbury. In direct address: My Lord or My Lady.
10. Baronet or Baronetess: Sir John Tilsbury or Lady Tilsbury. The children of a Baronet are not titled.
11. A King or Queen bestows knighthood upon an individual for some service performed. A male knight is referred to as Sir, thus Sir John Tilsbury. A lady who has been knighted is known as a Dame and is referred to as Dame Mary Tilsbury. This title cannot be inherited.
12. A Dowager is the widow of a deceased Duke, Marquess, Earl, Viscount or Baron. The title distinguishes her from the successor's wife. She is the Dowager Duchess of Chatworth.
13. The Honorable. All children, male and female, of viscounts and barons, and to the younger sons of earls. The Honorable Mary Tilsbury, daughter of Viscount Chatworth.

I have used only the English peerage. Titles in other countries are quite different. If you want to know more about peerage, I recommend the following books:
Miss Manners
The Amy Vanderbilt Complete Book of Etiquette
The Encyclopedia Britannica

"It takes a great deal of history to produce a little literature."
Henry James
* * *

For a writer of historical fiction, the greatest praise is to have a reader say, "You really took me back there."

Putting History in Your Historical

By Tori Phillips

Important dates, names of kings, generals, presidents, and locales are integral as they act as the backdrop for the action. Yet it isn't just the big events a writer has to worry about in a historical romance, but all the little everyday details. Think of your novel as a savory beef stew: the meat is the romance between the hero and heroine; the vegetables are all the subplots; the gravy is the historical time period. However, it is judicious addition of seasonings that gives the whole thing a wonderful flavor.

Historical details are those seasonings, but take care how much you use. If you coat your novel with too many historical facts, your readers will think they have been hit on the head with a documentary. Use too few, and your book will end up sounding like a contemporary in a time warp.

Sprinkled in the right proportions, colorful details can make the difference between a mediocre book and one that transports your reader to another time and place. As a writer of historical fiction, you must avoid the urge to slather your painstaking research on top of your plot. Instead, let the period bubble up through your story.

155

An example of slathered historical detail (set circa 1500-1800 AD):

The bed was made of ropes, tied tightly to the solid oak frame with a net-like pattern. On top of this lay a mattress made of canvas stuffed with fresh straw.

An example of bubbling historical detail (1500-1800):

When Rafe collapsed onto the bed, the tightly knotted ropes groaned in protest under his weight. He rolled over and held out his hand to Marie. Fresh straw in the mattress crinkled with his every deliberate movement.

Details, please. If your heroine enters a room, is it a drawing room, a parlor, a solar, a sleeping loft, pantry, distilling room, silver vault, or an Iroquois longhouse? She sits down on something specific. Is it a three-legged stool, plank bench, button-tufted ottoman, hob, daybed, stone garden bench, upturned nail keg, or an overstuffed wingback chair? Does she eat with a small, jewel-handled dagger, a two-pronged fork, chopsticks, a spoon made from a clamshell, a cutlery set of sterling silver, or her fingers? Does she drink from fine Venetian glassware, a clay cup, a wooden bowl, a teacup made of eggshell thin porcelain, a pewter mug, a polished cow horn, or a golden goblet?

If you've ever told a story to a child, you know that the first words out of the young listener's mouth are: "What did they eat?" Food truly is a very important detail in any story; tell me what you eat and I will tell you who you are.

As much fun as it is to describe feasts and formal dinner parties, remember people ate several times a day and the menu didn't usually include roast boar or petit fours. You will find that learning what the average person ate on an average day, and then inserting a simple meal or two into your story will add a subtle but essential flavor to your plot. In the case of most historical settings, the diet was fairly monotonous—with the possible exception of the upper class Victorians and Edwardians, who feasted at every meal.

Don't forget about preparation. How long do you think it takes to boil water over an open fire? Longer than you'd expect. Is your story set in the Civil War? Then your water would be in a coffee boiler. If your character were cooking over a fireplace in 17th Century Scotland, then the water would boil in a small hanging cauldron. And no, coffee wasn't yet available in Scotland.

Nothing jars the palate more than finding a foreign taste where it shouldn't be—like salt in your chocolate bar. So be sure to get the foods right.

People ate fruits and vegetables only in season, unless they were preserved or dried. Beef was a rare item on anyone's daily table during the Middle Ages. Fish, poultry, and wild game were much more in evidence. Vegetables were prepared less frequently than they are nowadays and everything was smothered in sweet sauces.

Ever read a story in which the heroine has a loaf of freshly baked bread ready and waiting for the hero when he rides over the castle moat and into her heart? Be reasonable. How did she know he was coming, and for how long? It takes an entire morning to get the coals in the fireplace to the right temperature for baking, not to mention mixing the dough, letting it rise, punching it down, letting it rise again and finally baking it to a crisp, golden brown.

An example of slathered historical detail (circa 1880):
From the fire in front of the chuckwagon came the inviting smells of freshly brewed coffee and hot buttermilk biscuits. Strips of sugar-cured bacon sizzled in the hot pan. Pansy kept a bowl of steaming flapjacks warm under a snow-white cloth just waiting for Hank. A bowl of fresh-picked strawberries, glistening with crystals of brown sugar and a cool pitcher of cream rounded off their prairie breakfast.

Poor Pansy would have had to get up at 3:00 am to have prepared this feast by 6:30. That is, if she had all the right ingredients in her wagon and everything had managed to stay fresh since the day they left Kansas City.

Example of bubbling historical detail (circa 1880):
When Hank looked down at the bubbling pot over the fire, a shadow passed across his handsome, sunburned face. "Beans again?" Pansy nodded, too intent on coaxing the last drops of molasses out of the bottom of the crock to voice a reply. He pulled his handkerchief out of his hip pocket, then wrapped it around his hand several times before he attempted to

grasp the coffee boiler and pour himself a cup of the strong brew. "Any milk?" he asked with a smidgen of hope. Pansy wiped the perspiration from her brow with her apron. "Went sour."

The menu, method, and realities of preservation are all incorporated in this passage. In addition, the reader learns a little something about the relationship between Hank and Pansy and the historical details become part of the story—instead of it being merely a descriptive paragraph.

Naturally, you will want to dress your characters in the proper period clothing. Have an accurate idea of exactly what they would wear, given the time of day and the situation. For instance, in the Renaissance (1485-1640), men wore two types of jackets: doublets and jerkins. Be mindful that there is a difference. Until the early 1920s, women's clothing was long-skirted, deliberately restrictive, and mostly uncomfortable to wear. Your heroine cannot outrun any man while clutching nearly nine yards of overskirts, underskirts, and three petticoats. Also, her corsets will keep her from taking deep breaths. In matters of the bedroom, women did not wear underpants of any sort until the 1800s. Men rarely had proper linen until the mid-1600s, and then most classes still did without for another hundred years.

Readers will not only want to know what your characters are wearing, but also what materials were used. Allow the clothing description to emerge during the action, rather than inserting a paragraph that lists every stitch. It helps to describe the clothes through the other characters' point of view.

Example of slathered historic detail (circa 1580):
Elizabeth's dress was a confection of billowing blue velvet. Her underskirt of cream satin peeped through the opening of outer skirts. Her five petticoats rustled with that new Dutch invention, blue starch. The padded bumroll around her waist lifted the heavy material into an attractive bell-shaped form. Under the cover of her petticoats, she was encased in a cage made of wire, wood and whalebone.

Example of bubbling historic detail (circa 1580):
In her haste, Elizabeth lost her footing on the slippery bank, falling headlong into the cold river. Her heavy velvet overskirt quickly weighed

her down. The fashionable bumroll around her waist greedily soaked up the water, pulling her beneath the surface. As she struggled to unclasp the hook of her woolen cloak, her pursuer grasped her around her waist, pulling her up against his chest. (From *Fool's Paradise*.)

Perhaps the most powerful herb you can add to your simmering story is the characters' manner of speaking. More than all the description, it is the diction in your dialogue that will make or break the historic flavor of your story. What accents, word usage, or idioms do the hero and heroine use? Remember, like a spicy seasoning, a little goes a long way. If you've created a character from the "Deep South," curb your desire to write the whole speech in dialect. One has only to read B'rer Rabbit to understand how difficult it is for an author to sustain this style, and, more importantly, for the reader to have the patience to decipher it. If your historical is set in the Scottish Highlands, a wee bit o' the burr will do. Avoid writing all of the dialogue using absolutely authentic Scots straight out of the poems of Robert Burns. You don't want your novel to become a wall-banger when your frustrated reader gives up on the "Scots wa hae wi Wallace bled." Instead, flavor your characters' speeches with hints of dialect over period idiom. One rule of thumb: Contractions did not come into common usage until the mid-19th century, and were not accepted until almost a hundred years later. In other words, don't use "don't," "can't," "won't," "ain't," "he'd," "I'll," etc. Nothing will blow your readers' sense of time and place faster than a contraction used in the middle of the 16th century or modern slang appearing in a Regency.

Inappropriate (1580s England): "*Your reputation will be shot, and I'll be hanged as your rapist.*"

Appropriate (1580s England): "*You will be disgraced forever, and I will dance my last jig on a gibbet for debauching you.*" (From *Fool's Paradise*.)

Now that you have the general idea, how do you discover all those delicious details? Read every book about your time period that you can locate. Excellent sources can be found in the children's section of your local library. *A Day in Tudor England* will give you the necessary information in much clearer detail (and with pictures) than an adult book on the same subject that is ten times as long. Peruse pictures, photographs, and maps.

To best capture the sense of period and place as well as the lilt and color of the dialogue, read biographies of people who lived during your chosen time period. Since I write stories set in Tudor times, my best reference book for language is a tattered copy of *The Shakespeare Phrasebook*, by John Bartlett (first published by Little Brown and Co. of Boston in 1881). It begins with the word "abandon," as in, "Abandon the society of this female or, clown, thou perish" (*As You Like It*); and goes to "zodiac," as in, "So long that nineteen zodiacs have gone round" (*Titus Andronicus*).

In my opinion, the very best way to research your details is hands-on experience. Ride double on horseback and discover just exactly where that saddle is going to be felt. Fire a flintlock musket (1750s) or an Enfield rifle (1860s) or a Winchester repeating rifle (1880s). Let all that black powder go up your nose and down your throat. Swing a broadsword, a cutlass, and a rapier. (Great exercise—once you recover from the soreness in your arms.) Wear a dress or gown, complete with all the underclothes, then try to walk, run, sit, lift your arms over your head, bend over, or complete other motions we modern folk take for granted. Don a suit of armor, then try to move. Cook in a fireplace or over an open fire. (Barbecuing with store-bought charcoal is cheating.) Find recipes from your time period and prepare a meal. Milk a cow, or a goat. Play the games of the period: cup and ball, chuck-a-luck (dice), poker and piquant (card games), roll a hoop, chess, mumbly-peg, or cricket. (I once managed a co-ed teenagers' cricket team and cherish the very memorable experience.) The truly adventurous can't wait for a cold, damp day in November so she can turn off the central heat, fill up a wash tub with fire-heated water, and take a bath in front of a fire just like all our heroines constantly do in our favorite novels.

How, you may ask, can we do these things? Where? War reenactments of the Civil War, the American Revolution, French and Indian wars. Your library will have a list of organizations that create just about every time period imaginable—including futuristic. If you are lucky enough to be able to attend a Renaissance fair, a Medieval feast, or have a chapter of the Society for Creative Anachronism nearby, go and pester the experts until they let you try. Seek out Scottish clans by utilizing your library. Museums can also be very helpful, especially if you tell them you are researching a book. Living-history villages and farms, as well as reenactments at national parks are very helpful. If you have a Native American hero or heroine, make an appointment with a village elder at a reservation. (Don't forget cultural sensitivity; show respect. Remember that these people don't exist merely as fodder for your novel.) Listen to people's stories, taste their foods, learn their songs and dances. Write your story with accuracy and specificity, but avoid stereotypes.

What are you waiting for? An engraved invitation, a fanfare of trumpets, a messenger on horseback, a garbled telegram, a military order, a note hidden in a tree hole or perhaps a smoke signal? Four thousand years await your explorations. The most important thing is to have fun—and it will shine through your prose. Good luck, and remember: when it comes to putting the history into your historical, sweat the small stuff.

Q and A

My Research Methods and Favorite Sources

Victoria Alexander

I did massive amounts of research for *The Perfect Wife*, partly set in Egypt in 1818, and enough on *The Princess and the Pea* to be able to build my own horse-less carriage. I recommend any dictionary with word origins, also *The Synonym Finder*, *The Regency Companion*, and *Character Naming Sourcebook* (Writer's Digest).

Amanda Ashley

Over the years I've done a great deal of research in the Old West, but my favorite sources include: *The Writer's Guide to Everyday Life in the 1800's* by Marc McCutheon, *The Sioux* by Royal B. Hasserick, *What Jane Austen Ate & Charles Dickens Knew* by Daniel Pool.

Jude Deveraux

I don't have a list of books, but recommend you use/buy "specific," rather than "general" books. For example, if you can afford only one costume book, get something on the history of shoes. You could then have your heroine mad about shoes and you could accurately describe shoes from her time period. This would be more interesting than quoting a general costume book.

Dorothy Garlock

I research very little, because I write in a time period that I am very familiar with. My favorite research tools are the telephone to call libraries and chambers of commerce, and the Internet.

Nancy Gideon

I love the Internet for research! It's so accessible. I also have at my fingertips: *Grammar for Grownups* by Val Dumond (Harper Collins), *Webster's Ninth Dictionary, The Order of Things* by Barbara Ann Kipfer (Random House) and *Character Naming Sourcebook* by Sherrilyn Kenyon (Writers Digest).

Dee Hendrickson

Write about something you know well . . . or do darn good research. If writing a historical, don't latch onto two or three "old" sounding words and use them to death. *The Oxford English Dictionary* will tell you whether the word you wonder about was used in the Regency—or whatever period you use. I also like *Life in the English Country House* by Mark Girouard (Yale University Press, 1978), *Private Palaces—Life in the Great London Houses* by Christopher Simon Sykes (Viking/Penguin, 1985), *Regency Design* by John Morley (Abrams, 1993), *English Women's Clothing in the 19th Century* by C. Willett Cunnington (reprint from Dover), other Cunnington costume books, and *Jane Austen's Town & Country Style* by Susan Watkins (Rizzoli, 1990).

Jill Marie Landis

I would suggest an historical romance writer worry more about researching place and setting, time periods and characters, than gowns, underwear and place settings.

I have a long list of research books, but my list changes with each book I write and setting I choose. I rely on diaries and accounts of the time period in which I'm working.

Johanna Lindsey

A lot of research you do is for you, not for your reader. You can have pages of notes, but that doesn't mean those notes are going to show up in your story. Aside from the *facts* you get out of research, you also get a *feel* for the subject, which you in turn can give to your characters.

Take a war for example, one that is in progress during the time of your story, but one that really isn't part of your plot. Your characters, being knowledgeable people, would know all about this war, so you must know about it, but your readers don't have to hear much about it, since it isn't pertinent to your story. They just need to know it's *there* and it *could* interfere with the characters, whether it does or not.

Research, aside from the facts you do actually put into your story, is more to give *you* a feel for the time period you're writing about, and the "every day" things that go along with that time period.

My research library, stocked over many years, is too large to list "favorites," so I will mention subjects.

You need a few good history books, of course, but also books on individual subjects and countries, transportation, weapons, architecture, historical costumes and antiques, etc. Get a few good "name your baby" books, but ones that mention historical names and country origin. And then there are books that cover specific races and people during certain time periods, i.e., Vikings, Anglo-Saxons, Indians, the Time Life books and "Life in Medieval Times" kinds of books, etc.

If you want to start your own collection, Barnes and Noble stocks great research books that can be obtained through mail order or over the Internet. However, your local library should also stock most of what you will need for most any subject.

Teresa Medeiros

I do as much research as it takes and always have my research books by my side. I'm always reaching for them to look up some obscure detail like, "Would this collar have buttons or hooks?" or "Where would they go to the bathroom?"

A historical romance should never read like a reference book. The details should be blended into the context of the story whenever possible and should never intrude on the story itself. That's just good writing.

I learned from Roberta Gellis that children's books are a wonderful source of concise information. Eyewitness Book's *Castle* by Christopher Gravett, *See Inside a Castle* by R. J. Unstead, and Stephen Biesty's *Cross Sections Castle* are wonderful sources.

Sharon Sala

First, the *Holy Bible*, because my storytelling is a gift from God and I draw strength from His words. Anything written by Zane Grey, because as a child, his books spoke to my heart and imagination. Erma Bombeck, because she used humor to deal with the tragedies and traumas of life.

I call the Chamber of Commerce in the city in which I've set my story and ask for any or all pertinent information regarding that hometown, including a city map. They are always willing to send lots of information that I may or may not use.

I like to know the geography of a place as well, so if I am unable to travel there myself, I interview people who live there or who have traveled through the area.

Bertrice Small

I do enough research so the flavor of the period comes through clearly to the readers. This means knowing political and religious history, kinds of food eaten and grown, kinds of crops and flowers grown, marriage customs, medicine, trade, etc. It's not as daunting as it seems. Children's history books are valuable sources because they give facts without being boring.

Ann Major

I do a lot of research . . . and headwork. Sandra Brown says she can just look at a TV show, watch the cops there and start a new novel. I must read all sorts of stuff about cops and interview cops and really *become* a cop before I can even start.

Martha Hix

I recently wrote a long novella, set in medieval Wales. My notes and research papers filled a thick three-ring binder, plus a quarter drawer in a file cabinet. I used only part of that research, but I still had to understand it all.

Some of my favorite/recommended research resources include: *The Peoples' Chronology* by James Trager and my old set of Encyclopedia Britannica, which I bought for $20 at a book sale. (Older encyclopedias aren't crammed with modern history or technology.)

Sara Orwig

My research subjects are widely diversified since I have written Regency, historicals and contemporary books. Historical atlases are valuable. I have used: *Timetables of History* (Touchstone), *Commanders of the Civil War* (Gallery Books), *The Writers Complete Crime Reference* (Writer's Digest), and The Old West series, Time/Life.

Deb Stover

I like Strunk and White's *Elements of Style*, *Self-Editing for Fiction Writers* by Browne (Published by Harper), Christopher Vogler's *The Writers Journey*, and by Debra Dixon, *Goal, Motivation and Conflict*.

Lorraine Heath

I am constantly researching: characters, settings, ideas and plots. When I go to the grocery store, I find myself studying the man and his young son who are waiting in line in front of me: Why are they there? What do they look like? How do they react with one another? I read a lot of books on Texas because I love the history of the state and enjoy weaving that history through my stories. Some of my favorite research books are: *Stagecoach Inns of Texas* by Kathryn Turner Carter, *Cowboys, Indians, and Gunfighters* by Albert Marrin, and *"I Do!" Courtship, Love, and Marriage on the American Frontier* by Cathy Luchetti.

Mary Balogh

The only research books I use with any regularity are: *The London Encyclopedia*, ed. Ben Weinreb and Christopher Hibbert

(Papermac Press, 1987), *The English Country House: A Grand Tour*, Gervase Jackson-Stops and James Pipkin (Weidenfeld and Nicolson, 1985), and *The Country House: A Grand Tour*, Gervase Jackson-Stops and Christopher Hibbert (Pavilion Books, 1987).

Lynn Emery

I like *The Cambridge Fact Finder* edited by David Crystal, *African Names* by Julia Stewart, *Building Believable Characters* by Marc McCutcheon, *Creoles of Color in the Bayou Country*, and *The Forgotten People*. I also use a variety of books like *The Illustrated Book of Symbols* and a book of African proverbs to give spice to my stories/plots.

Tori Phillips

My books take place in Tudor England (1485 - 1603). I have been a docent at the Folger Shakespeare Library in Washington, DC for the past 18 years. In my case, my research has taken 18 years. However, when I worked on an eighteenth-century pirate story set in the Caribbean, I spent a solid three months in the library and hours aboard several replica sailing ships of the period. Loved every minute of it, though my pirate book has yet to see the light of publication. For research I use *The Writer's Guide to Everyday Life in Renaissance England From 1485 – 1629* by Kathy Lynn Emerson (Writer's Digest Books, 1996), *The Wives of Henry VIII* by Antonia Fraser (Alfred A. Knopf, 1992), *Shakespeare's Insults* by Wayne F. Hill and Cynthia J. Ottchen (Crown Trade Paperbacks, 1995), and *Fabulous Feasts: Medieval Cookery and Ceremony*, by Madeleine Pelner Cosman (George Braziller & Co., 1976).

Suzanne Brockmann

My absolute favorite research resource is a book called *What's What: A Visual Glossary of the Physical World*, by David Fisher and Reginald Bragonier, Jr. published by Hammond, Inc. I use this book nearly as often as I use my dictionary. It contains labeled pictures of just about anything you might possibly need. Want to know the name of the "thingy" on top of the post at the end of a stair banister? (Newel cap) How about the parts of a door lock? (cylinder, case, bolt housing . . .) It's in there.

An Eclectic Selection of Turn of Century Sourcebooks

from the Library of Pamela Morsi

Andrist, Ralph K., ed. *The American Heritage History of the Confident Years, 1865 - 1916.* New York: American Heritage/Bonanza Books, 1987. ISBN: 0-517-63168-7.

Arnold, Eleanor, ed. *Voices of American Homemakers.* Indianapolis: Indiana University Press, 1985. ISBN: 0-253-20799-1.

Atherton, Lewis Eldon. *Main Street on the Middle Border.* Bloomington, Indiana University Press, 1984. ISBN: 0-253-20329-5.

Barlow, Ronald S. *The Vanishing American Barber Shop: An Illustrated History of Tonsorial Art, 1860-1960.* El Cajon, California, Windmill Publishing Company, 1993. ISBN: 0-933846-04-5.

Buenker, John D., ed. *Historical Dictionary of the Progressive Era, 1890 - 1920.* Westport, Connecticut: Greenwood Press, Inc., 1988. ISBN: 0-313-24309-3.

Carlile, Glenda. *Buckskin, Calico, and Lace: Oklahoma's Territorial Women.* Oklahoma: Southern Hills Publishing Company, 1990. ISBN: 0-9628214-0-3.

Clark, Thomas D. *The Southern Country Store: Pills, Petticoats and Plows.* Oklahoma: University of Oklahoma Press, 1944. ISBN 0-8061-1093-7 .

Coleman, Alexander, ed. *All there is To Know: From Abracadabra to Emile Zola . . . Here is the Highest Monument to Victorian Culture—Readings from the Illustrious 11th Edition of the Encyclopaedia Britannica.* New York: Simon & Schuster, 1994. ISBN: 0-671-50005-8.

Cooper, Patricia A. *Once A Cigar Maker: Men, Women, and Work Culture in American Cigar Factories, 1900-1919.* Chicago, Illinois: University of Illinois Press, 1987. ISBN: 0-252-01333-6.

Cunnington, C. Willett. *The History of Underclothes*. New York: Dover Publications, Inc., 1992. ISBN: 0-486-27124-2.

Daniels, Roger. *Coming To America: A History of Immigration and Ethnicity in American Life*. New York, NY Harper Collins Publishers 1990. ISBN: 0-06-092100-5.

Erickson, Charlotte. *Invisible Immigrants: The Adaptation of English and Scottish Immigrants in 19th-Century America*. New York: Cornell University Press, 1972. ISBN: 0-8014-9697-7.

Ferris, William R. *"You Live and Learn. Then You Die and Forget it all." Ray Lum's Tales of Horses, Mules, and Men*. New York, NY: Bantam Doubleday Dell Publishing Group Inc., 1992. ISBN: 0-385-41926-0.

Fischer, Claude S. *America Calling: A Social History of the Telephone to 1940*. Berkeley, California: University of California Press, 1992. ISBN: 0-520-07933-7.

George, Susanne K. *The Adventures of the Woman Homesteader: The Life and Letters of Elinore Pruitt Stewart*. Nebraska: University of Nebraska Press, 1992. ISBN: 0-8032-2141-X.

Gernsheim, Alison. *Victorian and Edwardian Fashion: A Photographic Survey*. New York: Dover Publications, Inc., 1981. ISBN: 0-486-24205-6.

Green, Harvey. *The Uncertainty of Everyday Life: 1915 - 1945*. New York: Harper Perennial, 1992. ISBN: 0-06-092414-4.

Hahn, Steven, ed. *The Countryside in the Age of Capitalist Transformation: Essays in the Social History of Rural America*. Chapel Hill, North Carolina: The University of North Carolina Press, 1985. ISBN: 0-8078-4139-0.

Himmerfarb, Gertrude. *Marriage and Morals among the Victorians*. New York: Alfred A Knopf Publisher, 1986. ISBN: 0-394-54303-3.

Hoy, Suellen. *Chasing Dirt: The American Pursuit of Cleanliness*. New York, NY: Oxford University Press, 1995. ISBN: 0-19-509420-4.

Hudson, John C. *Making the Corn Belt: A Geographical History of Middle-Western Agriculture*. Indiana: Indiana University Press, 1994. ISBN: 0-253-32832-2.

Hurt, R. Douglas. *American Farm Tools from Hand-Power to Steam-Power.* Manhattan, Kansas: Sunflower University Press, 1982. ISBN: 0-89745-026-4.

Jackel, Susan, ed. *A Flannel Shirt and Liberty: British Emigrant Gentlewomen in the Canadian West, 1880 - 1914.* Vancouver: University of British Columbia Press, 1982. ISBN: 0-7748-0180-8.

Jones, Joseph C. Jr., *America's Icemen: An Illustrative History of the United States Natural Ice Industry 1665 - 1925.* Olathe, Kansas: Jobeco Books, 1984. ISBN: 0-9607572-3-6.

Jordon, Terry G. *German Seed in Texas Soil: Immigrant Farmers in Nineteenth-Century Texas.* Austin, Texas: University of Texas Press, 1966. ISBN: 0-292-72707-0.

Kasson, John F. *Rudeness and Civility, Manners in Nineteenth-Century Urban America.* New York, NY: Hill and Wang, 1990. ISBN: 90-81229.

Lay, M. G. *Ways of the World: A History of the World's Roads and of the Vehicles That Used Them.* New Brunswick, New Jersey: Rutgers University Press, 1992. ISBN: 0-8135-1758-3.

Logsdon, Guy, ed. *"The Whorehouse Bells Were Ringing" and Other Songs Cowboys Sing.* Illinois: The University Of Illinois Press, 1989. ISBN: 0-252-06488-7.

Luchetti, Cathy. *Women of the West.* New York: Orion Books, 1982. ISBN: 0-517-59162-6.

Mason, Harry Morgan. *Life on the Dry Line: Working the Land, 1902-1944.* Golden Colorado: Fulcrum Publishing, 1992. ISBN: 1-55591-122-6.

McDannell, Colleen. *The Christian Home In Victorian America, 1840-1900.* Indiana: Indiana University Press, 1986. ISBN: 0-253-20882-3.

Mills, Betty J. *Calico Chronicle.* Lubbock, Texas: Texas Tech Press, 1985. ISBN: 0-89672-128-0.

Morlan, Michael. *American Automobile Collections and Museums: A Guide to U.S. Exhibits.* Shawnee, Kansas: Bon A Tirer Publishing, 1992. ISBN: 1-878446-10-X.

Moynihan, Ruth B., ed. *So Much To Be Done: Women Settlers on the Mining and Ranching Frontier.* Lincoln, Nebraska: University of Nebraska Press, 1990. ISBN: 0-8032-8165-X.

Nugent, Walter. *Crossings: The Great Transatlantic Migrations, 1870 - 1914.* Indiana: Indiana University Press, 1992. ISBN: 0-253-20953-6.

Peis, Kathy Lee. *Cheap Amusements.* Philadelphia: Temple University Press, 1986. ISBN: 0-87722-389-0.

Rae, Noel, ed. *Witnessing America: The Library of Congress Book of Firsthand Accounts of Life in America, 1600 - 1900.* New York: A Stonesong Press Book, Penguin Books, 1996. ISBN 0-670-86400-5.

Root, Waverly. *Eating In America: A History.* Hopewell, New Jersey: The Ecco Press, 1995. ISBN: 0-88001-399-0.

Ross, Pat. *Remembering Main Street: An American Album.* New York: Penguin Books USA Inc., 1994. ISBN 0-670-84784-4.

Schlereth, Thomas J. *Victorian America: Transformations in Everyday Life, 1876 - 1915.* New York, NY: HarperCollins Publishers, 1991. ISBN: 0-06-016218-X.

Stowe, Estha Briscoe. *Oil Field Child.* Ft. Worth, Texas: Texas Christian University Press, 1989. ISBN: 0-87565-033-3.

Stratton, Joanna L. *Pioneer Women: Voices from the Kansas Frontier.* New York, NY: Simon and Schuster, 1981. ISBN: 0-671-44748-3.

Sullivan, Mark. *Our Times: America at the Birth of the Twentieth Century.* New York: Scribner, 1996. ISBN 0-684-81573-7.

Teaford, Jon C. *Cities of the Heartland: The Rise and Fall of the Industrial Midwest.* Indiana: Indiana University Press, 1993. ISBN: 0-253-20914-5.

The 1902 Edition of Sears, Roebuck Catalogue. New York: Gramercy Books, 1993. ISBN: 0-517-00922-6.

Visser, Margaret. *The Rituals of Dinner: The Origins, Evolution, Eccentricities, and Meaning of Table Manners.* Canada: Harper Collins Publishers Ltd. 1991. ISBN: 0-8021-1116-5.

Weinberg, Cary, ed. *The Social Fabric: American Life from the Civil War to the Present*. Boston: Little, Brown and Company, 1981. ISBN: 0-316-130745.

Wiebe, Robert H. *The Search For Order, 1877-1920*. New York, NY: Hill and Wang, 1967. ISBN: 8090-8510-0.

Williamson, Ellen. *When We Went First Class: A Recollection of Good Times*. Iowa: Iowa State University Press, 1977. ISBN: 0-8138-1083-3.

Wolf, John Quincy. *Life in the Leatherwoods: An Ozark Boyhood Remembered*. Arkansas: August House Publishers, 1988. ISBN: 0-87483-055-9.

Rosemarie,
San Francisco Writers Colony

Dear Kathryn,
Thank you for forwarding my note to so many authors—the response was overwhelming. And, goodness, that research information has wiped any fantasy out of my mind that writers just sit down and, in a few weeks, out pops the great historical novel!

The articles and answers were so terrific and specific that I'm left with only one last research question: With all that time spent researching, how on earth do any of these authors find time to write?!!

I was so pleased to see the different kinds of books each author uses as research resources—especially that huge list from Pamela Morsi. I can tell exactly what kinds of books she must write (Texas, western, early settlers) from the library she has assembled.

If I am going to write about Scotland, I had better get busy on that research library of my own, as you suggested. I have started one already, actually, for I ordered Prince Michael's book through RomanticTimes.com. It has pride of place on the new Scotland-themed bookshelf I bought for my bedroom.

We are all getting so anxious to start. We are doing some writing exercises and reading, reading, reading. Jade is still jumping from sub-genre to sub-genre. She is a sweet will o' the wisp, ready to go anywhere and do anything to advance "her craft." Sierra, on the other hand, is the one of us who is really not the best for big changes (our apartment is only the second place she has ever lived in her whole life, and she is still working at the first computer programmer job she took after college.) She's starting to have a few doubts creep in as to whether or not she has the right stuff to pursue this.

She is the best of us at wonderful descriptions, but she didn't realize that there is so much time commitment involved in even getting *ready* to write. It might help her to feel there is a writing-light at the end of this tunnel.

Is there anything you might send us to get her back on track?

Rosemarie

P.S. Could we also request a list of do's and don'ts from some authors? We love those short tips.

CHAPTER VI

A WRITER'S LIFE—

INSPIRATION AND CONSOLATION

Kathryn Falk, Lady of Barrow
Romantic Times Magazine
Brooklyn, New York

Dear Rosemarie,

I haven't forgotten young writers' discouragement and impatience. Your first fledgling test flight is in the wings . . . I'm referring to the three of you finally sitting down and mapping out your first outlines. But, before you do there is a fair bit more to learn.

This is not meant to dash your spirits. You are in "preparation mode" with "practice sessions" about to begin. Remember those years of piano lessons and all the practice sessions before the final recital? You didn't become a pianist after only a few lessons, so don't expect to become a published novelist on your first try, either. There are exceptions to every rule, of course, but *don't count on this being one of them!*

Some writers are good; some are lucky. Sometimes they're both. Learn the difference as you go along. Some authors have only one book in them, like Margaret Mitchell who wrote *Gone with the Wind.* Others have one terrific book and several less mesmerizing ones after that, like the authors of *The Thorn Birds* and *The Bridges of Madison County.* Then you have authors like Barbara Cartland, Anne Hampson, Jayne Krentz, Janet Dailey, Heather Graham, and Nora Roberts, who each have more than 100 published works.

When you look at historical authors like Johanna Lindsey, Bertrice Small, Janelle Taylor, Connie Mason, Madeleine Baker, and others of their stature, you see a minimum of 30 bodies of work each, that in cumulative length compare to the output of some of the aforementioned, prolific, contemporary, category romance authors. Every author varies in writing time.

Ciji Ware and Diana Gabaldon work five years on each book. Others, such as Judith McNaught and Constance O'Day-Flannery need a minimum of three years. On the other hand, it is said Catherine Coulter can *dream* a book and it zaps onto her computer.

The next batch of selections is a "mother lode," and there is method to my madness. They are encouragement; they are success stories; they are well-worn writers' paving stones that, when laid all together, and studied carefully, may be a pathway to publication for each of you.

I've included the words of a warm and wonderful Texas teacher of writing, B. K. Reeves, who has inspired hundreds of "might be" writers to sit down in their chairs and actually WRITE their way to publication!

You'll be thrilled to know that after making you run a mile or two mentally, I will let you cool down with some inspirational messages and words of wisdom from Jennifer Blake, Linda Lael Miller, Jude Deveraux, and Heather Graham. Each is a legend, each is a uniquely different personality, and each is prolific. As you read through what they have sent you, listen carefully for the individual sounds of their "voices."

I forwarded your request for specific do's and don'ts to a group of excellent writers. Heed their answers well, for this is experience gleaned from years and years of struggle in the publishing biz.

In addition, I asked them to tell you what books influenced or inspired them to write. As you'll see from their varied answers, the foundation on which one builds a writing career can have some vastly different roots.

May your gray matter be stirred like never before.

Your romantic taskmaster!

Kathryn

All clean and comfortable, I sit down to write."
John Keats
* * *

"A Writer's Brain"
An Interview with Barbara 'B.K.' Reeves
Author/Teacher

Q. BK, when you teach writing, you often refer to something called a "Writer's Brain." What is it; how important is it; and how do you know if you have one?
You get the first clue when you are very young. You find yourself fascinated with the stories you read and the characters that you encounter through fiction. And you *always*, from childhood, have a desire to tell stories of your own. You will consider yourself to be "a storyteller." That is the first clue to knowing that you have a "writer's brain."

Unfortunately, many people lose the first inspiration and freedom they have as children. They grow up, go to work, possibly marry, have children of their own . . . and, at some point, turn away from the magic. Ahhh, but if you have a writer's brain you won't, for it will always be nagging away at you. Sometimes you will placate the writer's brain for long periods of time, by focusing on reading, but you will *never* get over the urge to write stories of your own.

Q. Can you write if you don't have a Writer's Brain?
You can, but you will never write from the soul.

Q. Do <u>you</u> have this Writer's Brain?

By the time I was eight years old, I was a dedicated writer. I wrote little stories, and I would take them into the newspaper in the small town near the ranch where I grew up. Those dear people at the paper would publish whatever I brought in. Now, I knew right then that BK *was a writer* . . . because I was being published. I've never stopped believing it since then!

Q. Does that imply that everyone who seriously <u>wants</u> to be a writer has a writer's brain?

If you are just a "wannabee," a person who only fleetingly wants very much to be a writer, then probably not. But, if this is a need that persists year in and year out; if you have a nagging, never forgotten inner voice that tells you that you could be a good storyteller, then definitely, yes . . . you have a writer's brain.

Q. Does reading help?

Goodness, yes! The one categorical statement I will say is, if you are not a reader, you will never be a writer. I was an avid reader. I taught myself to read at age three. About 1940, once a week, I would get on my pony and go after the mail, half a mile from the house, at the top of the lane. I would reach into the mailbox and draw out *The Saturday Evening Post*. With that in hand, I would turn my pony and not stop until I came to the first terrace with a view of the mountains, twenty miles away. I would drop to the ground and read the best short story in the magazine. Then, I'd put *The Post* down, drop my head into my hands and cry because I couldn't write like that.

Of course I couldn't, because at age ten, I was comparing what I was writing with Pulitzer Prize winners like Edna Ferber and John Steinbeck! (In those days, all leading writers wrote for *Colliers* and *The Saturday Evening Post*.) I couldn't write like them—but all the while, they fed my writer's brain. I would read their stories carefully and try to make mine sound just as professional, which meant that I had to be good in grammar, etc. I learned the basic craft of sentence structure, word usage, etc., right then and there. Soon, I knew all about where all those commas and semi-colons go.

Q. So if we've read a lot, and learned where all those commas go, what next? What's the first step to writing our own fiction?

What works for one person might not work for another, but I'll tell you what works for me and has since I was eight years old. I get the glimmer of an idea of a certain character, at a certain place, with a certain problem. I take out my ever-present legal pad or little fat, spiral notebook and start jotting down notes. Once I get the character fixed in my brain, right away I want to know the time and place and the year they were born and what age they are when the story will take place. Call it, say . . . a "life-bio."

All humans are defined by their place in time. How were they educated in 1487? Are they in the midst of the Civil War? What overall problems of humanity are present? How your characters respond to everything will be shaped by these external, time-related circumstances.

When you put a character in time and place, it is called putting your character "into context."

Q. What about a character who time travels?

That isn't easy. The writer has to take people shaped during different time periods and have them confront a different set of mores and cultural realities.

Q. All right, so we've chosen our character and time period—what next?

Characters. Plural. In writing a "real" romance, you will have a double protagonists: the first is the woman, second is the male. I try to stay away from cliché characters. For me that means I don't want my heroine to be too beautiful. I want the hero to love her because of her inner perfections, not her outer shell. This isn't always easy to write because, unfortunately, outer beauty affects the way other people respond to your character and, ultimately, the way your character feels about her/himself.

Orchestrate those characters. Have them be *very* different, so that whatever outer conflict there is, there is also inner conflict:

(Heroine/Hero) wants (Hero/Heroine) because _____ . But _____ and _____ .

Characters—motivation—conflict. Fill that out and get a "situation statement" that contains the story concept. Pretend that the story is finished and write a blurb on the inside cover or flap of the book. For instance, I have a four-book time-travel series in the works called "The Sinclair Women." There is a time gate, a time portal, and as I always make a blurb, the dramatic statement about this series is: "*Only the Sinclair women could travel through time . . . only the Sinclair men could call them.*"

Q. Ohhh, that's delicious!
Thank you darlin'. I think about those little blurbs all the time.

Q. BK, some writers say they don't have to do a story concept because they <u>see</u> the entire story from beginning to end.
"Mind Movies"!

Q. I beg your pardon?
I call them "Mind Movies." You *see* the story happen in your brain, like a movie. In teaching writing I have encountered only two people who <u>didn't</u> see mind movies, so I think that indicates that lots of people "see" their book laid out before them. People with "writer's brains" have an added advantage though; they also hear the dialogue. In that way, characters sound like themselves and speak with their own voices.

Q. What if the voices stop? What about "writer's block?"
First off, I don't believe in writer's block. Every once in a while, you just hit a wall. When you do, say, "This happens, it is not the end of the world, it is not the end of my writing career." Prepare ahead for when it happens; then you can do something about it.

In the early years when that happened to me, I didn't finish what I was writing, because I didn't think I *could*. I didn't write through it. Still don't. However, now I back off and make a detailed synopsis for the last chapters, or just the next few, so that I know how I am going to have a catalyst to turn the story around—how I am going to bring my characters into the climax and have a fast resolution.

Q. Does it work?
It does now. (*Laughing.*) After you have written 500,000 words, you

will know what you're doing. That is about five books.

Q. Your first published book was a Regency, correct?
Yes, and so was my second—both brought out in hard cover. I had a contract for a third Regency with Walker and Company, but shortly before it was to be published the head of the company died and the new owner—son or nephew, I'm not sure which—didn't want to do regency's. Walker sent me a letter saying, "We're turning back the (publishing) rights to you; keep the money." Then, I worked with an editor at Avon who wanted to back out of doing regency's, too. I consider myself a bit of an expert on the Regency period and love that period, so this was quite a blow. I have always said that if you absolutely love a certain genre and read it all the time—knowing your genre is very important—don't try to write anything else. But I learned there and then, it is best to write across genres.

In the years when I was determined to turn myself into a fiction specialist, I read with a catholic overview; I read everything. I read popular fiction, science fiction; I was even a western fan. I would set myself on a four, five, or six-year course where I would glean everything I could from those books. Then, I would write at least one book in that genre.

You can't learn to write in a genre you hate. Don't neglect periph eral writing, either. I write little articles. This has proved especially useful in letting readers know when my book will come out because I can say at the end of the article, "Barbara Reeves' next book will be published . . ."

I work on several projects at a time. My priorities right now are a historical set in the Regency period, a contemporary, a medieval novel that takes place before the battle of Hastings (which has taken me 20 years to finish), selling my traditional western series, and finishing up a screenplay.

Q. Whoa! That list brings up two questions right away! How did that screenplay sneak in there? And why has your medieval novel taken you 20 years to write?
This past summer I took an advanced course in screenwriting at Rice University, and I will take a couple more if I can. Studying screenplays

has made me a better teacher and writer. Hollywood people often have a handle on the code of a story better than we novelists do.

Q. And the medieval?
Oh, it's a wonderful book, I think!

Q. But, <u>20 years</u> . . .?
I was married for more than thirty years to a wonderful man I adored. He supported me in everything I ever wanted to do. However, there was a part of him that was threatened by my writing. So, I'd fit in time to write when he was at work. If he came home unexpectedly, he would try to *distract* me. While he was nuzzlin' me he'd say, "I know whatever you try to do you will succeed, and they will buy it and then you will get to be rich and leave me." Then he'd chuckle and lead me toward the bedroom with, "Come on in here, author, and let's do a little bit of research!" And I'd put aside what I was doing for that day.

Q. In all those years, did you ever think about just quitting?
Never. I was a *writer*. I just hadn't had that first novel published yet. I never doubted that I would, though—and neither did my husband. Shortly before he died, he expressed great remorse and said, "You have the potential to be one of the great ones; I don't want you to stop (writing)." I was sixty when my first book was published.

Q. In ways we can only guess, it must have been hard for you that it took so long, but it's <u>so</u> encouraging for the rest of us; shows there's hope for each of us yet! So now, you're writing up a storm and . . .?
Spending time with my family. I have some darling grandbabies! I teach (writing) four nights a week and give day-long or two-day seminars on writing. I find it's just not physically possible for me to do *everything* I want to do.

Q. Well, for goodness sake, that seems like more than enough! Most people wouldn't even have considered taking on the teaching when they were trying to get books finished. Do you especially like to teach?
I love it! It is the greatest joy to see people who have been living with

their "writer's brain" all their lives become more self confident. These are young housewives who have demanded the time from their family, and men and women who want to get all their rejection slips out of the way before they retire. It is tremendous to help them get a handle on their characters and their story and incredible to hear, "This has always been a dream, but now it's a *possible* dream."

Q. Do these people actually have potential as writers? Can you tell right away if they do?
Some of them have great potential, and yes I can tell right away. However, in the writing game, there are so many ways that you can be sidetracked; so much of life's garbage gets in the way of peoples' writing abilities. I want to be there when they get an overview and do their synopsis—to mentor as they stick to it and grow in their craft. I love to hear, "I'm sending it off." What joy then, for them to call me and say, "I just got the call. It sold!" Four of my students have sold their novels recently.

Q. Probably more of them could do so if they had more time to write.
That's no excuse at all. If you want to write, then write! People say, "I can write short stories but I could never find the time to write a novel." I tell them short stories are written one word at a time and so are novels. There was a time when my children were young and going to separate schools, and absolutely the only time I had to write each day was the fifteen minutes, sitting in the car after picking up my son, while we waited for my daughter. I finished the book in four months, *fifteen minutes at a time!* Of course, I never want to try THAT again!

Q. How long does it take to write a novel now that you have (slightly) fewer distractions than in the past?
Now I take three months to write a short book and five for a long one. That is good pacing for me. I once wrote a 90,000-word book in three weeks. And, I wrote *Much Maligned Lord* in three weeks. That was tremendous pressure. It was like being on speed. I wrote it start-to-finish and didn't have to restructure any of that book. I swore I would never do that again.

Q. Any last words of advice?

I have a handout for my classes called "Great Expectations." It deals with the fact that the person who expects the most of you and your book is *a reader*. Working within the genre in which you chose to write, that story and those characters must fulfill *all* your readers' "great expectations," including your own. For you are, after all, *your first reader*.

And if it don't work for <u>you</u>, honey . . .

Interview by Ann Peach

> *"There are three rules to writing fiction. Unfortunately, no one knows what they are."*
> —Somerset Maughan

> *"I want you to know that if your desire to be published is strong enough and you're willing to work hard and <u>never</u> give up, you can make it happen."*

God Doesn't Give You the Desire Without the Talent

By Gloria Dale Skinner

It's difficult to sell your book in today's tight markets, but it's not impossible.

First, your manuscript has to be better than all the other books that are landing on the editors' desks. It has to say, "Choose me! Choose Me!" However, that isn't enough. There are thousands of wonderful books that aren't getting published.

Whether or not you'll be published comes down to how badly you *want* to be published. You must have incredible excitement about your own work—and it needs to show in every page you write. If desire to write/publish is not eating away at you day and night with a burning intensity so hot you feel like you're on fire, you have drastically less of a chance to be published than someone who *does* have that feeling.

When I penned my first book more than ten years ago, I didn't know that I didn't know how to write a book. I only knew I *wanted* to write a book, and the day I began writing we didn't even have a typewriter in the house. I wrote that book in three composition notebooks with several different colors of ink, then paid someone to type it for me. It didn't sell. My second and third books were rejected, too. I just kept on writing.

Back then, Kathryn Falk held workshops in New York City on how to write a romance, and I took the train from Connecticut into the city for as many workshops as I could attend.

A published writer friend said, "Set a goal to sell a book in a year, and if you don't reach that goal—give up and go on to do something else."

I thought about that for a long time.

By then, I'd written three complete books and two proposals. They were good books. Special books. The best I could make them. But rejections were piling up. Friends and family members asked constantly, "Have you sold your book yet"? Again and again, I had to tell them, "No."

I began seriously to doubt if I was a good enough writer to be published.

I thought about other things I might like to do instead, since I had been a housewife and mother for fifteen years. I had no desire to be a secretary, a real estate agent, or a sales clerk. I didn't want to go to college and become a teacher, a businesswoman, or a nurse. And, I didn't want to join a women's club and play bridge, tennis or golf.

I wanted to be a *writer* . . . a romance writer.

A few days later, I told this to another published friend and she said, *"Gloria, God doesn't give you the desire without the talent to back it up."*

I had the desire, the talent and the skills I'd learned in the many workshops I had attended at conferences—and I had plenty of time. Why *should* I give up?

I didn't set a goal to give it one year more and quit if I wasn't published. I set a goal to be published <u>no matter how many rejections I received or how many workshops I had to attend</u> . . . *<u>no matter how long it took</u>*!

It took me another two years to sell that first book. I have just published my twelfth. Thank God I didn't give up.

"I don't want to just mess with your head. I want to mess with your life . . . I want you to miss appointments, burn dinner, skip your homework. I want you to tell your wife to take that moonlight stroll on the beach at Waikiki with the resort tennis pro while you read a few more chapters."
—Stephen King

* * *

"It's been a Long Ride"

An Interview with Linda Lael Miller
New York Times Bestseller-List Author

Q. Ms. Miller, have you been writing for a long time?
I have been writing since I was ten. I have been *published* since 1980. At first, I wrote confessions for the confessions magazines; I sold 33 stories. Writers of all genres tackle writing confessions because one can earn a decent living and get writing credits at the same time. (This gives credibility to a writer seeking an agent.)

My first *full* book was a romance, *Fletcher's Woman*, which sold to Pocket Books in 1983. When that happened, I was so excited at being accepted—and so hoping they would let me continue to do it—I probably would have written books for free! I sold six more books, which let me know I was *probably* going to "make it" as a writer; then I was divorced and suddenly . . . I *had* to make it as a writer—or quit.

You have to be prolific to make a living as a writer. So, I wrote "categories." They taught me to write fast, in the same way that working on the daily deadlines of a newspaper makes you work fast—you have to PRODUCE to make a decent living. It is important when writing categories that you not take yourself too seriously. I'm not minimizing the genre, or the skills required to write categories—they are fantastic training grounds for writers and a lot of my readers were acquired in my category years. You have to remember, it's a job, one you have to get to—and get done. When I was writing categories, I was putting out as many as five or six a year! I wrote Silhouettes (at least four, and normally six a year) and one or two *Tapestrys* for Pocket. I have written more than 50 category romances.

Q. Was that very first book easy to sell?
Eight publishers and a couple of agents rejected *Fletcher's Woman*. Most of the editors didn't say anything, just sent it back to me. Then Pocket bought it and it was a best seller! I had known that book was good and so I had persevered. If I had given up on it somewhere along that long line of publishers, I would not be a writer today. The point I am trying to make is that it is really important that _you_ believe in your book even when others don't seem to.

Q. It's wonderful that you've been such a successful romance author. Yet, a lot of people "pooh-pooh" the romance genre, comparing the books most unfavorably to works of "great" literature. Does this bother you?
Not at all, although it does gall me when people hate romances out of hand without ever having read any! A lot of so called "great" literature is so gloomy, which is idiocy. People are not looking for more pain in their lives; sometimes they need that happy ending. I am an entertainer . . . the literary equivalent of a Las Vegas lounge lizard. I am good at it. Besides, I chuckle to think of the naysayers' reaction to the fact that I take home *seven figures a year* writing romance!

Q. You must sell a lot of books! What has been your best seller?
Daniel's Bride. At the moment, I have 23 or 24 pocketbooks still in print.

Q. Do you ever worry that the story-well will dry up?
I don't worry about running out of stories, but I *do* worry about becoming complacent and not growing as a writer. Some books I write are better than others—some are better received—but every book is the best book I could write *at the time*.

Q. How do you ensure that you continue to grow as a writer?
I study all the time. I travel a lot, talk to people and keep my brain

fresh. I read copiously. I couldn't sleep at night if I didn't have a book to soothe me to sleep. I never go anywhere that I don't have a book with me. The idea of being on a plane without a book is horrifying. My Mom did that once and almost had a breakdown! (*Laughter.*) Growing up, I was considered to be a strange bookworm. Even now, if I go into Wal-Mart, I come out with seven or eight books.

Q. All right, we've established that you need to <u>read</u>, but how about writing—would you ever stop?
I write because I can't *not* write. I absolutely <u>have</u> to write; I think if I don't write, the stories will swell up my head and it'll explode!

Q. (Chuckle) But what about new writers who feel this same overwhelming need to write; isn't it nearly impossible for them to break into the romance genre today?
I don't think it is any harder now than it was when I started. At the very beginning of the rise to popularity of the romance genre, there was a totally different publishing climate. At the end of 1983, publishers were doing 800,000 print-runs on historicals they wouldn't even *publish* today. However, soon after I signed on, there was a crash; readers wanted good books and stopped buying things that weren't wonderful. I didn't let that stop me, though, I just kept sending in one submission after another. Starting writers today have to do the same thing. Send that proposal along. Then, work on another project so you don't obsess too much about the first one. Keep something in the mail at all times. And do the very best you can do. Talent is not something unusual; lots of writers have talent, but what sets the unpublished writer apart from someone like me is that they don't have my drive—and the ability to take it on the chin and get back up and keep going.

Q. Like the Energizer Bunny?
Exactly.

Q. What else would you tell a beginning romance writer that might help her/him toward that goal of publication?
Write in your own, authentic voice. Don't follow the market. If time travels are big, that means two years ago, there was a call for them—

not now. Jayne Krentz says that genre romances are simply human myths, and they all have basic psychological meaning. If you change them too much, people will pull back from them. Tomorrow's romance writer needs to understand all the myths and fairytales. Romance is still Cinderella and the Prince . . . with variations. Two people meet, fall in love, and work out their problems. The genre *is* the genre.

There are some writers/editors/publishers who want to push the boundaries of the genre and make it more like mainstream and more realistic. However, the reader reads for escape. What *I* want is to make my readers have an emotional experience, and in every book, that is what I strive to accomplish.

Q. What about some of those "toward-mainstream" changes? Any predictions on trends?
Many romance writers have had success with mysteries, but I'm not convinced that it is long term—although people like Linda Howard, with her great knack for romantic suspense, certainly do advance the popularity of that sub-genre. People will always like a good time travel. I'm not doing any more time travel, only because my ideas are taking me in a different direction. The other sub-genre that has a great future is Ethnic. It is a wonderful idea, whose time is long overdue.

Q. Do you write under your own name?
For the most part, yes. Years ago, Kate Duffy, then Senior Editor at Pocket Books, said, "Never use a pseudonym, because it is as if you are ashamed to be writing romance." If you choose a pseudonym, you do not own that name, the publisher does. So, if you are with a publisher and want to leave, you might find yourself hamstrung . . . writing books you don't want to write. However, having said that, I will add that I have two medievals coming out under a pseudonym. My regular readers like Americana, and that is good, but I have other stories in me, too. So, to reach a new readership, I have settled on the name *Lael St. James*.

Q. Anything else coming up for you in the future?
With my next book, I am beginning a scholarship program which I am funding, but which *Pocket* is administering. The money (three

scholarships of $5,000 each) will have no restrictions; the recipients can use it for college or trade school, computer repair school, day care while they start jobs, or testing facilities to help them get those jobs. We need to empower women if they are to be productive and happy. Women who apply for the scholarships will be required to write a two-page essay on what is their goal and what they want their life to be like. The initial judging as to who gets the scholarships will be done, in-house, at Pocket, but I will make the final decision. I hope to expand the program in the future.

I will give the bulk of my speaking fees to finance next year's scholarships. Possibly there are other authors who might be convinced to do the same?

I have been blessed in this business and I want to give back. This is my way to give thanks *to the universe*. It's really important to me.

Interview by Ann Peach

"Greetings from our writing group in New Orleans. Kathryn wanted you to know how my mother and I reached the point where we are today—finally published! Our journey wasn't easy, but we persisted."

Masters of Our Fate

By Christine Holden

"You write with your mother?"

That's been the resounding echo since she and I began actively working together seven years ago. Whenever I mention that we collaborate, I receive myriad reactions that run the gamut from down right perplexity to outright disbelief.

Working with your mother can be as easy as pie—and as tough as nails. Not only do we have creative differences, but also regular mother-daughter differences, which can put a tremendous strain on a working relationship, and vice-versa. Ours is no longer a relationship easily defined by the restraints of the parent-child label.

Motivation for the collaboration team of Christine Holden began with a chronic illness I have. From the age of 12 right up to college, most of my academics were done at home, during a period in which I was told I would never be able to work and my chances for having children were nil. Out of this emotional trauma, my mother and I became a team, first in battling my illness, and eventually in writing together.

For as long as I can remember, my mother has been a lover of the written word. She'd written on and off from the time I was six, and she passed on her love of words to me. During my darkest hours of despair, when I was alone in my room, books were my only comfort.

In 1991 an antebellum story began to grow in my head. Knowing I wasn't able to complete the story alone, I asked my mother to write it for me from the three-page synopsis I would give to her. She agreed, but since she doesn't type, she exacted my promise that I see the project through. Not only did she want me to type everything, she also insisted I do all necessary research and help her "write" the book.

I researched and read about the publishing industry—the romance genre in particular—and soon learned that what I thought I knew was miniscule in comparison to the slew of information we, as writers, *need* to know.

From the beginning, my mother and I decided I would handle the business side of our writing. She wanted to stay in the background. I have always been painfully shy and the long periods of isolation resulting from my illness compounded that, but she encouraged me every step of the way, so I gritted my teeth and just did it.

Our goal was to have the manuscript completed in three months. However, life got in the way of our grand plan. Between February 1992, two months after we were supposed to have completed the book, and May 1993, 15 months later, we were still writing and getting nowhere. I knew something wasn't right with the manuscript, so I joined a critique group. "Your heroine serves no purpose, except to aggravate the hero," the members of the group told us. "You're 'telling' the story, instead of 'showing' it." They also criticized those "extra scenes that aren't needed." We wondered seriously if we were cut out to be writers.

We sat down, did a great deal of soul searching, reassessed our goals, and decided to see it through. We also wrote down on index cards two lines from William Ernest Henley's *Invictus* and then, adopting those words—*I am the master of my fate. I am the captain of my soul*—charged forward.

We did character studies; we listened to our characters, and fleshed them out, giving them zodiac signs and birth dates, hobbies and histories. Then we threw away everything we had previously written, started from Page One, and reworked our story until it was finished.

Only then did we send that manuscript out again to be critiqued. Our partner in the critique group was a lady who was already published and busy with her own book. Still, she was willing to take a look at our "baby." What a pleasant surprise. She liked it! She is quite an outspoken woman and made no apologies for her critiquing tech-niques—and we didn't ask for any. She was good and made us bet-ter writers. In May 1993, after working and reworking that story, it was finished—all 789 pages of what we believed was a masterpiece! Whether or not that's true, that moment of achievement brought us a great sense of accomplishment.

By doing what writers do, we had become writers ourselves. After nearly two years of hard work, we had reached our goal; we were authors in the truest sense of the word. We were also collaborators . . . and friends.

Our next goal was to see the manuscript published. I perfected our query letter, and received a lot of positive rejections. We trimmed the manuscript to 683 pages. Then, we received 46 rejections from editors and agents, with reasons that included: "No reader base for that kind of book," and "We don't like the fact that you are un-agented." (Which was true at that time.) There were several that said, "The manuscript is too long."

So we put our "masterpiece" aside and came up with the idea for a *new* book called, *A Time for Us*, a time-travel that we decided to make light and humorous. After dealing with the intense characters and dramatic plot line we'd woven into our first book, we needed a breather. Ailith and Joshua, our heroine and hero, were perfect for that.

Although she is stranded 585 years in the future and doesn't know the fate of her parents who are left behind in 1413 Middlesbrough, Ailith is the type of person who knows there is a light at the end of the tunnel. Joshua can be quite conservative, but he has a wonder-ful sense of humor.

Since the time that I had printed "the end" to our first effort, there had been moments of disagreement and confusion, a "gazillion" disappointments and heartbreaks—and moments of incredible joy, which reached a pinnacle when I gave birth to the child I had been told I would never have!

A year later, that joy was nearly matched by the call my mom and I finally got from our agent at Jean and Dee. "Your manuscript has sold!"

A Time for Us was bought by Berkley, and came out in August 1998.

In the face of everything, we had somehow persevered. Through my illness, and five years later, my father's; through numerous rejections for all of our novels; through my marriage; my pregnancy which had me hospitalized twice and bedridden for five months; and finally my divorce, we had hung in there.

We had to. We were writers of novels.

We learned from our tragedies and thrived on our triumphs. In writing, as in our everyday lives, we celebrate our accomplishments and never willingly accept our pitfalls; we listen to each other; know our own strengths and weaknesses, and learn from one another.

Our system remains as it was with that first book we wrote together. After seven years and 11 books, some complete, some not, we still start our stories the way we began our very first one—I write a synopsis.

And so, we remain as we have been, steadfast in our faith . . . the masters of our fates, and the captains of our souls.

"Kathryn has known me for nearly 20 years and she wants me to tell you how I write several books a year for several publishers, in spite of having five kids. Writing fast is my solution. It also helps if you can work real well in chaos!"

On a Writing Life

By Heather Graham

I always wanted to write, though I majored in theater, and I loved it! After Derek was born (3rd out of 5!), I was bartending, doing dinner theater, and singing back-up on tapes for the entertainers who owned the club where I was working. Hours and hours of work and very little pay. I suffered the pains of the damned through every audition. (Little did I realize I would be stepping right back into the same audition thing when I started submitting manuscripts!)

At any rate, at the end, there I was doing a play called *The Perils of Poor Nellie*. I was Poor Nellie. The audience was supposed to throw rolls at the villain at certain parts of the play, but the audience usually had had a fair amount to drink—and somehow, they threw a whole lot more than rolls, and they never hit the villain. I used to come home from work wearing every food known to man. When Derek was born, it seemed time to find something else to do.

"Start writing," my husband Dennis suggested. He brought home a typewriter. It was missing the E. You can't begin to imagine how many E's there are on a page. Filling them in at night was definitely a challenge! However, I wanted to write. Desperately. I had loved books all of my life, loved the written word, and it was time to try. With all my heart, I embraced tenacity.

I had always been an avid fan of such writers as Dorothy Eden, Victoria Holt, Anya Seton and Mary Stewart—not to mention that I adored *Gone with the Wind*. I also loved horror, so I was writing in both genres, sending stories to *Black Cat*, *Twilight Zone*, and others, while also looking at romance. My first sale was actually in horror: fifteen dollars for a short vampire story.

When I started out, there was a huge category boom—all the companies were opening category lines. I read a Dell Ecstasy and liked it very much. My argument with category before that had been that the heroine tended to be very young (17 – 22), the hero very old in comparison (36 – 45). He tended as well to own a vineyard in France, and she didn't have much in the way of a life's ambition. In the late seventies and early eighties, the stories began to reflect modern life in a much more believable way.

I was very young when I started, and I could never see what the heroine saw in the old guy! Ugh! At that time, he was downright decrepit to me! Of course, I've caught up to the old guys, but that was then and this is now.

Anyway, it was the way romances were changing that I found so intriguing. I knew I wanted to write historicals—I felt that I lived the lives of British nobility thanks to some of the writers I so avidly read, and I wanted to give others that same feeling if I could. Also,

Kathleen Woodiwiss came out with her first book, and Bertrice Small wrote *Skye O'Malley* about that time. I was hooked.

Instead, I started off trying to write for the Dell contemporary category line. I was thrilled when I finally sold to them. It took me about two years; I knew neither a thing about publishing, nor a person involved. I just bought the Writer's Digest *Writer's Market* and started sending manuscripts off. Those two years seemed a very long time. For some people, it's an even longer road. I've met others who sold their very first effort. The only guarantee is the process will be different for everyone.

I love to write, and I'm grateful every day of my life that I am able to do something that I love so much and do it for a living. I'm grateful as well that I'm perceived as having "made it." I have goals, of course, but my main goal is just to keep writing and surviving at it until I drop dead. Of course, I want to make dozens of best-seller lists and write great books as well!

My favorite book is really always the book I'm working on because I'm most involved with it at the time. Books are special to me for different reasons. My "Civil War" series will always be near and dear, and close to my heart because I became so involved with so many re-enactors and spent so much time with my family, traveling to Civil War sites. I'm not so sure my *children* were thrilled to death with it all, but we did have great times, with Harper's Ferry, West Virginia remaining a favorite spot in all our hearts. My favorite period of history is the Civil War, and I've been at it again with the Florida series. (*Runaway, Captive, Rebel, Surrender*—and now, *Glory.*)

My Christmas books mean a lot to me, because I love Christmas, and the feelings and emotions I've tried to portray within them.

I was personally fond of my Viking books because my mother brought some of the research material I used for them with her when she emigrated here with her family from Ireland.

I also enjoy being Shannon Drake. *Ondine* is my favorite of that line, except that now I'm into another personal favorite theme— Shannon Drake is doing a series on the Graham clan, from the first use of the name through some of my more famous—and infamous— ancestors. The first of these books is called *Come the Morning*, and it was brought out in hardcover by Kensington in February of 1999.

I adored my Father and lost him right before my twenty-first birthday. These are for him, and for me.

In my contemporary work, *Slow Burn* and *If Looks Could Kill,* both from Mira, are favorites. Coming out in August from Onyx is a book called *Drop Dead Gorgeous,* and I used a lot of my own growing up in it, and it means a great deal to me too.

My main suggestion to other writers is to read, read, read, and read some more. Then be tenacious as hell. A dream is something you can never give up. Being published just makes you a *published* writer. (Great, of course, as I said, I'm very grateful for my living.) However, the *act of writing* makes you a *writer*.

Learn to be objective about your own material, which is hard. Listen to advice, then get rid of it if it doesn't work for you.

There is no "formula," and don't ever write "to formula." But *do* know your market—something you'll do naturally if you read, read, read.

It's a business world out there, so be savvy as to what goes on in a business sense. Join organizations—it's a truism that who you know can often help. Editors come to conventions, and sometimes what you learn from them is worth a fortune.

The market is always changing. When I started out, there was a huge category explosion. Publishers can be very "bandwagon" and they admit this. After all, they are out there to make money. After category flooded and began to wind down, historicals made a big boom. Then Patrick Swayze made a movie as a fabulously sexy and heart-wrenching ghost, and paranormals became big. Kevin Costner brought the western back in a big way with *Dances With Wolves.* Then Mel Gibson wore a kilt. A Graham was one of Wallace's best friends, by the way. How Mel missed that, I don't know, but don't worry, I intend to tell you all about it at a later date! *Remember that Graham series?* And now romance is making a big swing into romantic suspense.

Trends are great, and sometimes good to follow, if that's the book you want to write. I don't think that anyone should ever write what he or she doesn't want to write. A passion and love for what you write comes out on every page, and that, more than anything else, grabs a reader's heart, and his/her interest.

Of course, trends change. However, be aware that if you want to write about an obscure period of Hungarian history, it may be a hard sell.

"Hey," you say, "another author did exactly that!" Keep in mind, that author has a track record, was under contract, and had earned her publisher's trust before writing the book.

You still hear, "Write a great book, and we'll buy it." Well, of course, that's true. Write your great book, but always be aware of what is going on in the field. Target your market; know where to spin your wheels, because it is a slow, painful process with an awful lot of waiting involved. Know who is buying what and where to send what you want to write.

As I write this, I'm heavily into Scotland and the family, and turning more toward writing romantic suspense. Most of my first books had a touch of suspense to them, just like the old gothics, and I've always loved a good mystery or thriller. I have a vampire in the works for some later date, a book of which I'm exceptionally fond.

I like to think that my writing has matured as much as I have and I just want to keep doing it! I know that my writing changes as my life changes.

My children range from 8 – 21, and they remain the most important focus of my life, though I'm sure they're all certain they come from a highly dysfunctional family—we're always nuts as hell around here! But I love them with all my heart and I know that they love their dad and me as well.

People often ask me how I made it with so many children. Naturally, the concentration level can be hard, but they've given me so many new friends, such different experiences, and such a variety of thoughts and emotions that what I *couldn't* have done . . . is made it without them.

And Dennis, of course. We fight through half the process, but he's been there all the way. We disagree . . . we agree. He's known what I'm up against, and he's been at my side since he first brought home that E-less typewriter.

All in all, the best piece of advice I can impart (from many writers, with a bit of paraphrasing here and there) is this:

Attach butt to chair and work.
Read, read, read. Write, write, write.
And <u>never</u> give up your dream.

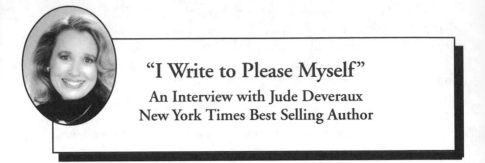

"I Write to Please Myself"

An Interview with Jude Deveraux
New York Times Best Selling Author

Q. You are one of the best-loved writers of Romance today, with millions of copies of your books in print. Will you tell us how this writing life began?

I started writing because I had stories in my head and I thought that if I wrote them down, they would go away. They did, but then more appeared. I still have stories in my head, and I still write them down, although, I used to have more of a compulsion to write than I do now. Before I was published, I had written about four books and had read every big romance that was published. I figured that mine were as good as anyone else's so I decided to go for it for five years. If I didn't make it to the top in that time, then I didn't have what it takes. So, I spent five years and seven months on the road. Hardly a TV camera turned on that I wasn't in front of it. I went to every conference, talked to every wholesaler and bookseller that I could and tried to learn everything I could. At the end of that time, I went home and haven't done any publicity to speak of since.

Q. You must have seen many changes in the years since you began . . .

Many. The best change is that there is less violence in romance novels now.

Q. What do you think about the increase in sex scenes?

I don't read much romance anymore, so I had no idea there was an increase in sex scenes until recently. How can there be more sex scenes in the books than there used to be? What a frightening thought. I wish these authors who get published on a platform of having really "hot" sex scenes would take the time to look carefully at the history of this genre. Over the 20 years that I have been writing romances, I have seen a "zillion" authors and their sex-filled books come and go. Sex does not sell books; stories do. People may read a book with long, erotic sex scenes in it once, maybe twice, but they don't read them over and over. And those books certainly don't stay in print for years and years. What lasts is great story telling, with characters that are more than their genitals. Quiz: Was it the hot sex scenes that have made Shakespeare's plays last, or the knockout stories?

Q. Jude, your book, _Knight in Shining Armor_, is just such a knockout wonderful story. As a matter of fact, it started the current trend toward time travel romances. Did your publisher suddenly ask you to write time travel?

No. I never write to please anyone. My publishing house doesn't tell me how to write and I don't tell them how to publish. _A Knight in Shining Armor_ is by far my best book. Everything in it worked: characters, place, plot . . . all of it.

Before I wrote that book, I read time travel books, but never felt satisfied by what I read. The heroine would go back in time and all she'd talk about was how stupid corsets were, or she'd go on and on about bloodletting.

I wanted to read about _everything_. I wanted to know how the music was different, what were the colors, smells, toilet habits, clothes, houses, etc. I wanted to know what people thought about raising children, about money, about any aspect of the era they saw. I wanted the heroine to see good things as well as bad. I didn't want her to set our age up as good and those people "back then" as bad and ignorant. Since I couldn't find what _I_ wanted to read, I decided to write a time travel that did its best to cover what I wanted to know.

I believe that publishers are wildly eager to publish anything that is a rip- roaring good story. They really don't care what the time period is, or the genre. If a publishing house says it's not doing time travel at this time, it's because they have been burned by really bad time travel novels. But if you write a great story with great characters, you can be sure they'll publish it—and they won't give a damn about the time period.

Q. Suppose a new writer has this great story and is about to have it published? Any advice?

Don't let success go to your head. I have seen more careers ruined by overwhelming ego than anything else. Don't think that you're somebody special when you become a "real" writer. If your first book is fabulous, readers are going to expect your next one to be even *better*.

Don't be greedy. Don't start demanding millions of dollars right away, and then get your feelings hurt because you don't get it. The *quality of your books* will earn you the money. Remember that! You *earn* the money you make; no one *gives* it to you, so don't try to bully your publishing house into giving you money before you earn it. If you're not getting what you think you should from your publishing house, it's because the quality of your books has not yet earned the money. Oh, but I wish I could get this through the heads of new writers!

If a writer wants to be in the "Whatever Happened To?" column of *Romantic Times* magazine, she should start thinking she's a great writer and making outrageous demands of her publishing house right off the bat.

Soon some slick-tongued agent will razzle-dazzle that writer by telling her she's the new "Queen of Romance," and her publishing house doesn't appreciate her. The next thing you know, she's left her backlist and gone to another house, and two years later that agent goes somewhere else, and the author can't get a verse printed in her church bulletin! I have seen this happen again and again.

Get a good publishing house and stay there.

Q. Those of us who love your books—and there are a lot of us out there—are waiting anxiously to find out what is coming up for you next.

What's next for me is more writing about what I'm experiencing in life. Since I recently gave birth, I would imagine my future books will have a lot more children in them. Specifically, I am inventing a town called Abernathy, Kentucky, and I plan to set several books and short stories in that town. I want to get to know the people both past and present, and see the town change over the years.

Since I had my son, I have had to learn to be more efficient in my writing. No more staring off into the clouds for hours while I think up what happens next. Now I plot while feeding him strained carrots. Since he was born, during daylight hours he sleeps on cushions by my side, where he is right now. Poor little thing thinks the keyboard click is a lullaby.

As for how he has changed me, my editor says that the plots I have come up with since his birth have been some of the happiest things I have ever done.

"Kathryn asked me to give you some background information on our genre—as it relates to my publishing career— and to encourage you. I will, by saying, if you want to make it, the talented and persistent usually shine like stars."

If I Can Make It . . . Anyone Can

By Jennifer Blake

My first book came out in 1970 and I have been writing ever since. Among the published romance writers of today, only Barbara Cartland goes back that far. I first appeared on the *New York Times* bestseller list in 1977. My books are in 18 languages and total more than 25 million copies in print.

It wasn't easy starting out, but I hope my life as a writer will inspire you. I always tell new writers, if I could make it, anyone can!

I was self-educated by reading everything and anything. I earned my G.E.D. by studying at night. (And I've never stopped learning.) I married at age 16, had three kids by twenty, and started writing at home with three small children underfoot. I wrote while rocking the baby or stirring soup. My youngest started first grade the year I started my first bestseller.

Writers starting out today need to know much more about the business end of publishing than when I started. In those days, most publishing houses were family owned and there was more of a family feeling. They were more involved with their authors than today when houses are owned by corporations and the "bottom line" is the important thing.

I've seen many changes in romance publishing. Books are getting shorter. I had been doing 125,000-word manuscripts. Now my most recent request was for a 100,000-word book. The writer who writes longer books can still publish, but with the cost of paper and publishers' costs going up, the shorter length, more like the length of a murder mystery, is becoming the norm.

There is more emphasis on suspense and slightly less on romance. I like doing 50/50; it is what I have always done. I like mystery, and I like a puzzle and something more than just the romance. In my own work, even when writing a historical, I add a certain element of suspense.

There is more of a trend to heightened "atmosphere" in today's romance novels—getting back to more of the settings that gothics had originally. (Although, never, ever use the word "gothic." It leaves a bad taste in the mouths of today's publishers.)

Southern atmosphere has become a large part of many novels. As a writer who intends to be writing for a long time, I have to have a small ability to look ahead and that is my general feeling about where the market is going.

Never say, "This is my magnum opus" to a publisher. They want to know if you are a writer for the long haul and that, although the book you are trying to sell them is wonderful, you have written (or have ideas for) three more that will be just as original, just as wonderful.

Learn how long the publishing process takes, keep in mind the publishing schedule and be willing to help with promotion, come up with angles for the marketing department and volunteer ideas for promotion. Promotion is now more of a cooperative effort between the writer and the publishing house. You can no longer sit back and leave everything up to the publisher.

I started out writing gothics as Patricia Maxwell. In the early days (1960's) they sold well; my first book had a copy print run of over 100,000. And it went back to print after that! However, the Gothic market went bust in 1974-75, so I had a slack period of a couple of years when I was searching for another genre for my writing.

My writing was "without a home" for two years. I wasn't doing well. I started a series of Louisiana antebellum romances, wrote a mystery and a couple of gothics that didn't sell. Then I had a request to do a historical. I wrote an outline, sent it off and sold the book. The publisher asked me for a pen name and I chose Blake, which was my Grandmother's name. The Jennifer was added to soften the name.

Before I ever sold a book I had written poetry, short stories, and articles. It was always a goal to do books. As all romance writers should do today, I studied the market and read all the romance novels I could find. I was a great fan of Daphne Du Maurier, Mary Stewart, etc. In all that I studied, I noticed no one using southern locale with dark, mysterious aspects such as swamps, Spanish moss, great old houses and families, etc., so I added this bit of novelty to the genre. Then I sent my manuscript to a publisher and it came back unopened because I didn't send a query letter first. I tried again, sent a query this time and after two months, they said, add 30 pages and we'll take it. That was it.

Having said all this, I have to tell you that, like many others, I have a book (in my case a 40,000 word nurse Gothic) that is sitting on my shelf to this day and it will remain in obscurity for all time.

Do's and Don'ts for Beginning Romance Writers

Victoria Alexander

Don't expect your life to change when you sell a book.

Amanda Ashley

Don't make changes in your story that you don't agree with (unless they come from an editor *who is willing to buy your book*!) And most important of all—don't get discouraged. I was rejected 31 times before I sold my first book. If I'd quit at 30, I'd still be shoving manuscripts under the bed. *Never give up!*

Write in whatever way is comfortable for you. If you don't want to write everyday, don't. I usually write everyday except Sunday, but if I'm not in the mood, I go do something else. I write in spurts. I usually write an hour or two in the morning, go run my errands, take a break to watch Andy Griffith reruns, then write another hour or two in the afternoon, and maybe a little more in the evening after dinner.

I don't feel guilty when I don't write. You shouldn't either. When the well is dry, take the hint and indulge in a movie, a book, TV, a long nap, lunch with a friend, whatever rejuvenates you . . .

Jude Deveraux

For over 20 years I have been telling new writers what to do and not do, but they don't listen. New authors are usually so infatuated with sex scenes that they go wild over them and think that the more sex scenes they put into the book, the more the book will sell. If you want to be an author for two years, then write lots and lots of really wild erotic sex. Shock the reader. It will get you lots of attention for one or two books.

However, if you want to still be making the *New York Times* list 20 years from now, do think about your plot and characters.

Unfortunately, too many romance plots are the same ones that I read years ago. How many times can one read about a raven-haired beauty captured by an Indian chief? Or a lady pirate? I think that if I have to read one more book with a hero named Hawk, I might go mad!

Dorothy Garlock

Use your own instincts about your story. Don't let your friends meddle with your plot. Write for the market if you want to sell your work. If not . . . write your family history.

Jill Marie Landis

Write every day. Take classes. Take classes other than those aimed strictly toward romance writing.

Don't keep polishing and re-writing as you go, get to the end of the book first—you learn a lot about the story and characters on the way.

Take your writing seriously if you want to succeed. Believe in yourself.

Johanna Lindsey

Make sure your hero and heroine are strong enough individuals for the reader to identify with. You can have a great plot, but if the reader could care less what happens to your main characters, then your story fails.

Don't make the mistake of throwing in boring filler material just because you're lacking "story." A few descriptions are necessary to set mood, but page after page of description can bring the smooth flow of your story to a blaring halt. If your main plot concludes too soon, don't pad what you have with filler, create new sub-plots. In other words, give your main characters new problems to sink their teeth into.

Advice I'll pass on from a great editor: *Don't "tell" your readers what is happening to your characters . . . "show" them.*

Keep in mind the old adage; *"Action speaks louder than words."* Character thoughts are often necessary, but too many can slow down the plot, too. Many thoughts can instead be addressed in dialogue or action. An example could be a minor death in your story. One of your characters could mention this death in their thoughts, or you could have dialogue that tells about the death in more detail so you can show the character's reaction to it, or you could also "show" the death and the character's reaction to it.

Don't overwhelm your reader with love scenes. Yes, you're writing a romance, and yes, one or two full love scenes will likely be pertinent to your story, but too many love scenes become boring very quickly.

Try to keep your two main characters together as much as possible. You're writing a story about them. Rather than having them "thinking" about each other, "show" them interacting with each other. They may not be getting along too well throughout most of your story, but they still need to get to know each other if you intend for them to fall in love.

Teresa Medeiros

Use professional courtesy in all your dealings with editors, agents, and booksellers. Form lasting friendships with other writers. They'll be a blessing for years to come. Don't ever criticize another writer's work in public, or on line, it will only make you look small.

Try to finish any project you start. That's what will set you apart from all those others who have "always wanted to write a book." Don't expect to be an overnight success.

Be prepared to write one good book after another and don't let anyone discourage you from pursuing your dream.

Dare to dream big.

Bertrice Small

Set a time to write at least five days a week, and then do it. Check your facts if you're writing historicals. Get an agent. If you get a publisher, deliver your work on time. No excuse except a death in the family is acceptable for being late.

Listen politely to your editor. You're not writing Faulkner, and the editor may have something helpful to contribute. However, if you disagree with an editor, just don't tell her "No," explain why you feel her suggestions wouldn't work, and do it diplomatically. Writing is, first, a business.

Keep track of your book once it's delivered, as well as you can. Don't be afraid to ask questions.

Deb Stover

Don't become a professional contest entrant—in other words, remember your goal is to write and sell books, and not to win writing contests. Write from your heart and your gut. Trust your instincts. Criticism is a smorgasbord—take what you want and leave what your don't.

And network, network, network.

Tori Phillips

Be prepared to spend more than 800 hours at a typewriter or computer when writing your first book.

DON'T let rejection slips get you down. They are a fact of a writer's life. It's called "paying your dues." Don't refuse to compromise. Be flexible enough to recognize when your work needs to be revised or completely changed.

Don't give up, don't give in, and never take "no" as your final answer.

Linda Cajio

My editor once told me five things that writers do which hold back the writing:

a). Tell too much background information in the first chapter. Writers should weave background in over the first three to five or more chapters.

b). Start the story before the (background) action begins. Instead of getting the hero physically *to* the heroine (and vice versa), start the story after they arrive. Put them at odds right on page one.

c). Not enough conflict. Conflict should be deep rooted. Everyone should know the problem right from the beginning and it should seem insurmountable.

d). Hero and heroine are apart too much. In a historical, one has leeway, but in a series romance, the hero and heroine should be together nearly all the time, talking, arguing, making-up, whatever. It's their story and they need to tell it, not Grandma, no matter how "scene-stealing" she is.

e). Wrong Submissions. Editors constantly receive work that is inappropriate for what they buy, such as historicals to a Loveswept or Silhouette line. Writers need to learn the market. (It saves them from needless rejection.)

Jennifer Crusie

Don't follow trends. Create them by writing the book you want to read but can't find. Don't consider writing as a job; it's a privilege and an art. Learn your craft. There's no excuse for sloppy writing, head-hopping, intrusive exposition, or any of the other amateur mistakes too many writers make. Do remember that you are taking your reader's money and—much more importantly—her time, when you ask her to read your book. In exchange you owe her the absolute best you can do, every time. "Good enough" is *never* good enough.

Do consider yourself a writer whether you're published or not. Being published is lovely, but it's not a determining factor in who's a "real" writer and who isn't. If you're serious about your writing and you write, then you're a writer. And remember, no one is going to take you seriously until you take yourself seriously.

Linda Lael Miller

Write. Just write, because there are so many people who want the life, but to actually write that novel is not as common as you might think.

Don't take no for an answer. Debbie Macomber tells this story of visiting her cousin in the hospital. She finally stopped a doctor and asked how to get to the cousin. *"See those doors marked 'absolutely no admittance'? . . . go through those doors."*

Don't be too influenced by what's going on in the market—there's *always* "something" going on in the market and there's *never* a good time to sell a book.

Do it anyway! Learn and grow or you will be eaten alive by the people behind you because they are sharp. Learn from other writers, but don't try to imitate them. Dorothy Dunnett has been writing wonderful books since the '60's, but if you try to ape her, it's not going to work. Find your own voice.

Christina Skye

No one can teach you how to write. That isn't to say that you can't learn, but learning will come directly from your own efforts. How? Commit yourself to the *task* of writing. Give the process value in your life, and then *expect* that you will succeed.

Read books that have moved you deeply—then reread them and analyze exactly why they worked. Don't try to copy them. Instead, find your own voice and tell a gripping story the way no one but you can.

Meanwhile, all the rules of strong writing apply. Be specific. Know your characters inside out. Immerse yourself in the details of locale. Make mood an intimate element of your plot. Do your research impeccably—then throw out half of it. Be present in your writing. Consider each word as if your life depended on it. (Your character's life *does* depend on it.)

Readers are always looking for something new, an old plot told in a new way or a completely fresh writing voice. Don't be afraid to spread your wings and soar, giving the world something that it doesn't yet have—you!

These are the Books that Influenced and Inspired

Victoria Alexander

The Eight by Katherine Neville, *The Chronicles of Narnia* by CS Lewis, *Gone with the Wind* by Margaret Mitchell.

Dorothy Garlock

A Lantern in Her Hand by Bess Streeter Aldrich, *Ramona* by Helen Hunt Jackson, and all books by Louis L'Amour

Nancy Gideon

The Writer's Journey by Christopher Vogler. *Do It: Let's Get Off Our Buts* by Peter Williamson. *Lightening* by Dean Koontz.

Teresa Medeiros

The Windflower by Tom and Sharon Curtis (aka Laura London), *The Little Princess* and *The Secret Garden* by Frances Hodgson Burnett. All of Anya Seton's historicals, Victoria Holt's gothics, and Mary Stewart's romantic suspense novels.

Jennifer Crusie

Linda Seger's *Making a Good Script Great,* Jack Bickham's *Writing Novels That Sell,* and Janet Burroway's *Writing Fiction.*

Johanna Lindsey

The books that most influenced me were the books that created our genre: Kathleen Woodiwiss' *The Flame and the Flower* and *The*

Wolf and the Dove, and Rosemary Rogers' *Sweet Savage Love*.

I was influenced/inspired to write when I got hooked on this new genre, and there weren't enough of these types of books available at the time to satisfy my craving for more. However, that wasn't why I wrote my first book, which really wasn't intended to be a book. I was just amusing myself while waiting for the next historical to come out by writing a scene about when a couple first meet. I had fun doing that, so I took that scene a bit further and soon had a few hundred pages that had developed into an actual story. It was at that point that I decided to finish what I'd started to see what could happen with it. Just as I was craving more historical romances on the market, so were the editors at Avon.

Sara Orwig

These Old Shades, An Infamous Army and *The Nonesuch*, all by Georgette Heyer.

Bertrice Small

It was the writers that inspired me. Ivy Bolton, the children's historical author of the late '30's-mid-'50's, Anya Seton, Taylor Caldwell, Jan Westcott, Sergeanne Golon, Frank Yerby, Samuel Shellenbarker, and Thomas Costain. These people wrote great historical swashbucklers, and I wanted to be like them.

Heather Graham

I still read voraciously—biographies, non-fiction, fiction, horror, suspense, the classics and, of course, romance.

Nan Ryan writes some of the more fabulous sensual books out there, as do Virginia Henley, Kat Martin, Joan Johnston and, of course, Bertrice Small. Tami Hoag is doing blockbuster suspense. I also love Carla Neggers and Sherry Woods.

There are so many of my friends who are fellow authors whom I read as well, I know I'll forget somebody, but here goes: Judith Ivory, Kathleen Eagle, Millie Criswell, Meryl Sawyer, Sandra Kitt, and Jennifer Green. Another author I love is Eileen Dryer. Lori Copeland writes wonderful comedy. I like Joan Hohl, Pap Gaffney, Pat Rice, and a new writer, Marcia King Gamble. She is writing the best of ethnic romance—words that touch us all, regardless of race, color, or creed.

In the horror genre, my favorite writer is Robert McCammon. Then there's Clive Barker and, okay, Stephen King and Michael Slade—positively chilling.

My favorite books of all time come from different places—*Killer Angels* by Michael Shaara (I cried my eyes out), *1066, the Year of the Conquest, Silent Witness, The Wolf and the Dove, Gone With the Wind, Katherine* by Anya Seton, *Sleep in the Woods* by Dorothy Eden, *A World Lit Only by Fire* (a fabulous research book), *Martin's Hundred* (another incredibly entertaining work of non-fiction), and many more. And I love Shakespeare.

Linda Lael Miller

All Dorothy Dunnett historicals. All Taylor Caldwell. Anything that fosters in me the magic of believing and that reinforces the power of positive thinking.

Amanda Ashley

I suppose the books that inspired me were Anne Rice's *Vampire Chronicles* and Lori Herter's books. Rice got me interested in vampires; Lori showed me you could write about vampires and still have romance.

Barbara Bretton

Everything Laurie Colwin ever wrote. Even her cookbooks. She was what I call a literary romance writer and her death left an enormous void. William Styron's *Sophie's Choice*. I read it in 1980 and its searing images of love and loss are still with me. Margaret Mitchell's *Gone with the Wind*. She's the mother of us all. She defined the sweeping romantic saga and, in my opinion, her achievement has never been topped. (Although Colleen McCullough's *Thorn Birds* came close.)

Marilyn Campbell

The Heart Listens by Helen Van Slyke, *Shanna*, by Kathleen Woodiwiss and *The Bourne Identity* by Robert Ludlum

Tess Mallory

Diana Gabaldon's *Outlander*, Lisa Ann Verge's *Twice Upon a Time* and Jennifer Crusie's *Anyone But You* in romance. In general, *Rifles for Watie* (a young adult book), Isaac Asimov's *Foundation* series, and one of the most beautiful pieces of literature ever written, the *Holy Bible*.

Suzanne Brockmann

Fancy Pants by Susan Elizabeth Philips, *Wild Swan* by Celeste DeBlasis and from Rachel Lee's *Connard County* series for Silhouette, *Intimate Moments*.

Tess Gerritsen

There's one book that really opened my eyes as to how wonderfully adventurous and sexy a good romance can be—and that was *Skye O'Malley* by Bertrice Small.

Meg Chittenden

Writers rather than books. John Galsworthy, Mary Stewart, and Sue Grafton.

Jane Toombs

Rebecca by Daphne Du Maurier, *Jane Eyre* by Charlotte Brontë, and *Burn, Witch, Burn* by Abraham Merritt.

Linda Cajio

Kathleen Woodiwiss' *Flame and The Flower* was the first romance I read, and I fell in love with the genre. I've been inspired by nearly all the writers I've read. Dick Francis is a joy to read for making the words count. That man knows how to do this better than anyone. I love Gary Jennings, for depth of story. He's fabulous to read, just sucks you into his characters and the time period.

Lucy Grijalva

When I was 16 and on a trip to Mexico with my parents, I ran out of reading material and bought the only English-language book I could find, *The Convenient Marriage* by Georgette Heyer. From then on I was hooked on romance. When I was 22, a friend gave me a copy of *Sweet Savage Love* by Rosemary Rogers. She said I wouldn't be able to put it down. She was right, and it opened my eyes to a whole new world of romance novels. When I was 34, I found a Harlequin *Temptation* by Jackie Weger entitled *Eye of the Beholder* that fundamentally changed how I looked at contemporary series romance. I guess those three would be my most influential books, although it's an odd little collection.

"A word is a bud attempting to become a twig.
How can one not dream while writing?
It is the pen which dreams.
The blank page gives the right to dream."
—Gaston Bachelard

Sierra Cole,
San Francisco Writer!

Dear Kathryn,

Sierra here. Okay, you got me with that last batch, darlin' girl! I read B.K. Reeves fantastic words and saw myself every time she talked about having a "writer's brain." From the time I was knee-high to my mama I have been a writer. I write short stories (and have even had a couple published) I write longer stories. I see the world in "descriptive phrases." I *love* to tell stories. Why, every once in a while I even tell stories to my dawg! And it's true that even though I may never get published again, I won't stop writin'.

Rosemarie just walked past and told me not to be so dog-gone negative! I try not to be, but where Rosemarie forges ahead and Jade jumps in with both feet, I have always been last man off the mark. But once I set myself a course, I always finish it. This latest batch of words of wisdom and encouragement was the final nudge I needed to stir my writing juices into full boil. If Heather Graham can start from scratch and make it to superstar status, so can I. She isn't the only one that struggled at the beginning; here are Linda Lael Miller, Gloria Dale Skinner, and Jennifer Blake all "workin' their way to the top"! And as for Jude Deveraux? I have been her biggest fan for longer than I can remember. She writes with such humor, and paints such pretty pictures of love, how can anyone who reads her, not become a fan!

I'll do everything you suggest, and walk each path you put before my feet to make this work. However, I do <u>need</u> that path. Rosemarie is pretty certain she wants to write historicals. Jade still changes from day-to-day, but always veers back to that romantic suspense category. And me? I don't have a clue what would be best for me. Maybe I'd be good at one of the new trends or out-of-the-ordinary plots and characters.

New age seems to be happening. There are many African-American, Hispanic, and Asian books in the stores now. However, as a part African-American, part Cherokee Indian, raised-on-a-farm, ex-North Carolina "Southern girl," where do I fit in? Kathryn, I need some more direction.

Re-committed-to-writing, but still confused in San Francisco,
Sierra

PART TWO
THE NEW MARKETS

CHAPTER VII

INNOVATIVE TRENDS

Kathryn Falk, Lady of Barrow
Romantic Times Magazine
Brooklyn, New York

Dear Sierra,

You definitely sound ready to move forward. Yes, it's finally time to think about the newest romance markets. However, in order to go forward, we first need to look back. A wise traveller peruses the path already trod, before forging a new one of his/her own.

When I first started in the romance novel industry nearly twenty years ago, there were few authors and a limited number of books. It was a fledgling industry, with readers who were awed by everything they read.

However, today's writers are dealing with avid readers who have already "been there" and "read 'em all." On average, romance readers devour between twenty and forty romances a month. It stands to reason then that some of them might be even just a tad jaded about what they read. Variety is essential to keeping them interested.

As Jude Deveraux said, "After 20 years or more of romances, many of the 'same-old, same-old' plots, heroes (and names) become repetitious." She is astute enough to keep up with the times. Her *Knight in Shining Armor* was considered a front-runner in the emergence of time-travel as a popular romance sub-genre.

In order to continually pique the interest of this audience, writers of romance novels, like fashion designers, must create excitement and "deliver new goods" with each new season. In fashion, changes are to hemlines and style of jackets, in romance novels, to plots and characters, with the ultimate goal being the creation of fresh twists for established—and new—sub-genres.

It's a challenge that has every writer throwing up his/her hands at one time or another. Where to come up with these new ideas? One way to create new plot twists in contemporary and historical novels is to incorporate subjects that reflect readers' *current* interests. For example: alcoholism, physically challenged heroes/heroines, or abusive treatment to a spouse are "modern" topics, reflective of today's society, but they also reflect problems that were in existence in the Regency era, medieval times, and throughout every other time period as well. For example, in Laura Kinsale's award-winning historical, *Flowers from the Storm*, the hero has suffered a stroke. Ms. Kinsale's book is a fine example of an author taking something currently of interest to the general population and placing it in the context of a historical setting.

The challenge is to look for ways to inject these currently relevant topics into your novel in new and *unique* ways, while at the same time keeping the story historically accurate and within the romance parameters.

For the romance industry to continue to grow, innovators must chart new directions and forge new paths—offering something fresh within the genre. Some believe that doing this is now the only way to break into the highly competitive (romance) writing game.

I've asked Linda Hyatt, a literary agent who deals daily with the selling end of romance manuscripts, to give you some insight into the state of the romance market today. Heed her well, for she's the one talking daily to editors and getting the inside scoop on what they are looking for.

I'm also sending you a "tasting menu" of articles on ethnic and inspirational romances, alternative realities, off-beat heroes, out-of-this-world settings, and romantic suspense. Then, a bit later, we'll delve into some of these categories at more length.

Among the "new" sub-genres, ethnic romance could prove to have the most growth potential in the 21st century. Heed well the advice of Sandra Kitt, a pioneer of the genre, who has written an essay for you.

You'll enjoy hearing from Jo Beverley, who is a cheerleader for younger heroes, and Jane LaMunyon, a popular writer of inspirational romance, who introduces this sub-genre and explains its growing popularity.

Alternative reality romances have been around for a long time. (Who can forget Anya Seton's *Green Darkness*?) However, within this sub-genre there are new angles worth pursuing. You'll be fascinated by the advice from Kathleen Morgan, who has nurtured the popularity of futuristic romances. Victoria Alexander and Jennifer Dunne, two authors who really "push the envelope" may inflame your imaginations as they introduce you to the many categories of alternative reality fiction. I doubt there is much more of outer space to cover, but . . . who knows what discoveries tomorrow will bring?"

Enjoy this explosive mix by a group of authors who have had the courage to go off the beaten path and create unusual characters and settings.

Affectionately,

Kathryn

> *"Never forget what I believe was observed by your Coleridge, that every great and original writer, in proportion as he is great and original, must himself create the taste by which he is to be relished."*
> —William Wordsworth
> * * *

"The one question that almost every writer, published or not, asks or should, is what kind of stories do editors want? I eat lunch with them, talk constantly on the phone with them, and negotiate money with them. I learn a lot about the wide range of editorial tastes and desires."

Overview of the Romance Market

By Linda Hyatt, Literary Agent

Most writers know the marketplace shifts. And, because everyone writes at a different pace, a manuscript created today may not have a market by the time it is completed. Five years from now, however, that same manuscript may be just what the editors are looking for.

During the '70's historical romances with alpha-heroes and heroines in distress were popular. Eventually dubbed "bodice-rippers," these stories took the market by storm. Contemporary romances as well as historicals from this era featured macho men who occasionally caused their women to cry, but who also always protected them from danger.

In the '80's, heroines became stronger, more assertive. Issue-based plots appeared in both contemporary and historical romances. Beta-heroes (the sensitive males) were preferred to the alpha male. These stories generally featured characters that dealt with past emotional baggage.

The '90's featured a good mix of romances. The short contemporary market published romantic comedy. Not necessarily bumbling, stumbling, slapstick humor, it was instead mature humor, with adult themes and witty dialog. Silhouette, *Yours Truly,* and Harlequin, *Love and Laughter* are two of the newest lines in short contemporary humor. Other houses are also acquiring humorously written stories.

The *Arabesque* line published by BET Books and the *Indigo* line by Genesis Press introduced African-American characters in stories written by African-American authors. The rapid growth of these lines soon indicated that these stories were definitely meeting reader expectation. (More about reader expectations later.)

Fantasy, time-travel, paranormal, futuristic, as well as traditional contemporary and historical romances, issue-based or not, continue to sell. Regency romances will always be popular with Regency enthusiasts. (Although their market, in number of readers, is very small.)

Any questions?

Writer: How can the market handle so many types of romances?

Agent: Are they really so different? What do the 90's have in common with the 80's and 70's? Do you know the answer? Take a guess.

Writer: Romance?

Agent: Yes. No matter where the story is set, whether on a Spanish galleon or a starship headed for undiscovered universes, no matter whether it is written with humor, dark emotional issues, or hot sizzling bedroom scenes—it will have a better chance of selling if it also has a heart-pounding (or at least heart-warming) romance at its core, for we are all familiar with the romance plot: Two people fall in love, fight the odds, and keep us, the reader, turning the pages until the very end.

Writer: But my story is different from many of the books I've read. It's more than just a romance. It has adventure. I like stories with adventure.

Agent: I've read and enjoyed many romance novels with adventure, too, but I will always caution writers to keep the focus on the romance.

Writer: But . . . I won't write love scenes. I just can't. What would I tell my mother?

Agent: Mothers like reading romances, too, but romances need not include bedroom gymnastics to be salable. Romance readers *do* expect sexual tension, however. For instance: the nun and the gambler. The longing between the two, if written well, may be enough to sustain the sexual tension and keep the reader turning the pages to the end, where he reforms and she rescinds her vows to be with him. Inspirational Romances, a new line for some major publishing houses, usually end with the couple pledging their love. Rarely do they consummate, and when, or if, they do it's never before marriage, and rarely in any detail.

Writer: My story sizzles. In my opinion there is nothing more romantic than a book with a lot of sex.

Agent: Tender, emotionally driven, and even detailed love scenes can be quite compelling in romance novels. However, I think most agents will agree with most editors and most writers that sex between the main characters, if born out of the relationship, is far more powerful in the romance genre. Readers expect that sex will never be gratuitous, promiscuous (multiple lovers), or vulgar. They expect that the romance between the two main characters will reign in the story—not necessarily the love scenes.

If the focus on the romance in your story becomes blurred by other elements, until the romance fades, consider offering your work elsewhere, to publishers who feature lines other than romance.

Writer: Why do editors seem to buy certain types of plots, or certain types of heroes?

Agent: Several reasons come to mind. Editors are drawn to certain writing styles, and themes, just like readers are. The writer simply hopes the editor who winds up reading her submission will be fond of it, for this would make the editor the best for that manuscript. Usually, they are, because they are the ones who acquire the manuscript, then read through it several times before the book appears on the shelves at the local store. Editors also appreciate the business side of the publishing world; they know what popular themes and types of heroes and heroines sell.

Aspiring writers will be better prepared to sell their first story if they take time to study the market. Except in rare instances, the first sale, or the first royalty statement, will usually end the new author's fantasy of overnight grandeur. So put away the Tiffany silver and study the catch phrases, "sell-through, print-run," and "reader-expectation." Keep an eye on the bestseller lists like those put out by Ingram, Waldenbooks, and B. Dalton. When readers buy many books of the same title, the author may be fortunate enough to appear on one of the most requested lists.

Writer: How do the compilers of the bestseller lists find out which titles are selling?

Agent: To clarify the concept: in essence, when a book is purchased, it is like casting a vote, not only for a particular author but also for the type of book she/he has written. The sales/votes are tallied by computer and are accessible to the publisher. The sales data is forwarded to the publisher, and eventually the author, via the royalty statement. Whether or not a title makes the bestseller lists, publishers will use each book's sales figures to decide if they will acquire future similar works from the author, and/or increase the size of any future print runs.

Writer: What good will it do me to read the books on those lists? Weren't the books on those lists purchased more than a year ago?

Agent: Manuscripts are purchased far in advance to allow time for revisions, copy-editing, and the production of the cover. However, staying abreast of the current market will help writers rediscover the common thread found throughout the genre, and understand why the books we find on the shelves today sold to an editor a year ago.

Writer: Romance is the common thread?

Agent: Yes. Romance, when written well, sells.

So, in conclusion, what *do* editors want? Good stories with characters that come to life on the page, surmount obstacles, and finally recognize their love for one another on the happily-ever-after last page. Why? Quoting my daughter who, at age five, after watching *Lassie Come Home*, tearfully sobbed, "I *like* that kind of story." Isn't that exactly what writers hope their future editors and readers will say about *their* stories?

Keep romance alive. Keep writing stories we love to read.

Reprinted with permission from *The Literary Times*

Nothing endures but change.
Heraclitus
* * *

"So you want to write a new kind of romance? Please consider some younger men with heroic values."

The Unusual Hero
Breaking the "Baby Boomer" Rules in the New Markets

By Jo Beverley

After watching the video of *Braveheart*, my 20-year-old son and I chatted about the real history behind the Scottish struggles against oppression. And as I watched his handsome young face, animated by this tale of battles won and lost, I suddenly realized how much better and thought-provoking the movie could have been if Mel Gibson had stayed in the director's chair and cast a younger man as William Wallace.

A much younger man.

Wallace moved onto the historical stage just past 20. At the time of that last disastrous battle, he was about 26. Robert the Bruce was even younger. On the screen, however, men nearly 40 were portraying them. Wouldn't it have been more moving to see the truth—youth fired by injustice and willing to suffer and die for it?

A friend watching a movie about World War II pilots said she felt uncomfortable about the youth of the actors. Then she realized the actors were older than the men who had fought and died in those planes had been.

Today, in a world dominated by baby boomers, we're in danger of stealing youth from the young, of denying them the qualities that make them great.

Consider another movie, *First Knight*. It's based on myth, but aren't we supposed to see it as the dashing young knight and the older, wiser man? Why was Lancelot played by a man of 50—one old enough to play Arthur himself?

Does this magical ability to translate youth into middle age apply to women? Oh no. The heroines are appropriately dewy-skinned young women in their twenties.

Tom Hanks and Sally Fields once played lovers. In *Forrest Gump,* she plays his mother. In an honest business, keeping the ages of the actresses close to those of the leading men, Meryl Streep, would have played the French princess in *Braveheart* and Cher would have played Guinevere!

So, we have two assaults here. One is on women, who apparently cease being romantic heroines at 30. (Thank heavens today's romance genre is firmly on the side of truth and justice on that issue.) However, the other injustice is against young men, who so rarely see their generation portrayed as heroic. Here, romance fiction is not entirely innocent.

Heroes in romance are getting older, because this appeals to many readers—again that baby-boomer bulge. There's nothing wrong with this, but we shouldn't forget that when it comes to fighting for dreams against impossible odds, it's young people who have historically led the way and spilled their blood.

Myths, as we all know, are important. Mythic heroes shape our dreams. What sort of dreams do our sons have if men with wrinkles and graying hair are doing all the daring-do? What sort of dreams do we have for them if the books we read are full of 20-year-old "knights-in-shining-armor"?

I hear writers say, "But I can't get interested in heroes as young as my sons." I can. Youth gives us great stories fueled by ideals and sensitivities not yet callused by time. For me, a romance isn't about me; it's about the interesting characters. First love makes a classic romance, and first lovemaking, a tender love scene.

William of Normandy seized control of his duchy and defeated France when just over 20. He was only 25 when he married Matilda, a story worthy of a romance—but not with Kevin Costner in the lead, please! And we all know about Mozart. Life certainly doesn't end at 30, but to imply it begins there is both unwise and unfair.

"The greatest thing in this world is not so much where we are, but in what direction we are moving."
—Oliver Wendell Holmes
* * *

"What does change have in common with death and taxes? It's inevitable. On the down side, change can be long, messy and filled with uncertainty. On the up side, it is always an opportunity for growth, enlightenment, innovation and progress."

New Faces, New Voices – Same Story

By Sandra Kitt

As an African-American reader AND writer of women's fiction, I have experienced both sides of "change." So, I can tell the story of what—in a uniquely *cultural* way—have come to be historic changes in women's popular fiction, especially romance. These changes include the introduction of stories that feature African-American main characters and story lines, written by African-American writers, and which are called "ethnic" romances.

Unfortunately, when "ethnic" romances were first identified as a sub-genre, many African-American romance writers found their efforts to be published blocked . . . by a resistance to the change these new stories represented. Not all efforts were unsuccessful.

In 1979, Candlelight Ecstasy romances from Dell publishing released *Entwined Destinies* by Rosalind Welles, a pseudonym for Elsie Washington who, at the time, was a writer for *Essence* magazine. This was the start of something new, but sales didn't take off.

Of the thousands of books published during the height of the market in the 1980's, less than 50 were romances that featured non-White main characters.

Oddly, not counted in the emerging ethnic category were books that had Indian male heroes and White heroines. These love stories were written and accepted as "historical." Only the contemporary stories by veteran writer Kathleen Eagle with similar characterization would escape being labeled as anything but simply "fiction." In the 1980's all others "need not apply."

A few Candlelight Ecstasy romances also were written with Hispanic or Latino characters, but they quietly and quickly disappeared. What was left, by sheer persistence of demanding Black readers, was the occasional romance with African-American heroes and heroines. ethnic romance, then, became a euphemism for "Black" romance.

So, what, exactly, is an "ethnic" romance? How is it the same and how different from the traditional romances of the past three decades?

First of all, at the core of the ethnic romance, love is all-important—the same as it is in a non-ethnic romance. This is the universal concept and common denominator of *all* romance fiction.

In ethnic romances, what changes is the voice and circumstances of the hero and heroine, affected by their histories, backgrounds, and societal influences. These stories are textured with cultural details that can be clearly attributed to a particular section of the population. These details can include word or phrase usage, hairstyles and fashion, holiday customs, entertainment, foods and even, specifically identified communities. For example: Black women referring to each other as "girlfriend," although currently popularized, is still used almost exclusively among African-Americans. So is the use of the celebration of Kwanzaa to mark a particular time during the year.

More than creating love stories in which the lead characters are simply "tinted brown," the writer of ethnic romances must be able to write with the voice of authenticity of an ethnic group and have an understanding of—and empathy for—that group. It is essential to have strong, first-hand knowledge of the culture being written about. This goes a long way toward convincing the reader that a writer knows what he/she is talking about. Readers are astute and sensitive to inaccuracies.

Besides having a convincing voice, an author must fight against creating stereotypical characters and story lines. Romances, for the most part, no matter the cultural orientation, are generally set in middle-class American values, and feature a heroine who is strong and independent, and a hero who is centered and capable of caring and gentleness. These stories present an opportunity to educate and enlighten all readers. Therefore, writers of ethnic romances have the added responsibility of being true to the culture they are writing about.

Writers must be voyeurs, astute observers of their own as well as other people's lives. With that willingness to see, writers must have an understanding of the similarities as well as the differences in these new stories, with new voices, and must show a willingness to portray non-white men and women as heroes and heroines, and as sexual beings. The characters must be portrayed as sympathetic, vulnerable, and sincere if the reader is to believe them. These are the same requirements of *any* love story.

The term "ethnic" has metamorphosed into "multicultural" in the last few years. As the nation becomes more diverse, the opportunities increase for varying ethnic groups to meet, become colleagues, co-workers, friends . . . and lovers. There exists the inevitability of another genre: the *interracial* romance. I explored this theme in a novella, *Love is Thanks Enough*, for Harlequin, and a full-length novel of more depth, *The Color of Love* from Signet. (Editor's note: The *Love Spectrum* line by Genesis Press is geared specifically toward interracial love stories.)

Writing an ethnic romance requires a belief that these characters, which you have created and, hopefully, brought to life, are at least your equals. It is hard to have empathy for characters and their plight if the writer condescends to, or feels sorry for them. In the final analysis, an ethnic romance is told through the eyes of someone who wants to present new faces and new voices . . . with a *twist*.

"You too may be interested in writing an inspirational romance for the growing readership. I write inspirational romances for the same reason I read romances—I love a great love story."

Romance with a Spiritual Dimension

By Jane LaMunyon

Inspirational romances have the same characteristics of all true romances: Hero and heroine meet close to the beginning of the story and are never separated for long, the emotional conflict is the story's focus and there is, of course, a happy ending.

Inspirational romances *differ* in that they have a spiritual dimension. Instead of the involvement and commitment of only two people, we have two people . . . and God.

Faith is a natural part of the characters in an inspirational romance; it is not something "tacked on" to make a generic romance inspirational. Sometimes that faith is the conflict, and sometimes it is the resolution.

I like writing a story with a lot of adventure that includes a scene where not only do the hero and heroine experience an awakening to the fact that they have fallen in love, they also realize they must make a spiritual adjustment so their lives are successful and compatible.

I enjoy responding to the challenge of writing a story that adds a spiritual journey to the plot and makes faith a natural, comfortable part of the book. It's satisfying to show that besides finding our "perfect life partner," faith in God can provide answers to the seemingly meaningless, often painful jumble of life's experiences.

Readers tell me they like stories that reinforce their own beliefs and values.

Being an inspirational romance writer doesn't mean I have to shrink back from portraying physical and sensual tension between a man and a woman falling in love; I just don't make it titillating and explicit. After all, God gave us the desire for the opposite sex, and there's nothing wrong with a romance with a hero who longs to hold and caress the heroine, and vice-versa.

It's a challenge to write high-quality, heart-touching, soul-stirring stories, but that's what inspirational romance publishers are looking for. Tyndale Publishing's Heartsong Presents, which published two of my inspirational romances (*Fly Away Home* and *Escape on the Wind*) have in their guidelines: "Our readers want to read about characters they can relate to, who face similar situations and deal with similar emotions. They want to be reminded that God is good, He is still in control, and the Bible holds true today."

As Americans revisit their bedrock Judeo-Christian values, houses which publish uplifting fiction—fiction which emphasizes fidelity and commitment between a man and woman and their God—have joined the romance marketplace in a big way.

"In all of mystery fiction, no other genre of literature has undergone as many changes in the last few decades as romantic suspense."

Suspense Has Changed

By Toby Bromberg—RT Mystery Books Reviewer

The essential ingredient in a romantic suspense novel is, as always, the heroine.

In books written during the '60's and '70's (and before), the heroine (constantly in jeopardy), was always portrayed as helpless . . . she *let* things happen to her. She was not able to problem-solve on her own, and needed the help of a man to see her through tough times.

Sometimes she inadvertently relied on the *wrong* man. But sooner or later, the right one came along to save the day.

However, in today's novels, there is still a romantic interest for the heroine, but now she is quite capable of getting through danger on her own. Of course, having someone amorous around never hurts.

It used to be the heroine was a virgin, and all the hero could hope for would be a chaste kiss or two. Today's heroines, on the other hand, are liberated—they are not immoral, but they certainly need more than just a kiss to satisfy the libido.

As we enter the 21st century, heroines in both sub-genres will grow stronger and more self-assured, reflecting not only the reading public's taste, but also, reality itself.

During the '90's, romantic suspense spun off into two different categories: romantic suspense novels that have the emphasis on suspense, and those where the emphasis is on romance. Traditional romantic suspense novels with more emphasis on the elements of intrigue and suspense still have a large and loyal audience. Authors writing in this sub-genre include Meredith Land Machlin, Alex Juniper, and America's national treasure, Phyllis A. Whitney.

Suspense novels with more emphasis on romance are growing steadily in popularity, especially as romance readers seek out and cross over into other genres. The superstars of the romance genre, notably Kay Hooper, Iris Johansson, and Nora Roberts, write many of these novels. These authors tell a good, intriguing, suspenseful story, but their tales always contain heightened romance scenes.

This sub-genre even has a "sub" sub-genre of sorts: the series suspense novels. Top publishers like Harlequin have been quick to jump on the suspense bandwagon, launching their own lines of softer mysteries, written by the top authors of the series world.

Rising sales indicate the public demands and enjoys both types of romantic suspense stories. It is now up to the aspiring author to decide if she is more comfortable with ROMANTIC suspense or romantic SUSPENSE, and then take it from there.

"Kathryn said you have expressed an interest in the paranormal romance sub-genre, and asked if I could give you some pointers. To begin with: I'm a 'wanna-be' believer. There I said it. Whew. What a relief. What's a "wanna-be" believer you ask? (I knew you would.) It's simple. Read on . . ."

Looking for Love in All the Odd Places

By Victoria Alexander

With my whole heart and soul I believe in second chances, the power of everlasting love, and happily ever after. And I *want* to believe in magic, time travel, reincarnation and fairy godmothers.

I suppose you can blame my condition on an upbringing filled with fairytales and classic myths, Jules Verne and H.G. Wells, *The Chronicles of Narnia* and *Gone with the Wind*. And how could I fail to mention Lois Lane and Superman. Eclectic choices? No doubt. Romantic? Absolutely.

For years, as a television reporter, I lived in the very-down-to-earth, just-the-facts-please world of journalism where good guys don't always win and few people live happily ever after. Then I discovered fiction, which was much more fun than real life. Now, I create worlds filled with humor and adventure, featuring heroes and heroines overcoming adversity and falling in love. Sometimes those fictional worlds pull from everything that my imagination-driven mind loved as a child: the excitement of traveling through time, the wonder of magic, the promise of eternal love and, of course, happily ever after. To date I've written time travel and reincarnation stories, and romances based on fairytales and legends.

One of the great things about writing in a paranormal sub-genre is that there are no hard and fast rules. However there are some risks. Concepts of reincarnation, magic, ghosts or angels are an integral part of many religious or secular beliefs. Readers will forgive a great deal, but there are some lines that even the best writer might not be able to cross. Where those lines lie depends upon the subject, its treatment, the writer and, ultimately, the expectations of the reader.

There are also some practical boundaries. If your hero is a ghost there's no way for him to be united with the heroine at the end of the book unless she dies, he comes back to life (difficult to pull off for any writer) or he reappears as a reincarnated soul or as his own descendant.

However, such problems pale in comparison to the nearly limitless possibilities. For a writer, there's an incredible amount of creative freedom.

For a reader, paranormal romances are a passport to a world usually found only in dreams.

For readers and writers alike, each sub-genre has its own allure. Among the most popular:

Time Travel

Time travel is the absolute adventure. You can take thoroughly modern characters and toss them into another century where they have only themselves to rely upon to survive. You can drag a historic character to the present and watch him discover a future he never dreamed of. You can even propel your unsuspecting protagonist a hundred or a thousand years ahead to a future that exists only in your own imagination.

Reincarnation

Who hasn't wished for a second chance at life or love? Reincarnation stories fulfill that desire in a way no other writing can. Here, you're able to watch a character live life again with lessons learned in a previous incarnation to guide her/him along the way.

Ghosts

This is the story told around a campfire, late at night when all things are possible . . . and possibly frightening. In every age, in nearly every civilization, people have believed that spirits of the dead walk the earth. It's a scary thought. Still, if those entities are intent not on harm but rather on helping the living, especially in finding love, what started as frightening becomes comforting.

Angels

There's a very warm, fuzzy feeling about the concept of heavenly beings watching over us and guiding the human race. It's the idea that we're not in this alone, that a power greater than man is concerned and involved.

Vampires

Dark, dangerous and erotic, a vampire hero is the ultimate bad boy. Would he be quite so sexy if we all truly believed in creatures that roam only by night and sleep in a coffin—or if he ordered a Bloody Mary and you had to wonder exactly what he meant?

There are different reasons for the attraction of specific paranormal plots, but they all share a universal idea: the lure of the unknown and the call of forces beyond the control of man. Paranormal elements pit characters against circumstances so far from the realm of real life they can only be imagined. These are situations fraught with excitement, adventure and danger, where the rules of the non-fiction world around us no longer apply.

Paranormal themes are classic; their power, timeless. Mark Twain wrote time travel (A *Connecticut Yankee in King Arthur's Court*) in 1889. Two of the most beloved Christmas tales of all time incorporate paranormal elements. Charles Dickens' *A Christmas Carol*, written in 1843, had a full cast of ghostly characters (Christmases Past, Present, and Yet-To-Come, not to mention Jacob Marley) and the movie *It's a Wonderful Life,* made in 1946, featured Clarence, the angel trying to "earn his wings."

As recently as a decade ago, paranormal themes were confined mostly to science fiction or horror genres. Today, romance shelves are filled with time traveling heroines and ghostly advisors. To predict whether or not the popularity of this trend will continue would require a crystal ball and more than a touch of magic!

History has shown us that each time mankind approaches the turn of a century, interest in the paranormal grows. History has also shown there has always been a market for stories that feature things that "go bump in the night." As I said before, they're classic. Add an element as timeless as love to the paranormal mix and the result will be a great romance that will always find readers.

I guess I'm a believer after all.

"That fairy kind of writing that depends only upon the imagination."
—Dryden
Dedication for *King Arthur*
* * *

"It was 'channeled' to me that you're contemplating sub-genres! Mixing genres works in today's marketplace. However, be careful what results."

Mixing Romance and Science Fiction
It's all in the Blend

By Jennifer Dunne

Take a pinch of science fiction; add a dash or a dollop of romance and, presto, you have whipped up a fascinating blend of science fiction romance. Or did you create romantic science fiction? Be careful. As with any blend, a successful result depends entirely upon the perfect mix of ingredients. And the final blend here will decide whether your books end up in the science fiction department or featured on the shelves under "romance."

Romantic Science Fiction

If you start with science fiction or fantasy novels and add romance, you'll end up with a romantic science fiction or romantic fantasy novel. You can tell that the fantasy or science fiction is more important, because it is the last issue to be resolved. These works are at one end of the science fiction romance spectrum. Anne McCaffrey, Mercedes Lackey, and Tanya Huff are examples of authors who often use strong romantic themes or subplots in their science fiction or fantasy novels.

Science Fiction Romance

On the other end of this spectrum are the books properly called science fiction romances. These are the romance novels that include fantasy or science fiction elements. Some are labeled simply as fantasy romances. The term science fiction romance is generally used to refer to those books where the romance and science fiction/fantasy elements are of roughly equal importance, but in which romance has the edge because it is the last issue to be resolved.

In one of the vagaries of publishing, many of these books are now coming out labeled science fiction or fantasy, and being printed by science fiction and fantasy publishers, rather than being labeled romance and printed by romance publishers. Those printed by romance publishers are usually subdivided based on the type of element added to the romance, e.g. futuristic, time-travel or paranormal.

Futuristic Science Fiction Romance

Futuristic romances are most often recognized by their settings on other worlds, and the use of interstellar travel. They look the most like science fiction. However, they also borrow some of the less obvious elements of science fiction and fantasy, frequently including a quest of some sort for either the hero or heroine, and, in the best works of the genre, commentary on the current world. Extrapolating existing social and/or political behaviors into a future world often does this. Writers who excel at this blend of romance flavored with science fiction include Dara Joy, Justine Davis, Marilyn Campbell, and Sherrilyn Kenyon.

"Once upon a time there was an aspiring writer—you! I would like to help you get published, make millions and live in castles, happily every after. Isn't fantasy great!"

Once Upon a Time—Writing the Fantasy Romance

By Kathleen Morgan

Everyone knows what goes into a fantasy romance, right? Take one twelfth-century castle complete with drawbridge, moat and pennants flying. Add an evil sorcerer, a fire-breathing dragon, a milk-white unicorn that can be seen only if one is "pure in heart," a gang of wart-nosed, greedy trolls who live under a bridge and threaten hapless travelers, and a race of ethereal fairies living deep in a nearby forest. To that, add a hero broad-of-chest and handsome-of-countenance riding a massive charger, and a beauteous, big-breasted heroine languishing in our pennant-flying castle. Easy enough, you say. Not so, *I* say; not if you want to *sell* that book, much less win over readers to this fun—if challenging—romance sub-genre.

Similarities Between Fantasy and Futuristic Romances

When I began my first fantasy romance, *Demon Prince*, I wondered if my loyal futuristic romance readers would follow me into yet another romance sub-genre. Moving from tales set in the distant future based upon scientific premises, to those arising from some imaginary past involving the decidedly *unscientific* inclusion of magic, seemed a great leap of faith to me. However, as I researched the elements of a fantasy romance, I began to realize there were more similarities than differences between the two sub-genres—similarities I felt confident my readers would recognize and accept. One still had to create a coherent, consistent world and maintain a harmonic flow to the language and the character names and words used. One still had to make a bit more effort, especially in the initial set-up, in building a world and the premises around which this world evolved. One still had to develop a culture that unfolded logically from the history and setting. And one still had to do research.

Definition of Fantasy Fiction

Though, in the broadest sense, all novels are fantasy since all fiction deals with things that aren't true, in a narrower sense—the definition I'll be using for the purposes of this article—a fantasy is a story containing elements that are fantastic or impossible. Science fiction isn't fantasy in this case, or vice-versa. Science fiction is fiction of the possible; true fantasy is fiction of the impossible, i.e., magic. Yet though magic is always an integral aspect of a fantasy, without certain other key elements, well thought out and presented, your story will, at best, be clichéd. At worst, it will be little more than a flat, lifeless imitation.

Like straight fantasy fiction, a fantasy romance should be set in a fantasy world. This can be based on a medieval model, set in a world of pure fantasy such as Tolkien's Middle Earth. It can take place on another planet entirely or on an "alternate Earth" in which, somewhere in the past, history has taken a different turn and magic—for whatever plausible reason you come up with—rules.

Your story can take the form of a quest in which a band of adventurers sets out to retrieve something of great value or to rescue a damsel in distress. It can take the form of a journey into unexplored regions (such as a lost city or labyrinth) or it can deal with characters living an everyday life while struggling to deal with the terrible power and responsibilities of magic.

You can have all kinds of monsters and non-human races—as well as the typical fantasy residents such as fairies, elves, trolls, unicorns, dragons, witches, and sorcerers—peopling your land. The inclusion of these kinds of characters is usually considered "high fantasy." You can devise all sorts of mechanical and magical traps to challenge your hero and heroine. You can have magical swords and jewels and talismans. The options and combinations are almost limitless; how you combine them is up to you and is what will make your story truly unique.

Types of Fantasy Fiction

In recent years, fantasy has expanded from the traditional "high fantasy" to include many interesting sub-genres, such as historical fantasy, urban fantasy, contemporary fantasy, humorous fantasy, science fantasy, and dark fantasy.

Demon Prince and my third fantasy romance, *A Certain Magic*, are both good examples of "high fantasy" romance—peopled as they are with all sorts of fantastical beings including, just to name a few, a war-horse named Lucifer, who can telepathically communicate with the hero (*Demon Prince*) and a black baby dragon named Paddy who bonds with the heroine (*A Certain Magic*).

On the other hand, *Fire Queen*, my second fantasy romance, is a good example of historical fantasy. Aside from a friendly female sorcerer as mentor, the only other magical aspects of the story arise from the heroine's gradual discovery of, and coming to terms with, her own magical powers. To add further to the diverse creative freedom offered by this romance sub-genre, my *Lovespell* fantasy romance, *Strands of Gold*, is both "high fantasy" *and* a fairytale, incorporating the *Rumplestiltskin* fairytale theme as a strong sub-plot, even if a bit modified.

Key Elements

There *are* certain key elements traditionally expected in fantasy fiction:

1. A pre-gunpowder setting.
2. Strange and unusual creatures with special powers.
3. A heroic protagonist who overcomes many obstacles to achieve an important goal.

4. A powerful antagonist—in most cases, one of evil inclinations—whom the hero/heroine must overcome.
5. Magic as an accepted part of the civilization, bound by logical, consistent rules.
6. An epic scope and feel.

Several issues should be considered in the development of your pre-gunpowder setting. All the details of your civilization should be consistently worked out. Your reader must believe that if magic *were* real and utilized in this way, this is the kind of world and society that would result.

However, do *not* overload your reader with all the details of your fantasy world up front. The reader may appreciate them in bits and pieces, but too much too soon will slow the initial and most vital flow of the story, which is not description, but characterization and plot. Start small. Begin with something commonplace to your characters but not to your readers, and gradually lead them deeper into the complexities of your world.

Maps can be useful, not only to keep yourself on track as a writer and to assure that your characters travel in the right direction, but also to help you generate story ideas. Once you can see your physical world clearly, you can also envision what might happen there, too.

The specific geography of your world can lend itself to various adventures and conflicts, not to mention add to the depth and descriptive richness of your story. Consider how capricious mountain weather can be, turning from pristine, sun-drenched beauty to a snarling, vicious hag of a storm in a matter of hours. Note how different the damp, balmy weather of an ocean shore is to that of the blistering, high desert in influencing the way people eke out their livings in these various kinds of terrain. These things affect the way people believe and behave, their legends that evolve, the way their societies develop, and their attitudes toward home and hearth, love, death and strangers.

A successful fantasy world is largely a matter of viewpoint—character viewpoint. There are two kinds of characters, the native-born and the outsider. Whatever the native-born sees and experiences will be in terms of the world he lives in. He won't explain a crow flying overhead as an omen. He automatically *knows* it as an omen, and any of his fellow "native-borns" will automatically know that as well. He'll simply say something like, "I saw a black crow yesterday, and I was afraid." He will *not* explain that a black crow is an omen which means the person who sees it is going to die, etc., etc. Your story should reveal nothing in any character's viewpoint that is outside their realm of experience—whether native born or outsider. If it does, the illusion of a fantasy world will be broken and the reader will be wrenched out of the story.

The appeal of an imaginary world also lies in its detail, detail so realistic the reader can immerse himself in it completely. A reader delights in detail. The more imaginary the lore the better. Help your readers experience your world—help them see it, hear it, smell it, taste it, and feel it. Help your reader *believe*. They want to believe. If they don't it's your fault—and your failure as a writer.

Deep Space to Brooklyn!
Note from Sierra

Oh Miss Kathryn,

Thanks so much for the wonderful "alternatives." Some of the authors and titles mentioned were new to us, but we're getting on RomanticTimes.com and ordering their books. This has really "set me to thinkin'." I had no idea there was so much leeway in writing romance today.

Rosemarie loved everything you sent, and is flirtin' with the idea of one day doing a Scottish historical that incorporates Celtic mysticism in a big way. Until then, she just wants to write true-to-history, big historicals, like those written by her Momma and Virginia Henley. Some standards to live up to, huh?

Jade, on the other hand, now wants to write time travel romances like Diana Gabaldon's "Outlander" series. (We have each read the entire series now and I swear to you, Kathryn, there was a moment when I was about halfway into *Outlander* that I knew I'd been touched by the hand of God. Wow, can that lady put words to a page!)

Anyway, here I am, flyin' too far from Miss Jade's tale. The main reason Jade has decided on time travel romances is she thinks she could make them historically accurate because she has a powerful belief in reincarnation. She's got herself convinced she can just call up memories of past lives any ol' time she needs 'em. She's certain she was a "bound-foot" woman in Beijing a couple of hundred years ago. That reincarnation stuff really excites her. (By the way, Kathryn, didn't I read somewhere that you collect "bound-foot shoes"?)

247

Jade has also been toyin' with an idea for a fantasy fairytale like *Strands of Gold* that Kathleen Morgan wrote. Who knows what next week will bring for that girl! I have a theory that because she is such a tiny thing, "any ol' wind picks her up and moves her around a bit."

As for me, this batch of articles, and in particular Sandra Kitt's inspiring words, clarified something I had mulled over a while back and then tucked deep away. I am now sure I want to write an authentic multicultural novel that *I would like to read*, and that every other person, regardless of race, creed, and color will find compelling to read, too. Could you give me more direction as to how to do this?

There are so many African-American and Hispanic books available now that the "ethnic" section of my local bookstore is enormous. Now this is a bandwagon I want to climb right up on and cheer!.

Throw it all at me, Lady Barrow; I am reeeeaaaddy!

Sierra

Chapter VIII

THE MULTI-CULTURAL MARKET

Kathryn Falk, Lady of Barrow
Romantic Times Magazine
Brooklyn, New York

Dear Sierra!

You have found the key for deciding what kind of book you should write: It's the book *you* want to read. I can't begin to tell you how many writers sat up one day and decided to do exactly that, and the results were bestsellers. If wanting to write what you *love* is your motivation, you're on your way to conceiving a powerful outline and an outstanding book.

About those bound-foot shoes—you were right. I have been collecting them, and now have 60 pairs. Except for one novel, *Golden Lotus Slippers*, published by the University of Hawaii press, I've never seen a lengthy work that incorporates this subject. I have found the study of other cultures opens our minds and hearts to so many interesting things.

We live in a changing world—John Kenneth Galbraith calls it a "Global Village." Ethnic groups are shifting and growing, affecting what we watch on television and in movies, and giving new direction to what we write.

An excellent example of this is found in the romance publishing industry, where there is now a new romance readership, reflective of a large segment of the younger group of readers—all part of the new multi-ethnic canvas of America, and the world.

Growing African-American, Hispanic, and Asian populations have demanded better representation in films, television productions, and literature, and moviemakers and publishers have listened.

At the present time, two publishers—BET Books and Genesis Press—produce both African-American and Latino/Hispanic romance lines. Genesis' *Love Spectrum* line of interracial love stories, introduced in 1998, has been a huge success. In the face of all this, other publishers are considering introducing multicultural lines of their own. Until that happens, there is already another market in place for ethnic romances as almost every publisher is buying multicultural novels on a "one-book" basis.

Sadly, Asian romances, with the exception of a few historicals, have yet to be developed. Oh, there are mainstream novels reflecting Asian culture: Amy Tan is one of the leading luminaries with her *Joy Luck Club*, and Linda Ching Sledge writes great multicultural historicals (*A Map of Paradise*, set in Hawaii, and *Empire of Heaven*, set in China.) But, a line of Asian romances? That hasn't happened yet. However, Genesis Press is launching it's *Red Slipper* line of Asian and Asian-American love stories in 1999, leading the way in a promising new writing field.

Genesis publisher, Wil Colom, originator of the Multicultural Romance lines, *Indigo, Tango 2,* and *Love Spectrum,* believes fiction requires a large middle class—people with some free time on their hands and money to buy books—in order to generate a great market for books. In sheer numbers alone, there is now a huge African-American middle class and a rapidly expanding Hispanic/Latino middle class. However, as yet, there is not as large an Asian middle class.

Read the enclosed articles, and then ask yourself two important questions: "Do I passionately want to write about any of these cultures?" and "Am I capable of writing a multicultural romance or Mainstream ethnic romantic novel?" (After all, you'll need to know the culture you'll be writing about inside out, backward and forward.)

A few authors, like Beverly Jenkins, are able to publish fascinating ethnic historicals within the genre, conveying large amounts of authentic history, affirming Emerson's dictum that, "There is properly no history, only biography." For the most part, though, the ethnic romances that are being bought are primarily contemporaries.

Romantic Times magazine has reviewed every African-American romance published since the beginning of the development of this sub-genre, and all the titles are listed on our web site.

Many exciting ethnic writers have emerged since the mid-90's. I have asked a wonderful line-up of African-American authors, as well as Hebby Roman (latino romances), and the great Kathleen Eagle (Indian romances) to give you their views on this rising sub-genre of romance.

In order to give you some insight into the changes which have taken place in ethnic publishing, and also to give you a peek into what motivates publishers, I have included an interview with Wil Colom—the tall, gorgeous publisher of Genesis Press, Inc. He is a true romantic, and a publisher who takes a decidedly personal interest in the books that are chosen for his firm!

Best Wishes,

Kathryn

"I wanted characters that reflected my experiences. So, I sat down and constructed multi-layered, textured characters. My women have the three S's—Sense, Sanity and Self-esteem…and I give them men who deserve them."
—Gay G. Gunn

The Changing Face and Voice of Romance Publishing
An Interview with
Wil Colom, Publisher, Genesis Press, Inc.

Q. Without having your accomplishment in publishing Ethnic Romance come across as being one of those, "bravely-go-where-few-have-ever-gone-before" sorts of things, nonetheless, we do need to emphasize that you have been one of a handful of pioneers in the advancement of this sub-genre. How did you, in particular, take up this flag to wave?

I like new ideas; I have a brain that is never still. A few years ago, my daughter, Nyani, came to me with an idea to start a company that would publish "ethnic" romance. It was a terrific idea. The result was Genesis Press and its Indigo line. Then, after things were underway, graduate studies beckoned my daughter to Paris. I took charge of the company and instantly loved the people I met (who were involved with the genre), found them to be interesting and exciting. Publishing is fun. I enjoy it tremendously.

Q. Why this genre?

I *live* in that universe. The idea to publish "ethnic" romance originally came from my wife, Dorothy, Nyani, and others who were reading all these romances and not finding any Black heroes and heroines. I visited large publishing houses and would see on their slush piles, many unpublished romances written by Black authors. Now, realize…romance *readers* are romance *writers*, so I knew there was already a demand and a market out there for these books. So far, I've been proven right.

Q. Why now? Why not 20, 30, 40 years ago?

One of the big, "un-kept" secrets in this country is this: Due largely to the success of the civil rights movement and the resulting greater assimilation of Blacks into society, there is now a huge, well-educated, literate, Black middle class in America. For the large part, these are people who were directly affected by the civil rights movement—people who lived through the sixties…and *their* children. They are professional people; doctors, lawyers, and business owners with—*for the first time in history*—enough disposable income to allow them to buy books and read romance. They move in professional circles where the contemporary stories of romance between successful people are now meaningful for them. We have such distorted images of Blacks through the media, but the reality is, there are large numbers of Blacks in America going on cruises, to the theater, etc. There are more Black millionaires in the United States than in several small European and African countries, combined. However, this is a phenomenon of this time and a newer generation. If you look at Blacks over age sixty, only 4% have college degrees. If you look at Blacks in their 20's, a large percentage have college degrees. In Mississippi, where I practice law, there isn't one Black lawyer older than 55.

Q. What sets "ethnic" romances apart from others?

Some say that all a writer has to do to write an Ethnic or Multicultural Romance is take any tale of two people in love, change any reference in that romance from "blonde and blue-eyed" to "black-haired and brown-eyed" and that changes the ethnicity of the characters. There is a part of me that agrees that all situations should apply to all people, but Black women write in a different way, more in the passive voice— "We be this way"—that goes way back to Africa. The cadence in the writing is different. The Black women I know tend to have "public" and "private" voices. My wife, who is a judge, sounds one way when she's at work and another way when she's at home. This "voice" is hard to imitate and critical to the portrayal of any character or group.

Also, there is a reaction to sexuality that is different in many Black women. They can be more sexually aggressive, more direct in what they want. Having said that, I must temper it by saying the Black woman of today is more and more assimilated into a larger culture and moving closer to the mainstream.

Q. Well then, is it even <u>possible</u> to write cross-culturally? Does a writer have to be Black to write romances for Blacks, Asian to write for Asians, etc.?

I don't think it's necessary to be White to write a White character, any more than it is necessary to have lived in the eleventh century to write a Medieval Romance! Research, research, research! For the most part, romances are *read* and have been *written* exclusively by women. Publishers feel—and sales have concurred—romances sell best if the writer is thought to be a woman. Men who write romance do so (for the most part) under pseudonyms. Will the same thing happen with ethnic/multicultural romances? Will they sell better if the reader thinks the writer is African-American/Hispanic/Asian? We'll have to wait to see. Will my company publish a story about one ethnic group, written by a writer of another ethnic group? Try me.

Q. What can a writer of a different culture/race do to increase his/ her chances of selling a cross-cultural manuscript?

Above all else, have the right ethnic voice—and you absolutely *can* write "a voice."

Q. How can you find this "ethnic" voice?

The same way you "find" characters. Use someone you know. Listen to him or her; pick up his/her voice. Get pleasure out of writing that is not in the same cadence and voice as your own. In the end, it all comes down to what the author feels comfortable with…and writing a darn good yarn.

Q. A number of the agents and publishers equate "ethnic" with African-American or Black. If <u>they</u> feel this way, then it is probable that this is the public's perception, as well. How difficult is it going to be to change this perception—to pull Hispanic/Latino and Asian under the umbrella of the ethnic genre?

It will be slow. It will take time, but eventually it will happen. The same thing is happening with Latinos now as happened to Blacks fifteen years ago: economic growth and a corresponding rise in the middle class. Now that Hispanics have risen to a certain economic level where they have enough disposable income to spend on books, they will *demand* books whose characters mirror their own ethnic groups.

Q. Where does Genesis Press come in?
In addition to Indigo, our line of African-American romances, we have added two new romance lines: Tango 2, a line of Hispanic-themed romances and, Red Slipper, written for the Asian-American market, which will debut in 1999.

We have shown there *are* good writers of African-American ethnic fiction and there *is* a market for these books. We want to do the same with Hispanic and Asian fiction.

Q. At Genesis, it seems as though you encourage new writers.
We do. Recently, we ran a contest asking for manuscripts and received some very good submissions. In general, there is still a shortage of *excellent* manuscripts, and improving on that will take time, but there are also some wonderful writers of the genre such as Donna Hill, Gay G. Gunn, Sandra Kitt, and Gwynn Forster.

Soon there will emerge a Black, Hispanic, or Asian writer who is just about the sauciest writer around and she'll capture the historical romance market. Then there will be the "swooner," and she will be the best at that and capture the next wave of the romance market ...and so on

Q. Is there anything really different you would like to receive?
I would love to see more stories with a White female and Black male. Let's face it, though, romance writing is all about fantasy—getting a woman's fantasy onto paper, and I don't feel that the Black male/White female relationship has been a fantasy for a lot of women out there—Denzel Washington being the exception, of course! Having said that, let me just add, we've just launched our *Love Spectrum* imprint with Dar Tomlinson's *Forbidden Quest,* which features a Black Jamaican hero and a genteel Southern White heroine, and sales have been quite brisk.

These books are a female fantasy of relationships. Some people say "female pornography," but I would definitely dispute that. I believe every woman has one secret fantasy—a scene she relives over and over in her mind—and she will buy any book that writes about it.

Q. Female fantasy, hmmm? Do you really believe in that?
Completely! I tell men I know, "Learn your woman's fantasy. If you fulfill that fantasy, it will pay back tenfold." You don't even have to exert yourself in a great way. Do something, like write your wife a little note in the morning that says, *You were asleep when I left and I stood for a while and adored you while you slept. I didn't disturb you then . . . but I intend to tonight.* Then, leave the note where she'll find it!

Q. Romance must be important to you, personally, Wil. And not just the romance found in your books!
Oh, it is...it is! I say to people all the time, "I love my wife more now than when I married her and there isn't anything I wouldn't do for her." She's a beautiful woman, I love the smell of her breath . . . the turning of her head . . . the curve of her arm . . .

Q. Whew! No wonder you publish romance!
(Laughter!)

Q. Wil, upon thinking this one over, I conclude you <u>have</u> "bravely gone . . ." and all that; you <u>have</u> been a pioneer in advancing the genre. What next?
I intend to publish more broad-based books, more sensuous, more traditional books, children's books and non-fiction. I also want to do some things related to theatrics: produce plays, movies, etc. Technology will make it such that within two decades a small group of people in Mississippi will be able to make movies just as well as the millionaires in Hollywood. I am trying to carve out my own special niche.

Q. It sounds like you already have.

Interview by Ann Peach
* * *

"We're pulling for you to write an ethnic/multicultural romance. Perhaps one day you will write one about you and your roommates? It sounds like your writers' colony is a mini-United Nations."

Researching and Writing a Multicultural Romance

By Shirley Hailstock

The ethnic/multicultural romance sub-genre has developed and burst onto the "screen" much like a movie star's career. Writers of ethnic fiction have been trying to sell their stories for decades; now, suddenly, they're overnight sensations.

Since everyone is part of one culture or another, for publishing purposes we define the multicultural romance sub-genre as, a romance in which at least one of the main characters is a member of one of the minority races in the United States. As of this writing, these books have featured mainly African-American characters as the major players.

Spanish translations of some category and Indian romances, which had previously been considered historicals, are suddenly popping up in the "ethnic" classification.

The basic elements of an ethnic romance novel are the same as they are for any well-written romance novel: great characters, fascinating, well-thought-out plot, interesting setting, sexual tension, and taut pacing, etc. The only difference between non-ethnic and multicultural romances is: Books written by African-American, Hispanic, or Indian women bring a new perspective to the genre, a new view to tried and true relationships.

First and foremost multicultural romances are love stories. At the core of each is the one-man-one-woman romance. Around it, nurturing it, helping it grow is the inclusion of the culture, foods, clothing, and lifestyles of the characters. Everyday living is interpretive and open to use, but the differences between a romance with an "ethnic" slant and one of the non-ethnic novels we've been reading for years, encompass the following:

Background is probably the most significant difference. Life experiences that define character are part of the culture that formulates ethnicity, whether African-American, Hispanic, Indian, or Jewish, etc. For example, I have heard writers say, "It's impossible to understand guilt if you weren't raised Catholic."

Many African-Americans grew up in the Baptist Church, which presents its own set of taboos and restraints. Most people who grew up in a Southern Baptist community probably spent from sunup to sundown at church on any given Sunday. Everything from three significant meals to courtship and marriage occurred at church functions. Those communal experiences can be used to give unique attributes to ethnic heroes and heroines.

Growing up is different for every individual—even members of the same household do not have the same experiences. However, the experiences they do share are culturally separable, and used in the definition of character.

Traditions further enhance the "ethnicity" of a romance. These rituals usually revolve around holidays. Many families celebrate holidays with specific ceremonies or practices that are unique to them.

Since 1966, the concept of Kwanzaa, a celebration in kinship for African-Americans, has begun to be practiced in addition to, or in place of, Christmas.

The eating of specific foods as a first meal on New Year's Day is part of my family tradition. Each food has a meaning geared toward the coming year. This holds true in other cultures as well. In the Chinese culture there are many traditions which are practiced to ensure prosperity for the New Year, or to rid the family of bad omens that will cloud the future. These include beginning the year with no clothes in need of mending, and owing no debt. Many days of preparation go into the celebration of the New Year.

Making elements which are taken for granted by one culture part of the makeup of the characters adds flavor and makes for a better read.

Methods of Speaking and Expression are combined because they go hand in hand. While expression can be hard to describe, it can play a strong part in a story. You might think expressions are universal, but think of the use of hands in speaking by Italian-Americans and you realize there are differences. Without question, the "feet-apart, hands-on-hips, cocked-head" stance is a patented gesture of the African-American female showing her disapproval or disbelief. In addition, we mustn't forget the mere raising of an eyebrow, the subtle turning of a head in a certain direction, or the lifting of an arm to curtail an action while sitting in church.

Speech Patterns provide for a wide range of colorful characters. Among African-Americans alone, there is street language; the King's English; proper American English; and the drawling accent and cadence of the American South. The use of slang is sometimes prevalent in the African-American community. We no longer call each other "sister," but we do use words like "girlfriend," and expressions like "You go 'gurl'!"

Language is also used differently within each setting. At home there is a more relaxed method of communication than will be found in the workplace, or in a mixed cultural environment. While phonetics or dialect is difficult to read and write, voice is clear, and when set apart can be quite identifiable.

Description can be easy or difficult to convey. Physical attributes can be anything. African-Americans run the full gamut of color schemes and features. They can be as patrician and angular as traditional heroes and heroines, but they can also be softly rounded.

Color of Skin is usually dark, and often likened to food, such as coffee or honey. Coffee when mixed with cream ranges from black to off-white, and this gives a huge variety of descriptive areas to draw upon. New words to describe color have cropped up in the writers' vocabulary, where "tanned" used to be the only version of dark. "Sienna," "palomino," and "peanut butter" have joined "wheat," "straw," and "porcelain" as descriptions of skin color.

Hair is another area that is as varied as the weather. Today, African-American women have everything from chemically straightened or relaxed hair to the natural look. Elaborate designs of braided hair and in a few cases even baldness can be done. Hairstyles don't so easily come undone as they do for non-African-Americans. Hair doesn't usually "flow like curtains or panels" to hide expressions, although this is not totally out of the question.

There are also African-Americans with hair that is fine and flowing, and that needs little or no relaxation. They may be the most difficult to describe as "ethnic" because they have many of the features of traditional heroines.

Occupation is open. African-Americans occupy all levels of the economic chain in the United States, and outside. From industry Vice Presidents and CEO's of major corporations, to workers at social development agencies such as Manpower, you can find African-Americans.

Setting can be in any part of the world. The ethnic books I've read tend to be limited to African-Americans, and are set in the United States or Caribbean Islands. Yet there is a large population of people with West Indian heritage living in England. In Paris there are war babies from the Second World War of Black descent. These war babies are over fifty years old with grown children of their own who would be perfect featured in multicultural romances.

Any of these cultures can bring new vision to the multicultural romance sub-genre and be the basis of wonderful love stories. And do not forget the Vietnam War, one of the results of which is a population of African-American/Vietnamese children who are now in their twenties or thirties. They will bring an even greater cultural background to the multicultural romance—turning it instantly into a "rulti-cultural romance."

Writing the multicultural romance is a challenge, but it is no greater a challenge than writing any good book. Begin by crafting a wonderful love story incorporating the diverse characters and cultures present in the world around us, whether in the world of today, the historical past, or at a future time period. Enrich that story with customs, language, traditions and lifestyles unique to the characters' backgrounds; exclude stereotypes; and you will have a book that appeals to everyone, regardless of their personal culture.

"Your words are like pebbles tossed into a lake. Who knows what far reaches the resulting ripples may make? Share your culture, your experiences, your dreams and your perceptions with the reader. Toss those pebbles, and you may change the world—one reader at a time."
Mildred Riley

* * *

"Ten years ago I never dreamed that I would be writing romance for one of the fastest growing markets. However, today, at last, I am."

How I Finally Got Published

By Marcia King Gamble

I was raised on Mills and Boon books, the only series romances you could get your hands on in the Caribbean. When I moved to the United States, I graduated to Harlequin. When I was a teenager, all of the heroes and heroines in the books I read were Caucasians. While I enjoyed the novels, and fantasized about the exotic locales, as a Black woman I found it difficult to identify with the heroine whose *"long blonde hair swayed in the breeze while the hero's warm blue eyes regarded her with passion."*

One thing, though, I knew I wanted to write, and always firmly believed that there was a market out there somewhere for people like me.

My initial efforts in the early '90's were, of course, directed to Harlequin, Silhouette, and Bantam, because those were the only houses I knew about. By then, I had become an educated reader and knew that to sell, I would have to make my heroes and heroines Caucasian. Even knowing that, I would occasionally slip in a heroine of mixed race, and though rejection after rejection followed, I remained optimistic, reminding myself of the "nice" rejections I'd received. That was at least the way I interpreted the gentle "No-thank-you's" that followed. I always considered myself one of the lucky ones; editors reading my work seemed to like my voice, even if the storyline wasn't quite right for their line.

In July of 1994, when the Arabesque line launched, I was immediately drawn to the sepia covers. I spent hours in bookstores, staring, touching covers, and flipping pages, unable to believe these books were real. While it might have taken some time, we Black people had finally been recognized, both as readers and as people who fall in love. During those months of staring and touching, I never left the store without purchasing the two books per month that Arabesque offered.

When I read the stories, I became filled with an indescribable pride. Page after page was filled with African-American role models, people to whom I could relate. I knew within my heart I wanted to write for that line, and I focused all my efforts toward that end—spending a great deal of time visualizing. I saw myself at book signings, speaking to inner city kids, educating the reading public, and serving as a role model.

Somewhere in the back of my mind it registered that I probably would have a better shot of being published if I directed my efforts at this new line, which actively solicited new authors. Ironically, I had met Monica Harris, the editor responsible for launching Arabesque, at a conference and had even had a lengthy conversation with her.

Here's where I learned a painful first lesson about keeping abreast of the market. When I spoke with Monica, I was under the impression her sole focus was historicals. I didn't write historicals, so I thought I had nothing to pitch. However, she *did* accept contemporary romances, and I had lost out on a perfectly good opportunity to sell the manuscript I was currently working on. Talk about wanting to kick myself.

Several months later, after my first two manuscripts were rejected, I had called myself every name in the book. By then I had acquired an agent and, with both of us working to promote me, I am certain the publishing company was sick of hearing my name, and promptly discarding my submissions.

My first Arabesque effort, an interracial romance set on a fictitious Caribbean island, got nixed. I called it my "Eliza Doolittle/ Henry Higgins" tale. My second attempt—a reluctantly retired hero (a soon-to-be-retired basketball player with a bad knee) and his love interest, a lead singer of an all-female rock band—fared no better. Lesson number two? Athletes and artsy types rarely sell. With rejection number two under my belt, it took everything I had to remain optimistic. I constantly reminded myself that Monica had kept this latest manuscript almost eight months. She'd even encouraged me to submit additional work.

Buoyed by the thought there was hope, I embarked on my third Arabesque novel. In my quest to find the missing ingredient, I read every romance novel I could get my hands on. As a result, my first romantic suspense was born. I wanted this story to be poignant, to be something every woman could relate to—a real "gut-wrencher." I've always been a sucker for stories in which long-lost lovers reunite, but my plot would have a twist to it; a pervert, who just might be the love interest, would stalk my heroine. I called this love story, *Coffee Mates*, getting the idea for the title from a New Jersey dating service with the zippy name, "Chocolate Singles." I put my heart in this book and my emotions on the line. I submitted the first three chapters to Monica and waited.

Dear Ms. King-Gamble;

Thank you for your patience and allowing me to see your partial manuscript. I like your voice, the cruise idea, and the mystery angle. However, I am quite disturbed by the stalker who taunts our heroine …the sexual taunts are too heavy-handed for this list. Therefore I will not make an offer on this version.

I hope I am not too discouraging; you are a strong writer. Please keep me in mind for any other fiction you may have.

Sincerely,
Monica Harris, Arabesque Line

It was hard to remain positive, but I focused on the words, "I will not make an offer on *this* version." Did that mean if I submitted *another* version, she would be interested? I made the recommended changes in ten minutes, and shipped the manuscript back with two brand new chapters. Several weeks passed.

Then I got the call.

When I heard Monica Harris's voice on the other end of the line it took every ounce of self-control not to scream. With a fourth monthly Arabesque slot now open, my dream was about to be realized.

One revision later, *Coffee Mates* became *Remembrance*. I felt lucky; my third title was chosen. Many authors never have any say in what their novels are named. What I think made this story sell was the suspense interwoven with nostalgia. I'd relied upon my memories of attending a small liberal arts college in upstate New York . . . of being in love with love . . . of the way women bonded with each other. I counted on the fact that a woman never forgets her first lover, or his first betrayal. Even though some of us may deny it, years later when we meet again at a reunion, whether he is overweight and bald, rich or poor, married or unmarried, the sight of him creates havoc on our hormones and dredges up a lot of lustful/hurtful emotions.

When I created my hero, Devin Spencer, I had a particular man in mind. He was the man of my dreams: successful, sensitive, and devastatingly handsome. I'd recently connected with an ex-boyfriend after several years, and though I was never in love with the man, I can tell you, that first sight of him caused my knees to buckle. I tried to bring the same electrical connection to my heroine's first encounter with her ex-lover.

Here's an excerpt.

At a loss for words, Charlie stared into his soft gray eyes. What she saw in their depths forced her to look away. Had time also made Devin forget the reality of the situation?

A woman also never forgets good sex, and since most good sex is mental, it is especially memorable between two people who care about each other. When lovers reunite, they're bonded by memories, and overly sensitive to each other's touch. I tried to bring this heightened sense of awareness to Charlie and Devin's heated sexual reunion. Do you think I achieved it?

His fingers lingered at the nape of her neck before turning her around to face him. When he spoke, his voice was low and urgent, his eyes intense. His kisses left her unable to concentrate, much less respond. Little jolts of electricity ricocheted through her body, leaving her tingling all over.

*Rational thought disappeared. Reality lost its meaning as the rhythm
picked up. Charlie whirled out of control.*

At one point, my heroine, Charlie, reminisces about meeting her
college roommates for the first time. I used that opportunity to remind my readers that my characters were Black.

Here is an excerpt from this first encounter.

*Charlie still remembered her first day at Mount Merrimack. She'd
walked to her assigned suite and damn near died. It had been plain old
Charlie Canfield's luck to be matched with three of the best looking
women the college had recruited.*

*The first to introduce herself had been Lisa Williams, a petite cof-
fee-skinned beauty with a wild mane of hair and the personality of
bubbling brown sugar. She'd then shook the hand of Onike Hamilton,
a half African/half British combination of classic good looks, and subtle
sex appeal. Her cafe au lait complexion, cluster of freckles, and amazing
brain had kept the men drooling all that year.*

*Then she'd met Kim—Kimberly Morgan, who became her best friend
and worst nightmare. Statuesque Kim, who in her stocking feet fell short
of six feet by only half an inch, whose bra size was a smidgen short of
thirty-eight D, and whom all the men desired and ultimately had.*

I am not alone in my desire to reach out to "our" Black readers.
Like me, most ethnic authors write about Black people who, although originally from various socio-economic backgrounds, have
now "made it." We portray middle class Blacks with careers and families; people with productive lives, who travel, meet, fall in love, and
eventually marry; and men and women who practice safe sex, live
independent of welfare, and aspire to be happy, productive beings.

Of course, I can only speak for myself, but I use my stories to
educate, to eradicate the myth of the chauvinistic, insensitive, Black
male unable to show feeling. I aim to educate my Caucasian readers
and dispel the stereotypes that prevail in the media. We are not all
from the ghetto and dependent on a welfare check to get by. Our
people come in myriad shapes and sizes. Many have gray, green, or
even blue eyes. Our men are not all in jail, nor do all our women end
up teenage casualties, i.e., babies having babies.

Those who have read *Remembrance* have told me they feel a remarkable bond with both hero and heroine. Women have told me especially, that Devin, my hero, is a dream come true. I've also been told my heroine, Charlie, represents the strong, vulnerable, working single parent not uncommon in many Black households. I've also been told I could have made the book "more Black." Whatever that's supposed to mean.

Readers apparently agree with my take on these romances. I once again find it increasingly harder to find multicultural romances in stores, but this time it is because our books are flying off the shelves so fast that if you're not in the store at the beginning of the month, you're compelled to special order. Word has since spread in the mass market that our books are well-written romances, dealing with topical issues. Readership has shifted, and we are starting to break the color barrier. Our books are no longer pigeonholed as "those romances Black people read."

My fellow authors each bring something different to the table. I have become interested in them as people, and eagerly read their biographies before reading the works they pen. Ethnic authors seem to have several things in common: most are educated, successful, confident, and driven by the need to share their experiences. Several hold master's degrees, and, in addition to writing several books a year, hold down full time jobs. Their stories are rich in detail, and deal with the positive side of the Black experience.

I am proud to be one of the growing number of writers of multicultural romance, for we've filled a much-needed niche in the romance market. One in every five people in the United States is non-White—a reality that cosmetics companies acknowledged years ago when they expanded and enhanced their product lines, thus ensuring a profitable bottom line.

The publishing industry has finally come to recognize these shifting demographics as well. Romance novels, after all, account for nearly 50% of all mass market paperback book sales, and more than one third of those buyers are women and men of color. Who could doubt that multicultural romance is here to stay?

"Throughout history, there had to have been beautiful, creative Black women, who were intelligent and filled with passion. Not all Black women could have been domestics, farm wives or nursemaids, as portrayed in so many books. The Black women I knew personally, were experiencing love, thinking about happiness, and dreaming about better lives. However, this was never shown in the books I was reading. So, I decided to pen my own stories, creating popular fiction with Black heroes and heroines who would sweep me into their lives."
—Anita Richmond Bunkley

* * *

"I have made a niche for myself as a writer of historical romances, and I think other writers can do the same. I would like to help you add authenticity to your 'ethnicity.'"

Writing the Historical Multicultural Romance

By Beverly Jenkins

Ten years ago, the number of romances targeted towards minority readers was . . . nil. Publishers had not yet awakened to the fact that minority women—particularly Black women—were a potent force in the book-buying market.

Then, the unprecedented, best-seller success of Terry McMillan's *Waiting to Exhale* effectively killed the myth that Black women did not buy books. As a result, publishers began looking for ways to tap into this juggernaut.

The summer of 1994 is often referred to as, "The Summer of Black Romance," for it was then that BET Books introduced its new Arabesque line—contemporary romances, written by Black women, primarily for Black romance readers. The novels were immediately embraced. Avon books also entered the minority market that summer with the release of its first African-American historical romance, my first published novel, *Night Song*.

These "new" romances were met with much fanfare, and a flood of Black romances followed. Almost overnight, minority women not only had stories that reflected their own cultures but also, for the first time, were afforded the opportunity to pen their own.

There's been a lot of debate as to whether multicultural romances can, and should, be written by authors outside the culture. I have no plans to weigh in on either side, but my advice for anyone attempting multicultural romance for the first time is to please, know the culture you plan to write about. Some writers believe changing eye color is all that is necessary. Wrong! If that's your only "ethnic" touch, ethnic readers will be able to tell right away how familiar/unfamiliar you are with their culture, and will judge you accordingly. There is no way I could have written, or even attempted to write, a book such as Amy Tan's *The Joy Luck Club,* because I know nothing about the rhythms and influences which shaped the life of the Asian-American author and her family. All writers thinking of entering this subgenre need to ask themselves if what they know about any culture is based upon an intimate knowledge, or on the very misguided stereotypes offered to us by the media. Just as "Beavis and Butthead" do not represent most mainstream American teenagers, most of what is being fed to us as "Black life" by Hollywood and the television networks, does not accurately reflect the lives of Black Americans, either today . . . or in the past.

HISTORY

In order to write African-American historicals, extensive research is absolutely necessary. Blacks were more than just slaves. They fought bravely in all of the nation's wars—from the American Revolution to the Gulf War. Black men were whalers, explorers, and outlaws. They mined gold in California in 1849 and helped open the west. Black women owned businesses before and after slavery, taught school, and in 1832, a Black woman named Maria W. Stewart stepped up and became the first American woman to ever lecture before a gender-mixed audience.

Where do you find this information? Begin with the basics. A great source of information is *Before the Mayflower* by Lerone Bennett Jr., published initially in 1962. This book is still in print. It has been updated more than a few times since the early sixties (my newest edition is the sixth), and each new release offers more information on the prominent yet often neglected role Black Americans played in the history of this country. After reading Mr. Bennett's book, pick out a certain period or aspect of Black history you wish to highlight in your novel, and start focusing your research toward that goal. If you decide you want to do a Black western, then you need books on Blacks in the west. Two of the best are *The Black West*, written by William Loren Katz, and *Black, Red, and Deadly*, by Art Burton.

Perhaps you want to concentrate on Black women of the nineteenth century? The book you must have is *We Are Your Sisters*, edited by Dorothy Sterling. This book has fueled more than a few ideas for the characters and settings in my novels. I highly recommend you *purchase* your history books if at all possible, so that they will be readily available.

I write about everyday Black people, whose hopes and dreams are no different from the hopes and dreams of mainstream Americans. However, I would be doing my readers a disservice by pretending my characters were not impacted by Black history. The laws of the nineteenth century limited access to transportation, schooling, and employment for America's Black population, both slave and free, so my characters' lives must reflect that fact, while still showing the strides the race made in spite of these social and legal limitations. The post-Civil War Jim Crow laws of the nineteenth century kept us from carrying the mail, voting, and traveling first class, among other things, but did not stop us from founding all-Black towns, building colleges, or from celebrating holidays.

I use books like *The Black Press*, edited by Martin E. Dann, to put me in touch with nineteenth-century Black thought. It offers not only the history of nineteenth century Black newspapers, but also letters to the editors, and editorials as well. Mr. Dann's book gives a unique look at how members of the race viewed the world around them. The writers of both the editorials and the letters intelligently debate everything from emigration to Africa, to the Redemptionists in the South, to the rise of Jim Crow; but none employ the stereotypical dialect used so prevalently by Blacks portrayed in movies and on television. There were many articulate and well-educated Blacks in this country, and writers of Black historicals need to keep that fact in mind.

The Journal of Negro History, which can be found in both public and college libraries, is also an excellent source for the history of the Black race. Its articles, written by many prominent historians, shed light on everything from the Black lawmen of the west, to the Black slave-owners of antebellum Louisiana.

CHARACTERS

In Sterling's *We Are Your Sisters*, the author cites three elements as the fuel for the unprecedented strides Black women made in the years after the civil war. These "gifts," passed down by the Black women before the Civil War, are a strong work ethic; a commitment to community through social activism; and the penchant to push beyond the boundaries of race and gender.

A short history lesson: If you were a Black woman in the US before the Civil War, you were either enslaved in the South, or free in the segregated North. Both classes of women had something in common—both worked. In the South, slave women worked right beside their men and, like men, were expected to pull their weight. After work, she went home, prepared meals, and saw to the needs of her family.

In the segregated, free North, women also worked, not because they had a feminist desire to prove themselves equal, but because—as shown in the diaries of these women—they already knew they were equals. They worked because it was necessary. If you didn't have a man, you worked to feed yourself and/or your family. If you were married and your husband did not own his own business or property (and many did), you worked. The additional income was needed because the menial jobs forced upon men of color were usually not enough to make ends meet.

When opportunities for all women increased after the Civil War, these women were able to take advantage of the opened doors, because they were already accustomed to being in the work place.

The second part of the legacy revolves around political and social activism. In 1840, there were nearly 400,000 free Blacks in the major cities of the segregated North, and the numbers would climb higher as more and more slaves either escaped or purchased their freedom. Contrary to popular belief, William Lloyd Garrison and Harriet Beecher Stowe were not the first, and only, abolitionists.

Blacks began petitioning the US government for equal rights in the 1700's, and were at the forefront of the struggle through the 1840's and 50's as the country slid down the slippery slope to war. Standing right beside these Black men were Black women.

This nation's first Female Anti-Slavery Society was formed in 1832 by the Black women of Salem, Massachusetts. Another early Black women's group was the African Female Benevolent Society of Newport, Rhode Island, formed in 1809. In 1821, a group of Philadelphia washer women and domestics calling themselves Daughters of Africa, pooled their pennies to pay the sick and death benefits for the needy in the community, thus forming what could be termed one of America's first insurance enterprises.

Abolitionist activity was also an offshoot of this second gift. Black women raised funds, solicited clothing for impoverished runaways, and gave anti-slavery speeches. In 1831, the Black women at Philadelphia's Bethel A.M.E. began to embrace a movement known as Free Produce. Supporters of Free Produce hoped to impact slavery by boycotting all items made by slave labor, such as American grown cotton and sugar. These foremothers of the 1840's and '50's routed slave catchers, marched in rallies, and helped "rescue" from courtrooms escaped slaves being tried under the Fugitive Slave Act. Black women were so active during the 1850's, that at one point, the *Colored American*, one of the leading Black newspapers, urged Black men to please keep their women at home.

The propensity Black women have for pushing beyond gender and race is what I consider the most lasting and important gift of the elements cited by Sterling. Our refusal to be told what we can and cannot accomplish gave rise to such women as the aforementioned Maria W. Stewart, Mary Shadd, one of the first women on the North American continent to edit and publish her own newspaper, and the many Black female physicians who hung up their shingles after the Civil War.

It also gave rise to me. *Night Song* would never have been published had I taken "no" for an answer.

All of these gifts have served the race well, and continue to mold Black women today. Use them to mold your own characters. Use them to give your characters strength, dignity, and purpose, no matter the story you intend to tell. Cara Lee Henson in my first novel, *Night*

Song, is a dedicated schoolteacher; Viveca Lancaster of *Vivid* is a physician; Hester Wyatt, the heroine of *Indigo* is an Underground Railroad conductor and an active abolitionist. In my fourth novel, *Topaz,* Katherine Love is an investigative reporter and women's rights crusader. They are each in their own way embodiments of the three gifts.

My heroes are always men of action who mirror these same qualities. We hear very little about the positive roles Black men have played in the forming of the nation. History <u>does not</u> support the myth that they were shiftless, wife-beating, non-contributing, members of American society. However, research *does* support their bravery, their commitment to education and family, and their never-ending quest for justice.

SETTINGS

Every writer weaves stories in unique ways. I like to weave mine atop the real paths Black people walked. In that way, I don't have to answer the oft-asked question, "Did Black people *really* do that? I include the bibliography so the facts can be verified. I hope that as more and more African-American history rises and is rediscovered, such questions will cease to be necessary.

Where my stories are set is never a problem. There were all-Black communities in nearly every state in the nation following the Civil War. Before the War, nearly 400,000 Black folks resided in the major cities of the northeast such as Boston, Philadelphia, and New York. Each of these communities is an excellent place for launching stories. Most Blacks had their own churches, schools, and community activities, all elements you can use to give your stories depth and background. There were Black-owned theaters, hotels, and Mississippi paddleboats. There were Black hospitals, colleges, and social clubs. I have yet to come across any aspect of mainstream society that was not mirrored by the Black race, in some form or another.

I am often challenged on my insistence upon capitalizing the word Black when referring to the race. My response is this: I find the non-capitalization of the word Black when referring to the race quite offensive because, we are a race of peoples—we are not black cars, black crayons, or black shoes. I usually ask people to write this sentence: At the party were a Hispanic woman, two Asian men, a Jewish professor and three black people sitting on a black sofa. Once the sentence is written down and read, my point is usually made. I don't care to debate with the language and grammar police over why the word, Black, is not capitalized when referring to the race. I know their reasons, and I also know it took these same fools nearly a half century to finally sanction the capitalization of the word Negro, so I do not wait for others to empower me; I empower myself.

Remember, the following are essential if you want to pen a multicultural romance all readers will love:

Don't settle for stereotypes in any shape or form.

Finish the book.

*"I entered publishing in the area of romance because the
genre dictates that the hero is honorable and must have
integrity, and the heroine has wonderfully redeeming
qualities. In that regard, for African-Americans, the romance
genre is much more progressive in accepting this axiom for
'our' heroes and heroines than any other genre at this time."*
—Leslie Esdaile

* * *

*"Stir up a pot full of 'Multicultural
Gumbo' with me and you just might
find you've got exactly the right
recipe for publication."*

Stir up a Strong Multicultural Romance

By Leslie Esdaile

When considering the ingredients for a strong multicultural
romance, much like stirring up a spicy gumbo, you must first start
with the basics. The essence, or "stock," of your story must have all
of the initial elements of a good read: a solid plot, heroes and heroines whom you root for (hoping they'll win), and, ultimately, a plausible story structure that moves quickly through beginning and middle
to thrilling, victorious conclusion. Now this may seem bland . . . too
simplistic, leaving you asking, "Those are the ingredients for *any* good
romance. So, what makes a multi-cultural romance any different?"

Ahhh . . . herein lies the art of adding cultural spice and flavor
to your "ethnic gumbo." First, let's dispel the myth that only people
of color have "ethnicity." *Every* culture has its own variations on a
theme—eccentricities and beautiful nuances that make it wondrous,
and culturally identifiable. This is where you, as a writer, must en-
deavor to capture the five "senses" of that culture in order to give your
readers a realistic, palatable, gourmet blend.

Once the story has been outlined and plotted, and long before you give your characters a color shade or hue, begin by focusing on the five primal senses. What does that culture's dialogue *sound* like? What does that cultural environment, or that culture's food *smell* like? What does it *taste* like? What do the people who make up that culture *look* like? What do the textures of their lives *feel* like? Sight, sound, taste, smell, feel . . . factoring in these elements gives your multi-cultural characters full-bodied dimension that rings true, without having to make multiple and tedious references back to that singular dimension of their being—their appearance.

Taking a narrow view of your characters, such as focusing on them only from a visual perspective, will make them read as "flat," and your readers will come away unfulfilled. Imagine that you are making a Cajun dish and only add red pepper . . . the dish will be unbalanced, too hot and one-dimensional. However, if you add in a delicate blend of Old Bay seasoning, some onions, green and red peppers, a touch of this, or a pinch of that; serve it on a platter that resembles the New Orleans environment and perhaps pipe in Jazz from that region to complement your dinner; and then pick a good, local wine . . . Voila! You have just created a "Cajun dining experience." This is what you want to give your readers—an *experience*— not just a plate of gumbo.

For example, in writing about the African-American experience, I shift dialogues based upon the subtleties of age. Older women and men come from a different era, thus their speech patterns may reflect older, more southern-based colloquialisms than their younger, northern-educated counterparts. Their phraseology may seem cryptic and "parable-istic," utilizing many biblical references such as, "Chile, you gonna have to wait on THE LORD!" Or, an older person might quip, "Honey, you'd better let sleeping dogs lie," where a younger heroine might say, "Girlfriend, this is too deep. You'll have to wait to find out what the deal is. Until then, leave that man alone!" Cadence. Sentence structure. Identifiable reference points. This is a subtle blend.

Other issues that point to the complex workings of socio-economic and educational differences within a culture are things like diet. What people ate one generation ago has changed. Whereas Grandma might have made chitterlings and greens and grits, a young, upwardly mobile heroine might be a vegetarian. These are tension points that give your characters definition. Draw lines within the culture, between age groups, education, belief or religious systems, family structure, etc., to round out your heroes and heroines.

Another example of how family structure affects your characters, might be the difference in how your heroine acts just coming from a wine and cheese business affair, as opposed to how she acts when she goes home to visit her parents. This is true within many, many cultures. Pick one: old-world Italian family, versus new, traditional Irish, Native American, African-American, Caribbean . . . the list is endless. The clash of family culture versus "Westernization" is the perfect introduction to the use of the five senses in your story.

Take the case of the young African-American attorney who is Caribbean-born, in my book, *Slow Burn*. Nate McGregor does not believe in ghosts, magic, or the old belief systems resident in his mother-culture. His diet is different and his education has made him diametrically opposed to accepting these "Old World" beliefs. His speech patterns are most certainly different. The same holds true for the heroine in *Sundance*, who cannot conceive of being psychic—or of giving credence to the "old wives tales" she grew up hearing at home.

The element of developing cultural tension is another interesting aspect of "adding flavor" to your recipe for story success. Wherever there is tension in a story, you have excitement. Writers within the multicultural sub-genre have extra colors and textures to add to their palate, thus creating exotic blends and having fun in the process. Listen to the rhythms, the music, the language, the cadence of movement, the wondrous vapors that come from the kitchens, and the exciting tales from eras gone by. Then, capture them on the page, close your eyes and get lost in a foreign exchange that enlivens your being! Good Luck, Bon Appetite, and Bon Voyage!

"If you write about the things and the people you know best, you discover your roots. Even if they are new roots, fresh roots...they are better than...no roots."
—Isaac Bashevis Singer

* * *

"Kathryn asked me to tell you about my experiences writing Latino multicultural romance. There's plenty of room for new writers in this sub-genre. Editors are desperate to fill some slots. So come on in, 'la agua es buena'."

How to Write Latino Romance

By Hebby Roman

Love is a universal emotion. It knows no boundaries, cutting across all of humankind, young and old, rich and poor. All cultures experience romantic love, but each culture is unique in the way it *manifests* this feeling. One only has to think of Eskimos rubbing noses to realize that love, although a universal emotion, has strong cultural ties.

The key to writing any multicultural romance is research, whether that research is as informal as being born and raised to a particular culture, or as difficult/in-depth as researching a story that goes outside a writer's individual cultural experience.

Researching a Latino romance can take many forms. There's always the traditional method of researching books and articles in the public library. The Internet can also be a rich source of information. To write authentically of the Latino/Hispanic experience, you should also read Latino literature, study books on speaking Spanish (which should include vernacular and common phrases), talk with Latinos, and, if possible, visit Latino countries. These latter forms of research breathe "cultural life" into the books you'll write.

To assure the cultural authenticity of what you write, meticulously research the following: background, history, setting, physical characteristics, language, and culture.

Background and History

Determine whether you want to write contemporary or historical romances. If you've decided to write contemporary Latino romance (the most sought after), not as much historical research is necessary. For historicals, on the other hand, you'll need to do <u>plenty</u> of digging.

The best way to begin a historical Hispanic romance is, settle on a setting. Historical research is much easier to focus once the setting and time period are finalized. To make your romance more exciting, pick a setting and time period that contain significant historical events. It's not coincidental that many American historicals are centered on the Civil War, which was a time of strife and profound change in the United States. Revolutions also serve as excellent historical backgrounds. Using a turbulent backdrop for your romance strengthens both your internal, and external, conflict(s).

Setting

Setting is no less important for contemporary romance. Familiarize yourself as thoroughly as possible with any setting you choose. If you can't afford to visit the locale, read tourist guides and obtain maps of the area(s) where your romance will be set. Some of the best resource materials are those originally written in Spanish, and now translated into English.

Don't choose an inappropriate location or time period. Try to set your Latino romance where there is/was a large Latino population, with an established culture. For example, a contemporary Latino romance set in Boston, with its limited Latino population, probably won't have the same appeal as one set in Texas, California, Arizona, or New Mexico where there are huge numbers of Latinos/Hispanics and the Latino culture is present and visible everyday.

Physical Characteristics

All successful romances today are character-driven, and the smart writers of these books, from the beginning, have a strong sense of how they want their characters to appear. In multicultural/ethnic romance, the importance of appearance takes on added dimension. You want your characters to be true, ethnically speaking, to their cultural or racial origins, but you also want them to be striking, to stand out in the reader's imagination.

It's axiomatic to say that Latinos have dark hair and eyes; however, even within the confines of the predictable norms of dark hair and eyes, there are subtle differences. The hero can have warm brown or ebony eyes. The heroine's hair color can range from a rich mahogany to midnight-black.

Research reveals there are divergences from this "norm." Many Hispanics are blonde, particularly in South America, which has a history of intermarriage between the native peoples and the Europeans who settled there.

To make a character "stand out," and provide greater contrast with most of the Latino characters in your book, make limited use of unusual (but not abnormal) hair or eye color. This is a wonderful way to supply added flair to your manuscript and your characters. Give the hero deep-blue, Castilian eyes, or the heroine fiery red hair, and watch your characters come alive.

Many Latino women tend to be petite and have voluptuous figures. Roman noses, broad foreheads, and high cheekbones are other common physical characteristics of Latinos. The simple inclusion of one or more of these common characteristics in a description of one of your characters can instantly bring his/her Latino/Hispanic heritage to the mind of your reader.

Language

Your Latino manuscript should reflect the cadence and rhythm, if not the actual Spanish words, of the native tongue of your characters. In both dialogue and narrative, it's important to keep this rhythm in mind. By doing so, you give your story that special tone that highlights its ethnic authenticity.

How do you achieve this effect if you're not a native speaker? Invest in at least two books: a Spanish-English dictionary, and a Spanish phrase book. Study these books, particularly the latter, for sentence structure and common phraseology. A beginner's course in Spanish can also be helpful, although not strictly necessary. What you want to learn are simple elements: native expletives, commonly used words such as "Si" for yes, and formal titles of address, as in, "Señor, Señora," and "Señorita." Be aware that sentences that are questions in Spanish begin and end with question marks. The beginning question mark is upside down. This is also true of exclamatory sentences.

Another investment, which can pay dividends, is a software program for your computer that gives you the flexibility of displaying Spanish accent marks, as those illustrated in "Señor", above. (If you work with Word for Windows, the international marks can be easily accessed through your software.)

Sprinkle your text with Spanish words, but use them sparingly. You're publishing an English language book with an ethnic flair, not a Spanish textbook, so, guide yourself accordingly.

Historically, the Spanish language was both written and spoken more formally than the English language was. Your Latino/Hispanic characters must speak more formally when addressing other characters, particularly if they're speaking to someone older. Limit your use of contractions and faddish sayings. If you're writing contemporary multicultural romance and feel you must use "hip" language, purchase a book on vernacular Spanish idioms. Be certain of the common expressions or expletives you use. For example, if you're writing a Latino historical romance, your hero would use phrases such as: "Por Dios," or "by the Blessed Virgin Mary." He wouldn't say, "Bloody awful," because this is an English expletive.

Use Latino given names and surnames for your characters. Acquire a character-naming book that contains Latino names. Spanish literature is also a good source for authentic names.

Culture

Be careful not to stereotype! Research the culture carefully, then include enough of Latino culture in your story to make it believable and set the mood, without making caricatures of your characters.

Three broad elements of Hispanic/Latino culture need to be taken into consideration for writers of these romances: social structure, customs, and beliefs and morals.

Modern Latino life, in general terms, is much more informal than in previous time periods. Historically, social hierarchies were of extreme importance. Much like the British peerage system, these social hierarchies tended to be rigid and fixed. Unlike the United States' fluid system of upward mobility, Latinos tended to measure their worth based upon the name and background of their ancestors. When it came to making appropriate matches for their children, social status was often the key element considered.

Any place that Latinos/Hispanics settled outside of Spain, those with less than illustrious backgrounds had chances to "make good," by acquiring land and amassing fortunes. However, this new "aristocracy" clung just as tenaciously to wealth and power, as had the old guard in Spain. They relinquished their "aristocratic" positions only through major upheavals such as wars or revolutions.

Another aspect of Latino social structure that is especially relevant to the romance writer is the position women traditionally held in society. Unlike the second-class property rights historically afforded women in other cultures, Latino women owned property in common with their spouses. This is how the concept of community property originated in the Southwestern United States.

Many Latino children took their mother's maiden name, as well as their father's name. For example: A son who was named Juan, born to Señor Mártinez and Señora Pérez (mother's maiden name) would be baptized as Juan Mártinez y Pérez. In some Spanish countries, today, the mother's name is dropped in common usage, but the legal name of the child still retains it.

Customs add flavor and texture to your story. Immerse your reader in a Latin culture by building your plotline around native customs. Holidays peculiar to Latinos, such as *Las Días de Muertos* (the Day of the Dead) and the Christ child's *Posada* at Christmas are two examples of Latino holidays. A *quinceanera* is the coming-of-age party given for a young lady when she reaches fifteen years of age—and it's steeped in rich tradition and rituals. Rather than using the timeworn element of a ball for one of your pivotal scenes, why not include a *quinceanera?* However, be sure to do your research so the presentation is authentic.

Other customs cover native cuisine, fashion, and ethnic dances. To sprinkle cultural spice into your manuscript, don't show your Latino characters cutting into a thick steak, instead show them eating *tamales, empanadas, cabrito,* or *arroz con pollo.*

Fashion, depending upon the time period, has always followed that of other cultures, especially for the upper class. However, in historical eras, there were differences to the fashions worn in non-Latino countries and societies. Latino women wore mantillas (head-coverings). Full, hooped skirts, common in the United States before the Civil War, continued to be fashionable in Latino countries long after straight skirts were adopted elsewhere. Now, due largely to the advent of global communications, fashion differences between Latino cultures and others, have largely melted away.

Include Latino/Hispanic dances in your story, as another way to incorporate Latino customs. Instead of showing your hero and hero-ine waltzing, show them doing the *fandango* or *tango*.

The final element of culture—beliefs and morals—is crucial, because of its influence on character development. Characters must have compelling internal and external conflicts to make readers want to finish your story. Morals and beliefs are the value system, which guide your characters through their challenges and joys, and enhance this conflict.

Latinos do not all have the same value system, but they do have common beliefs that influence their culture. Probably the foremost belief is in God. With few exceptions, most Latinos are Roman Catholic. This is important, particularly with regard to customs surrounding marriage and divorce. Even today, a divorce by two Catholics who are married by the Catholic Church isn't sanctioned. The Catholic Church recognizes a divorce only by annulling the original marriage, a lengthy and costly procedure.

The sanctity of marriage in Latino culture places a high value on the family unit. Latinos tend to have strong familial ties and often live in large, extended families. This was particularly true in past times. Today, large extended families are less common due to modern mobility, but the family unit is still cherished.

Although Latino women have enjoyed a superior legal status with regard to property rights for hundreds of years, their social lives have been carefully circumscribed. The *dueña,* or ever-present chaperone, is one example of this. In the past, single Latino women, especially those of noble birth, were guarded like rare treasures. Although this practice is outmoded today, as little as a generation ago, in some Latino countries, wives rarely accompanied their husbands to public places in the evening. Incorporate just some of these unique cultural aspects into your Latino multicultural romance and you will be able to make your readers "see," and ultimately fall in love with, the fascinating characters you present, and the story they tell.

From the Desk of Kathryn Falk

Indian romances have been around for a long time under the straight "romance" banner, and fall into that nebulous "are-they-or-aren't-they-'ethnic'?" area. If, by definition, an ethnic romance features a culture that is non-White, then, yes, technically, Indian romances must be considered "ethnic." Deciding whether or not this is true has been a bone of contention with writers and publishers of romantic fiction for some time. I did not include Kathleen Eagle's wonderful and perceptive article in this bunch to stir up the controversy further, but rather to give prospective authors a chance to see how cultural differences can be integrated into a manuscript so that the magic in another culture shines through.

"As the traveler who has once been from home is wiser than he who has never left his own doorstep, so a knowledge of one other culture should sharpen our ability to scrutinize more steadily, to appreciate more lovingly, our own."
—*Margaret Mead*
* * *

"I am usually defined as being "a writer of Indian-themed romances," and so feel I might be just the one to set your feet along this writing path."

Writing the Indian Romance

By Kathleen Eagle

So you want to write an "Indian romance"? The first question you should ask yourself is why have you chosen this particular sub-genre? Is it because you love to write, you love romance, and you are an American Indian? If so, you don't need any advice from me. Start writing. You are the perfect candidate.

If you fit the first two criteria, but not the third—and let's be honest, if you've recently discovered that your great-great grandfather married an Indian princess, that probably doesn't qualify—then welcome to the club. I love to write, love romance, and have not a drop of Lakota blood in me. (Well, I did when I was pregnant.) Read on.

Is this the book you want to write because it's the one you most enjoy reading? If so, that's a check in your plus column. One of my favorite pieces of advice to any writer is that you ought to first think about writing the kind of book you enjoy reading.

On to the next question. Do you want to write an Indian romance because you've always been fascinated with American Indian history and culture? This is certainly a plus. If you were not born into a culture, if you have not lived it daily (and probably even if you have), then you will be reading, investigating, interviewing, listening, looking, and learning all you can from the people you want to write about, so your interest in their culture is vital. Notice I say from the people you *want* to write about.

You'll read material written by non-Indian writers, too, but don't ever forget that the best source is a primary source. We non-Indians are a bold lot. We are presumptuous. We tend to put words into people's mouths without first listening to what they have to say. I know I've done it, even though I've spent a lifetime trying to remember to hush my mouth and open my ears.

Next question: Is this the book you want to write because you fell in love with the "Noble Savage" on TV and in the movies? Uh-oh. Red Flag! Time to fall back and regroup. The Hollywood Indian is largely a stereotype. This is the version of the American Indian that we non-Indians hold dear because we invented him. Not that there aren't some kernels of truth in this icon—there are bits of truth buried in most stereotypes—but this is not the character you want to write. Stereotypes are flat, one-dimensional characters. They are not particularly memorable, not as interesting as the flesh-and-blood characters that a good writer discovers by meeting people rather than simply by reading about them. And stereotypes can be harmful too— as in, "Gee, it's too bad those people aren't like their noble ancestors. Guess all the real Indians must be dead."

Not that there aren't lessons to be learned from Hollywood. Look to the characters played by American Indian actors in movies like *The Outlaw Josie Wales* and *Dances with Wolves*. However, don't base your characters on someone else's fiction (and that includes mine). Your fiction comes from your vision of life, the people you know, places you've been, your education—formal and otherwise—coupled with your creativity, your imagination, and your ability to take the human experience with which your reader can identify into a world of your making.

By now you're probably saying, "What does this woman know? She's not Native American, and she's not even using the politically correct term." Well, that's because most of the American Indians I know have gone back to using "American Indian" because "Native American" caused a lot of confusion. When it appears on, say, a form, people who were born in the U.S. routinely choose it to describe themselves. My husband is Hunkpapa (band) Lakota (nation) from Standing Rock (reservation), so he prefers to tell people he's Lakota, and if that doesn't ring a bell, he'll say Sioux, and then he'll explain that he's from Sitting Bull's band. Everyone knows who Sitting Bull was. But he uses the term *American Indian* more naturally than *Native American,* because that's what he's lived with, and *American* is no more native to this continent than *Indian,* so why split the hairs? Clyde Eagle says with a wry smile, "I sure wish you guys would make up your minds what you're gonna call us."

Incidentally, the editors at the Minneapolis *Star Tribune* consulted with tribal leaders in this area, who asked the newspaper to use *American Indian* rather than *Native American.* That is now the policy at a newspaper that refers to sports teams by city if the team name is considered offensive by, and to, American Indian people. Therefore, the question of using the correct term is a proper one; it's a matter of respect, and the debate continues. Times change. People change their minds. Which gives you some idea why a writer must get to know the people she's writing about, see them in the flesh, hear them, and listen to them with her heart.

Now, I'm not saying that only Indian people and their spouses can write good fiction about Indian people. Far from it. But I can't tell you how many letters I get from people who say, "Love your books, love Indian romance, want to write one because I just love Indian people. Of course, I've never met one, but I'd love to." My question is, if you've never met an American Indian, whom are you going to write about? Where will your characters come from? If you've only heard the drum in a movie theater, you haven't really heard the drum. If you've never eaten "frybread," how will you describe it? Repeat after me: "I shall not write an Indian romance until I have tasted frybread." There, I said it.

Last summer I had the pleasure of meeting a reader and his family who were on their way back from touring the Dakotas for the first time in their lives, and they took the trip because he enjoyed my books. He was intrigued. He wanted to meet the people I wrote about. He wanted to *taste the frybread* for himself.

They drove all the way from Maryland to the Black Hills. They called and asked me where they should go to see a powwow, and I said, "Standing Rock, of course!" (Yes, Pine Ridge was closer, but I have no compunction about sending people a few hundred miles down the road. In the Dakotas, that's a Sunday drive!) The adventuresome family from Maryland went to Fort Yates, put up their tent in the campgrounds, and they met people. They listened to the drums, and they partook of the frybread. They had the time of their lives, and they weren't even writing a book.

That's one bit of advice. Take the trip. Meet the people. I'm fond of saying that I don't speak for Indian people. My stories are what I like to call "bridge stories." Love is the best bridge between cultures. I often depict a non-Indian-viewpoint character sojourning in Indian Country—hey; I did it *before Dances with Wolves*. I took a trip that became a lifelong sojourn. You don't have to go quite that far, but do take the trip. You'll never regret it.

Learn about the language. See if you can find it on tape, perhaps through a state library or college.

Learn about the music. Purchase tapes and listen to them. While you're writing, there is nothing more romantic than American Indian flute music. (I recommend music by Kevin Locke from Standing Rock.) I'm sure you can find tapes of powwow music in any well-stocked music store. Every state historical society or museum has a bookstore, and in a state located in Indian Country, they should have tapes. The North Dakota State Historical Society is located in Bismarck; South Dakota's is in Pierre. Both state libraries have been enormously helpful to me in doing my research. Ask for the Reference Librarian.

Learn about the food. Indian people eat more than just frybread. Have you tasted buffalo? *Wasna*? *Wojapi*? How about wild turnips and sun-dried corn?

Experience Indian humor. This austere Swede has been the straight woman for a certain Indian humorist for nigh onto 28 years now, and I still walk right into his traps—Clyde's own Dale, in blinders.

Read Native American writers. This, by the way, is where the term Native American is most commonly used—the literary or academic world. Some of my personal favorites: Louise Erdrich, Simon Ortiz, James Welch, and Sherman Alexie—to name a few. These are the voices you need to hear. These are primary sources. Read their fiction, their poetry. Read nonfiction from the American Indian perspective, in addition to the profusion of references you'll find written by non-Indian scholars.

One excellent place to find personal contacts is through the Indian community college or tribal college, and most western reservations have one. Get the phone number. Make friends with the librarian. The tribal college system is supported, in part, by the American Indian College Fund (1-800-776-FUND). Consider making a donation to this worthy cause when you call them for more information about the tribal college on the reservation that the people you're writing about (or their descendants) call home.

So, you still want to write an Indian romance, do you? Then do it. Yes, do! Write what you love to read. Write what you know. (And if you don't know, go to the source.) The bottom line is, tell us a good story. Write, write, write. Writers write.

And I'd better get back to it!

"The collective hope is that all ethnic authors create good stories, and not just good "ethnic stories." These fully rounded, ethnic characters enhance novels, giving real insight into other cultures, without just giving history lessons. The next time readers stand in the romance aisle browsing the titles, let's hope they don't judge our books by their color. "
—Shirley Hailstock
* * *

Do's and Don'ts for Writing
Ethnic/Multicultural Romance

Anita Richmond Bunkley

As I started to write, I developed guidelines to help me craft my novels.

A. Base stories on compelling, real life events and people.
B. Use time periods that have never, or rarely, been used to showcase Black characters.
C. Strive to create positive, attractive characters.
D. Incorporate an educational approach to the story.

Lynn Emery

If you are not a member of the ethnic group you are writing about, use resources written by them *in their own words*.

Read magazines (such as *Essense* for Black middle and upper class women) targeted for specific ethnic or cultural groups. The articles and letters to the editors give pictures of the fashions, music, issues, and hobbies Black/Asian/Hispanic women are into—information that can be used to flesh out characters.

Make your characters full-bodied people. Give them childhood memories, best friends from high school, first love—all that and more. However, they don't need to be preoccupied with their ethnicity (or civil rights, racism, etc.).

Don't write ethnic fiction simply because you think it's "hot" right now. Readers, especially members of the ethnic group your fiction involves, will know you don't really care about the story.

Gwynne Forster

Do understand the socio-cultural context within which your characters interact. Do understand there is more variation *among* African-Americans, for example, than *between* them and other groups.

Books that Influenced & Inspired

And Authors We Love

Bridget Anderson

Terry McMillan, E. Lynn Harris, and Nikki Giovanni. In romance, Felicia Mason, Maggie Ferguson, and Beverly Jenkins. My list goes on . . .

Shirley Hailstock

The only romances which came out in the 1980's with black characters: *Entwined Destinies* by Elsie Washington, *Adam and Eve* by Sandra Kitt, and *A Strong and Tender Thread* by Jackie Weger. (The latter was not written by an African-American.)

Chassie West

In general: Karen Kijewski, Gar Anthony Heywood, Valerie Wilson Wesley, Walter Mosley, Sue Grafton, Dorothy Gilman. Within the romance genre: Rebecca York, Susan Elizabeth Phillips, Sandra Kitt, Maggie Ferguson and Anna Larence.

Gay G. Gunn

Early Maya Angelou who, despite her circumstances, always wrote with such hope and so positively, and Gloria Naylor. I like Ms. Naylor's way of taking the classics and reworking them into relevant themes for our community. Her *Bailey's Café,* is likened to Chaucer's *Canterbury Tales,* and her *Linden Hills* was *Inferno*-esque, ala Dante. I enjoy Anita Richmond Bunkley and Beverly Jenkins.

Crystal Wilson Harris

Legacy by Shirley Hailstock, *Rhapsody* by Felicia Mason, and *Only Hers* by Frances Ray.

Lynn Emery

Ernest Gaines, J. California Cooper, Gloria Naylor, Octavia Butler, Walter Mosely, Terri McMillan, Valerie Wesley Wilson, Vernise Berry and Barbara Neely.

Gwynn Forster

Langston Hughes, Lawrence Durell, E.B. White, Paule Marshall and, among romance writers, Donna Hill, Sandra Kitt, and Linda Howard.

Sinclair LeBeau

Night Song, Vivid, and *Indigo* by Beverly Jenkins; *Black Gold* and *Wild Embers* by Anita Richmond Bunkley; *Seduction* and *Body and Soul* by Felicia Mason; *The Color of Love, Significant Other,* and *Suddenly* by Sandra Kitt; *Whispers of Love* by Shirley Hailstock; *Forever Yours* and *Only Hers* by Francis Ray; *For All Time* by Angela Benson; *Fever Rising* by Maggie Ferguson; and, *Happily Ever After* by Rochelle Alers.

Kayla Perrin

Read Margie Walker for romantic suspense and Angela Benson for a highly emotional story. Also read Carmen Green, Shirley Hailstock and Lynn Emery.

Hebby Roman

Gone with the Wind, The Thornbirds, and *House on the Lagoon.* In the romance genre, I like to read Jodi Thomas.

"The sole substitute for an experience which we have not ourselves lived through is art and literature."
—Alexander Solzhenitsyn

Sierra,
Writers Colony, San Francisco

Dear Kathryn,
    You overwhelmed us! Whoooeee! That was a book in itself. Wait
...no, I stand corrected; it was a *whole encyclopedia*! Everyone just
surely tapped right into the multi-colored tapestry of today's
population. What a fine group of writers (and Mr. Colom too, I
might add)! So intelligent and passionate. No wonder they're proud
of bein' the pioneers of ethnic romance writing of the 90's, just like
you're proud of having been there in the early 80's, with Barbara
Cartland, Jennifer Blake, Rosemary Rogers, and Jennifer Wilde.
    I would be honored to follow in the footsteps of Sandra Kitt,
Kathleen Eagle, Donna Hill, Anita Richmond Bunkley, and Beverly
Jenkins. Multicultural romance suits me to a "T."
    Miss. Kathryn, thanks for being the first to stimulate this
perspective. Your articles are a perfect way to help us with de
cisions about what—and how—to write, and for getting us ready
to start on this journey to being published authors.
    After all ... anything can happen, right? One of us might even
get to the next step. (???)
    Okay, okay, Rosemarie is right behind me again shoutin',
"MIGHT? ONE OF US *MIGHT*?!!! ALL OF US *WILL*! NOT *MIGHT*,
BUT *WILL*!"
    Now *that* is one dedicated lady!
    All right, let me re-phrase that ... "*When* we get to the next
step ..."
    Jade says, "I don't know if I'm up to creating a whole market
for Asian romance," and thinks maybe she should learn about the
Inspirational market, instead. I told her I don't think "reincarnation"

293

is part of the Inspirational/Christian Romance guidelines! (And furthermore, I don't think her idea of "spiritual" is the evangelical sort, if you know what I mean.)

Anyway, she says inspirational romances are selling well—she learned that on the Internet. Maybe this is something we should *all* think about. There does seem to be a cry for people to return to "good-old-fashioned family values."

Believe it or not, my great-grammie always read Grace Livingston Hill because Miss Hill thought lipstick was something used only by fast women! Grace could write a mean story if you could get past the "no smoking, no lipstick, and no-fast-men-or-women" part.

We all want to know more about the inspirational romances we see reviewed in *Romantic Times.* Please ship this information out to us—Lord willin', it will get here soon!

Sincerely,
Sierra

Chapter IX

INSPIRATIONAL ROMANCES

Kathryn Falk, Lady of Barrow
Romantic Times Magazine
Brooklyn, New York

Friends:

So you think you could be "inspired" to write Inspirational Romance? Hallelujah! If you have the faith, this rapidly growing market may be for you. As a religious resurgence sweeps America and attendance in its churches grows, sales of inspirational romances are rising.

One possible new variation of this sub-genre may boost sales even higher. Until recently, inspirational romances have been almost exclusively Christian-themed. Now, however, Jewish readers are asking for romances that feature Jewish characters dealing with, and being helped by, *their* religion. It shouldn't be long before a publisher or two answers the call.

Several established Romance genre authors, such as Lori Copeland and Robin Lee Hatcher, have "crossed over" and are now writing in this category. This is sure to provide a tremendous boost for sales of inspirational romance. Although their readers may at first reach for their books primarily due to name recognition, that will change as soon as readers discover that the books Lori and Robin Lee (and other fine writers like them) are writing, are not only delightful *inspirational* romances, but, simply, delightful *romances*. Period.

Soon it will follow, as it always has in the past, that the more people read something, the more they want of the same.

I have asked Lori and Robin to tell you why they have chosen this new direction. They are now firmly committed to writing these uplifting, inspirational stories and helping to promote this sub-genre.

One of my researchers, Danny Sinopoli, will lead you through the in's and out's of inspirational publishing. The best-selling inspirational author of the 1990's, Janette Oke gives you insight into her background and motivation for writing. (Her novel, *Love Comes Softly*, is considered the all-time best-selling paperback inspirational romance novel, and her total book sales top 14,000,000.) I also recommend you look for Francine Rivers' inspirational romances. She started out writing time-travel and historicals in the 1980's and has totally switched to this sub-genre.

There are strict guidelines for writing inspirational romance and publishers of inspirational fiction are unanimous in wanting only authors who are clearly committed to writing "clean," uplifting stories that show a commitment to their (so far mainly Christian) religious faith. Submission guidelines are available by sending the publishers a SASE (self-addressed stamped envelope).

Keep the Faith,

Kathryn

"Many people will never enter a church, but they might pick up a good book that a friend has recommended. If that book presents a gripping tale that speaks to a searching heart, what could be better? I like to think of inspirational fiction as entertainment with a soul."
—Elizabeth Goldsmith Musser

"Although I'm an author of 25 historical romances, two historical novellas, and one contemporary category romance, I'm a neophyte in the inspirational romance field. As I write this, my first CBA (Christian Booksellers Association) novel has yet to be published. But perhaps my newcomer status makes me an excellent candidate to answer the question, 'Why this market and why now?'"

Writing the Inspirational Romance
Why this Market? Why Now?

By Robin Lee Hatcher

Inspirational romances are written primarily for the CBA marketplace, although many have made their way into mainstream bookstores. As a sub-genre, inspirational romance has truly come into its own in the '90s. Many factors played into that new popularity, but two come immediately to my mind:

- Many of today's CBA romance writers, among them Francine Rivers, Lori Copeland, Catherine Palmer, Carolyn Zane, and Lorena McCourtney, honed their craft in the ABA marketplace.
- There is a strong commitment from CBA publishers to bring out and promote Inspirational Romance.

The primary difference between an inspirational romance and a mass market, genre romance, is that themes of faith and God are integral to the overall plot of the Inspirational Romance. A second difference is the absence of explicit and/or premarital sex in the inspirational. (Writing must be evocative of sexual feelings and experiences rather than graphic.) There is also an absence of strong language (curse words).

However, there are far more *similarities* than *differences* between mass market and inspirational romances. Inspirational novels tackle tough issues, like all other successful fiction does. In recent years, I've read inspirational stories about a woman trapped in the ugly and crippling world of prostitution; about a man blinded in the same accident that killed his wife; about a victim of rape who is pregnant by her assailant; and about a man who is falsely accused of a crime and thrown into prison for many years. I've read stories set in Ireland, the mid-1800s, ancient Rome, Gaul and Egypt, in the California Gold Rush era, Depression-era Oregon, and in contemporary times. Inspirational books are limited only by the imagination and skill of the writers who pen them.

Readers of Christian fiction are not looking for "namby-pamby" stories; they want true-to-life situations and conflicts. They also want to see what role God plays in those situations. For example, how many women have faced the heartache of an unfaithful husband? Countless. It happens every day to someone, and is a reality of today's world. Vows are broken. Families are torn apart. Bitterness can eat away like a cancer at the person betrayed. In my first CBA novel, *The Forgiving Hour* (WaterBrook Press, February, 1999), I use the painful subject of adultery to demonstrate that God's love is greater than any betrayal and that forgiveness is better than bitterness.

Francine Rivers, a Romance Writers of America RITA Award winner for inspirational romance, and an inductee into RWA's Hall of Fame, is among my all time favorite authors. I love her books because they are realistic and make me believe in and learn from her characters. In early 1992, not long after reading her novel *Redeeming Love* (which was re-released in 1997 by Multnomah Press), I was blessed to meet Francine. That day was the first time I toyed with the idea of writing Christian fiction, but to be honest, I didn't think I was good enough. I thought it took a master craftsperson of

Francine's caliber, and I was certain I could never measure up. God had other things in mind for me.

Moving into this market was a natural next step in my 17-year career, for my belief and faith in God is an important part of who I am. In recent years, it became a frustration to be restricted in how I portrayed matters of faith. What an author believes cannot help but work its way into her books; the things that are important to her—the way she views courtship, marriage, children, hope, loss, abuse, death, survival and a host of other things—wind up affecting the readers. This doesn't mean any writer needs to beat readers over the head with personal beliefs. No novelist can afford to forget that her job is, first, to entertain. If she "preaches" anything (not simply religious beliefs, but *any* belief) she will lose her readers forever. The faith message in inspirational fiction must be so intricately woven into the fabric of the story that the reader is unaware a message is there. A character's actions must ring true and not be manipulated simply to get a point across.

Writing *The Forgiving Hour,* was a departure from my "comfort zone"—it's my first big contemporary novel and my first CBA novel. I believe very strongly that this is the story I needed to write. I had plenty of reasons to feel nervous over this book, but a verse in the Bible that restores me to a place of comfort whenever I'm feeling unsure of myself is: "And I will lead the blind by a way they do not know, in paths they do not know I will guide them. I will make darkness into light before them and rugged places into plains." (Isaiah 42:16)

The meaning is very clear to me. Even when I don't know where I'm going, even when I don't know what I'm supposed to write, Someone bigger and wiser than me does. So, I just trust in Him.

Which brings me back to the original question: Why this market and why now? The answer must be more than "because the number of inspirational romances published is on the rise." Writers must tell the stories that are in their hearts; if they try to force a story to fit some preconceived slot, it shows. That's true for every genre and sub-genre. But if, like me, you are "called" to write an inspirational romance, if you believe with your whole heart the tenets of your faith, and you want to include that element in your stories, then this market is for you and the best time is now.

"The inspirational romance genre will grow along with our attention to the approaching millennium. This significant occurrence in history causes us to pause, reflect, and take a barometer reading on the personal meaning we are carving out of life. It is this that has made the television show, 'Touched by an Angel' popular, kept 'Simple Abundance' by Sarah Ban Breathnach on the bestseller list for two years, and caused 'The Cloister Walk' by Kathleen Norris to be a New York Times best seller and selected as a New York Times Notable Book of the Year."

—Peggy Jaegly

* * *

The Inspirational Publishers

By Danny Sinopoli

According to the Bible, God is everywhere—including, it seems, at a bookstore near you!

Over the past few years, authors from James Redfield (*The Celestine Prophecy*) to Norman Mailer (*The Gospel According to the Son*) have explored religious and spiritual issues in a steady stream of commercially successful (if sometimes critically savaged) mainstream works.

Not to be outdone, the publishers (both small and large) of romantic fiction also appear to have seen the light, taking so-called inspirational romances (romance novels that incorporate themes of faith and spirituality) beyond the Christian bookstores, which until recently were their exclusive domain. In the process, they present fresh marketing opportunities for both new and established writers.

In fact, the degree to which the inspirational has penetrated the mainstream can be gauged by the array of commercial and entirely secular booksellers—giants like Barnes & Noble, Wal-Mart, B. Dalton and Kmart—on whose shelves they have started to appear. Of course, finding such novels on a bookstore shelf may be no small feat, considering the rate at which some of them have been selling. In Christian bookstores across the country, inspirational novels are quickly becoming a significant source of revenue for those outlets.

Perhaps the biggest indication that inspirational romances have arrived was the unprecedented launch of the *Steeple Hill* imprint by Harlequin Enterprises Ltd., the world's most famous publisher of romance novels and the first non-evangelical house to put out an inspirational line. Harlequin was followed by Bantam/ Doubleday/ Dell, whose autonomous subsidiary, WaterBrook Press, debuted its own inspirational line recently. In trying to break into the inspirational romance sub-genre, outfits like Steeple Hill have recruited such well-known inspirational authors as Carole Gift Page and Jane Peart—whose novels are already familiar to the readers of such works—to write romances.

Almost everyone in the industry, especially at the mainstream houses, seems to feel that inspirational romance is a rapidly growing market—one which will likely call for the services of more and more new talent as its audience expands.

So how, then, does an aspiring author of inspirational romance break into the category? As a *Romantic Times* survey of the top publishers in the field shows, this sub-genre is deceptively complex, combining the traditional elements of a conventional romance novel (love, action, intrigue) with religious content (faith, prayer, the goal of spiritual salvation). It is written for an audience that can run the gamut from born-again Christians to less conservative readers who are simply in the market for a sweet and affecting love story. At least to date, almost all of the inspirational romances that have appeared on the market over the past ten years have been centered around— as top publisher Heartsong puts it—"a conservative, evangelical, Christian world-view." As such, the contents of an inspirational novel must typically conform to strict guidelines on lovemaking, drinking, violence, and foul language.

Among the top publishers, Ohio-based Heartsong, and Illinois' Tyndale House, appear to rank as the most proscriptive. Each requires its writers to adhere to lengthy lists of dos and don'ts, including bans on: the depiction of dancing (except, possibly, in historical novels); unsavory settings like bars; a divorced hero or heroine (secondary characters who are divorcees are acceptable); and in the case of Heartsong, even the use of euphemisms like "heck, darn, golly, gosh" and so on. By contrast, publishers like Steeple Hill, Waterbrook, Oregon-based Multnomah (publisher of the *Palisades* romances and the longer *Alabaster*), and Bethany House of Minneapolis, generally allow more leeway, emphasizing "unique themes," "interesting settings," and the "light and natural" chronicling of "passionate yet chaste relationships."

When it comes to sex, premarital relations are almost always frowned upon in inspirational novels, and even married couples' most intimate scenes are to be left, in the view of Heartsong (which also reflects the other houses' approach,) "to the reader's imagination."

At the same time, none of the various houses is in the business of publishing novels that are either boring or preachy. As Multnomah puts it in their writers' guide, "The plot should not be too harsh; we want readers to be uplifted, not depressed. Successful storylines are entertaining, and portray Christian values."

In terms of storylines, each of the houses does have its own specific editorial focus, like contemporary romances at Steeple Hill; both contemporaries and historicals at Waterbrook, Heartsong and Tyndale; stories involving "mystery, intrigue and social issues" at Bethany; and the two lines (*Palisades* for romance and *Alabaster* for mystery, suspense, and comedy) at Multnomah.

Trickiest among the various demands of the genre—and it is among the most demanding, according to veteran inspirational author Tracie Peterson (a.k.a. Janelle Jamison)—is striking the right narrative balance between the romantic and the religious . . . pairing an attractive hero or heroine, and a persuasive spiritual reckoning that doesn't overwhelm or offend. As Peterson, who is also a columnist for the *Kansas Christian*, told *Romantic Times*, "I've read manuscripts in which the religious aspects were just slapped on. In order for the book to be believable—and also effective—they have to be included naturally, from the heart."

To that end, Tyndale provides its authors with perhaps the most constructive advice on the genre by urging them to regard most inspirational romances as involving "three plotlines—an action plot (involving a problem, villain, obstacles, climax and resolution), an emotional plot (dealing with the developing love relationship of the hero and heroine), and a faith plot (showing the growth of both of the main characters' Christian walks in the Lord)." This "three-thread plot," the publisher adds, contributes to the Inspirational Romance's "complexity," making it both more challenging to write, and more interesting to read.

By any standards—and for writers both new and established—that is indeed a heady mix, a fine and tricky line to walk. When it works, as it has in the instance of the genre's best and brightest, it can be, well . . . inspiring.

"Faith is a natural part of the characters in an inspirational romance, not something "tacked on" to make a generic romance inspirational. Sometimes that faith is the conflict, and sometimes it is the resolution."
—Jane LaMunyon

* * *

"The inspirational romance novel market is blooming and all signs point to a growing trend. I don't profess to know what all inspirational publishing houses are looking for in romances—they each have strict guidelines—but I will share with you an important part of what my publisher, Tyndale House, is seeking."

Writing Romance for a "Blooming" Market

By Lori Copland

Tyndale targets the discerning romance reader who craves inspirational love stories that minister to spiritual needs. For Tyndale to publish a work of fiction, it must have a Christian purpose beyond that of its entertainment value. In short, it must be *Christian* fiction.

Like all inspirational fiction, Christian fiction vividly portrays the work of God in people's lives; it provides characters that are moral and spiritual examples; depicts situations in which characters confront sin and evil; and demonstrates the effects of characters' moral and spiritual choices. Unlike other (non-Christian) inspirational fiction, Christian fiction also illustrates how characters follow Christ in challenging situations. Most of all, it inspires readers toward faith and commitment to Jesus Christ.

Christian romance is about relationships, love, courtship, character, family, children, nurturing, marriage, and faithfulness—all high values to Christians.

"Hey! I can write on one of those!" you say.

Whoa, not so fast. Writing the Christian inspirational romance novel might sound good, and be an attractive alternative to a world-weary secular writer who shies from the graphic love scenes, but there's more to Christian inspirational romances than writing a "clean" book.

"Hey! No love scenes! I can do that too!" you contend.

Christian romances are more than the absence of love scenes. Christian romances contain sensuality, but on a different plane than the secular romance writer is accustomed to writing. Many Christian readers want to know there is more to a romance than an alpha-male, a strong-willed heroine, and a sizzling magnetism between them—they want to read romance that resonates with their values, their lives and their souls.

Sexual content in fiction can carry a power beyond that of other fictional content. Whereas fictional depictions of pride or murder or selfishness are not likely to lead a person into sin, descriptions of sexual situations can all too easily arouse a person and lead him or her into the sin of lust. Tyndale believes that author, editor, and publisher alike hold a significant responsibility in avoiding graphic descriptions of sexual interactions between characters.

Tyndale observes a difference between "description" and "reporting." Show and tell. Christian romance fiction doesn't forbid sexual content, only the *description* of such content. The Bible "tells" the story of David having an affair with Bathsheba, but does not "show" or describe the details of that affair. Likewise, Tyndale insists that when its fiction must contain scenes of sexual content, that content should be "reported" or "told about" rather than described or shown.

Christian publishing is in the business of publishing romances that lead women to a deeper understanding of God and themselves, therefore, no "gratuitous" or "prurient" descriptions of sex or sexuality are to be used. (For the purposes of publishing this category of romance, "gratuitous" means that which is "thrown in" and not integral to the story, and "prurient" means that which is included for the express purpose of arousing the reader to lust.)

Because Tyndale believes romance fiction has moved beyond the "bodice ripper" and is becoming a life-changing genre, they discourage the use of scenes in which sexual content is combined with bedroom setting.

No sexually descriptive references to specific parts of the human body. In other words, a Tyndale Christian romance will not contain the use of the word "breast" in a sexual characterization of a female character.

No descriptions of sexual acts between characters. In Christian romance, sex outside marriage is viewed as sin. Premarital and extramarital sex should be considered likewise. Sexual sin will never be fortified or made enticing.

Rebekah Nesbitt, Acquisitions Editor for Tyndale, explains it like this: "I have a vision for women who have never read a romance to be pleasantly surprised by the genre…and recommend it to friends and their daughters. I want the books to stick with women, so they ponder the material long after the book is closed. In short, I want Christian romance to be a genre that positively changes the way we view God, our selves and our relationships."

*"Redeeming Love was my first Christian novel,
and writing it was an experience of being tutored
as I went along. The Lord instructs through His
Word—and that book was based upon Hosea from
the Bible, an awesome story that broke my heart.
As a Christian writer, you should know The Word
so well that it will flow into your work naturally.
But, don't preach."*
—Francine Rivers

* * *

*My journey as a writer has been
long, and blessed. In telling a part of
it, I hope to inspire more of you to
write romantic fiction from your
hearts . . . and from the depths of
your souls. God bless.*

A Long and Blessed Journey

By Janette Oke

My family lived on the Canadian prairies and in the long, cold
winter evenings, or the extended twilight hours of summer, I sat and
listened to stories my parents and grandparents told...stories of settlers and pioneer life.

I also read every Western I could get my hands on. However, it
was frustrating reading, for there was something important missing
in what I read. None of the stories dealt with the "commitment to
faith" that many pioneers carried with them as they journeyed across
North America.

If you go to a small town in Canada—and I use Canada here only
as an example, for it would be the same in any small American
town—you can tell which nationality settled first in that town by
finding the oldest church. In many towns, the church was the first
building that went up—even before people built their homes. "Faith"
shaped town after town from one end of North America to the other.
That pioneer "commitment to faith" shaped my Christian mother's
life—and mine, too.

As an adult, I attended Bible College to further my perception.
Eventually, I married a young gentleman who went first into the
pastorate and then into prison education. Through the years, his
commitment has remained as deep as my own. God has always figured as a major part of my life. It is only natural that He would be
a big part of my writing, too.

In the beginning I tried to find a Canadian religious publisher, but they were few and far between. So, I turned to American publishers. I sent my whole book to Bantam, and then found that is an expensive exercise in futility, as they do not accept unsolicited manuscripts.

I did my research, discovered that a new writer should send a query letter first and then, only if the editor requests it, a synopsis and the first few chapters.

So, off went my query letter, and back came a reply from one publishing house asking to look at my sample chapters. I was elated. But, as so often happens in publishing, nothing moves exactly in a straight line. The book just wouldn't fit into their present publishing schedule. That was deeply discouraging.

I do not stay down for long though, and soon sent the query out again. Before I knew it, Bethany House accepted my manuscript!

Bethany was taking a big chance because at that time, they were doing mostly non-fiction, biographies, study books, etc., and my novel was a totally new venture. They didn't know if fiction—romantic fiction—would be accepted or not in the Christian community. Would Christian readers feel that one should spend more time reading self-help and not "wasting time" on mere fiction?

My book, *Love Comes Softly*, was published in July of 1979. By December, it was on the bestseller list.

I write for Bethany to this day—and my books continue to sell.

The biggest percentage of my (fan) mail comes from the United States. I don't think my own country has fully accepted what I write. The secular press, as an example, has been willing to totally ignore me. I don't feel any animosity about this—I guess it is their right to ignore the growing numbers of readers of inspirational fiction.

When I write, I plan the spiritual journey of my characters quite early in the process in order to determine the spiritual lesson that I want to emphasize in the book. It is tempting for a Christian writer to want to cover a lot of things in the book. Trying to narrow whether the lesson will be on "how to forgive" or "accepting difficulties with your faith still intact," and figuring out where the various plot lines might lead us so it all ties together is a great challenge.

Above all, each book is the characters' story. If I can't journey with them—if my readers can't journey with them—and experience with them and root for them, then no matter how exciting the plot, the book doesn't make it.

In my book about a young Indian girl, *Drums of Change*, the last of a series about women of the west, I brought more actual history into that than in my other stories, because so much of what has disappeared was so pertinent to her situation—the loss of the buffalo and resulting change of lifestyle because of the coming of the White man.

I have found that working with these characters in the situations they need to work through has sharpened my own reactions and attitude and I have grown right along with them. There are still many lessons God needs to teach me that will come through the characters of my books.

Where do my stories come from? I can't say for sure, but everything in life you experience first-hand helps to feed the idea-bank. Small ideas sometimes spark great beginnings. I'm never sure exactly what will trigger a story. I do a great deal of praying and I'm sure I get lots of help even though I'm not aware of. I have more ideas than I will probably ever use.

In the mind-set of "writer," I see ideas for stories everywhere. If I were a photographer I would look at the world through a camera lens and see wonderful *pictures*. As a writer, I go through life with ears and eyes for ideas—my "writer's lens." Through it I see wonderful *stories*.

I have been writing inspirational romance for close to twenty years and for me the timing has been perfect. In the beginning it may have looked like it was a difficult road, but as long as there was a publisher to take that risk with me, there were opportunities out there. Now, however, it is more difficult. There is almost a flooding of the market and much copying of ideas. Many authors have chosen to write about the same time periods. So new authors of inspirational fiction will have to discover new ways to present their stories; they will need new twists and turns to capture readers.

Do I feel there is hope for new writers in this sub-genre? Indeed. For "good" writers, there will always be opportunities. But bear in mind, publishers and agents are able to pick only the best because so much is being written now.

Luckily, there is also a growing readership for inspirational books. As secular romances have begun to pull in more and more that is a little bit raw and risqué, there are people who feel this is not right. Isn't it our responsibility to give them a choice?

Writing, though enjoyable, is very hard work. There isn't anyone to push you to the keyboard every morning. If you don't have determination and drive, you'll not make it.

There are always those who say they will write *when they find the time*. That never works; if you are going to be a writer, you have to *make* the time. If you have to get up at 4:00 AM and work for two hours because that is the only time you have free, then do it! Be prepared to deal with the comments and suggestions that editors make, do a lot of praying and never, ever give up.

(as told to Ann Peach)

"A writer strives to express a universal truth in the way that rings the most bells in the shortest amount of time."
—William Faulkner

Jade Young,
San Francisco

Dear Kathryn,

That inspirational material was so illuminating and helpful—
it inspired us all. We would love to write beautiful books like
Janette Oke and the others do—books that leave readers feeling
wonderful to the bottom of their souls. Inspirational romance seems
to be the perfect venue through which to do this.

Sierra, who was raised as a devout Southern Baptist, wants
to know what are the chances for an ethnic inspirational?
Rosemarie, on the other hand, says she's sticking to her Scottish
historicals, and isn't at all sure how to reconcile the two for religion was viewed so differently and played such a different role in
people's lives in the past. But she does want her characters to be
good people with strong commitments, so she is going to do a bit
more research and reserves the right to withhold judgement for
the present time.

I don't know for sure if I have exactly the beliefs and commitment that it takes to write one of these books well, but, even if I
don't write a book that is completely classed as an inspirational
romance, I would still like to inject the essence of all that is good
in inspirationals into whatever I write.

Okay, you know me by now . . . I seem a little "wishy-washy,"
right? Well, I'm not, actually. Mostly, I'm so greedy for everything
life has to offer, I just don't want to give up anything!

I love so many of the romance sub-genres, and think I might like
to write a romance that is as complicated as my brain is. To that
end, I think I want to blend genres, the way Sierra is talking about
doing. Can I do that? How about an Asian/inspirational romance

with a Eurasian, Christian missionary heroine, and a Chinese hero? I'll inject it with suspense and touches of the paranormal, like in *Lady of Hay* by Barbara Erskine. In that story (which is a fabulous book and one of my all-time favorites), there's a suspenseful conflict in the past that occurs again in characters who are reincarnated in the present.

Ooh, there are so many ways to go that my head is spinning. Wish me luck; my over-active imagination needs it!

Your "ever-devout" student,
Jade

P.S. I am serious about writing that book I just mentioned, Kathryn, but suddenly realize that if I *do* write it, I'm not yet really ready. We haven't learned much about writing paranormals. I know that I love to read them—all kinds of them, and I know all my friends do too. I fell in love with Jude Deveraux's *Knight in Shining Armor*, and am so familiar with the ghost of Draycott Abbey in Christina Skye's books, that if I ever met him face to face, I feel we'd just stroll off into the sunset together. (Moonlight?)

These are wonderful books, wonderfully written. Oh, I pray I can write like that someday! Help me, Kathryn. Please teach me some of the in's and out's of writing a paranormal romance and eventually, I just might be able to conjure up a fantastic, original story of my own.

"We have only to believe."
—Pierre Teilhard de Chardin

CHAPTER X

ALTERNATIVE REALITIES

Kathryn Falk, Lady of Barrow
Romantic Times Magazine
Brooklyn, New York

Dear Jade,

You have chosen an awful lot to handle for your first book. Blending genres is the equivalent of writing two (or, in your case, three or four) books. Doing this is more complex than you can imagine—and very difficult for a beginning writer—but it can be done.

To see how a master blends genres, take a look at Katherine Neville's amazing book, *Eight*, in which she blends at least eight genres and layers them with puzzles and myths. In addition, read Robert McCammons' *Wolf's Hour*, which is a combination of a World War II adventure, with romance, spy/intrigue, and more. (I don't want to ruin the plot!)

You are going to complicate your blend <u>enormously</u> by introducing time travel to your multi-sub-genre mix. If you choose to have your hero or heroine move to another time period, he or she will carry along a modern sensibility that will react against the alternative reality—definitely not easy for a new writer to pull off. (Although, try to tell that to Diana Gabaldon after the tremendous success of her first book, a time travel called *Outlander.*)

Another way to explain the complication in trying to write time travel is, your first chapter is a contemporary romance, and the rest is a historical romance. Or vice-versa.

To help you figure out how to do it well, I offer you advice from some of the pros—Barbara Bretton, Marilyn Campbell and Sandra Hill—who each pen wonderful romances in the time-travel category—romances that introduce an element some people call "paranormal." Others call these unusual occurrences "alternative reality." (The idea being that they are not *abnormal*, just unusual.) Whatever moniker we give them, they are extremely popular elements in romance novels.

During the past several months, I questioned hundreds of readers, and almost without exception, they told me they love time travel books. (They also love ghost stories, stories of reincarnation, and vampires.) Now, this presents somewhat of a paradox when paired with the information that I received during the same time period from the distributors who decide what books (and how many) go to the various big bookstores around the country. They said, "We don't want 'em." (Meaning paranormal/alternative reality romance.)

But <u>readers</u> want them. Booksellers tell me readers do not just *want* them, they are <u>clamoring</u> for them. Hello? We have a major breakdown in communication somewhere along the road from great-book-idea to final purchase. Bookseller Merry Cutler mirrors the circumstance of plenty of booksellers when she says, "We started with one shelf for time travel/paranormal books, and now have fourteen!"

I see a fine future for the author who can do these books well.

I also want you to take to heart the words of Christina Skye, who writes the immensely popular *Draycott Abbey* series of ghostly romances. (You're definitely not the only one who loves her work). Jane Toombs will teach you to write "magically," and Susan Krinard will show you the fine points of several of the categories. Amanda Ashley calls upon romantic vampires and Katherine Sutcliffe conveys the sensuous power of the werewolf! All of these categories of alternative reality romance have dedicated followers.

Susan Bontley and Carol Sheridan who have literally "written the book" on alternative reality romance finish this group of articles by defining all the categories of alternative reality romance. Are you interested? Does the spirit move you, as it were? Read on...

"There may always be another reality to make fiction of the truth we think we've arrived at."
—Christopher Fry
* * *

"Time travel is one of the hottest romance novel sub-genres of the '90s and shows every promise of remaining strong into the new millennium."

Time Travels On

By Sandra Hill

Quality time-travel novels stir up quite a bit of hype. Look at new author Dara Joy, whose sexy, offbeat paranormals have garnered tremendous reader support and landed her on most bestseller lists! She is the first to admit it was not publisher support or distributor incentives that put her there; rather, it was word-of-mouth. Take Eugenia Riley. She wrote many well-received historical and contemporary novels before her first time-travel romance. To her amazement, she received a thousand fan letters after its release. Who knew there was such a demand for this sub-genre? Fans knew. Time travels are nothing new in the science fiction genre. H.G. Wells wrote one of the best known time travels ever—*The Time Machine*—in 1895. Other popular examples are R. A. MacAvoy's *The Book of Kells*, 1985; Richard Matheson's *Bid Time Return*, 1974 (made into the film *Somewhere In Time*, starring Christopher Reeves and Jane Seymour); and *The Doomsday Book* by Connie Willis in the early '90s.

Time travel has long had a home in the science fiction genre. But what about romance? The all-time greatest time-travel romance is, of course, Anya Seton's *Green Darkness*, published in 1972. Aspiring time-travel writers of all genres would do well to study this classic. Also worth exploring are the works of June Lund Shiplett, who wrote two splendid time-travel romances in 1975 and 1976, *Journey to Yesterday* and *Return to Yesterday*, respectively. Constance O'Day-Flannery began writing her wonderfully humorous time-travel romances in the late '80s, thus launching this sub-genre into full-fledged popularity and credibility. I can personally say that when reading *A Time For Love*, I experienced a feeling of synchronicity, sensing that this was the kind of book I could write—a perfect vehicle for my off-beat sense of humor. In this story, the heroine is sitting in a dentist's chair when she's thrust back to the Old West. The 19th-century people she encounters are astounded to meet this strange woman with a huge swollen cheek; saliva dribbling from numb lips, wearing what they think is a paper necklace—a real hoot! If Ms. O'Day Flannery catapulted us into this fascinating new arena, Jude Deveraux firmly planted us there with her 1989 masterpiece, *A Knight in Shining Armor*. Then there was Diana Gabaldon's powerful, endearing and enduring *Outlander* series, different from all other time travels written, straddling romance and mainstream fiction.

One indication of the strength of this sub-genre—aside from the fact that it has jump-started the careers of some now-famous authors—is that so many well-known historical and contemporary romance writers, including Linda Howard, Linda Lael Miller, Brenda Joyce, Georgina Gentry, Parris Afton Bonds, and Virginia Henley have dipped their ink into its waters.

Why are time travels so popular? In my opinion, the best combine some of the following desired components, (preferably all eight):

1) Creativity
2) Second Chances
3) Magic/Miracles/Fantasy
4) Destined Lovers
5) Live View of History or the Future
6) Humor
7) Romance
8) Sizzling Sex (Optional, but a personal favorite of mine!)

Creativity is at the crux of the best time-travel novels, and this sub-genre gives writers free rein to push their wildest ideas. Consider my book, *Frankly My Dear*, in which a high-fashion model obsessed with the movie *Gone with the Wind* gets to go back in time, searching for Rhett. Or *Sweeter Savage Love*, in which I poke fun at Rosemary Rogers' classic *Sweet Savage Love*. My heroine, a famous psychologist, thinks she's met Rogers' outrageous rogue, Steve Morgan, and plans to alter him and his modus operandi, forceful seduction. Boy, is Harriet in for a rude (or rogue!) awakening!

317

In Susan Sizemore's *In My Dreams*, a druid sorceress in Ireland conjures up a hero to save her people from the Vikings. To her amazement, he comes zooming through time on a motorcycle. Maggie Shayne brought an ancient Viking forward to the present, frozen in ice, in *Miranda's Viking*. Virginia Henley transported her enslaved heroine from Regency England to Roman Bath—in other words, she traveled *further back* on the time line. Donna Valentino uses the inventive ploy of tossing a medieval knight smack dab into the Kansas prairie. How about Deb Stover's *A Willing Spirit*? Imagine how you would feel being thrown back in time with your ex-husband's detestable (though irresistible) divorce lawyer?

Second chances are the heart and soul of many romance novels, and time travels lend themselves perfectly to them. In my first novel, *The Reluctant Viking*, a modern heroine is distraught over the break-up of her long-term marriage. When Ruby is transported back to 10th-century England, she meets Thork, a Viking man who looks just like her beloved husband, Jack. It's what Ruby learns in the past that helps her solve her problems in the present. Susan Macias gives us another view of second chances in *Courtney's Cowboy* when a husband and wife, about to be divorced, get shot back in time together and learn to treasure their existing love.

Magic is a lure that tantalizes all romantics. We want to believe that there is the possibility of some miracle that can bring about fantastic events. Unlike science fiction that relies on technical explanations for why the time travel occurs, romance readers must accept that by some magical fluke, a door through time has opened.

On the online bulletin boards, aspiring and published authors often argue points about how time travel occurs. They mention such complicated details as coexisting time periods, paradoxes, time dimensions, string theories, etc. I just shake my head at all this mumbo-jumbo. Romance readers want romance, not technological detail in their novels. In fact, Alicia Condon, senior editor at Dorchester Publishing, which puts out more time-travel novels than any other company, says she rejects novels out of hand for this very reason—scientific explanations of time travel. The only exception in recent years that she can think of is one involving a computer as a time-travel vehicle, and it only made it because the story was so well written.

I heard Anne Stuart say that if she were ever going to write time travel, she'd use the revolving door at Bloomingdale's. Hey, it works for me! Eugenia Riley mentioned one of her time travels where the heroine walks around a street corner and ends up in another time period. As long as the writer gives a reason for the time travel, there is no need for super hi-tech details.

Destined lovers are the stuff of which romantic dreams are made. One of the strongest elements of time travels is when the couple is separated by time. Talk about insurmountable obstacles! I like to think that Raine Jordan, the modern female physician in my book, *The Outlaw Viking*, was destined to go back to 10th-century Britain to "heal" Selik, a Viking man tormented by the gruesome murder of his wife and infant son.

Living history is a tantalizing prospect. Imagine what it would be like to witness, in person, the Civil War, the Battle of Culloden, the Gold Rush, a pirate ship, a medieval court, the Old West, the Gay Nineties, or a 17th-century witch hunt! These have all been explored in a variety of time-travel novels.

Humor is time travel's ultimate strength, for it lends itself particularly well to laughter. Consider these examples from my books: a modern woman teaching 10th-century Viking women how to make homemade condoms; a feminist psychologist and a male chauvinist rogue; a female military officer mistaken for a prostitute with a talent for something called "cork-screwing;" or a Viking warrior thrust into modern America who thinks Tim Allen and Martha Stewart are the ideal man and woman. Other authors, such as Dara Joy, have found a niche with humorous novels. She provides many laughs for us with a Regency lady and a cat/changeling who doesn't know how to drink milk from a saucer (*Rejar*). Deb Stover had a Dirty-Harry-meets-Scarlett-O'Hara scenario in *Some Like It Hotter.*

However, in the end, it's all about romance, isn't it? Humor, outrageous transport methods, creative themes and enticing settings are all fine, but they must remain secondary to the romance. Readers pick up a time-travel romance just as they do a contemporary or historical romance, because they want to escape into a love story.

Many aspiring authors believe there is a formula for writing saleable time travel, but there isn't one—just editor preferences, which change from year to year. Numerous manuscripts have been rejected simply because they used settings or historical reenactments that were just "overdone."

Though the time traveler should be shocked and wonder what has happened, authors must not belabor characters' acceptance of the fact. In addition, characters should not be changing actual history. This is more the realm of science fiction, not romance.

Other than publishers' pet peeves, transcontinental time travel, revolving door time travel, and language barriers are all fine elements as long as a reasonable explanation is given as to the how and why.

Anya Seton concluded more than 25 years ago in *Green Darkness*, "No matter what human errors may occur in the future, several tragic wrongs have been redressed by love, by knowledge and by the grace of God in whatever form we envision the Supreme Being."

In support of time-travel romances, I couldn't have said it better.

"Toto! I don't think we're in Kansas anymore!"
—Dorothy
The Wizard of Oz
* * *

"You might one day find yourself in a predicament. You may have a sneaking suspicion the story you're writing is going nowhere. If that happens, maybe what you need is a 'touch of magic' in your romance."

A Touch of Magic

By Jane Toombs

Introducing elements of fantasy, including magic, into a contemporary or historical romance can provide that special spin that adds to a reader's enjoyment. The term magic, as used here, covers paranormal traits such as PSI abilities, witchcraft, and communication with spirits, plus magical creatures such as werewolves and other were-beings, dragons, elves, fairies, gnomes, and trolls—but not ghosts, demons, or angels. In the same way Berkley-Jove separates their lines to include ghosts in one and magic in another, this essay is limited to magic only.

If you are trying to decide in favor of some kind of magic or magical creature to spice your novel, think your choice over carefully. Publishers believe that most romance readers don't care to be faced with dark magic in what is essentially a relationship story. So, keep that precept before you when choosing your particular magic spin.

Were-creatures fare well as heroes or heroines in romance lines that allow magic. PSI talents and witchcraft can be viewed as traits of some humans, so are not problematical. The beings of fairytales—

fairies, elves, and the like—are often thought of as "little people" but they don't have to be depicted that way.

Don't become so fascinated with the fantasy that the love story is neglected. Never forget that romances are about man-woman relationships. The werewolf hero may have major difficulties with his beast self, but his primary focus should be on his growing love for the heroine. Perhaps the mermaid heroine (who somehow will have to grow legs or else be able to shape-shift into human form) struggles against her intense feelings for the hero. This must remain the focus of the book.

Keeping the plot focused where it belongs doesn't mean you can't have fun with the magic you've inserted, or use it to create obstacles to the relationship. In a story where the magic is not connected directly to the hero or heroine, care must be used not to allow the magical creatures (elves are cute!) to take over so much that they overshadow the main relationship. If the magic is of a threatening nature and used as suspense, again remember where the emphasis belongs.

Conflict should not all be external. As a writer, you must think about how the magic aspects of the hero and/or heroine hinder or enhance their romance. For instance, would you fall in love with a person you suspect can read your mind? (On the positive side of that magic situation, with two PSI lovers, their coming together can be mental as well as physical, adding a new dimension to lovemaking.)

If you plan to write a single-title romance release, the mix of magic to romance can be looser, but even there, don't forget you're first writing a romance, not a story intended for the science fiction/fantasy shelves, where the criteria are entirely different. Think of it this way: In a magic romance, the magic provides the ambiance, most of the conflict and much of the excitement—but all this is background for the man and woman struggling to reach out to one another in unusual circumstances. The magic is the vehicle, the hero and heroine are the drivers, and the destination is love and commitment.

"Let me make my contribution to your education about today's paranormal romances. You know the ones I mean..."

Close Encounters of the Paranormal Kind

By Christina Skye

Brooding ghosts. Sexy vampires. Hunky, futuristic space pirates and spunky, century-jumping heroines. Right now they're hot, hot, hot. Nearly everybody has a story in the planning stage or has been nursing an idea for one. And with good reason. By all accounts, readers are stalking these "romances with a twist" with all the avidity of vampires pursuing fresh blood. Editors, however, do not necessarily echo this enthusiasm. So what does this mean for you, the writer, as you face a blank page and ponder trying your hand at this new area of romance?

1. First and foremost, all the rules of good writing still apply. Be sure convincing characters with believable strengths and weaknesses propel your story. Even if your hero does have the strange propensity for growing hair on his forearms and loping along on four legs whenever the moon is full, be sure that he is a flesh-and-blood human male in all the ways that count.

2. Think concrete. Think simple. The paranormal requires a solid, realistic framework since you'll be dealing with elements that strain the normal rules of logic. How do you manage this sleight of hand?

Keep the majority of the story operating within the normal boundaries of everyday experience. When you introduce paranormal elements, create a logical sequence or predictability to these occurrences. Don't fling things in indiscriminately. In my contemporary ghost stories for the "Draycott Abbey" series, the appearance of the guardian of Draycott Abbey is heralded by church bells that toll thirteen times. This pattern creates a believable basis for other unusual events.

3. Be accurate. Never underestimate your readers. The readers who enjoy romances today are an extremely sophisticated audience (no matter what some media pundits would have us believe.) Many have had personal experience with the paranormal. Events such as a near-death experience or the image of a loved one appearing moments after death are common today. As part of the mass consciousness, they raise the level of sophistication and expectation about descriptions of the unusual.

4. Just because you're writing a paranormal doesn't give you license to ignore all the rules. You can only break certain rules at certain times. When you do, show your characters baffled and disturbed by these events, just as you or I would be. Their surprise and shock will make everything that follows more compelling.

5. Show; don't tell. If your hero can "shape-shift," paint that world for us in vivid, full-color detail. Let us feel his atoms tumbling through space and then jolting back together into a new form. Let us smell the hundred scents that would besiege an animal of prey on a summer's night. Make our senses expand bit-by-bit until we capture the elusive phantom sounds that a "clairaudient" would perceive. Make us hear it, smell it, taste it. If you can't get inside your character's skin, then chances are your readers won't be able to either.

6. Tell us why right from the start. Set out what is at stake—and be sure that it's dangerous and emotionally gripping, something so intensely important that we believe it truly might distort the normal rules of time and space. That kind of drama—compelling, intense, and well defined—will make believers of us all. With paranormal fiction, believing is half the battle.

7. Whatever you do, make it fresh. Editors agree that the popularity of time-travel stories in particular creates a danger of repetitiveness. You'll need a convincing device to explain your hero or heroine's jaunt through time—but be sure it's something that hasn't been used before.

8. If you are describing paranormal or psychic abilities, make them unique to your character's personal experience. Research your subject thoroughly and find an area of skill that accords with the sum

total of your character's nature and motivations. A surgeon who dabbles in palm reading is not necessarily convincing. A surgeon who is intrigued by possible subtle energy forms that can influence his patients' health is far more believable.

In addition, be sure that the paranormal elements are not the basis of *all* the conflict in the book. These can lend tension to the greater story, but they should never be the *only* story. Your romance is the heart of your book—as it always should be.

Above all, give your story your heart.

"The most beautiful thing we can experience is the mysterious. It is the source of all true art and science."
—Albert Einstein

❋ ❋ ❋

"I'm sending you one of my favorite themes, about 'Once upon a time. . . .' Who doesn't love a story that starts with those words?"

From "Once Upon a Time" to "Happily Ever After"

By Victoria Alexander

"One upon a time . . ." is the password to a world of fairies and dragons, of damsels in distress and princes in disguise. It's a guarantee of magic and happy endings. In short, it's a fairytale. At first glance, you may simply think of fairytales as stories for children. The

American Heritage Dictionary defines a fairytale as: "A fanciful tale of legendary deeds and creatures, usually intended for children." For children??? I don't think so. Just look around.

The impact of fairytales is evident everywhere in society, even in the words and phrases we use. Going back to the dictionary: a "Cinderella" is defined as "one who unexpectedly achieves recognition or success after a period of obscurity and neglect." (Cinderella was obviously a romance writer.) A "Prince Charming" is defined as "a man who fulfills all the romantic expectations of a woman." (Can we say romance hero?) Even the word "serendipity" comes directly from a fairytale. It was coined in 1754 by English author Horace Walpole, who took it from the Persian fairytale, *The Three Princes of Serendip.*

The influence of fairytales extends throughout our culture to music *(Peter and the Wolf)* and ballet *(Sleeping Beauty)* and, here it comes…literature. Fairytales even play a role in our assessment of moral values. Critic Lionel Trilling (1905-1975) warned against their impact in a marvelous tongue-in-cheek quote:

Educating a son I should allow him no fairytales and only a very few novels.

This is to prevent him from having:

1. A sense of romantic solitude (if he is worth anything he will develop a proper and useful solitude), which identification with the hero gives.

2. Ideas of right and wrong, absurd systems of honor and morality which never will he be able completely to get rid of.

3. "Ideals," desires, emotions. He should amuse himself with fact only: he then will not learn that, if the weak younger son does the magical and honorable thing, he will win the princess with hair like flax.

Maybe Trilling pegged the appeal right there: In fairytales anything is possible. When you think about it, the pairing of fairytales and romance novels is a natural. What's more romantic than an enchanted beauty rescued by a handsome prince? Or an unreachable princess falling in love with a humble woodsman?

The themes embodied in these folk tales are timeless. (Did you know Cinderella first appeared in a centuries old Chinese book?) In many ways, you could call some fairytales early versions of romance novels. A prime example is *Beauty and the Beast*. (Hah! You thought I was going to use *Cinderella* again didn't you?) It has wonderful external conflict (after all, the man is a beast and that's bad for the neighborhood), internal conflict (does he keep her because he needs her or let her go because he loves her?), an exquisite black moment (he's dead . . . isn't he?), and the wonderful pressure of a time limit. It's a classic.

So how do you take a classic and modify it for today's romance reader?

1) Re-tell the story in its original setting.

2) Re-tell the story in a completely new and different setting.

In *The Princess and the Pea*, written for Love Spell's *Faerie Tale Romances*, I set the story at the end of the nineteenth century amidst the backdrop of the frenzy of American heiresses seeking British titles. I decided my hero had to actually want to do something with his life (an unusual twist for British aristocracy in this period, but appealing to modern readers) so I gave him horseless carriages to tinker with. Then I turned to the original story as written by Hans Christian Anderson. Yow! His version of *The Princess and The Pea* runs a page and a half. A page and a half??? How was I going to turn a page and a half into a 400-page novel?

Actually, the brevity of the story turned out to be a blessing. I didn't have to worry about following the fairytale too faithfully because there wasn't much to follow. I made sure the basics were there: a hero looking for a wife, a heroine worthy of his love, and an interfering mother determined to get the best for her son. Beyond that, I pretty much did what I wanted.

This story worked out beautifully in 1895 with an America heiress and a British earl, but it could have just as easily been set in its original, much earlier era. However, be careful when you pick a time period for a fairytale. I'm not sure you could set a story about a mother meddling in her son's love life in a contemporary setting without being very cautious not to make him seem, well, un-heroic.

In *The Emperor's New Clothes,* I started with the story itself and determined its basic theme; people don't always see what's right in front of them. Then I studied the fairytale. When you come right down to it, it's the story of a scam, a rip off, and a con. Now, in terms of a historical novel, what would be a good setting to rip people off in? Of course! The Old West in the 1880's. A town looking for civilization and respectability. Dead End, Wyoming was born.

I had the setting but what about the romance? This fairytale is one without a prince or princess so I was free to concoct that in whatever way I wished. I didn't want to have the hero the target of the scam—you can't have your hero looking stupid. So I made him the nephew of the victim and mayor of Dead End and pitted him against the heroine who is working hard to sell something that doesn't exist. In the fairytale, it was a suit of clothes made from a magical cloth. In my version, it's a title, an estate, and a castle.

Because of the nature of this fairytale, it would probably work just as well in a contemporary setting. Maybe even a high tech rip-off with computers and virtual reality and…hmmm. Now there's an idea!

Whatever fairytale you decide to retell as a romance, follow the basic themes of the story, and choose an appropriate setting. A word of warning though: If you choose an obscure fairytale, one people aren't familiar with, you're going to have to explain the fairytale itself somewhere in your book.

In short, people love fairytales. They always have and they always will. One of your best benefits as a writer of fairytales is that even before you begin, you already know how it's going to end. How else?

And they lived happily ever after.

"Do you believe in fairytales? The Sandman? Magic? My take: The more realistic it is to you, the more likely the reader will buy into the unusual situation you have created."

Making the Extraordinary Seem Ordinary

By Marilyn Campbell

Alan Guth, an MIT theoretical physicist, disclosed in an article in *The Washington Post* (August 1991), that based upon modern physics, there is *no reason* time-travel can't happen! Rich Gott, of Princeton, has even developed an accepted theory on how it could be done involving speed, gravity, and cosmic strings.

Objections to time-travel are primarily philosophical. What would happen to the world if someone went back and made a change of some kind? Movies like *Back to the Future, Millennium,* and *Time Cop* suggest possible repercussions from causing a paradox (i.e., going back and meeting yourself). Before you even begin to write your story, you need to decide what you believe would happen.

The simplest scenario that works in fiction—but is also the most naive in reality—is that a slight alteration can be made that only affects the character's direct descendants or an isolated situation in the future. Other, more scientific theories are:

A. The pebble-in-the-pond ripples theory, where even an insignificant change in the past could have widespread repercussions in the present.

B. The separate time-line theory, where history as we know it does not change, but from the moment an event was altered, a new, separate reality is created.

C. You can go back, but no matter how you try to change history, something will prevent you from doing so.

D. You can change an aspect of history, but not the ultimate result. For instance, you might prevent John Wilkes Booth from assassinating Lincoln, but someone else would still commit the act.

I referred to each of those theories in my futuristic time-travel romance *Stolen Dreams*. However, none of them mattered in the end because the couple's time hopping caused a tear in the time-space continuum which resulted in disastrous changes in their own future time.

In *Just in Time* and *Out of Time*, which were time-travel romances set entirely in the second half of the twentieth century, I used the simple route. The change and limited effect was justified because in both stories a wrong was made right by a character's interference.

Besides deciding which theory you believe in, you need to select a device for the actual time traveling. A time machine is easy, but hardly original, so in *Stolen Dreams* I made the device faulty, making the travel more complicated. *Just in Time* had a gypsy and a magic potion, and *Out of Time* utilized spontaneous combustion and heavenly intervention.

The first time-travel romances I ever read were by Constance O'Day Flannery. They all involved present-day women going about a century back into the past. One device she used was a car accident and another was an old portrait.

To help the reader make the transition, it is best if there is something that ties together the moment in the present with the moment at the other end of the time-travel. In *Just in Time*, I have a woman from 1958 coming forward into the present time. The tie for the first journey was her listening to a new (at that time) Elvis Presley hit when she took the potion. When and where she lands, the same song is being lip-synched by an Elvis impersonator at a male strip club.

In *Out of Time* the traveler is a man who is being electrocuted for a crime in 1965 when he is zapped forward. The connection is that a romantic suspense author in the present is researching his case for a new novel.

As you can see, time-travel doesn't have to take place from the present to the distant past, nor does the traveler have to be the heroine. Whatever route you take or devices you choose, it is still imperative that you remember that you are writing a *romance,* and the best romances have plenty of conflict between the hero and heroine. Obviously, there is a conflict if one half of the couple could vanish at any moment, or the stationary one thinks the traveler is insane, but the author is challenged to get past the obvious quickly and think of an additional conflict between the two to keep the tension going.

In *Stolen Dreams* I couldn't rely upon the obvious because the couple travels from the future together. Instead, I had her going back to an ancient time on Atlantis to change history with him forcing his way along to stop her from doing so.

One warning: Don't get too caught up in showing how surprised or frustrated the traveler is about everything he or she encounters. A few good shocks are enough to make your point to the reader. Then, get on with the story.

Another question that needs to be answered for the readers' satisfaction is what happens to the family and friends left behind. I would suggest you read as many time-travel stories as you can, then come up with something new to handle this problem.

No matter how you accomplish it, however, I am certain you will agree that doing a time-travel romance is a terrific way to write both a contemporary and historical, or even a futuristic, all in one book.

"I heard from Kathryn that time travel articles are burning up the air waves between the east and west coasts thanks to the girls at the SF 'Writers' Colony.' (Sounds like you have a creative think-tank set up!) Let me make my pleas for the heart and soul of time travel."

The Heart and Soul of Time Travel

By Barbara Bretton

Location, location, location. In real estate, that's everything. For writers, "everything" is character, character, character.

Let me stop a second so you can re-read that last sentence. Sounds simple, doesn't it? It is. If you don't have wonderful characters, you don't have anything at all. The most intricate plot, the most fascinating setting—none of it matters one bit if you don't give your readers characters they can love. Characters who grab our hearts on page one and don't give them back until "The End." Characters who grow and change and make mistakes but always, always make the decision to love.

Would you want to spend four hundred pages with characters you don't care about? Would their love story matter to you if you didn't like them? Of course not. However, if you take a man and woman who somehow touch your heart then show them their true destiny—well, it doesn't get any better than that. My favorite romances are romances that resonate with destiny, kismet, fate, whatever you want to call that bone-deep certainty that a man and woman were brought to this place, at this time, for a reason—and that reason is to join their lives together for eternity. That inevitability lies at the heart of all romance, all love stories, and it should be at the heart of any time travel or paranormal romance that you write. Ask yourself: Can this romance happen in any other way, at any other time? If the answer is no, then you've got yourself the beginnings of a great time travel.

That was a question I had to ask myself when I wrote my first time travel *Somewhere in Time*. Emilie and Zane had to go back to a time period she loved and was familiar with, a time of commitment and passion where Zane could discover a better self. A time where the talents they both possessed could be put to their best use. Most important of all, a time that restored the balance to their relationship and made the future possible. The characters determined the plot. The plot didn't determine the characters. It's a critical difference. I think that's very important, in time travel or any other paranormal element you might introduce in a romance. Don't look at time travel (or ghosts or vampires or whatever) as simply a clever plot device designed to help you bounce your characters along for two, three, or four hundred pages. Sure, the element of time travel is going to provide you with lots of opportunity for all sorts of cute bits of business that a straight contemporary or historical could never provide. However, there's more to it than that, much more. Unless you're John Updike, you'll never have a chance in your contemporaries to skewer all that's ridiculous about modern life—at least, not unless you're willing to risk sending your readers running away in droves. By sending a character from past to present, you can make all manner of observations, both overt and sly, about the nature of society in a way that is entertaining and telling. However, make sure that each and every observation pushes the plot along in some way, even if it's only to illuminate another part of your character's personality. Lectures are for the classroom, not the pages of a novel.

Most important of all, listen to your characters. Follow their lead. Open up your heart and fall in love with them and your readers will do the same. I guarantee it.

It Works Like This

1. You create a fictional world and the rules that govern it, but be consistent with those rules. You're writing fantasy, but even fantasy needs a strong foundation.

2. If you're bringing a character from past to present, remember you're bringing a lot of intricate psychological baggage. Attitudes toward sex, for one thing, were very different in the eighteenth cen-

tury than they are in the twentieth. Thomas Jefferson was brilliant but he wasn't a feminist. Keep your characters in step with their own upbringing. That's part of the fun—and the conflict.

3. Unless you're a physicist, be careful what plot device you use to initiate the time travel itself. I've heard editors say that if one more character bumps his/her head and wakes up in another century, they'll scream.

4. Remember that in romance, most readers are more interested in what happens after the characters travel through time, not in the mechanics of *how* they traveled through time. Be clever, be inventive, be somewhat grounded in possibility, but don't inundate the reader with ten pages of information on the existence of wormholes in deep space. That's not what she or he is looking for. These are still character-driven stories, not plot-driven.

5. Much of the fun in reading time travels is experiencing the unfamiliar world through the eyes of your time-traveling character. Keep in mind that as the popularity of time travel novels increases, the boredom threshold of time travel readers will decrease. Simply put, I'm beginning to hear rumbles from readers these days that say "enough with the angst over the lack of running water, let's get on with the story!" Give the reader the experience she's looking for, but strive to do it in a way that's fresh and different.

6. Go back to my first suggestion about setting up the rules and sticking to them. Good advice, sure, but in the long run don't be afraid to ignore everything I've said and go with your gut instinct— because that's what we're really talking about. When you venture into the world of the paranormal, you're heading down a long dark road and you can't see beyond your own headlights. The road twists and turns, there are steep hills and hairpin curves, but that only adds to the excitement. Trust your characters! Trust yourself!

Whether it's time travel or reincarnation, things that go bump in the night or guardian angels, we're talking about writing from the heart. And isn't that what romance writers do better than anyone?

"I write alternative reality fiction because I love a dark and dangerous male. Here's why..."

Vampires! You Love Them! You Hate Them!

By Amanda Ashley

Anne Rice reawakened my fascination with them. Lori Herter gave them a romantic twist. Yes, I'm talking about vampires. Not the blood-sucking fiendish ones who send shivers of fear down our spines and give us nightmares, but the dark, tortured heroes who give us shivers of delight and dreams of undying ecstasy, who can promise forever—and deliver it!

I can remember how entranced I was when I read *Interview with the Vampire*, yet how disappointed I was that Anne's vampires were unable to make love. All that charm and charisma, all that raw sexuality, gone to waste! Then along came Nancy Gideon's hero, Louis. He was everything I wanted in a vampire—he was handsome, mysterious, sexy, lonely, and haunted, with just the right blend of danger and tenderness, a vampire who wanted to be mortal again. Oh, yes, I loved Louis!

About the time I was discovering vampires, I reached a point in my career when I needed a break from writing western historicals, and as vampires were much on my mind, I wrote a short story for a Topaz anthology titled "Masquerade." Well, a short story merely served to whet my appetite, and so I wrote my novel *Embrace the Night*.

When I began researching vampires, I discovered there were many myths and beliefs that I'd never heard of before. For me, one of the things that makes writing about vampires so much fun is that you can pick and choose the characteristics you want to use and ignore the rest. Some of my vampires cast a reflection, some don't. Some can move about during the hours of daylight, some can't; some are repelled by crosses; some aren't. Some become mortal again. Half the fun of writing stories about ghosts and vampires is letting your imagination run wild.

The vampire in my book *Deeper Than the Night* was not a true vampire at all, but an alien from another world, suggesting that vampires were not really native to Earth, but were outcasts from a distant planet.

In my book *Moonlight,* my hero was to be a sacrifice to a vampire goddess. Instead of dining on him, she gave him the "Dark Gift." It was interesting for me as a writer to take my vampire from the distant past to the present. This was a rather dark tale, and yet I loved Navarre.

My favorite book is *Embrace the Night.* The book opens in Old England. My vampire falls in love with a young woman and eventually he marries her and they live together until she dies. Heartbroken, he burrows into the earth and sleeps beside her coffin for many years, and when he rises again, it is to a new world where he finds his old love again, reincarnated.

In *Shades of Gray*, my characters time travel to the past for a short time. Again, you can do pretty much anything you want, as long as you make it logical and believable.

The main thing to remember in writing about a vampire hero is that he must be sympathetic and romantic. Dark and tortured by what he is, separated from the rest of humanity by a secret he cannot share, nonetheless, he still yearns for love, for that one woman who can see past the monster to the man inside. The heroine, of course, is both attracted and repelled.

Vampire heroes are mesmerizing. They can hypnotize the heroine with a glance, bend her will to his with a word, yet they should have a sense of honor that prohibits them from taking advantage of her. In addition, there must be that sense of danger, the awareness that loving this man could be hazardous, even fatal, for the heroine.

If you want to pursue writing a vampire romance, the good news is, there is a devoted readership out there. The bad news is that it's small, and that it's getting more and more difficult to sell a vampire romance. However, I believe that rules are made to be broken, and

that a good book will find an editor who will appreciate it, and—
hopefully— an audience.

*"According to the dictionary, gothic
is a work of fiction set in a remote
setting with an occurrence of mysterious incidents. I agree. Sort of."*

My Hero is a Werewolf

By Katherine Sutcliffe

Any story with any degree of heightened anticipation and an
element of not only "who done it," but "who is going to do it again,"
and "when is it going to happen," has the sweet taste of a gothic to
it. I don't care if it's set in uptown Manhattan—if it raises the hairs
on the back of your neck, it's a gothic. If it screams attitude and atmosphere, it's a gothic.

I cut my teeth reading gothics...*Jane Eyre, Wuthering Heights,
Frankenstein,* the all-time classics that made us fall in love with foggy
moors and heroes with Godzilla-sized chips on their shoulders. I
truly believe it was the mystery of the male characters in those novels that were the most compelling elements of those gothics. Emotional upheaval and high drama kept us turning the pages.

Even as I began my writing career, and the rejects began piling
up, one of the main comments that was passed along to me was,
"Your writing smacks of gothic." There was also, "This is a great
story, but it reads like a gothic," and "Not sure the romance market
wants such a dark tone to their romances."

So I tried my best to ditch the dark, the brooding, the atmosphere. That lasted for one published book.

Then came *Windstorm*, a semi-creepy story of black magic on a Caribbean island. That was followed *by A Heart Possessed*, then *Love's Illusion, Forever Your*s with a vampire hero, and *Shadow Play* with Amazonian drums beating and a supernatural Boto hero who walked the Brazilian docks seducing virgins. Not exactly *Jane Eyre*.

Around that time Anne Rice appeared with her vampire series, and suddenly it was very cool to have blood sucking sexy heroes though, in no way were her books written as romance.

However, for those of us who craved the tortured bad boys who could not help hurting those they love, and relished in destroying those they loathed, Lestat's adventures brought us closer to reaching out and grasping the unattainable—the ones who could not be saved by love-ever-after.

In 1998, I began a story about a werewolf, Lycaon, for an anthology of Halloween stories called Moonglow. My novella is titled "The Wolf Keeper." The hero is a doomed man whose only chance at being saved would have to be by such purity and goodness that evil could not prevail. Enter the heroine, a nun. It is the classic case of good and evil colliding. Can the nun, in all her divine virtue, save his soul? And how faithfully does she believe that God will save him? Is she willing to sacrifice her own soul to break the awful curse that has plagued his family for two hundred years?

I was fortunate that my editor allowed me to write the novella the way it needed to be written. It's dark. It's nearly a Gothic.

*"The difference between fiction and reality?
Fiction has to make sense."*
—Tom Clancy
* * *

I heard through telepathic means (only joking!) that some new writers are looking for new heroes. May I offer one of my favorite "new guys of romance."

Writing Paranormal Romance

By Susan Krinard

If you've decided to write paranormal romance, you've chosen both endless possibilities and a real challenge. The challenge lies in the fact that this kind of romance has an additional factor to consider—that of the "fantastic." As a result, you not only have to tell a good story and make use of polished writing skills, but you also have to understand what makes paranormal romance unique.

The fantasy/paranormal element in a romance novel may be in the setting, as in futuristic or fantasy romance. It may be incorporated into the hero or heroine, such as when he/she is a vampire, werewolf, ghost, or fairy protagonist, thereby enhancing the mystery and attractiveness of the character. Or, it may be an obstacle the hero or heroine must overcome, from within or without. It may comprise a background element or involve only secondary characters.

Most paranormal writers find that they simply *have* to write this kind of romance; it's in their blood. Some paranormal writers have read science fiction and fantasy as well as romance and have a desire to combine the two in a love story.

Because of the unique position of the paranormal sub-genre, an unpublished writer entering this market needs to feel strongly that this is the kind of novel she or he *wants* to write, indeed, *must* write. It's not a matter of trends; trends come and go. It's what truly inspires you, carefully balanced with the demands of the current market, which can shift over a period of years. As is true with all sub-genres of romance, the prospective writer of paranormal romance needs to be aware of the current market climate.

Futuristic romance has always been a harder sell than other paranormal romances set in the past or present. Futuristic or "sword and sorcery" fantasy romance deals with world building, taking the reader away from "reality" and into a totally unfamiliar time and place. This is not a place the reader has been reincarnated from; this is not a place the reader has "gene memories" about. This is a brand new, completely unfamiliar world. If this world is not completely drawn and made real by a skillful writer, it will be too alien a world for the reader to embrace with any comfort. For this reason, it's probably going to be more difficult to build an audience for a new futuristic romance. To reach a wider market, the writer may want to focus on contemporary or historical paranormals, or time travels. However, in all cases, it's important to find the kind of story that truly moves you. Ultimately, what you *love* will shine through in a much clearer voice.

If you're determined to write this kind of romance, there are several factors that are important:
- Choosing a subject.
- Making it real through research and setting.
- The balancing act between the love and the fantastic.

Choosing a subject may seem obvious if you already have your heart set on a vampire, ghost, or time travel romance. It may already be clear to you that you prefer to set your story in the present, or in a historical period. (If the latter, you'll want to be aware what time periods and settings have market appeal. Books that take place after the 1920's or before medieval times are hard to sell.)

Vampires have long been considered romantic subjects, though in the romance genre they must be handled with an eye to toning down the horror aspects. Werewolves seem less likely subjects, yet my own books, *Prince of Wolves* and *Prince of Shadows,* have helped establish "shape-shifters" as viable romantic protagonists.

Ghosts have frequently been used in paranormal romance, and angels can make good subjects, though more often as secondary characters rather than hero or heroine. Witches and warlocks have made appearances, as have the occasional wizard, shaman, or druid, each with his or her own kind of magic. Reincarnation is an often-seen theme in paranormal romance, and can include elements of magic or time travel. Telepathy is another common topic, especially in the contemporary paranormal.

If you're in search of an idea, consult books on mythology, fairytales, legends, and New Age subjects. Any of these can provide the germ of an idea.

Let's say you've settled on writing about a romantic vampire. You can decide on the traditional direction, the type of vampire suggested by Bram Stoker's *Dracula*, or you may choose to use your own variation. In *My Prince of Dreams*, I created a race of vampires who fed not on blood but on the invisible life force of humans often skimmed from dreams.

One of the most important things to remember is, you need to establish the rules and stick to them. They need not be those of folklore or other works of fiction; they may be entirely your own, as long as you carefully define them and make them work sensibly within the context of your story. If you give your vampire certain powers, be consistent. Don't let him walk in daylight one day and fear it the next. By establishing rules that make sense, you'll enable the reader to suspend disbelief.

Keep in mind that some subjects are always going to be easier and more commercial than others are. If you choose an obscure or unusual subject, it may be harder for a publisher to market and thus for you to sell. It also has to lend itself to romance, to an enthralling love story, without lapsing into horror.

Once you've settled on a subject, you'll want to consider all the basics of good storytelling common to a strong romance novel. However, since this is paranormal romance, you need to pay special attention to grounding your story in reality so that you can allow the reader to suspend his or her disbelief. The more "real" you can make the background and surrounding characters, the more your reader will accept the less real aspects of your story.

In a contemporary, convincing the reader that the setting is our world, the real world, makes the paranormal element that much more interesting and believable. In an historical, taking special care with the accuracy of your details will only enhance the paranormal flavor. Just because you're writing about the fantastic, don't believe that everything is fluid and arbitrary. Quite the contrary: You must work even harder to make it real.

You also need to strike the right note between explaining enough about your paranormal element to make the reader feel comfortable and not explaining too much. Keep that air of mystery, but don't leave the reader confused and wondering how your paranormal character functions or what your "rules" are.

Let's say you've chosen your subject and established a setting and characters that are sure to make your reader "believe." The next task—and it's an important one—is to balance the romance with the paranormal elements. You must always remember that this is primarily a love story and it's more of a challenge in this sub-genre than in any other, except suspense. The biggest danger in paranormal is to lapse too far into horror or lose the romantic focus.

Let's return to our vampire. If he's traditional, he's likely to take blood from his "victims." If he's to be sympathetic, he's going to be a vampire with ethics, with vulnerabilities. He's probably going to have very mixed feelings about the way he survives. The horror angle is going to be played down; instead, the erotic aspects are played up and the reader will be reasonably comfortable that the hero-vampire is redeemable and won't violate the "heroes' code of ethics."

No matter what, our vampire hero's main focus is going to be the heroine. Their love will be the central thrust of the story, even if his "redemption" (whatever form it may take) is a secondary theme. In fact, the heroine, and his love for her, is probably at the center of his redemption.

In my werewolf novels, I created a hero who had the best qualities of the wolf along with those of a man, while avoiding the typical horror aspects so often seen in movies. The werewolf aspect is always an important part of the stories, but it does not overshadow the romance between hero and heroine. It's simply another way of telling the classic *Beauty and the Beast* tale.

What makes paranormal romance so exciting is precisely the fact that a new "twist" can be given the tried-and-true archetypes of romance. This added dimension makes the sub-genre both more difficult to write in many ways, and also very rewarding for the writer willing and able to take the necessary time and effort to create a compelling and believable story.

"Without this playing with fantasy no creative work has ever yet come to birth. The debt we owe to the play of imagination is incalculable."
—Carl Gustav Jung

* * *

"Although 'alternative reality' romances only become sought after in the late 90's, various elements can be traced back to the gothic and romantic suspense romances, as well as some science fiction/fantasy (SF/F), and even to a few of the literary classics."

Expanding Romance Boundaries:
Alternative Reality Romances Come of Age

By Susan W. Bontley and Carol J. Sheridan

Kristin Ramsdell, librarian and romance coordinator, first coined the term "Alternative Reality" for the *Library Journal*. We have applied it to all books that feature one or more of the following elements: fantasy, including fairytales/legends and myths; futuristic; angel/guardian angel; ghost; extrasensory or sixth sense powers including healing, telepathy, visions, precognition, etc.; vampire; werewolf; monster; shape-shifter; magic; witchcraft; American Indian mysticism; and time travel.

This sub-genre is sometimes referred to as supernatural or occult romance, but this is a misnomer, because only a portion of the books in this sub-genre actually fall under those headings.

A Little History

Early beginnings of AR romances can be found in such classics as *Wuthering Heights* by Emily Brontë and Daphne du Maurier's *Rebecca*. More recent history shows the readers' enchantment with

AR starting to blossom with the many gothics written during the '60s and '70s by authors Virginia Coffman, Dorothy Daniels, Marilyn Ross, and Florence Stevenson. Haunted houses, spectral visions, and unspeakably evil rituals were foundation plot devices used by most gothic writers. Popular romantic suspense authors (Victoria Holt, Barbara Michaels, Mary Stewart, and Phyllis A. Whitney) also played their part in AR romance's origin.

Favorite SF/F writers like Marion Zimmer Bradley, Carole Nelson Douglas, Sharon Green, Ann Maxwell, and Anne McCaffrey all had strong romantic sub-plots threaded through their earlier works. AR elements can also be found in some of the more mainstream historical and contemporary fiction as far back as the 1970s (Daphne du Maurier's *The House on the Strand*, Mary Luke's *The Nonsuch Lure*, Trevor Meldal-Johnson's *Always*, and Anya Seton's *Green Darkness* and *Smoldering Fires*).

Using data gathered from the 1,100 books and 200 short stories we have profiled in our AR reference set *Enchanted Journeys Beyond the Imagination (An Annotated Bibliography of Fantasy, Futuristic, Supernatural, and Time Travel Romances, Volumes 1-3)* as a basis, we have gained an understanding of this unique sub-genre's most recent history. This has enabled us to make some general predictions on future trends. For example, the top AR categories that have been published are powers, ghost (& reincarnation) and witchcraft/ magic. In the Time Travel category, journeys to the American West time period are the most frequently written about, followed closely by the contemporary and early English time periods.

Based upon their publishing track records, current AR-friendly publishers include Leisure/*Love Spell* and Kensington/Zebra, with Harper, Pinnacle, Bantam, and Avon all practically tying for third place. Among the series lines, Harlequin *American Romance* and *Temptation*, and Silhouette *Intimate Moments* and *Romance* have published a large number of books with AR elements.

What's Current

To get a clearer picture of the current state of AR romances, we informally polled about 80 readers, authors, and booksellers for details about their reading, writing, and selling habits. This is not by any means a statistically valid survey, especially because readers' tastes seem to vary from region to region, but it does highlight some interesting points we have discovered in other similar discussions.

AR fans are a small but <u>voracious</u> group of devoted readers. Several readers said the majority of the books they read are AR. Time Travel seemed to be the topic of choice, followed by powers, ghost, and vampire. The biggest reader complaint was there were not enough of these types of books available to meet their demands.

One reader wrote, "There are very few new books being released in the miscellaneous paranormal genres, so most of my reading is either straight historical or fantasy/horror." Another said, "I find it frustrating when looking for new books to read! I feel as though they are not getting published or are few and far between." Several readers also lamented strongly about the poor writing and lack of futuristics. Numerous readers responded that they have had to switch to SF/F to find quality books to enjoy.

We also interviewed the booksellers, who find AR romances to be *very* big sellers. Their customers' top requests? time travel, futuristic, and fantasy. More than one bookseller said that, "We continually sell out of time travel, futuristic, and vampire." Another bookseller wrote, "I receive a lot of requests for time travel and I find that they are hard to get hold of."

A storeowner said her readers were tired of reprints and non-substantial story lines. They don't want rewrites of existing books, or historicals masquerading as time travels. They want fresh voices and "meaty" plots.

The Future

Some editors and publishers would have you believe the popularity of AR romances has peaked and begun to wane. Not so. In scanning past issues of our newsletter, *The Alternative Reality Romance Connection,* which includes a monthly listing of upcoming AR books, we discovered that in 1997 alone, 248 books that included AR elements (148 historicals, 56 contemporaries, 12 Regencies, and 56 series) were published.

Of those, 58% were marketed as primarily AR books, i.e. as part of an AR-oriented line or series sub-category like Love Spell's *An Angel's Touch* line or Harlequin American's *More Than Men* series. In addition, 32 previously released AR books were reprinted. That averages out to be almost 21 new books and three reissues per month for 1997.

In a recent survey, we asked our mailing list about likes and dislikes. Readers told us which AR categories they wanted more of and which ones they'd had enough of. Booksellers let us know what their readers were saying. Authors were asked about what the publishers and their readers were telling them. Here is the result:

AR fans are begging for new stories and faces. On the readers' "Want-More-Of" list are ghost, time travel, powers, futuristic, and fantasy. Vampires are also pretty high, but not every reader who responded liked this type of book. The only category that was listed on the "Not Interested" list was angels.

Booksellers responded that their readers definitely want more time travels and vampires. The vote was split on the futuristics and Anthologies, and we have discovered, as in the case with vampires, readership tends to be more regional. One bookseller said readers complain that in anthologies, "the story just starts and it's time to end." Another bookstore owner commented that, for her area, "Vampires are still popular but the reading group is narrowing."

Authors gave us insight into what their publishers are telling them to write. The average time from delivery of their manuscript until publication is usually about a year, so these authors are working on books that readers won't see for at least another 12 months.

Most publishers appear not be too interested in angels (as were the readers) or futuristics (which is contrary to what the readers have shown they wanted). Many editors have told their writers to stick to straight historicals or contemporaries with limited or no AR elements. Only one or two have been encouraged to continue to write AR books, even though a majority of the authors we contacted are multi-published with both non-AR and AR books.

On the other hand, authors told us that their readers are constantly pleading for more AR books—particularly vampires and futuristics! Ironically, when asked what type of book they'd like to write if they knew it would sell well, writers were split among the various categories, with one noted exception: angels. No one wanted to write about angels.

Finally, we used the "stats" we gathered from the books we profiled, plus a list of confirmed AR books we have not yet cataloged, to give us somewhat of an indicator of what the future market may hold for aspiring authors. Reviewing almost 1600 titles, we found that in the past four years, publishers have collectively brought out an average of 250 books per year with AR elements in them.

There is some indication, from conversations we have had with authors as well as industry rumors, that publishers believe readers' interest may have peaked, but we expect there to be only a gradual reduction in the number of AR marketed titles. Books that include AR elements as secondary plot devices should compensate for this.

Historically, Leisure and Zebra have shown a steadily growing interest in producing AR romances, and should continue to produce about 30 books apiece per year. Harlequin has published a majority of the series romances with AR elements, and we expect they will continue this trend, with 35-40 titles per year. Silhouette's highest year for publishing AR romances was 1994. They have since slowly reduced their AR titles to 15-20 books per year.

If you are determined to write a book with AR elements, target these publishers. You'll need to ask which of their editors are in charge of their various lines and series.

Our Recommendations

First and foremost, write a GOOD story with engaging characters and a strong, romance-driven plot. Many authors mentioned that those were the keys for selling to publishers, even when a specific type of story was not considered to be in vogue. Readers confirmed this with comments like "don't 'dumb down' the story line" and, "I want more stories that are so good I can't put them down—even to go to work!"

AR category romances will be easier to sell if the AR elements are secondary to the story. An overwhelming majority of the books in our reference set are not specifically designated as AR romances. In fact, several authors we contacted were surprised that we classified their books as AR. since that was not their intention. Granted, there are several publishers that have lines that feature AR-driven plots (Jove's *Time Passages* and *Haunting Hearts*, Love Spell's *Heart's Magic* and *A Faerie Tale Romance*), but there is no guarantee that these lines will still be published once your manuscript is finished. Many an AR author lamented the demise of Silhouette's *Shadows* series, suddenly finding him/herself with a non-saleable manuscript or work in progress because their story was too dark or too spooky for any of the other series lines.

It also seems, in general, that historicals with AR elements are much easier to get published, especially those set in Scotland or Ireland, or during medieval times. In fact, fantastical or mystical elements are almost *expected* for books written about those places and times. However, with the current high interest in contemporary romantic suspense, using psychic powers, American Indian mysticism, or New Age elements seems also to be acceptable.

Another point made clear was that authors with an established following, who have already proven their salability to publishers, are more likely to convince their editors to include strong AR elements in their books. Most readers buy books to begin with because of the topic, but they continue to buy books by a specific author because of their writing style. This is why immensely successful writers like Jayne Ann Krentz and Nora Roberts use pseudonyms to differentiate their vastly diverse writing styles.

So if it looks like your straight historical is more popular with your editor than your time travel, don't despair. Create a loyal following of readers, and then come back to present your AR book. Your editor is more likely to hear you out if you have already proven yourself as a marketable writer.

Read what you're planning to write, and know your competition. Find out what's already been written and what areas still need to be explored. Going back to the "stats," we found that the following AR categories have the least number of books available: fantasy, futuristic, UFOs, super-natural, werewolf, and time travel (American wilderness/American Revolution & Regency England). This means that there is less competition for your reader's attention and a greater potential for success.

Some prime examples of cherished AR "keepers" that readers have asked for more of are: Jessica Bryan's "merpeople" trilogy, *Across a Wine-Dark Sea, Dawn on a Jade Sea*, and *Beneath a Sapphire Sea*; Cheri Scotch's trilogy *The Werewolf's Touch, The Werewolf's Kiss,* and *The Werewolf's Sin*; Kate Donovan's American Wilderness Time Travel duet, *Timeless* and *Time Weaver*, and Kasey Michael's Regency Time Travel, *Out of the Blue.*

Finally, we ask interested new writers not to give up the ghost. (Pardon the pun). What's not hot today may be in demand tomorrow.

One thing is for certain, though—those who like AR romances can't seem to get enough of them. The numbers seem to be growing, not diminishing as more and more readers discover this fascinating sub-genre. In fact, there's a whole new era of readers to look forward to writing for. As one author put it, "the up and coming generation of readers are avid AR fans, if R.L. Stine's phenomenal success is any indication. If we could steer these young readers toward AR romances, we'd have them for life."

Jade, the finally committed
San Francisco

Dear Kathryn,

No more twisting in the wind; I have decided what to write—maybe. (Just joking!) Actually, this last group of things you had us read clarified a lot of things—to the point that we finally know what categories of romance are best for each of us.

You mentioned the difficulty of combining sub-genres, and then Kathryn Sutcliffe says that it is easier to put unusual elements in a romance novel <u>after</u> you have a book or two published, so I've decided you are both right, and now is not the time for me to attempt my complicated combination.

Rosemary was thrilled to read Susan Bontley's and Carol Sheridan's observation that "fantastical or mystical elements are almost expected" in historicals, because she has a fumbling, endearing grandmother with second sight, and the ability to cast spells—albeit extremely limited ones—planned for the historical she is beginning to formulate. (Get this . . . the people the grandmother is casting the spells over actually have to somehow wish for the spell to happen.)

Don't scream, Kathryn, I said, she's formulating, not *writing!* No, she has not turned on that computer yet; she is just thinking things through very carefully—says she's starting to play some of those "mind movies" through her brain.

Sierra, on the other hand, says to tell you (and I quote), "I surely do mean to add a few 'other-worldly' elements at some time—just not yet. There has always been a strong mystical base of belief throughout Africa and I aim to do a book includin' some of it one day real soon." She's "chompin' at the bit" to get to an outline for her ethnic romance.

Actually, we're all "chomping" at this stage, Kathryn.

For me that means chin up, shoulders back, size five shoe poised to take the first stride. I have made a commitment to follow one path all the way to the end.

Bet you thought that would never happen! Sometimes I felt that way too, but something important happened last night, that has been the final bit of "guidance" I needed to set me in the right direction.

I think very spiritually and look for the signs that I believe are out there for all of us to see. So, when I had a dream last night that showed me moving confidently forward on a familiar-looking, winding path, I took that as a sign that I am to write a book that also takes a twisting path . . . a mystery. I'm going back to my original idea to write a romantic suspense. (Get it? That's the "familiar" part of the path.) Only this time, I am starting from scratch. That manuscript I started previously "is toast," as they say.

Your articles and advice have opened my eyes to new plot twists and a whole universe of possible story ideas. In the long run, I don't really have to give up any of the many paths I have flirted with taking—I just have to let my imagination swing open the gate to a secret garden filled with myriad magical pathways leading me in infinite directions! None of these pathways are right or wrong; they are simply there to beckon me forward.

I will write this first romantic suspense in a straightforward manner. Then, when I have studied more, and have several successful manuscripts under my belt, I will begin writing romantic suspense stories that will also include time travel—maybe even a shape-changer or two. These are the elements of romances that I love to read. These are also the elements my readers will love to read.

However, that's tomorrow's journey . . . for now, I need your help to begin this one.

Thus far, you have only teased us with references and information about the romantic suspense sub-genre. I read that romantic suspense is one of the most popular categories of romance. Is that true? If you go by the three of us, it is, for we all love romantic suspense.

This in-depth "writing course" you're putting us through is taking longer than we thought it would and we feel we're almost ready to go. But, we hear you Kathryn—all the way from Brooklyn! First we have to outline. And, we can't outline if we don't know which category to write in! And so on. I know ... Rome wasn't built in a day. (I bet that was what you were about to write back to me. Beat you to the punch!)

I'm ready for a mystery Kathryn; Surprise me!
Jade

"Upon this twisted path I set my pointed toe.
Nor damsels lost, nor hidden foe
Shall stay the way I go
. . . To discovery."
—Anon.

Chapter XI

ROMANTIC SUSPENSE

Kathryn Falk, Lady of Barrow
Romantic Times Magazine
Brooklyn, New York

Dear Jade,

You caught me at a good time to mention suspense, because I'm in the midst of interviewing Thomas Perry and Linda Barnes. They write such great yarns! The books are not too romantic, but they do have memorable female detectives. After all, aren't memorable characters the most important part of a book? Also at *Romantic Times* magazine, we've launched a new feature capitalizing on the amazing increase in the number of female sleuth series. We're calling it, "Mystery, Suspense and Thrillers."

The popular new intrigues, suspenses, and mysteries—lump them under romantic suspense if you will—are a definite blending of the romance and mystery genres. With these books, the heroines portray strong, independent women who, along the way, encounter romantic relationships. They do not necessarily have happy endings, nor do they have languid love scenes. However, readers of romances love them. They offer reading variety for the female psyche.

Sales of romantic suspense/Intrigue are strong, partly because men who wouldn't admit to reading one of those women's books (meaning traditional romance), will pick up a copy of an intrigue/romantic suspense/thriller novel without a second's hesitation. This makes for a broader readership base and *that* translates to healthy sales which, in turn, account for why dozens of romance authors (Nora Roberts, Catherine Coulter, Tami Hoag, Janet Evanovich, Tess Gerritsen, and others) have crossed over to this genre, and now have books that have either "Mystery" or "Fiction" on the spine.

Romantic suspense and gothic romance remain the classic categories of romantic fiction, and are still published regularly within the romance genre. For example, the Harlequin *Intrigue* line brings out four titles each month, and every other major publisher produces at least one gothic (historical) or romantic suspense (contemporary) monthly, all strictly following the romance parameters (monogamy and happy endings).

The mystery/thriller genre, on the other hand, which has no such romantic restrictions, was once an exclusive male domain—the exception being the "cozy" category mystery writers, such as Agatha Christie.

In the 1990's, the mystery genre was "invaded" by female writers and female sleuths. This was after an enterprising group of young women writers, with a wide membership from the romance genre, formed "Sisters in Crime" in the late 1980's for the main purpose of storming the walls of a heretofore "male bastion," and promoting their books.

They have more than succeeded.

The founding mothers of this group included Sharyn McCrumb and Sue Grafton, who paved the way for female mystery writers to make the prestigious New York Times list. Today their books, as well as those by Patricia Cornwell and Mary Higgins Clark, rank in sales with Tom Clancy and Michael Crichton.

Not surprisingly, women readers flocked to these books with female protagonists. What is surprising is the fact that this crossed-over female readership has mushroomed and now accounts for 60% of mystery sales. An even more extraordinary fact is that there are now more than 600 mystery series books featuring female sleuths, written by women! Janet Evanovich, Sparkle Hayter, and Linda Barnes rank among the top performers.

There is even an all-encompassing reference work, *Detecting Women*, that lists all the female sleuth series written by women, in a format that breaks the list down by the special categories mysteries fall under today. The sleuths are categorized under each book's specialized theme, or each sleuth's special interest, such as law, gardening, music, rare books, antiques, cooking, chocolate, and herbs, etc. Cats are popular. Many mysteries take place in special settings, such as an English pub, a bookshop, or an antique center. Regions also figure heavily in the plots—with crimes taking place in cities and towns from Lake Tahoe (home of the Perry O'Shaugnessy legal thriller series written by two sisters, one a lawyer) to Boston (home of Carlotta Carlyle, Linda Barnes' great PI). There's even a beekeeper sleuth and several American Indian private eyes. So far, the only angle not addressed, as far as I can detect, is a series spun around garage sales!

Male writers—discovering that more women buy fiction than do men—have answered the siren call of the female reader, and are at last including more romantic elements in their novels. It's working—their sales have increased. Some have even created excellent female-sleuth series, one of the best being the Karren Whitefield series by Thomas Perry. The heroine is part American Indian and specializes as a guide who helps worthy people disappear.

Writers have been combining romance with suspense and having it sell well in the popular marketplace, for just about as long as there have been published novels. Fine examples of this include Ann Radcliffe who published five well-received gothic romances before 1797, and Charlotte Brontë, who chilled readers more than a hundred and fifty years ago with her romance between Jane Eyre and the brooding, mysterious Mr. Rochester.

One of the leading heroines of the current romantic suspense trend is the indomitable Mary Higgins Clark, a recently-remarried widow with five children, who started out writing radio commercials and worked herself up to the first $35,000,000 contract in

American publishing. She works romantic elements into rip-roaring good mysteries that regularly make the bestseller lists and are turned into TV films. She cleared a path to popularity, so romance writers including Heather Graham, Sandra Brown, Iris Johansen, Megan McKinney, and Karen Robards are also now profiting greatly from writing suspense.

Publishing houses are seeking out suspense in all forms because these books, with their limited numbers of characters and—in most cases—contemporary settings, can be turned into relatively inexpensive movies or TV shows, thus giving publishers another chance to make money. Of course, all this means the authors will make more money too!

To really get a feel for this writing, I recommend you study some of the early classic gothic authors such as Mary Stewart (who is retired and living in Scotland), Virginia Coffman (now retired and at home in Nevada), and the late Victoria Holt (who spent months every year writing aboard luxury liners like the QE II). Ms. Holt actually died in her 90th year on a Mediterranean cruise and, per her instructions, her ashes were strewn at sea!

On the subject of blending mystery and romance, there *are* differences, as you will discover when you read the following articles. It is no mystery that this batch will include terrific "how-to" advice. However, I will keep you in suspense by not telling you what all is included—except to say, I've sent along a favorite essay of mine that I published when a romance author of many fine traditional contemporaries finally saw her dream of landing on the New York Times best seller list come true. This was followed by her first profile in *People* magazine when her book was made into a much-watched TV film.

I say it could happen to one of you!

"I enjoy weaving suspense into my romance novels and find the readers like that extra dollop of tension and conflict. The following article explains some key characteristics that define romantic suspense. Are you ready for some action?"

Melding Romance and Suspense

By Merline Lovelace

Spine-tingling action with a strong heroine at the center, a sexy hero in the wings and a smattering of secondary characters, all woven artfully together have made romantic suspense one of the hottest selling sub-genres in our business. Classic gothics and women-in-jeopardy tales (ahhh, for another Rebecca); police thrillers; psychological twisters; or paranormal and futuristic suspense stories—all of these categories of the Romantic-Suspense sub-genre have legions of followers.

Romantic suspense novels contain the same essential ingredients as all other romances—strong characterization, wrenching conflict, escalating tension, crisp dialogue, and most importantly, a stirring love story. However, over and above these basic requirements are certain key characteristics that set romantic suspense apart.

Action! First and foremost, you must have plenty of action. Generally, these books are more plot-driven than character-driven. Startling events occur, keeping the characters and readers on edge.

Faster Pacing. With increased action, the story moves fast. There's less introspection, more dialogue. Watch for long chunks of narrative (I look for three pages or more.) You may be wallowing around in your characters' heads too much. If so, introduce some event or interchange that gets the players back on stage and interacting with each other.

High Levels of Tension. Elements of danger and vulnerability are the key to romantic suspense. The characters must be at risk, physically and/or emotionally. Watch out for what I call the "Perils of Pauline" syndrome, where the poor characters never get a chance to laugh or breathe; but do keep their nerves tingling.

Dramatic Tone. In keeping with the high-tension levels, these novels exude a strong sense of atmosphere. The tone may be brooding or reflect danger and excitement. Your word choice and setting should enhance that tone. For example, strong action verbs increase the drama at critical points. A nerve-shattering thunderstorm or soul-sucking heat can add to the mood.

Larger Number of Characters. Romantic suspense novels usually include a larger cast of characters, often designed to keep the reader guessing as to the identity of the villain. Yes, Virginia, it's okay to get in these sub-characters' heads. A word of caution here, though. I have trouble keeping large casts of characters straight, so I try to introduce them slowly (one per chapter) and give them tags—a limp, a mustache, a squeaky voice—that make them immediately recognizable.

Strong Female Protagonist. This is my favorite part, because I would have trouble writing any other kind of female protagonist. In a romantic suspense, the heroine is a very active player. She doesn't have to call in the cavalry to save her. The trick is to devise a way for both the hero and heroine to participate in the resolution of the conflict or mystery. Remember, you're writing two stories, the romance and the suspense, yet these two stories can't be separate and distinct. Everything that happens in one has to affect the other. Leslie Wainger, Silhouette's *Intimate Moments* Senior Editor, described them as two strands of a braid—closely interwoven and interdependent.

Weaving these two strands into a coherent, dynamic whole requires more plotting than normal. I use a plotting arc to track the main events, chapter by chapter. This is a simple curving line, with key elements of sexual tension on one side, and action elements on the other. If you find blocks of empty space on either side of the arc, you should consider tightening the plot or heating up the relationship. Your mission—should you choose to accept it—is to keep something happening on both sides of the equation in every chapter.

Sounds daunting, doesn't it?

It's hard work, often frustrating, yet totally exhilarating when—against all odds!—those tightly woven strands actually result in a fast-paced, action-filled tale that keeps readers coming back for more.

"I switched from writing straight romance to romantic suspense. The response has been terrific! I'd like to share with you my own 'how to' list for writing edge-of-your-seat romantic suspense."

A Step by Step Approach to Writing Romantic Suspense

By Tess Gerritsen

After a dozen years of writing romantic thrillers and mainstream suspense novels, I've developed my personal "formula" for tackling a novel that goes beyond the usual advice of simply creating wonderful characters and plotting out a great mystery.

1. START YOUR BOOK ON A CRISIS POINT

Otherwise known as "the hook," this is the very first scene, and it should immediately snare your reader's interest. The classic hook, of course, is a murder, but the hook need not be violent. It can be as ordinary as an argument between lovers, or a husband walking out on his wife without explanation. Some of the hooks I've used:

- *Presumed Guilty.* A woman discovers her married lover's dead body in her bedroom.

- *Life Support.* A surgeon goes berserk in the operating room.
- *Whistleblower.* A man is pursued by a killer through the woods.

  If you can lead off with a great first sentence, so much the better!

2. ESTABLISH A BELIEVABLE REASON FOR YOUR HEROINE TO GET INVOLVED IN THE MYSTERY

There is nothing as irritating to me as the heroine who goes to great lengths to endanger herself purely out of curiosity. (Or is it sheer stupidity?) Put yourself in your heroine's place. What would motivate you to become involved in a dangerous situation? Here are some possibilities:

- Threat to life. The heroine is forced to investigate because her life (or a loved one's) is at stake.
- Vengeance. The heroine is righting a terrible wrong against her.
- Her reputation or her career is at stake.
- It's her job; she's a cop/spy/FBI agent.

3. WEAVE THE MYSTERY AND ROMANCE TOGETHER IN SUCH A WAY THAT ONE DOESN'T EXIST WITHOUT THE OTHER

Achieving a satisfying balance between romance and suspense may be the hardest thing of all for the writer to accomplish. Involve both your hero and heroine in the mystery in such a way that neither can afford to walk away. The danger should threaten them both, not just as a couple, but as individuals as well. The love affair will be sped up by the perilous situation; use danger as an aphrodisiac!

4. FORCE YOUR HEROINE TO MAKE CHOICES THAT COMPLICATE HER LIFE

Your heroine should not be merely battered by events; she should be actively trying to find her way out of the crisis. In the process, she will make mistakes and she'll choose paths that may worsen the crisis. In *Life Support*, my heroine is a doctor who wants to know why a certain patient died. Against the wishes of everyone involved, she demands an autopsy. The result is a cascade of events that eventually threatens her life.

5. INTRODUCE CONFLICT AT EVERY TURN

There's no better way to keep your scenes lively than to have every piece of dialogue, every interaction between characters, tinged with conflict. This doesn't mean you have to create a prickly heroine who argues with everyone. The conflict can be subtle (irritation between mother and daughter, for instance) or out-and-out war (heroine against a murderous villain). Between hero and heroine, conflict should be a major source of tension. I usually try to pit my lovers against each other, on opposite sides of an issue. In *Under the Knife*, my heroine is a doctor accused of malpractice, and the hero is the plaintiff's attorney. In *Harvest*, my heroine is a doctor accused of murder, and the hero is the homicide cop. They have to make it through many hurdles (and hundreds of pages) to finally end up happily ever after in each others' arms.

But that's the point of a romance novel, isn't it?

6. THE VILLAIN'S MOTIVES ARE AS IMPORTANT AS THE HEROINE'S

If your villain is "masked," then he'll remain unknown until the end. What the writer must do is keep him well concealed, while laying down all the clues needed for the reader to understand his motives. In trying to hide my villains, I use the "Let's Make a Deal" game show approach, in which I give my reader two "wrong doors" to open. Behind one door is the suspect who is obvious to everyone. Behind the second door is a suspect the "clever" reader will choose as the culprit. However, the real culprit stands behind door three waiting to be unmasked at the climax.

If your villain is revealed to the reader from the start, you have more chances to fully flesh him out. This is the interesting part, crawling into the bad guy's skin and viewing the world through evil eyes. Most mystery writers find this the most fun of all. Your responsibility is to make your villain real, to endow him with emotions, to make us understand and even sympathize with his reasons for evil. Remember: Give your villain a life!

7. INTRODUCE COMPLICATION AFTER COMPLICATION

Hollywood calls these "plot points." I call them "Oh, sh*t!" points, when I introduce yet another crisis, another disaster for my heroine. I use these crises to help me sail past any mid-book slump. Examples of plot points: another dead body turns up; there's another crime; there's a reappearance of a long lost character; or, a major character turns up dead.

8. BE AWARE OF THE DIFFERENCE BETWEEN SURPRISE AND SUSPENSE

Surprise: The bomb goes off in the theater without warning. Suspense: The reader knows the bomb is ticking and knows the heroine is struggling to find it in time. Of the two of these, suspense is the most powerful tool for keeping your reader turning the pages.

9. IF YOU'RE FEELING BLOCKED, TRY SWITCHING POINT OF VIEW

This is the reason I don't write first person novels. I have a very short attention span, and I couldn't possibly stay in the head of only one character through an entire book. A new character can also introduce a different perspective on the plot, and can witness events your heroine couldn't possibly witness. Be careful, though, not to head hop. I usually try to stick to one POV per scene.

10. TO SCARE YOUR READER, WRITE ABOUT WHAT SCARES YOU

The climax is where I reveal, as a writer, my deepest fears. In *Harvest*, I reveal my fears of paralysis and intubation by putting my heroine on the operating table, helpless to stop a surgeon with a scalpel in his hand. In *Call After Midnight*, I reveal my fear of heights by putting my heroine on a rooftop, inches away from death. When you write about your own fears, you transmit that tension to your story, and you scare your readers as well. I also try to think cinematically, asking myself, "How can I set up this scene in a flashy way that will have a movie audience gasping?" You never know when Hollywood will come knocking, asking for film rights to your book!

11. THE RESOLUTION SHOULD NOT SOUND CANNED

I have never been a big fan of Hercule Poirot style speeches at the end. I prefer to let the solution to the mystery be uncovered bit by bit, revealing it to the reader without long-winded explanations by the sleuth. I don't feel compelled to tie up every single loose end. If I've paced it right, and the groundwork of my mystery has been laid, then the reader should be able to tie up those loose ends without my explaining it all to her.

12. RESOLVE THE MYSTERY BEFORE YOU RESOLVE THE ROMANCE

Every good book involves two separate resolutions. First, it must give the reader intellectual satisfaction; the mystery is solved, the puzzle is explained. Second, it must give the reader emotional satisfaction; the hero and heroine resolve their conflicts and find a happy ending together.

The real "payoff" for women readers is the emotional satisfaction, so I save that for last. This is what gives your ending the happy "Ahhh…" factor. This is what makes your reader eagerly go off in search of your next book!

"Tension is the element that keeps the reader turning the pages, and to have tension, you must build suspense. Four ingredients are of paramount importance: Problem, Purpose, Conflict, Goal."
--Phyllis A. Whitney
From *Guide to Fiction Writing*
Reprinted with Permission
* * *

"Kathryn is going to great lengths to collect articles and what a tapestry of romance writing! I hope this essay helps to illuminate the fun of writing romantic adventures. Roller-coaster thrills <u>should</u> be scary as hell."

It's Not Just Another Suspense
—It's Romantic Adventure

By Suzanne Brockmann

The hero is trapped on a ledge on the side of a cliff. He's got one arm around the heroine, and the other arm clutching a sub-machine gun. The heroine's holding her terrified four-year-old daughter.

She's also holding her own gun because, hey, she's a modern romance heroine and she can take care of herself. Still, in this situation, she's probably a little glad that the hero's around to help out.

On top of the cliff are the bad guy, a mob heavy, and his gang. They, too, carry significant firepower, and their goal is to blast the heroine—the only witness to a murder—off the side of that mountain. So as not to leave any further witnesses, they'll pop the hero and the innocent four-year-old while they're at it.

What's the sub-genre: romantic suspense or romantic adventure? More importantly, what exactly is the difference between the two?

Suspense novels usually have characters that are intent upon achieving their goal, which often involves crime solving. Because the crime is usually of a serious nature and the hero and/or heroine is usually either a suspect or a law-enforcement official on the case, there's not a lot of room for levity. The story is often told with a rather quiet voice, using neither flowery description nor many one-liners for comic relief.

Then there's the plot. A suspense usually has a mystery involving one of what I call "modern day terrors"—serial killers and other murderers, stalkers, kidnappers and the molesters of our children, terrorists, or the threat of biological warfare, to name a few. Yikes! These are all things that "go bump in the night" of our modern lives. These are very real bogeymen who walk our streets and scare the hell out of us.

We whip through the pages (if they're well-written) because we can't bear to put the book down before we find out who the killer is, or how the heroine manages to track down and defuse the anthrax bomb before it wipes out half of Baltimore, or how the hero finds his kidnapped child.

At first glance, suspense and adventure seem similar. Both have a life-threatening dilemma to resolve. Both have fast-paced plot lines. The main characters' lives are always in jeopardy. The real difference lies in the information that is revealed both to the reader and to the characters. Think about "Star Wars," a classic adventure. Darth Vader is the bad guy, and as he approaches the rebel moon in his Death Star, he's not worried about concealing his identity! There's no mystery as to where the threat is coming from—it's there, in plain view. In an adventure, suspense is created as we wait to see not who the bad guy is, but how and if the bad guy will be defeated.

Adventure novels can be lighter in tone and mood than suspense. Since the main plot isn't a dark and scary whodunit, there's more of an opportunity to add comic relief. The characters can be less intense as well.

The characters are the focus of an adventure. In fact, one way I define a romantic adventure is a book in which plot twists are used to enhance a character-driven romance. In a suspense novel, it's the characters who enhance a complex plot.

When writing an adventure, I'm not so much concerned with exactly how any mystery elements are solved, as I am with how my characters react to the information that has been uncovered, how they react to the new problems that arise, and how they react as a situation goes from bad to worse.

Even though a romantic *adventure* is not a romantic *suspense,* it's nonetheless suspenseful. Suspense is necessary in any book. As writers, we have to keep readers worrying about what happens next.

That—along with truly believable, compelling characters—is what keeps those readers from turning off the light on their bedside table until three in the morning.

Right now, romantic suspense sales are booming. So why write Romantic Adventure when everyone else is trying to break into the world of romantic suspense? Well, there's an answer right in the question, isn't there? These days there's an overflow of dark and scary books on editors' slush piles as all styles of writers attempt to hop ontothe suspense bandwagon.

If your writing voice is not naturally dark and scary, if you can't easily creep out readers with your tone and your word choices, then the romantic suspense that you write may sound forced and unnatural. Maybe you do have that extra Stephen King gene that gives your writing that gut-tightening edge, but maybe you want to stand out from the crowd by writing something a little different. Or, maybe you're not interested in reading or writing a book that is as dark as a true suspense needs to be.

Let's go back to my opening example—that man, woman, and child on the ledge. Is their story romantic suspense, or adventure? Depends upon the mood, tone and characters, and how much of the threat is revealed—right?

Here's how I see the scenario played out as a romantic adventure:

Kerrie was understandably upset. "You promised you'd keep Molly safe!"

She all but kicked him.

The four-year-old was clinging to her, her baby-soft platinum curls sharply at odds with the dulled black metal of the sub-machine gun.

Kerrie was still held loosely in her other arm.

"She's safe. We're all safe now," Murphy said, checking the clip on his own gun.

"We're trapped by seven men with guns," she practically spat at him. "Unless you've got an entire cavalry up your sleeve, ready to come to our rescue, I wouldn't exactly call us safe. God! Why did I ever agree to go anywhere with you?"

Murphy scratched the back of his hand with the two days growth of stubble on his chin. "It was probably my irresistible smile and magnetic charm."

She snorted. It was not an affirmative sounding snort and it was accompanied by a venomous glare. So much for his idea of seducing her by the light of the fire after the kid was asleep.

Murphy squinted as he scanned the harshness of the surrounding countryside. The ledge they were on was not easily accessible from above. That was good. A sheer wall of rock went up at an outward angle, shielding them from the guns of the men at the top. That was good, too.

However, they were vulnerable and exposed from the vantagepoint of the mountain across the ravine. It wouldn't take more than a few hours for Fiore to send one of his sharpshooters down the other side of the mountain, across the river flowing below, and over to the neighboring mountainside. At a distance of only a quarter mile, they'd all three be easy targets. That was not good at all.

"What if I told them I wouldn't testify?" All of the sarcasm was suddenly gone from Kerrie's voice and Murphy knew that she finally was scared to death. Her eyes were the same almost painful shade of blue as the sky. "What if I promised I would take Molly and go to Mexico? Do you think they'd believe me?"

Murphy touched Molly's white-blond hair. Somehow, the kid had fallen asleep, the paths of her tears clearly visible on her dusty little face.

She was a miniature version of her mother, with the same porcelain-perfect angelic features.

He met Kerrie's gaze as he shook his head. "No," he said quietly. "It's too late for making deals. If you want to get out of here alive, I'm the one you've got to trust. One hundred and ten percent. And you've got to start now."

She didn't want to trust him. She didn't even like him—Murphy could see that in her eyes. But she didn't have a choice and she nodded. "Does Molly know how to swim?" he asked, pulling the shoulder strap of his gun over his head and leaning the weapon against the side of the cliff.

"She's four. She's had a few lessons, but..." Kerrie shook her head. "Why do you ask?"

"How about you?" he asked. "You can swim, right? I mean now would be a really great time for you to tell me all about how you trained for the Olympic swimming team when you were thirteen."

She looked down at the river flowing far beneath them and then she looked back at him. "Please tell me you're kidding."

"If you're not a real strong swimmer, you better let me hold the kid."

Kerrie made a sound that was more a sob than a laugh. "You want me to give you Molly to hold while you jump off the side of a cliff into a river?"

Like a 250-page roller coaster ride, the adventure rages on. Bad guys with guns, incredible odds, and the growing trust between a man and a woman that eventually becomes love…all provide non-stop action.

If both sub-genres were park rides, romantic suspense would be "Space Mountain", i.e., a roller coaster ride inside a dark mountain with dizzying drops and frighteningly sharp curves that come out of nowhere. Romantic adventure, on the other hand, would be the "Loop-the-Loop." You're going to get turned upside-down and taken for the ride of your life—you know you will, because it's broad daylight and you can see it all coming at you down the track.

Like these amusement rides, both romantic suspense and adventure are equally thrilling. There are other similarities. Adventure needs to have the same relentless pacing as suspense. Both need excellent, multidimensional characters.

I love writing romantic adventure. I can create the kind of heroes I adore: those larger than life, sexy, smart alpha males (usually Navy SEALS!) I can also use elements of comedy in my books that I wouldn't be able to get away with were I writing romantic suspense. I can stand out in the crowd because my voice is my own.

For me, romance is not just a job—it's an adventure.

"Kathryn always remembers the time I first made the New York Times list, after writing for many years in the romance genre. Before then, I'd always wondered exactly what it took. This essay will give you an example of the kind of romantic suspense stories that publishers are looking for. I wish you all the best of luck. "

Making the New York Times Bestseller List

By Tami Hoag

"Are you sitting down?"

I always imagined that's exactly what Nita Taublib, my publisher at Bantam Books, would say if she ever called to tell me I had made the *New York Times* bestseller list.

Still, when she did call me with those very words one December, I wasn't at all prepared for what followed: "Guess who's Number 11 on the *Times* list?"

A spot on the *New York Times* paperback list is what every romance writer dreams of, whether they admit it or not. The title "New York Times Best-selling Author" opens doors, eyes, and pocketbooks. It comes with a built-in prestige writers simply can't get anywhere else. Even though we're the very same writers we were a week ago, we've suddenly gained legitimacy in the eyes of a great many people.

Night Sins is part psychological suspense, part police procedural mystery. It is a mainstream thriller with all the expected nail-biting, page-turning power promised on the back cover. However, the book also has the complex personal relationships and strong romantic element that readers have come to expect from me.

Set in the fictitious rural Minnesota college town of Deer Lake, the plot revolves around the search for a missing child. With each passing hour the search for Josh Kirkwood takes on a more ominous intensity.

For heroine Megan O'Malley, the new regional officer of the state criminal investigative unit, it is the first test of whether she can cut it in the all-male world of local cops.

For the hero, Police Chief Mitch Holt, it is an unwelcome and frightening reminder of the big city crime that devastated his life before he found sanctuary in Deer Lake. And all the while someone watches, preparing the next move in a deadly game to which only he knows the rules...

For me, having *Night Sins* make this list as a paperback bestseller had an added bonus. The following February, the much anticipated sequel, *Guilty As Sin* would hit the stands in hardcover. With luck, the book would catch that wave of momentum created by the success of *Night Sins*.

Guilty As Sin plunges the reader into a rural county court system dealing with a big-time crime: child abduction.

The task of bringing Josh Kirkwood's abductor to justice puts Ellen North in the hot seat—a position she thought she'd left behind in Minneapolis. However, politics and ulterior motives lurk even in rural Minnesota. Ellen knows she's the best prosecutor in the office and, in the eyes of her politically paranoid boss, the most expendable. Complicating her life further, any control over the media frenzy surrounding the case is shattered when her boss grants best-selling true-crime author Jay Butler Brooks access to the case.

Jay is by turns cynical, mercenary, and selfless. He is a classic, tarnished knight. A man convinced of his own disinclination to heroines, which makes him, ironically, all the more heroic.

Ellen, however, will take some convincing. She looks around and sees nothing but wolves: her boss, Brooks, and, arguing for the defense, the last man she wants to face in court or out—her ex-lover, Tony Costello.

While the wolves circle her, Ellen knows that there is another in the shadows watching her with deadly intent. When a second child is kidnapped while Ellen's prime suspect sits in jail, she realizes the game isn't over. It's just begun—again.

While *Guilty As Sin* is a sequel to *Night Sins*, the book stands on its own. I think anyone who enjoys a good court thriller will be drawn into Ellen's struggle to win justice, discover the truth, and stay alive in the process. In fact, I'm counting on it, because I would certainly love to always get calls that start with "Are you sitting down?"

"Start writing now! If you write one page a day, you will have written a short mystery in less than eight months!"
—Toby Bromberg

* * *

Rosemarie,
Writers' Colony, San Francisco

Dear Kathryn,

Another treasure chest of information! We are thrilled that these authors took the time to help us. It looks like Jade has been very smart to zero in on writing romantic suspense. What a ripe market she will have for her ideas.

Jade may be the only one of us planning to write books that are strictly romantic suspense, but it looks like we will all do better if we inject some suspense into whatever plots we create from here on in. We haven't forgotten that great advice you sent us about the importance of writing a page-turner! What better way to do it than keeping readers "at the edge of their seats," as it were?

By the way, talk about edge-of-your-seat—my "waiter," Alex has asked me to return to Scotland with him when he goes back nest week! However, it's suddenly become so complicated. It turns out Alex was once married. They divorced, but his ex- wife vanished about the same time the money began to disappear from his restaurants.

Yesterday, a man Alex trusts called him to say he is certain that a woman he saw getting onto a ferry in the north of Scotland—is Alex's ex-wife!

Suffice it to say, this has both of us in a total jumble and, as a result, I have *no* idea what I should do. What a complicated plot twist *this* is!!

I know, I know, you're saying, "Sounds like a great idea for a book." Speaking of which...

Is it time yet for us to develop our outlines? We've each chosen our niche, we've read the past and present recommended books for our particular categories, and we've studied and re-studied Al Zuckerman's lessons on creating an outline. You have given us so many mental challenges, and new plot ideas with all the articles and advice you sent, that each of us feels we are primed and ready to write the next best-selling romance novel!

What do you say Kathryn, may we start?

Your grateful protegee,
Rosemarie

* * *

Kathryn Falk, Lady of Barrow
Romantic Times Magazine
Brooklyn, New York

Dear Rosemarie, Sierra, and Jade,

I am happy to say the time has indeed arrived to take the next step! You are now ready to sit down and plot. And may I remind you…not a word of dialogue until your plotting is completely thought out and you know how this book is going to "play" right to the very end.

Did I ever tell you many readers look at the <u>last</u> chapter first? I think it's appalling, but several of my reviewers swear by it. You will be ahead of the game if you can think about that part of the book first; it will mean you have really done your advance calculating.

Even though it is not yet time for you to write your book—<u>only the outline</u> at this stage—I want you to keep in mind that you are going to be aiming this finished work at the agents and publishers who are looking for new writers. Each publishing house has its own code of submissions. Some want only a query letter (they have small offices and believe me, if you can sell them with a one-page letter they'll be impressed); others want a partial manuscript (the outline and the first three chapters). A small number want the entire manuscript.

The same submission rules usually apply to agents: some want short submissions before they will decide whether or not they want to represent you, and some want long. Some have a reading fee. If an agent agrees to handle your work, the usual percentage he/she will take is 15% of your advance and royalties. Some publishers will not look at your manuscript unless an agent presents it.

Going on the assumption that an agent or an editor will eventually buy your book, you then have another pile of work in front of you—how to promote, how to get booksellers to recommend your book, how to get on the lists, how to attract a following of readers, and how to build your career from the first book onwards.

I'm getting way ahead of things. Due to the fact that you are fledglings, I was wondering if you would be interested in keeping in touch with me? Perhaps, when your outline is finished, we can correspond again? It would be fascinating to me to look over your outlines and help you with your first three chapters (and the last one, of course). I am sure my coterie of publishing pals can help you take the book from outline to final form. We can even do some of those writing exercises you love!

There is self-publication to consider, and publishing on the Internet. We need to come up with a thorough resource list for you. I want you to know the books to read if you're going to be writing for the ethnic market, and the best Internet sites to research Haggis (you just might need that if you go off to Scotland, Rosemarie.) You will need to know exactly how to write a query letter, and what agents/editors/publishers are seeking.

Then, we can start from scratch on the promotion highway. You'll have to study book covers, and learn about illustrators. Did you know that eventually you might even be able to choose your cover models?

You might become so erudite that, like Johanna Lindsey and Virginia Henley, you figure out which month you would prefer to have your book(s) come out to guarantee maximum sales exposure.

We should discuss the advantages of sending your book to Hollywood agents and producers.

There are promotional materials like bookmarks to think about. (They are what made Brenda Joyce a big name in romance publishing. Each of her first five books came with a handsome, headless hunk that everyone talked about.) Nora Roberts, to this day, sends out gifts to booksellers and reviewers with each new book. We've received champagne bottles filled with candy, Kleenex boxes that say, "Don't cry over my book," mugs, pens, and T-shirts.

Heather Graham creates some of the most colorful posters, and she even has her husband Dennis posing with her for her book covers. The great Sci-Fi and fantasy artists, The Hildebrandt Brothers (who did the "Star Wars" poster) designed a fabulous illustration, with Dennis included, for Heather's debut Vampire Romance, *Beneath A Blood Red Moon*.

I don't mean to run on with this letter, for I know you said you're "chomping at the bit" to get to your outlines. Tuck the information I've sent to you deep inside your brains and let it percolate. *We're not done yet.* I have such confidence in each of you, that I am busy putting together the *rest* of the articles you will soon need to get your exciting novel idea from manuscript…to publisher…to booklovers' hands.

Love,

Kathryn

Appendix I

Etiquette for Manuscript Submission

By Kathryn Falk

Most publishers and agents agree upon one important thing: Unpublished authors should *not* send in full manuscripts. Instead, an untried writer should first send a publisher or an agent a query letter (one to three pages), giving a description of her/his book's plot, setting and characters, along with any personal information that is relevant to that individual's writing experience.

If your book has a plot set in Scotland or Saudi Arabia, and you've lived, worked, studied, or researched there, mention that in your query letter. Life experience interests editors. If you are a long-time romance reader, let an editor know the scope of your reading, and your familiarity with the genre.

If an editor or agent likes what you have sent, he/she will then request a "partial," i.e., the first three chapters, or the first fifty pages of your book. Most publishers (and even many agents) will not read full, unsolicited manuscripts, so you're wasting your time sending something beyond a partial.

Do not *ever* send a random chapter, or your favorite chapter, unless that is specifically what an editor asks you for. Most editors like to start reading from the beginning, and—like readers who pick up books in book stores—if they don't like the beginning, they won't buy the book.

Don't worry that you are not submitting your "most interesting" chapter. Most editors are looking for a "voice" and they know immediately if a writer has that "voice" by reading those first 50 pages of a manuscript.

Some publishing houses go step-by-step after giving a favorable nod to a query letter. They will request a brief synopsis. If you pass the synopsis test, you must then pass the test of the synopsis and first chapter. After that, if not rejected at that stage, you will be requested to send in the first half. And so on. The process can take many months. The entire editorial team decides whether or not the book is viable at each phase. In other houses, individual editors can buy what they like, without getting the whole team's approval, and the process is sped up enormously.

Most publishing houses do not take unsolicited manuscripts, usually due to their small offices! If you want to hear back from a publishing house regarding your query letter or partial, it is more than polite, it is *essential* to include a SASE (self-addressed-stamped-envelope). Use the proper postage on the correct size envelope, so the editor can send it back to you with a note.

As far as getting what you've submitted returned to you, I don't know of any publisher who will guarantee the return of a partial manuscript without the proper postage included.

If a romance is what you have written, it will certainly help to have a *romance* editor's name on the envelope. Editors move around, but even so, I have included the current roster of names below. When your book is finally ready to be sent off, it wouldn't hurt to call beforehand to see if the person named on that list is still the romance or fiction editor.

If you haven't verified by phone or another source exactly who is buying romances at which company, then at least put "Romance Editor" or "Romance Acquisitions Editor" on the envelope.

Query letters, outlines, and partials are not read overnight. Do not expect to hear from an editor for weeks—or months. The "turn-around" as the expression goes, can be as short as six weeks, or as long as three months.

Some publishers will send you a form letter of rejection. Others, who think you have talent, will write a note that may say, "Your dialogue is good but the plot is predictable." That's encouragement, which means you would probably succeed in making another submission to that editor.

Some publishers have a standing policy not to comment on *any* manuscripts they reject. When asked why this is his policy, the Editor-in-Chief at Genesis Press, Gary Frazier, said, "Because I, or our Romance Acquisitions Editor could be wrong. I've seen plenty of books in print that I would not have published in a million years. So when it comes to any one of those books, some editor somewhere liked it, bought it, and published it. I would not want any comments we would make to an author—a new author especially—about a manuscript we reject, to discourage her or him from continuing to write and continuing to try to get published. For another editor at another house that author's work may be just what he/she is looking for—and the only way the author will know that is to keep submitting."

Some editors require that you have an agent make the submission for you. ("You must be 'agented,'" is the expression.) Many editors feel that if an agent represents your manuscript, then it's worth the time to consider it.

What happens to your manuscript if you disagree with these suggestions and send the whole manuscript in anyway? It literally ends up on a pile—what is commonly known in publishing as a "slush pile." This consists of the manuscripts sent in unsolicited and piled high for some new editor to go through. (I want you to realize why your manuscript may never be returned if you send it unsolicited to a publisher.) Gold has been found in those piles, but for the most part, manuscripts piled there are sent in by people who have no idea of either publishing protocol, or how small an editor's office really is!

If an editor likes your work, most likely she/he will call you and make an offer. I would advise you not to agree to an amount of money or any terms at this point. You will probably be too excited to negotiate a deal for your book with any sense of self-preservation. That's typical, as anyone involved in publishing knows. (I might add that if you have already agreed to any conditions, such as an advance or royalties, etc., your about-to-be-acquired agent would most likely be bound to that amount.)

So, if you think your manuscript is ready to sell, put this post-it note on your telephone:

**"Don't agree to an amount until I have
an agent or call *Romantic Times* for advice."**

When that editor calls, it is professional for you to say, "I am deciding upon an agent at the moment, and will have one get back to you." Whatever you do say—don't accept terms then and there over the phone. Call me at *Romantic Times* and if you don't have an agent, I will get one for you.

Finding an agent is similar to finding an editor. You submit a query, an outline and the first three chapters with a SASE, and then wait for a response. Agents and editors are like marriages, some work out and some don't. Few authors currently have the same ones they started out with.

One more tip. Many agents and editors ask that you not make multiple submissions. I believe that your hair will turn white if you wait one-by-one for everyone to read your query letter or partial. (The worst that can happen is that everyone wants you!) This multiple submission bonanza has happened to only one writer I know of, who followed my send-it-to-everyone suggestion. She had her pick. If you're fortunate and receive several offers for publication, call me and I'll help you choose which editor or agent to try first.

When I solicited publishers in the 1980's for my first romance reference book, *Love's Leading Ladies,* I blanketed the market with my query letter and outline. Avon contacted me first, but then decided not to publish the book. However, a little publisher named Pinnacle wanted it. If I had waited and gone one-by-one through the publishing houses, I might not have gotten to Pinnacle for years.

I would suggest that your multiple submissions *not* look like carbon copies. Put the editor's name on each one, don't use Xerox copies that are obvious, and *don't forget the SASE!*

Finally, nothing infuriates editors more than having unpublished authors explain that they have chosen their pen name. Wait until after you get a contract before addressing that sore point!

Appendix II

Romance Publishing Houses

Editor's Note: Except for Harlequin and Silhouette (actually the same company but different divisions of that company), there are not any publishers buying the short, "series" romances at the present time. If a publishing house says that it accepts "all types" of romances, it is referring to sub-genres or categories of romance, and not book length. Inspirational, and some smaller regional publishers do sometimes have the series length.

Avalon Books
401 Lafayette St., NY, NY 10003
Tel: 212/598-0222
Ellen Mickelsen-Publisher; Executive Editor-Veronica Mixon
Interested in: Sweet romances, contemporaries and mysteries for the library market.
Submission Requirements: Query letter or agented. No E-mailed submissions.
www.avalonbooks.com

Avon Books
1350 Avenue of the Americas, NY, NY 10019
Tel: 212/261-6800
Carrie Feron, Executive Editor; Lucia Macro, Senior Editor; Ann McKay Thoroman, Editor; Lyssa Keusch, Editor; Micki Nuding, Associate Editor
Interested in: All types of romance.
Submission Requirements: Query letter or agented. No E-mailed submissions.

Ballantine/Fawcett/Ivy Books
201 E. 50th St., NY, NY 10022
Tel: 212/751-2600

Shauna Summers-Senior Editor; Elisa Wares-Senior Editor;
Charlotte Herscher-Edit. Ass't.
Interested in: All types of romance.
Submission Requirements: Prefer agented but will look at a query
letter. No E-mailed submissions.

Bantam/Doubleday/Dell Books
1540 Broadway, NY, NY 10036
Tel: 212/354-6500
Bantam: Beth de Guzman-Senior Editor; Wendy McCurdy-Senior
Editor; Stephanie Kip-Editor; Kara Cesare-Ass't. Ed.; Wendy Chen-
Ass't Ed.;
Dell: Christine Zika, Editor; Maggie Crawford-Editorial Director
Dell Mass Market
Interested in: All types of romance.
Submission Requirements: Prefer agented, but will look at a query
letter (no more than three pages).

Barbour (Heartsong Presents)
P.O. Box 719, Uhrichsville, OH 44683
Tel: 740/922-6045, Fax: 740/922-5948
Rebecca Germany-Managing Editor
Tracie Peterson, Acquisitions Editor - Historical and Contemporary
Inspirational Romance.
Interested in: Historical and contemporary inspirational romance
novellas between 19-20,000 words. Also, looking for ethnic christian
romances. (African-American, Hispanic, Asian, etc.)
Submission Requirement: Partial manuscript with SASE included.
www.barbourbooks.com

Bethany House (*Portraits* Series)
11300 Hampshire Avenue South, Minneapolis, MN 55438
Tel: 612/829-2500
Barbara Lilland-Senior Editor Adult Fiction; Sarah Neirman-Fiction
Editor
Interested in: Inspirational mystery/intrigue/social Issues, with only
a thread of romance.
Submission Requirements: Partial manuscript with SASE.

BET Books/Arabesque
All submissions to be made to Kensington Books at the present time.
Karen Thomas, Romance Editor
Interested In: Multi-cultural contemporary romances of 80,000 -
100,000 words.
Submission Requirements: Include a cover letter that mentions any
previously published work. Include a two or three page detailed
synopsis covering the plot points. Send the first three consecutive
chapters of your manuscript for evaluation. Your name and address
must be in the first page of the manuscript, which should be typed and
double-spaced with one inch margins. Do not send computer disks or
hand-written material. Please allow 10 to 12 weeks for a reply.

Dorchester Publishing Co., Inc.
276 Fifth Avenue Suite 1008, New York, NY 10001
Tel: 212/725-8811, Fax: 212/532-1054
Alicia Condon-Editorial Director; Chris Keeslar-Editor
Lines: *Leisure* and *Lovespell* imprints
Interested in: Historical, futuristic, time travel, fairy tale and
paranormal romances of approximately 95,000 words.
Submission Requirements: Query or submit synopsis and first three
chapters.

Forge/Tor Books
175 Fifth Ave., 14th floor, NY, NY 10010
Tel: 212/388-0100
Melissa Ann Singer-Senior Editor Romance; Natalia Aponte-Editor
Romance
Claire Eddy-Editor science fiction/fantasy romance.
Interested in: Romance and straight historicals.
Submission requirements: Partial with synopsis.
www.tor.com/forge.html

Genesis Press, Inc.
315 3rd Avenue North, Columbus, MS 39701
Tel: 601/329-9927, Fax: 601/329-9399
Gary M. Frazier, Editor-in-Chief; Susan R. Simpson, Assistant Editor
- Romance

Interested in: Multicultural romance, erotica written by women for women.

The Lines: *Indigo* (African-American), *Tango 2* (Latino/Hispanic), *Red Slipper* (Asian/Asian-American), *Love Spectrum* (Interracial), *THERION* (Erotica for women).

Submission Requirements: Query letter, first three chapters, and synopsis. SASE for a reply. No queries by e-mail, fax, or phone.
www.genesis-press.com

HARLEQUIN, MILLS & BOON, SILHOUETTE, MIRA and STEEPLE HILL BOOKS

Harlequin and Silhouette offer detailed tip sheets. These guidelines are available by sending in a SASE to the addresses/divisions listed below. They are also available on the various Harlequin web sites.

Originally, all editorial work was done through Mills and Boon in London. Writers are still welcome to submit to Mills and Boon. (They alone publish medical romances, which are not sold in North America, but that are a library staple in England and Australia, in particular.)

Alternatively, writers can submit to editors either in New York, in the Canadian office. The tip sheets detail which lines are edited where.

Harlequin Books — Canada
225 Duncan Mill Road Don Mills, Ontario, Canada M3B 3K9
Tel: 416/445-5860, Fax: 416/445-8655
Diane Moggy-Senior Editor; Malle Vallik-Senior Editor; Birgit Davis-Todd-Senior Editor; Paula Eykelhof-Senior Editor;
Series Romance, Historical romance
Submission Requirements: Write for tip sheets or check web site.

Harlequin Books — United States
300 E. 42nd St., NY, NY 10017
Tel: 212/682-6080, Fax: 212/682-4539

Debra Matteucci-Senior Editor; Tracy Farrell-Senior Editor;
The Lines: *American, Intrigue, Love and Laughter, Presents, Romance, Superromance, Temptation*
Submission requirements: Write for tip sheets or check web site.

Harlequin/Mills and Boon Ltd.
Eaton Heights, 18-24 Paradise Road, Richmond, Surrey TW9 1SR
England
Tel: 011-44-181-948-0444
Gillian Griffiths; Elizabeth Johnson
Series Contemporary Romance and medical romances.
Submission requirements: Write for tip sheets or check web site.

Mira
225 Duncan Mill Road Don Mills, Ontario Canada M3B 3K9
Tel: 416/445-5860, Fax: 416/445-8655
Diane Moggy-Senior Editor
Mainstream Romance
Submission requirements: Write for tip sheets or check web site.

Harlequin/Silhouette Books
300E 42nd St. 6th floor, NY, NY 10017
Tel: 212/682-6080
Leslie Wainger-Executive Senior Editor; Mary Theresa Hussey-Senior
Editor; Joan Marlow Golan-Senior Editor; Karen Taylor Richman;
Tracy Farrell-Senior Editor; Ann Leslie Tuttle, Ass't Editor
Interested in: Series/Contemporary Romance.
The Lines: *Inspirational, Romance, Desire, Special Edition, Intimate Moments,* and *Yours Truly*
Submission requirements: Write for tip sheets or check web site.

Harlequin/Steeple Hill (Love Inspired)
300 E. 42nd St., NY, NY 10017
212/682-6080
Anne Canadeo-Editor; Tracy Farrell, Senior Editor
Interested in: Contemporary inspirational romance. Circa 70,000
words.
Submission Requirements: Write for tip sheets or check web site.

Harper Collins
10 E. 53 St., NY, NY 10022
212/207-7000
Interested in: All types of fiction
Submission requirements: No unsolicited manuscripts.

Kensington/Pinnacle/Zebra Publications:
850 Third Ave. NY, NY 10022
Tel: 212/407-1500
Ann LaFarge-Executive Editor; Carolyn Marino-Senior Editor; Kate Duffy-Senior Editor
Karen Thomas-Multicultural Editor for BET's Arabesque line.
Interested in: Historical, contemporary, and romantic suspense, as well as African American and Latino Hispanic romance.
The Lines: *Arabesque*, and *Precious Gems* (historicals and contemporaries sold exclusively through Wal-Mart).
Submission Requirements: Cover letter, synopsis, and partial with SASE.

LionHearted Publishing
P.O. Box 618
Zephyr Cove, NV 89448-0618
Tel: 702 588 1388
Email: admin@LionHearted.com
Submissions to: Acquisitions Editor
Mary Ann Heathman President and CEO
Interested in romance (historical/contemporary/regency/western/time travel/paranormal/futuristic)
Submission Requirements: Query letter, 1-5 page synopsis and first three chapters. No faxed or electronic submissions please. Electronic query letters okay.

Multnomah Publishers: *(Palisades and Alabaster)*
P.O. Box 1720, Sisters, OR 97759
Tel: 541/549-1144
Karen Ball-Editor Palisades Romance Division
Interested in: Romance/mystery/humor/inspirational romances

Submission Requirements: Query letter with personal history including statement of faith, short 2-3 page synopsis and three sample chapters.

Penguin/Putnam Publishing
(Topaz, Onyx, Berkley, Signet, Dutton, Jove)
375 Hudson St., NY, NY 10014
Tel: 212/366-2000
Hillary Cige-Senior Editor; Hillary Ross-Executive Editor and creator of the Regency Romance Line; Audrey Le Fehr-Director of Editorial for Topaz
Interested in: Historical, contemporary, Regency, and suspense
Submission Requirements: No unsolicited manuscripts at this time.
www.penguinputnam.com

Pocket Books/Simon & Schuster
1230 Sixth Ave., NY, NY 10020
Tel: 212/698-7000
Linda Marrow—Executive Editor and VP; Caroline Tolley-Senior Editor;
Catherine Collins-Editor; Amy Pierpont-Associate Editor
Interested in: Historical, contemporary and suspense romance.
New imprint in 1999: *Sonnet Books* – Historicals only.
Submission Requirement: Agented only. Manuscripts more than 100,000 words.
www.simonsays.com

Red Sage Publishing
P.O. Box 4844, Seminole, FL 33775
Tel: 727/391-3847
Alexandria Kendall-Editor
Interested in: Looking for sexy romance, all sub-genres. Novella length (23-30,000 words). Intense love relationship with an equally intense sexual relationship.
Submission Requirements: One page synopsis and the first ten pages of the story; include writing credentials.

Robinson Publishing (Scarlet Books)
7 Kensington Church Court, London W8 4SP England
Tel: 011-44-171/938-3830
Sue Curran-Editor; Colleen Collier-Editorial Ass't.;
Frances Whitehead-Editorial Consultant
Interested in: Sensual contemporary romances.
Submission Requirement: Query, synopsis and first 20 pages, plus
personal information.

St. Martin's Press
175 Fifth Ave., NY, NY 10010
Tel: 212/674-5151
Jennifer Enderlin-Exec. Editor; Jennifer Weis-Exec. Editor
Glenda Howard-Editor
Interested in: All commercial fiction.
Submission Requirements: Query, synopsis, and partial with SASE.

Rubenesque Romances
P.O. Box 534, Tarrytown, NY 10591-0534
Joanne K. Morse, Ph.D., Publisher
Interested in: Stories for and about plus-sized women.
Submission Requirments: Synopsis and partial. Ms length: 40,000-
50,000 words. Heroine has to overcome problem about her weight.

Tyndale House
P.O. Box 80, Wheaton, IL 60189-0080
Tel: 630/668-8300
Submit to: Manuscript Review Committee
Interested in: Historical and contemporary inspirational romance.
Submission Requirements: Agented preferred, or query letter and
detailed outline with a sample chapter. SASE required.
www.tyndale.com

Warner Books
Time and Life Building, 1271 Ave. of the Americas, NY, NY 10020
Tel: 212/522-7200
Claire Zion-Exec. Editor Romance; Sandra Swedeen-Ed. Ass't.;
Tina Moskow, Consulting Editor; Danielle Dayen, Ass't Editor

Interested in: All commercial fiction
Submission Requirements: Agented or query letter. No electronic submissions

Waterbrook Press
5446 North Academy Blvd., Suite 200, Colorado Springs, CO 80918
Tel: 719/590-4999, Fax: 719/590-8977
Lisa Bergren-Executive Editor for Fiction
Interested in: Contemporary and Historical Inspirational Romance.
Submission Requirements: No query letter necessary. Send two-page synopsis and first three chapters.

Appendix III

Agents and Agencies

Aaron Priest Literary Agency
Aaron Priest
708 Third Avenue, 23rd Fl.
NY, NY 10017
Tel: 212-818-0344
Fax: 212-573-9417
apriestlit@aol.com

Ahearn Agency, Inc.
Pamela Ahearn
2021 Pine Street
New Orleans, LA 70118
Tel: 504-861-8395

Alice Hilton Literary Agency
Alice Hilton
13131 Welby Way, Suite. B
N. Hollywood, CA 91606
Tel: 818-982-2546
Fax: 818-765-8207

Alice Orr Agency
Alice Orr
305 Madison Avenue, #1166
NY, NY 10165
Tel: 718-204-6673
Fax: 718-204-6023
orragency@aol.com

Alison J. Picard
P.O. Box 2000
Cotuit, MA 02635

Anita Diamant Agency
310 Madison Avenue
NY, NY 10017
Tel: 212-687-1122
Fax: 212-972-1756

The Axelrod Agency
Steven Axelrod
54 Church Street
Lenox, MA 01240
Tel: 413-637-2000

Cherry Weiner Literary Agency
Cherry Weiner
28 Kipling Way
Manalapan, NJ 07726
Tel: 732-446-2096

The Cohen Agency
Rob Cohen
331 W. 57th Street, #176
NY, NY 10019
Tel: 212-399-9079
Fax: 212-246-4697

Curtis Brown, Ltd.
Maureen Walters,
10 Astor Place, 3rd Fl.
NY, NY 10003
Tel: 212-473-5400
Fax: 212-598-0917
mw@cbltd.com

Daniel King Literary Agency
Daniel King
5125 N. Cumberland Blvd.
Whitefish Bay, WI 53217
Tel: 414-964-2903
Fax: 414-964-6860-fax

Denise Marcil Literary Agency
Denise Marcil
685 W. End Avenue, #9C
NY, NY 10025
Tel: 212-932-3110

Ethan Ellenberg Literary Agency
Ethan Ellenberg
548 Broadway, 5-E
NY, NY 10012
Tel: 212-431-4554
Fax: 212-941-4652
eellenberg@aol.com

The Evan Marshall Agency
Evan Marshall
6 Tristram Place
Pine Brook, NJ 07058
Tel: 973-882-1122

Francine Ciske
Patricia Dietz
P.O. Box 555
Neenah, WI 54957
Tel: 920-722-5944

Great Titles, Inc.
Tina Tsallas
18 Greenfield Drive
Etobicoke, Ontario
M9B 1G9

Tel: 416-231-6686

Hyatt Literary Agency
Linda Hyatt
Box 730
Holden, ME 04429
Ldhyatt@aol.com

Jane Rotrosen Agency
Andrea Cirillo
Meg Ruley
318 E. 51st Street
NY, NY 10022
Tel: 212-593-4330
Fax: 212-935-6985
jrotrosen@aol.com

Joyce Flaherty Literary Agency
Joyce Flaherty
816 Lynda Court
Street Louis, MO 63122
Tel: 314-966-3057
Fax: 314-965-7043

Kellock & Assoc., Ltd.
Joanne Kellock
11017 80th Avenue
Edmonton, Alberta
T6G OR2 Canada
Tel: 403-433-0274

Knight Literary Agency
Diedre Knight
P.O. Box 550648
Atlanta, GA 30355
Tel: 404-816-9620
Fax: 404-237-3439

Lowenstein Associates
Nancy Yost
121 W. 27th Street, Suite. 601
NY, NY 10001
Tel: 212-206-1630
Fax: 212-727-0280
nancy@bookhaven.com

Marcia Amsterdam Agency
Marcia Amsterdam
41 W. 82nd Street
NY, NY 10024
Tel: 212-873-4945

Maria Carvainis Agency
Maria Carvainis
235 West End Avenue
NY, NY 10023
Tel: 212-580-1559
Fax: 212-877-3486
mcainc@banet.net

Meredith Bernstein Literary Agency
Meredith Bernstein
Elizabeth Cavanaugh
2112 Broadway, Suite. 503 A
NY, NY 10023
Tel: 212-799-1007
Fax: 212-799-1145

Natasha Kern Literary Agency
Natasha Kern
P.O. Box 2908
Portland, OR 97208
Tel: 503-297-6190
Fax: 503-297-8241

Northeast Literary Agency
Mary Hill
69 Broadway
Concord, NH 03301
Tel: 603-225-9162
Fax: 603-255-3774

Patricia Teal Literary Agency
Patricia Teal
2036 Vista del Rosa
Fullerton, CA 92831
Tel: 714-738-8333

Patti Steele-Perkins
38 Eastview Mall Drive
Victor, NY 14564
Tel: 716-223-2250
Fax: 716-396-3579
pattiesp@aol.com

Pegasus International
Gene Lovitz
Box 5470
Winter Park, FL 32793

Pema Browne Ltd.
Perry Browne
HCR 104B Pine Road
Neversink, NY 12765
Tel: 914-985-2936

Perkins Literary Agency
Esther Perkins
Box 48
Childs, MD 21916
Tel: 410-398-2647

Pesha Rubenstein Literary
Agency
Pesha Rubenstein
1392 Rugby Road
Teaneck, NJ 07666
Tel: 201-862-1174
Fax: 201-862-1180
peshalit@aol.com
(No downloads)

Richard Curtis Agency
Richard Curtis
Laura Tucker
171 E. 74th Street, 2nd Fl.
NY, NY 10021
Tel: 212-772-7363
Fax: 212-772-7393
ltucker@curtisagency.com
rcurtis@curtisagency.com
www.curtisagency.com

Ruth Cohen Agency
Ruth Cohen
P.O. Box 7626
Menlo Park, CA 94025
Tel: 650-854-2054

Sandra Watt & Associates
Sandra Watt
8033 Sunset Blvd., #4063
Los Angeles, CA 90046
Tel: 213-851-1021

Scott Meredith Literary Agency
845 Third Avenue, 15th Fl.
NY, NY 10022
Tel: 212-751-4545
Fax: 212-755-2972

Sharon Jarvis & Co.
Sharon Jarvis
Roxy LeRose
Toad Hall Inc.
Rural Rte. #2, Box 16B
Laceyville, PA 18623
Tel: 717-869-2942
Fax: 717-869-1031
toadhallco@aol.com
www.toadhallinc.com

Writer's Edge Inc.
Albert Link
112 Neptune Court
Indialantic, FL 32903
Tel: 813-797-5530

Writer's House, Inc.
Albert Zuckerman
Amy Becktower
Robin Rue
Karen Solem
21 W. 26th Street
NY, NY 10010
Tel: 212-685-2400
Fax: 212-685-1781

Appendix IV

Romantic Times Magazine

Each month *Romantic Times* magazine is published in Brooklyn, and reviews and rates more than 120 new book releases. The magazine is read by booksellers, publishers, and their sales forces, editors, agents, readers of romance, aspiring writers, and published authors. It is an invaluable guide to Hollywood moguls looking for script ideas and writers, for foreign editors looking to buy American books, and to librarians (who tell us at *Romantic Times* that romances are the most checked-out genre).

Aside from reviews, RT previews all the romance lines three months ahead of time, delivers the latest news and gossip about the genre, profiles authors, and includes news on editors and agents, as well as passing along the latest writing tips.

Address all correspondence to:

Romantic Times Magazine:
55 Bergen Street, Brooklyn, New York 11201
Tel. No.: 718/237-1097, Fax No.: 718/624-4231
E-Mail: Rtmag1@aol.com

To Subscribe to *Romantic Times* Magazine:

Price per issue—$4. (A sample copy will be sent
first class for $5.) Six Month Subscription, US, $21;
Canada, $33; Europe, $43. (Foreign subscribers
requested to pay in US funds, drawn on a US bank.)
Major Credit Cards Accepted: Amex, Visa, MC, and
Discover.

Appendix V

Romantic Times Annual and Regional Conventions & Lady Barrow Tours

By Kate Ryan

Almost every weekend, groups of romance writers gather somewhere to hold conferences. It's hard to believe that in 1981, when *Romantic Times* magazine began publishing, this didn't happen! It wasn't until Kathryn Falk launched the very first romance writer's conference in New York, that romance writers were finally able to gain access to this kind of sharing of personal and professional information that is now so prevalent worldwide.

Before that first conference, writers holed up in homes or offices, with only a typewriter for company. There was no easy way of networking with other writers as a means of sharing encouragement or trading insider tips on writing and the pitfalls of publishing. Few of them knew what to expect as a monetary "advance" for a standard contract, how to market and publicize themselves; or how to sell a multi-book contract. Their access to agents and editors in the field of romance was limited.

With the advent of the first *Romantic Times* Booklovers' Convention, that all changed. Soon, aspiring authors, booksellers and readers flocked to these annual conferences in New York. Published authors delighted in the opportunity to cross-promote to readers and booksellers, and aspiring authors learned skills from the masters of their craft, and had opportunities to network with industry professionals. The result was a happy romance for all involved!

Who could have imagined that these first conferences would become the largest industry parties and networking opportunities in the field today?

Each year *Romantic Times* holds a conference in a different city. In conjunction with the conference, multi-tracks of seminars are held, for everyone from aspiring to published authors, to booksellers, and readers.

Readers and booksellers flock to the conferences for the opportunity to meet their favorite authors, and because the conferences are FUN! They ooh and ahh during the Mr. Romance Novel Cover Model pageant (where the next Fabio is chosen), dress up as their favorite romance novel characters for the Costume Competition, and get to pose with the author who created the character!

Last year, an Autographing Book Fair, where over 300 authors autographed and sold books to fans from all over the country, was linked to the convention.

The 1999 convention is to be held in Toronto, Canada during the weekend of September 16-19. In October, 2000, the convention will take place on board a Carnival Cruises' cruise liner, which will depart for the Mexican Caribbean for seven days! The first year of the next millenium, 2001, marks the first International Booklovers Convention, to be held June 30-July7 in Cambridge, England.

In addition to the giant, annual conferences, *Romantic Times* has begun to offer smaller, specialized, regional conferences called "Booked on Romance, "which are held in conjunction with the Independent Bookseller Association meetings. The first of these conferences was held last year in San Antonio, Texas.

At a time when publishers are consolidating, and new writers are finding it increasingly difficult to get published, "Booked on Romance" brought together independent publishers (as well as some of the large publishers), and featured the first all-day industry tracks on new genres, multicultural publishing, and Internet publishing. Writing workshops incorporated actors dramatizing scenes as writers wrote them, and booksellers and readers participated in interactive programs where they had opportunities to voice their opinions directly to published authors and industry professionals.

The next *Romantic Times* regional conference will be held in Portland, Oregon in 1999, and will combine romance-writing programs with the "Pacific Northwest Booksellers Forum." Two book fairs will be held at the same time: one organized by the PNBA, hosting authors from many genres, and a second, organized by *Romantic Times*, featuring romance authors. Conventions are also planned for Las Vegas and Houston, TX (Nov 9-12, 2000).

Fun, fantasy, fabulous parties and the opportunity to meet thousands of other book lovers from around the world, keep romance readers and writers returning to these incredible networking events again and again.

As an addition to each of these conventions, Kathryn Falk, Lady of Barrow, has created "Lady Barrow Tours." Originally introduced strictly so conference attendees might extend their stays, learn more about the cities in which the conferences were being held, and have more time to get to know one's fellow writers, the tours have now expanded to include "stand-alone" booklovers' tours to many exotic locations.

Whether toasting the New Year in the Land of the Midnight Sun in Iceland, or whirling on the arm of a handsome Scot during the ball following the opening of the Museum of Scotland, members of Lady Barrow's tours never lose sight of the real reason for the festivities—to bring together book lovers everywhere in a festive, fun way.

The most recent convention and tour calendar is available by calling Romantic Times at 718/237-1097.

A schedule of events is also available on RT's website:

RomanticTimes.com

Appendix VI

Recommended Reads

How to Write a Romance and Get It Published
By Katherine Falk
A Signet Book, Published by Penguin

How to Write a Blockbuster Novel
by Al Zuckerman
Pub. by F & W. Publications

Enchanted Journeys Beyond the Imagination: An Annotated Bibliography of Fantasy, Futuristic, Supernatural, and Time Travel Romances, Volumes 1-3
by Susan W. Bontley and Carol J. Sheridan
(Available through Blue Diamond Publications, 937/320-1642)

Writing Past Dark
By Bonnie Friedman
Pub. by Harper Perennial/Harper Collins

The Writing Life
By Annie Dillard
Pub. by Harper Perennial/Harper Collins

Listen to Their Voices
Mickey Pearlman
Pub. by Houghton Mifflin Company

Writing Down the Bones
Natalie Goldberg
Pub. by Shambala Publications Inc.

The Artist's Way
Julia Cameron with Mark Bryan
Pub. by Jeremy P. Tarcher/G. P. Putnam Sons

The Writer's Journey
Mythic Structure for Storytellers & Screenwriters
By Christopher Vogler
Pub. by Michael Wiese Productions

The Art of Fiction
By John Gardner
Pub. by Vintage Books/Random House

Bird by Bird: Some Instructions of Writing and Life
By Anne Lamott
Pub. by Pantheon

Write Right!
By Jan Venolia
Pub. by Ten Speed Press

The Elements of Style
By William Strunk Jr. and E.B. White
Pub. by Allyn & Bacon Incorporated

Guide to Fiction Writing
By Phyllis A. Whitney
Pub. by The Writer Inc.

All *Romantic Times* Top Picks

for this year

Pub. By *Romantic Times* Magazine
Available on *RomanticTimes.com*

Appendix VII

Contributors to this book

Ed. Note: Profiles of authors who have published from 1996 on are listed on *RomanticTimes.com*, along with reviews of their books and the ratings they received. The site also lists any awards they may have received from *Romantic Times*.

Victoria Alexander has spent much of her life as an award-winning TV reporter. She's covered presidents, the Pope, and movie stars. When she discovered fiction was more fun than real life, she turned to writing full time. Victoria lives in Omaha with her husband, two children and a canine comedian named Sam.

Bridget Anderson was born and raised in Louisville, Kentucky, but now lives in Atlanta, Georgia. She has a master's degree in clinical therapy. She sold her first book, *Soul Mates*, to Pinnacle Books in 1997. She enjoys reading, music, movies, and the least amount of exercise possible.

Amanda Ashley (aka Madeline Baker) was born in California and has lived there ever since. She is married and the mother of three and grandmother of five. Amanda's first grandchild and first book were "published" on the same day 12 years ago. She has since published 26 books with Leisure Books, and just recently sold her first full-length book to Topaz. Amanda is obsessed with vampires and *The Phantom of the Opera*, which she has seen 19 times.

Mary Balogh grew up in Wales and moved to Canada to teach after graduation. Love and marriage intervened when she was on the brink of returning home, and she is still in Kipling, Saskatchewan (pop. 1200) more than 30 years later. Mary and her husband Robert have three grown children scattered over the continent and three energetic grandchildren close by. She is an incurable optimist who lives with her head in the clouds and ignores the banana peel underfoot.

Gerry Benninger is a life-long reader of romances who has been reviewing mainstream & new reality/historical romance novels for *Romantic Times* for more than five years. During that period, her enthusiasm for the genre has increased, proving her assertion that "only romance provides the heroine inside each of us" with a satisfying outlet. Currently, Gerry is a resident of Phoenix, Arizona.

Jo Beverley, a *New York Times* best selling author, has won nearly every award in romance, and is a member of the RWA Hall of Fame. She is also one of the authors featured with profile and article in the reference book, *North American Romance Writers*. Born and raised in England, and with a degree in English history, Jo writes historical romances set in her native land. She lives with her husband and sons in British Columbia, on Canada's West Coast.

Jennifer Blake (aka Patricia Maxwell, Maxine Patrick, Elizabeth Trehearne, and Patricia Ponder) is often called the "Steel Magnolia of women's fiction". She is a seventh generation Louisianian who married her teenage sweetheart when she was fifteen and he was nineteen. She published her first book in 1970. She and her husband live in a lake home patterned after the houses of the Louisiana French colonial era. Hobbies for Jennifer include growing antique roses, painting, and needlework.

Susan W. Bontley and Carol J. Sheridan are co-authors of the alternative reality romance reference set, *Enchanted Journeys Beyond the Imagination: An Annotated Bibliography of Fantasy, Futuristic, Supernatural, and Time Travel Romances, Volumes 1-3*. They also publish a monthly newsletter, The Alternative Reality Romance Connection, devoted exclusively to upcoming and newly discovered AR romances.

Barbara Bretton reigns happily over her Caribbean kingdom, a lush and private island south of Barbados. She spends her days relaxing in the tropical sunshine while biddable nubile men (in the guise of unemployed publishing executives) keep her in SPF 30 sunblock and pina coladas. She spends her nights doing the merengue with an assortment of lovers, all of whom are named Antonio. Her *good* twin stays home in New Jersey with her husband and writes books.

Suzanne Brockmann writes contemporary series romance for Silhouette *Intimate Moments* and single-titles for Ballantine. She lives west of Boston with her husband and two children, both of whom are professional actors. Her daughter has appeared in films and videos, and her son prefers the stage. Suzanne is vocal arranger, co-director and one of the lead singers in the Boston-area, nine-voice, a cappella group "Serious Fun."

Toby Bromberg is RT's reviewer of mystery books. She genuinely finds her reviewing to be "one of the most satisfying things I do." She also enjoys the fact that she is always ahead of the general reading public. "I never run out of reading material," Toby says, "and I'm always one of the first to know what's going on in the mystery world." Toby resides in Rumford, Maine.

Anita Richmond Bunkley's first novel, *Emily, the Yellow Rose*, was turned down by several publishers because of questions regarding its "marketability." Undeterred, Anita and her husband, Crawford, used their savings to create Rinard Publishing and self-published the book in 1989. It received wonderful praise and sold nearly 10,000 copies. Based upon that tremendous response, Dutton/Signet signed Anita to a two-book contract. She has two grown daughters and lives in Houston with her husband, Crawford.

Linda Cajio sold her novel *All is Fair* to Bantam Books in 1985. Published in June of 1986, *All is Fair* topped the Waldenbooks Bestseller List for series romance. Linda's books have been consistent best-sellers, with her fourteenth book, *The Reluctant Prince*, an August 1992 release, garnering the #1 spot on both the Waldenbooks' and B. Dalton's best-sellers lists. She is the author of the popular Kitteridge Family series for Bantam/Loveswept.

Stella Cameron (aka Jane Worth Abbott and Alicia Brandon) hails from Scotland. She and her husband, Jerry, live in Washington State. They have a son and two daughters, are animal "nuts," and raise orchids. She started her career writing for Harlequin/Silhouette and is the author of more than 40 contemporary and historical romantic suspense novels as well as several novellas. She is a *New York Times* and *USA Today* bestseller.

Marilyn Campbell (aka Marina Palmieri) is based in south Florida. Besides being a prolific, multi-genre author, she is a popular public speaker and lecturer on topics ranging from writing and getting published to metaphysical studies. Having personally experienced the phenomenon of "passing into the light," she has also gained a respected reputation for her unique insights and work as a Spiritual Guidance Counselor.

Margaret (Meg) Chittenden (formerly aka Rosalind Carson), English born, has been writing since 1970. She has published short stories and articles, three children's books and more than 25 novels in various genres. All of her novels have been reprinted around the world. She is the author *of How to Write Your Novel,* published by The Writer Inc. *Dying to Sing,* the first book in her Charlie Plato Mystery Series, was published in hardcover by Kensington Publishing in 1996.

Wil Colom is the founder and publisher of Genesis Press, Inc. He practices law in Columbus, Mississippi, where he lives with his wife, Dorothy (who is a Chancery Court Judge and avid romance reader), and their twin sons.

Lori Copeland is happily married to her high school sweetheart, Lance. She lives in the Ozarks, and values the hours she spends with family. Lori has three grown sons, Randy, Rick and Russ, three gorgeous daughters-in-law, Maureen, Shae and Shelly, and three absolutely perfect grandsons, James, Joe and Josh. Bridge, water aerobics, lunches with friends, and long phone chats with writing buddies are among a few of her favorite things.

Millie Criswell is a winner of the Romantic Times Career Achievement Award. She began writing when her husband suggested: "Why don't you write one of those romances you're always reading." (Millie contends that Larry has a brilliant idea once every decade and this happened to be the one for the 80's). Residing in Fredricksburg, Virginia, Millie has two grown children and one neurotic Boston terrier.

Linda L. Crockett (aka Linda Castle, aka Linda Lea Castle) is a third generation New Mexican who started writing in 1992. She is the founder of *Four Corners Literary Alliance and Cornucopia,* a monthly, international newsletter for writers. She is married to husband/hero Bill Crockett and is the mother of four. Two grandsons and one granddaughter have made an appearance as well as three sales to Harlequin *Historicals.*

Jennifer Crusie holds a master's degree in professional writing and women's literature. Her best-selling novels have won numerous awards and she has garnered a Romantic Times Career Achievement Award. Jenny lives in an historic district in southern Ohio with three dogs and three cats. Daughter Mollie moved near Jenny in 1997, and now Jenny says her life is "almost perfect." She is currently in the Ph.D. program at OSU. Jenny's first hardcover novel, *Tell Me No Lies*, came out in March of '98.

Emma Darcy has had a life journey that has taken as many twists as those of the characters in her stories, whose popularity worldwide has resulted in sixty million books in print. Born in Australia, she currently lives on a beautiful country property in New South Wales. Before taking up writing, creative urges were channeled into oil-painting, pottery, designing and overseeing the construction and decorating of two homes, all in the midst of keeping up with three lively sons and the very social life of her businessman husband. She has recently taken a new direction in writing mainstream women's fiction.

Jude Deveraux has created a tradition of best selling success with each of her novels surpassing the last in audience recognition and sales.

Born in Fairdale, Kentucky, she first gained notoriety in the 1980's with her historical romance saga "The Montgomery Annals," which won the Romantic Times award for best historical romantic series. Readers dubbed these books the "Velvet Books" because of their titles: *Velvet Promise, Highland Velvet, Velvet Song* and *Velvet Angel*. Since then she has delighted millions of fans with the continuing saga of the Montgomery clan. Her books are perennial favorites on the *New York Times* bestseller list. Son Max now fills her hours with delight.

Thea Devine, a Zebra author, has been called "The Queen of Erotic Romance." She is the author of more than a dozen steamy historical romances, the most recent of which have been reviewed as erotica. And yes… it's her real name.

Jennifer Dunne writes romance and science fiction, and edits the *Science Fiction Romance* newsletter. Her novel-length fiction has garnered numerous awards, including first and second place in the Silver Heart competition. In addition to writing, Jennifer holds a full-time job playing with numbers, and spends far too much time spoiling her cat.

Kathleen Eagle was an English teacher on the Standing Rock Sioux Indian Reservation in North Dakota when she met and married Clyde Eagle, a "handsome, charming, irresistible" Lakota cowboy. The Eagles have been married for more than 28 years and have three children. Since the publication of her first Silhouette *Special Edition* (a Golden Heart winner) in 1984, Kathleen has published well over 30 romances. She has won virtually every prize in the romance industry. She lives in Minnesota with her husband and children.

Lynn Emery is a native of Louisiana. She has long been an avid student of history, loves collecting and viewing art, and gardening. Lynn has a masters degree in social work and sold her first book, *Night Magic,* in 1994 to Kensington for the *Arabesque* line under the Pinnacle imprint.

Leslie Esdaile is VP of Creative Projects for All America Film and Video, and has a Masters of Fine Art in Screenwriting and

Filmmaking. Leslie got into writing when she stayed home to look after her six-month-old daughter who, having been scalded in an accident at a day-care center, required multiple surgeries. Leslie finished a novel, *Sundance*, which was printed by Kensington Publishing as part of its *Arabesque* line.

Gwynne Forster published her first romance novel in 1995. She was formerly head of research in fertility and family planning at the United Nations, and published widely as a demographer. Gwynne lives in New York City with her husband, who designs her promotional materials and is her solid rock. She raises vegetables, is a gourmet cook, loves to entertain, fish, sing, and read. She lectures on fiction writing, haunts museums, and spends her Sunday afternoons answering fan mail.

Suzanne Forster started writing, literally, by accident when a car crash ended her dream for a career in clinical psychology. She started writing during the recovery period and before she was well enough to go back to graduate school had sold a novel, and launched a new career. She has since written more than 20 women's fiction novels, specializing in thrills, chills and passionate romantic suspense.

Lori Foster has a husband who is the funniest man she knows, and her three sons (just like their father) keep her happily on the brink of insanity. Luckily, Lori likes being a little zany... and a little risqué. Harlequin *Temptations "Blaze"*—the hotter *Temptations*—allow her to write the kind of books she loves. (Which is exactly why she sold her first 10 books to *Temptation*.)

Dorothy Garlock (aka Dorothy Phillips, Dorothy Glenn, and Johanna Phillips) has published 38 novels, which have been translated into 18 different languages and sold in 35 countries around the world. Currently she has 12 million books in print. It was while working as a newspaper reporter that Dorothy, at age 49, wrote her first book. Her writing is still inspired by the world of wagon trains and the adventures of the Old West. To her fans she is known as the "grand mistress of the frontier novel."

Julie Garwood has earned a solid position among fiction's established stars with over 20 million books in print worldwide, 14 consecutive *New York Times* bestsellers, and a #1 *New York Times* bestseller. She is an active supporter of the Toys for Tots Foundation that collects toys for needy children each holiday season. In addition, she is a champion of literacy, serving as a tutor, a classroom storyteller, and as author of two children's books. Julie's first historical romance, *Gentle Warrior*, was published by Pocket Books in 1985.

Tess Gerritsen was a practicing physician when she sold her first romantic thriller in 1987 to Harlequin *Intrigue*. A Reviewer's Choice award winner, she wrote nine romantic suspense novels before switching genres in 1996 with her first medical thriller, *Harvest*, which was a *New York Times* bestseller. It was followed by *Life Support* and *Bloodstream*. When not writing, Tess is an avid rose gardener and fiddler in a dance band. She and her family live in Maine.

Nancy Gideon (aka Dana Ransom) is a prolific author with more than 35 sales to her credit since 1987. She is a Waldenbooks bestseller for Silhouette, has written an award-winning vampire romance series for Pinnacle and is currently dabbling in the motion picture industry after writing a horror film "novelization" and having her first original screen play optioned. She writes for Zebra as Dana Ransom, and under her new name, Rosalyn West, she's begun a series for Avon called "The Men of Pride County."

Heather Graham (aka Heather G. Pozzessere, and Shannon Drake) has more than twenty million copies of her books in print. In addition to being a New York Times best-selling author, Heather has received numerous awards for her novels. Her books have been selections for the Doubleday Book Club and the Literary Guild. She has been published across the world in more than fifteen languages and has produced more than 80 titles including anthologies and short stories. She lives in Florida with husband Dennis and their five children.

Lucy Grijalva (pronounced gree-HALL-va) has lived in the San Francisco Bay Area all her life. Her interests include her two children, quilting and needlework (in her dreams), playing trivia games (as long as she gets to win), catalog shopping (okay, no one ever said she's normal), and, of course, reading. She loves writing stories about cops.

Gay G. Gunn began her literary career when, for five years, she wrote a monthly column, "Personal Reflections," for *Washington Living Magazine.* Her first book was *Dotted Swiss and Gingham*, a series of essays about growing up and coming of age as a Black female in 1950-60's Washington, DC. Gay has two sons and lives with her husband in Maryland.

Shirley Hailstock, best-selling, award-winning novelist has been writing for more than ten years. Holding a bachelor's degree in chemistry and an MBA in marketing, Shirley's initial wish was to join the space program. Living in Plainsboro, NJ with her two teenage children, Shirley has been an Adjunct Professor at Rutgers University and at Middlesex County College.

Sylvia Halliday has been published since 1982. In addition to writing, she is a free-lance editor and book doctor. A trivia nut, she has appeared on "Jeopardy," and is a gourmet cook and skilled seamstress. She is the mother of four grown children and the grandmother of four, an accomplishment she prizes far more highly than her publishing output! She lives happily alone in Forest Hills, NY.

Crystal Wilson Harris is an Assistant Professor of Developmental English at Sinclair Community College in Dayton, Ohio. She holds a Master's degree from the University of Dayton. Her first novel, *Dark Embrace*, was released in 1991 by Odyssey Books and was reprinted in 1998 by Genesis Press. Despite a schedule that has her juggling two kids, a dog, a cat, and a full-time job, she is currently hard at work on her next novel.

Robin Lee Hatcher (aka Robin Leigh) is an author of both historical and contemporary novels, she is a past president of Romance Writers of America and namesake of "The Robin Award" given by Laubach Literacy International. Robin, a native of Boise, and her husband,

Jerry, like to escape the city and take refuge at their mountain cabin in central Idaho. Robin is the mother of two and the (very young) grandmother of three. Hobbies include golf and musical theater.

Lorraine Heath had no idea when she received her BA in Psychology, that she had gained a foundation that would help her create believable characters—characters that are often described as "real people." She received a Romantic Times Career Achievement Award for Americana historicals. She is currently working on another historical. Lorraine enjoys hearing from readers and can be reached via E-mail at LorraineHe@aol.com.

Dee (Emily) Hendrickson lives in Reno, Nevada with her retired airline pilot husband. Of all the many places she has traveled around the world, England is her favorite and the most natural choice as the setting for her novels. In addition to her many Regency romances, she has written a Regency reference book.

Virginia Henley is the *New York Times* best-selling author whose authentic medievals about England, Ireland, and Scotland, have received critical acclaim and garnered her many awards. Virginia and her husband Arthur were married in 1956. They have two handsome sons and three beautiful grandchildren. Virginia lives on the Gulf of Mexico in St. Petersburg, Florida and spends her summers in Canada.

Donna Hill began her writing career crafting short stories for confession magazines. Her first book, *Rooms of the Heart,* launched Odyssey Books contemporary romance line in 1990 and was reprinted by Genesis Press in 1998. A Brooklyn resident and mother of three, Donna manages her own publicity and promotions company, Annod Productions. She gives workshops around the country and works full-time for the Queens Borough Public Library as a Public Relations Specialist.

Sandra Hill (aka Harper Allen) is known for the humor she injects into her outrageous, award-winning novels. She is the wife of a brokerage executive and mother of four sons. As a former newspaper journalist dealing with serious issues, she discovered the merits of seeking the lighter side of even the darkest stories. Sandra loves to hear from her readers at shill733@aol.com.

Martha Hix has written numerous internationally-published, best-selling novels, winning awards along the way. This married mother of two ranks her extended family as Priority #1. A sixth-generation Texan, she considers herself a learned genealogist, a passable whitewater rafter, and "lousy at dieting or housework." *MAD Magazine* is her favorite reading material.

Tami Hoag claims writing is the ideal profession because "You get to go to work in your pajamas, tell lies all day, and get paid for it. There aren't many other jobs where a person can do that kind of thing without danger of prosecution." Tami began her writing career with Bantam's *Loveswept* line and has since moved on to pen numerous *New York Times* best-selling thrillers. She lives on a horse farm in Virginia.

Christine Holden comprises the duo of Leslie-Christine Megahey and Shirley-Holden Ferdinand, a mother-daughter writing team who have been working together since 1991. Seven years and 10 manuscripts later, they're living their writers' dreams.

Linda Hyatt is an agent and author who has written several articles about writing and the writing business. She founded Hyatt Literary Agency in 1993, and she and associate Roberta Brown, represent many talented and successful authors.

Beverly Jenkins is an African-American historical romance writer. She and her family live in southeast Michigan. Her first novel, *Night Song*, was published by Avon.

Peggy Jaegly is multi-published in various newspaper and trade and city magazines on a wide variety of topics. She co-authored the booklet, *Miscarriage: A Book for Parents Experiencing Fetal Death*. She has compiled three editions of *Romantic Hearts: A Personal Reference* *for Romance Readers*, a comprehensive collection of romance authors profiles, publications and pseudonyms.

Donna Julian enjoyed a successful career in international finance before becoming a writer. Her favorite pastimes include spectator football, reading, travel, and dance (especially when travel involves the opportunity to watch her granddaughters dance). Donna is a best-selling, award-winning author. She is the mother of three children and lives in a St. Louis, Missouri suburb with her husband, Jerry.

Marcia King-Gamble was born on the island of St. Vincent in the sunny Caribbean. She resides in Florida and holds a degree in psychology and theater. Marcia is currently an executive with a major cruise line. She is the author of three multicultural romantic suspense novels: *Remembrance* and *Eden's Dream* released in 1998 and *Under Your Spell* scheduled for release in 1999.

Mary Kirk is the award-winning author of seven novels, including *Miracles* (1990 - Romantic Times Reviewers' Choice Award); and *Embers* (1991 - Romantic Times Lifetime Achievement Award). Ms. Kirk says, "I feel very much a part of the dialogue among women who are questioning what they want out of life and love. As a writer, I strive to present the most hopeful visions this dialogue has to offer."

Sandra Kitt is considered to be the foremost African American writer of romance. She was the first black author to publish with Harlequin with the classic *Adam and Eva*. Her twelfth novel, *Serenade*, launched the *Arabesque* ethnic romance line. As an artist with degrees in fine art, she has exhibited across the U.S., illustrated a number of books, and created greeting cards for UNICEF.

Karen Morrison-Knox graduated Summa Cum Laude from the University of California, Davis, and has a Master's Degree in Art History. Currently, she is writing a medieval romance. Ms. Morrison-Knox lives in northern California with her husband and daughter.

Judith Kohnen is a freelance editor and former newspaper columnist. Though also a registered nurse, she spends most of her days as an editorial consultant. She's a novelist and poet, and editor of her own inspirational newsletter, *Whispers Of Hope*. She lives in Virginia with her husband Mike, and is the proud mom of three daughters and two stepsons.

Susan Krinard combined science fiction and romance in *Prince of Wolves*, which made several bestseller lists. She's since written two other paranormal romances, a "futuristic," a fantasy-historical novella and a time-travel romance. A native Californian with a BFA in Illustration, Susan lives in the San Francisco Bay area with her husband, Serge Mailloux, a dog and a cat. She collects wolf-related items, vests, and fanciful costume jewelry.

Jane LaMunyon writes inspirational romances "for the same reason I read romances...because I enjoy a good love story." Barbour Publishing's *Heartsong Presents* published two of her inspirational romances *Fly Away Home* and *Escape on the Wind*. Along with award-winning author Vince Brach, she writes an inspirational newsletter, *Herein is Love*.

Jill Marie Landis is the multi-award-winning author of numerous national best-selling historical romances and short stories. She claims to be bi-coastal and lives in both Southern California and Hawaii with her husband, actor Steve Landis, and their cats. Her main goal in life is to stay tan. Besides sunning, her hobbies include reading, quilting, painting murals, growing tropical plants and playing the ukulele.

Sinclair LeBeau has been a freelance writer of magazine articles for several years. She had her first novel published in October of 1997 by Genesis Press. She has lived in Norfolk, VA all her life. Sinclair and her husband Edward have been married for 25 years and have three children.

Johanna Lindsey began writing in 1975 on a whim, just to amuse herself. As quoted, "It was like a Cinderella story, having that first book accepted by the first publisher it was sent to," which was Avon. She has been with Avon ever since. Raised mostly in Hawaii, she still lives there with her family. She is the mother of three sons, and now a grandmother as well.

Merline Lovelace spent 23 exciting years as an officer in the US Airforce before she began writing romance. She is the author of more than 30 romances, most of which combine elements of romantic suspense and action/adventure. She and her husband of 30 years enjoy travelling, golfing and long, lazy dinners with friends.

Tess Mallory saw her first romance, *Jewels of Time*, published by Leisure in 1994. Her second book made Ingram Books' Top 50 Romance Novels A-List. Tess has been a reporter, disk jockey, theatre costume mistress, and storyteller specializing in Irish, Scottish and English folktales. Tess lives in the Texas hill country with her two daughters and son, where she runs a small gift shop specializing in— what else?—Irish and Scottish gifts.

Teresa Medeiros is a former army brat and registered nurse, who wrote her first novel at the age of twenty-one and has since gone on to win the hearts of readers and critics alike. She currently lives in Kentucky with her husband, four cats, and one floppy-eared Doberman. Writing romance allows her to express her own heartfelt beliefs in faith, hope, and the enduring power of love to bring about a happy ending.

Linda Lael Miller is a single mom of daughter Wendy who is "the light of my life" and has written more than 20 novels, including the *New York Times* bestsellers *Princess Annie, The Legacy, Yankee Wife,* and *Daniel's Bride*. With over five million copies of her books in print, she is considered to be among the finest romance authors writing today. Ms. Miller resides in Washington and Arizona.

Jeanne Montague is the author of 36 books. She has published gothics, historicals, teenage romances and, her latest venture, erotica, with 11 erotica novels published in the past four years. She was married very young and then married for a second time 20 years ago.

Jeanne has four children, nine grandchildren and two great grandchildren. She lives in Warminster, Salisbury in England.

Kathleen Morgan is the author of 14 award-winning romances, including six futuristic romances, four fantasy romances, four historical romances, and one futuristic novella in a paranormal anthology collection. She is a registered nurse with a master's degree in counseling, married to a former US Army helicopter pilot, the mother of a teen-aged son, a breeder of English cocker spaniels, and a passionate water gardener.

Pamela Morsi introduced herself to the world with her first book, *Heaven Sent*. She has nearly two million books in print. Morsi has a BA in Humanities from Oklahoma State University and a Masters in Library Science from the University of Missouri. She worked as a librarian for 17 years before becoming a full time writer. An Oklahoma native, Morsi now lives in Texas with her daughter. All of Morsi's novels remain in print.

Elizabeth Goldsmith Musser is a native of Atlanta, Georgia. She and her husband, Paul, are missionaries with International Teams in Montpellier, France where they live with their two sons, Andrew and Christopher. She is the author of two novels, *Two Crosses* and its sequel, *Two Testaments* (Chariot Victor). She is working on her third novel, *Two Destinies* which takes place in present day France.

Constance O'Banyon (aka Micah Leigh) is the proud mother of four children. She is also a fold-out, picture-carrying, grandmother of seven. Constance lives in San Antonio, Texas with husband, Jim, and son, Jason. She is a voracious reader of mysteries. Constance has received numerous awards including Romantic Times' Career Achievement Award. She is the author of the highly acclaimed Savages Season series.

Janette Oke (pronounced Oak) is a best-selling author who has sold more than forty million books. She is the mother of four children, three boys and a girl, and the grandmother of 10. She and her husband live just north of Calgary, Alberta, Canada.

Sara Orwig (aka Daisy Logan) and her family live in a book-filled house in Oklahoma. When the writing career began, Sara gave up the corners to cobwebs, found a cubby in which to stash the ironing, and collected recipes of no more than four ingredients. The family survived. Sara's still writing as well as growing peppers, walking more than 700 miles each year and trying to find another spot to build more bookshelves.

Catherine Palmer is the daughter of missionaries. She grew up in Bangladesh and Kenya. She is a Summa Cum Laude graduate in English and holds a master's degree in English from Baylor University in Texas. Catherine has taught at both the high school and middle school levels. She, her husband and six-year-old son, Geoffrey, live in Bolivar, Missouri. She enjoys gardening, sewing and reading.

Susan Paul is the award-winning author of four romances, and a sensual historical novella in *Secrets Vol. II,* which was featured by Doubleday Book Club. Susan lives in Albany, Georgia with her family. A former model, she holds a black belt in Tae Kwon Do and received a gold medal at the 1995 US Nationals.

Ann Peach is a former newspaper editor and interior designer. She is currently a freelance editor, author and manuscript evaluator. Ann is married to "the love of this life, and every other one I have lived, too!"—her high school sweetheart, Ralph. She is the adoring mom of daughter Corrie, son-in-law Robert, and grandbabies Shelby and Christopher. Ralph and Ann live in New York city.

Chris Peirson is the Dallas-based head of her own 300-person law firm. She is nationally acclaimed as a speaker on the psychology of romance writing. Chris is married and the mother of two sons. Her interest in evolutionary psychology, anthropology, ethnology and culture has led her to develop an active consulting business in the application of science to romance.

Kayla Perrin lives in Toronto, Canada with her husband. She has a Bachelor of Arts in English and Sociology, as well as a Bachelor of Education degree. Kayla has starred in stage plays as well as in television and film productions. She sold her first novel, *Again, My Love*, in 1996 to Genesis Press. She has since sold two other novels.

Susan Elizabeth Phillips (aka Justine Cole) is a *New York Times*, *Publisher's Weekly*, and *USA Today* Top 50 best seller, whose books have been published in 14 foreign languages. She is a recipient of RWA's Favorite Book of the Year Award and holds Romantic Times' Career Achievement Award. She taught high school, and has two grown sons. She currently lives in the Chicago suburbs with her husband.

Tori Phillips received her degree in theater arts from the University of San Diego, then worked at MGM Studios, and appeared in Paramount Pictures' "The Great Gatsby." She is a published playwright. Tori's poetry is included in several anthologies. Tori is the mother of Tori and Philip, the mother-in-law of Rick and Elizabeth and the grandmother of Konrad. She lives happily ever after with her husband Marty in beautiful Burke, Virginia.

B.K. (Barbara) Reeves is a highly acclaimed author of several books, a well-loved teacher of writing, and an aspiring screenwriter. She lives near Houston Texas, and is a proud mom and grandmother.

Mildred E. Riley is a native of Connecticut. She graduated from Boston City Hospital School of Nursing and received a BA degree from Framingham State College. She retired after forty years of nursing and began writing. Her first published romance, was *Yamilla*. Her hobbies include ceramics, quilting, traveling and reading. A grandmother of six, she currently lives in Massachusetts.

Evelyn Rogers is the award-winning author of more than two dozen historical and contemporary romance novels and novellas. Evelyn credits family, friends, and experience (from crime reporter to teacher/librarian) as her inspirations. Besides family (husband, two children, one grandchild) and friends, she is passionately fond of books (all kinds), opera (nineteenth-century), and travel (England/ Scotland, France and Italy head the list).

Hebby Roman is a native Texan, who graduated from the University of Texas at Austin with both her bachelor's and master's degrees in business administration. Born and raised on the border of Old Mexico, she is a product of the dual culture of her upbringing, both American and Latino. Hebby currently resides in Arlington, Texas with her husband and son.

Kate Ryan is an avid romance reader who is coordinator of the Lady Barrow tours. She also coordinates Romantic Times' Annual Symposiums, and the Booklovers' Conferences. Kate writes several monthly columns for *Romantic Times* magazine. In addition, she writes a newsletter for the 1,000 Independent Bookstores that are part of the *Romantic Times* "Bookstores that Care" network. Kate lives in Brooklyn with her husband, Chris.

Sharon Sala (aka Dinah McCall) is a native Oklahoman whose home is in Eastern Oklahoma in the heart of the Creek Nation. Her son and daughter are grown and married, and her three granddaughters are the delights of her life. The love of her life is a native Oklahoman as well. He's half Creek Indian and half Irish, and as they say in Oklahoma, "all cowboy and then some."

Dallas Schulze is the award-winning, best-selling author of more than 40 novels. She sold her first book when she was 24, and has never looked back. Her work is known for its strong, likeable characters and quick-paced dialogue. She has written books with a fantasy theme and books told solely through the male's point of view. Her novels have been both contemporary as well as historical. She has been marrief for 26 years to a "wonderful" man.

Danny Sinopoli is a free-lance writer based in New York.

Gloria Dale Skinner (aka Charla Cameron) has been married to her high school sweetheart for over 25 years. In a writing career that began in 1990, Gloria has been a winner and finalist of numerous awards. Her books have been sold to several European countries. She has won the coveted Maggie award for her writing. A native

Floridian, Gloria likes flowers, candlelight, sweet smiles, gentle laughter and sunshine. E-mail: gloriadaleskinner@worldnet.att.net

Christina Skye is a China scholar with a doctorate in classical Chinese poetry. She has translated for Chinese generals, dissident poets, folk artists and fifth-generation puppet virtuosos. Skye has appeared on Geraldo! ABC Worldwide News, Travel News Network, the Arthur Frommer Show, Voice of America and Looking East. Her multi-award-winning romance novels are sold worldwide.

Bertrice Small is a *New York Times* best-selling author of historical romance, and the recipient of numerous awards for her work. She lives with her husband, George, and their two cats, Pookie and Honeybun, on the eastern end of Long Island, in the oldest English-speaking town in New York State. Known as "Lust's Leading Lady," she says she is really just a nice quiet lady who writes books.

Heywood Smith found it took a midlife crisis to motivate her to write a book. Burned out from selling real estate, she decided to quit her job and pursue her dream of writing despite dire predictions for the book market. Six years and three acclaimed historical novels later, Heywood is living her dream and loving every minute of it, especially meeting her readers and getting their letters.

Deb Stover wanted to be Lois Lane until she grew up and discovered there was no Clark Kent, let alone Superman. She gave up her monthly newspaper column to write what she loves to read— romance! Deb shatters genre and gender boundaries, braiding her novels with high adventure, sizzling passion, and wicked humor. This Colorado author has received several Readers' Favorite awards.

Anne Stuart has won every award in the business, has appeared on Entertainment Tonight and been quoted in *Vogue, People,* and *USA Today.* As naughty as she is nice, Anne lives in Vermont with her husband and two children, and is currently writing contemporary romantic suspense for Mira, historical romance for Kensington, and series romance for Harlequin *American Romance.*

Katherine Sutcliffe is the author of more than 10 novels. She won the Romantic Times 1987 Reviewers' Choice Award for her historical romance, *Windstorm*. A native Texan, she currently lives in Texas with her English-born husband and three children.

Jane Toombs recently moved from upstate New York to Carson City, Nevada, where she lives very happily with a man from her past and a calico kitten named Kinko. She is the author of 50 published books and the co-author of six others. Jane has written contemporary, historical, Regency, gothic, suspense and fantasy romance, as well as horror and fantasy, for many different publishing houses.

Chassie West is a Harper Paperback writer whose last two books were mysteries. Her three previous books, written for Silhouette *Intimate Moments* were romantic suspense. She once wrote young adult romances for Silhouette and is working on a sequel to the first of her Harper Paperback mysteries.

Al Zuckerman has been literary agent and book doctor to some two dozen blockbuster novels. At Writers House, he presides over a firm that represents hundreds of leading writers in all categories. Author of two published novels, winner of the 1964 Stanley Drama Award and former writer for three television series, he years ago also taught playwriting at the Yale School of Drama. He lives in New York with his wife.

Appendix VIII

From the Desk of Kathryn Falk

To Aspiring Authors Everywhere:

I am so excited about this book—and Volume Two, which is due out soon! Please join me, and Jade, Sierra and Rosemarie, as they continue on their journey to publication.

In order to help them take their ideas from outlines to finished novels, I have asked many friends to help. In response, my writing pals have already sent in writing exercises and "how-to's," sample synopses, insider tips on promotion, tips on self-publication, interviews with editors and agents, advice on the "new kid on the block" (electronic publishing), and the latest updates on the new markets, in-depth publisher tips and more…

In essence, they have sent a mini-encyclopedia of terrific information covering each important aspect of the romance novel writing and publishing process. Oh yes, and I will have a resource section that will knock your socks off!

Information is rolling in daily. All I will say about this two-volume set is: If it isn't in here…it isn't about romance writing!

Look for Volume II soon…from Genesis Press.

Kathryn

In memory of Pamela Macaluso,
Nancy Richards Akers, Ann Wassall
and too many victimized women
before them and since . . .
May angel winds lift you, may true
love enfold you.